BRITISH VESSELS LOST AT SEA 1939-45

A reprint of the original official publications
*Ships of the Royal Navy: Statement of Losses
during the Second World War* and *British
Merchant Vessels Lost or Damaged by Enemy
Action during Second World War*

 Patrick Stephens, Cambridge

First published in combined case-bound edition—1976
Reprinted—1977
First published in combined softbound edition—1980

ISBN 0 85059 420 0

Printed in Great Britain on MF Printing 80 gsm and
bound by The Pitman Press, Bath, for the publishers,
Patrick Stephens Limited, Bar Hill, Cambridge, CB3 8EL.

Contents

Publisher's introduction

In 1947 two major reference books were published by HMSO on behalf of the British Admiralty. One was entitled *Ships of the Royal Navy: Statement of Losses during the Second World War,* and the other *British Merchant Vessels Lost or Damaged by Enemy Action during Second World War.* For many years, original editions of both these volumes have been extremely hard to find, yet they contain a wealth of important historical data on the Royal and Merchant Navies of the last war.

Now these two excellent and highly detailed books have been combined into one case-bound volume, and are reprinted exactly as they first appeared, but in a smaller, more practical format.

The information is presented in clear and concise tabular form for ease of reference. Section I, which is devoted to the Royal Navy, gives the following data on warships and auxiliary vessels: class, name, tonnage, date of completion, date of loss, and how lost and where, while there is also a useful feature on landing ships, craft and barges. In the second section, similar information is given on merchant and fishing vessels, together with a list of vessels that were damaged by enemy action but not lost, and a brief summary of casualties to personnel of British merchant ships.

We are certain that this long-awaited reprint of two rare collector's items will be much sought after by naval historians and shipping buffs everywhere.

Special note:
Both sections of this book are separately numbered and indexed, as were the original volumes.

SHIPS OF THE ROYAL NAVY STATEMENT OF LOSSES DURING THE SECOND WORLD WAR

3rd September, 1939 to 2nd September, 1945

CONTENTS

PART I

WARSHIPS AND AUXILIARY VESSELS

List of Losses
Arranged according to Year and Class

(This return excludes Ships of the Dominion and Royal Indian Navies)

NOTES

(i) (R) Signifies that the vessel was requisitioned for Naval Service.

(ii) Tonnage is Standard displacement unless otherwise stated.

(iii) Gross Registered Tonnage is shown in italics.

(iv) The list excludes Steam and Motor boats and small requisitioned and acquired Craft when the known tonnage is below 10 tons.

LIST OF ABBREVIATIONS

A/C	Aircraft.
A/S	Anti-Submarine
D/C	Depth Charge.
(E)	Estimated.
E/B	E-Boat.
E.M.B.	Explosive Motor Boat.
S.C.	Surface Craft.
S/M	Submarine.
T/B	Torpedo Boat.
U/B	U-Boat.

Class	Name	Tonnage	Date of Completion	Date of Loss	How Lost and Where
				1939	
BATTLESHIP ...	ROYAL OAK	29,150	1. 5.16	14 Oct.	Sunk by U/B, torpedo in Scapa Flow, Orkneys.
AIRCRAFT CARRIER (ex CRUISER).	COURAGEOUS	22,500	1.17 As A/C Carrier 5. 5.28	17 Sept.	Sunk by U/B, torpedo, West of Ireland.
DESTROYERS ...	BLANCHE	1,360	14. 2.31	13 Nov.	Sunk by mine, Thames Estuary.
	GIPSY	1,335	22. 2.36	21 Nov.	Sunk by mine off Harwich.
	DUCHESS...	1,375	27. 1.33	12 Dec.	Sunk in collision, W. Scotland.
SUBMARINE ...	OXLEY	1,354	22. 7.27	10 Sept.	Sunk by accident off Norway.
ARMED MERCHANT CRUISER.	RAWALPINDI (R) ...	16,697	1925 As AMC 10.39	23 Nov.	Sunk by SCHARNHORST S.E. of Iceland.
MOTOR TORPEDO BOAT.	No. 6	18	17.11.36	16 Nov.	Foundered in bad weather off Sardinia.
TRAWLERS ...	NORTHERN ROVER (R) ...	655	1936	31 Oct.– 5 Nov.	Overdue at Kirkwall, Orkneys.
	MASTIFF	520	16. 5.38	20 Nov.	Sunk by mine, Thames Estuary.
	ARAGONITE (R)	315	1934	22 Nov.	Mined off Deal.
	WASHINGTON (R) ...	209	1909	6 Dec.	Sunk by mine en route for Yarmouth.
	WILLIAM HALLETT (R)...	202	1919	13 Dec.	Mined, Tyne area.
	JAMES LUDFORD ...	506	30. 4.19	14 Dec.	Sunk by mine off Tyne.
	EVELINA (R)	202	1919 ⎫	16 Dec.	Sunk, probably by mine, Tyne area.
	SEDGEFLY (R)	520	1939 ⎭		
	DROMIO (R)	380	1929	22 Dec.	Sunk in collision, North of Whitby.
	BARBARA ROBERTSON (R)	325	1919	23 Dec.	Sunk by U/B, gunfire, North of Hebrides, W. Scotland.
	LOCH DOON (R) ...	534	1937	25 Dec.	Sunk, probably by mine, off Blyth.
BOOM DEFENCE VESSEL.	BAYONET	605	16. 3.39	21 Dec.	Sunk by mine, Firth of Forth.
TUG	NAPIA (R)	155	1914	20 Dec.	Sunk as result of explosion, probably caused by mine, off Ramsgate.

A 2

Class	Name	Tonnage	Date of Completion	Date of Loss	How Lost and Where
				1939	
DRIFTERS ...	RAY OF HOPE (R) ...	*98*	1925	10 Dec.	Mined, Thames Estuary.
	GLEN ALBYN (R) ...	*82*	1909	} 23 Dec.	Mined, Loch Ewe, W. Scotland.
	PROMOTIVE (R)	*78*	1908		
OILER	BIRCHOL	*1,115*(E)	12. 9.17	29 Nov.	Wrecked, Hebrides.
AMMUNITION HULKS	LUCY BORCHARDT ...	*1,850*	1905	14 Sept.	
	CARLO	*1,737*	1911	15 Sept.	
	MOURINO	*2,165*	1906	15 Sept.	} Cause and place unknown.
	STANLARD	*1,737*	1912	15 Sept.	
	DUNMORE HEAD ...	*1,682*	1898	29 Sept.	
				1940	
AIRCRAFT CARRIER (ex CRUISER).	GLORIOUS	22,500	1.17 As A/C Carrier 10. 3.30	8 June	Sunk by gunfire, SCHARNHORST and GNEISENAU, lat. of Narvik, Norway.
CRUISERS ...	EFFINGHAM	9,550	9. 7.25	18 May	Struck submerged rock, wrecked Vestfiold, Norway.
	CALYPSO	4,180	8. 6.17	12 June	Sunk by U/B, torpedo, South of Crete.
DESTROYERS ...	GRENVILLE (Leader) ...	1,485	1. 7.36	19 Jan.	Sunk by mine, North Sea.
	EXMOUTH (Leader) ...	1,475	9.11.34	21 Jan.	Sunk, probably U/B, torpedo, Moray Firth.
	DARING	1,375	25.11.32	18 Feb.	Sunk by U/B, torpedo, off Duncansby Head, N. Scotland.
	GLOWWORM	1,345	22. 1.36	8 Apr.	Sunk by ADMIRAL HIPPER, gunfire, off Norway.
	GURKHA	1,870	21.10.38	9 Apr.	Sunk by A/C, bombs, off Stavanger, Norway.
	HUNTER	1,340	30. 9.46	10 Apr.	Sunk by S.C., gunfire, in battle of Narvik.
	HARDY (Leader) ...	1,505	11.12.36	10 Apr.	Driven ashore, gunfire, Narvik.
	AFRIDI (Leader) ...	1,870	29. 4.38	3 May	Sunk by A/C, bombs, off Norway.
	VALENTINE (Leader) ...	1,090	27. 6.17	15 May	Bombed, grounded and abandoned in River Schelde.
	WHITLEY	1,100	14.10.18	19 May	Damaged by bombs, beached, between Nieuport & Ostend.
	WESSEX	1,100	11. 5.18	24 May	Sunk by A/C, bombs, off Calais.
	GRAFTON	1,335	20. 3.36	29 May	Sunk by E/B, torpedo, off Dunkirk.
	GRENADE	1,335	28. 3.36	29 May	Sunk by A/C, bombs, in Dunkirk Harbour.
	WAKEFUL	1,100	20.11.17	29 May	Sunk by E/B, torpedo, off Dunkirk.
	BASILISK	1,360	4. 3.31		
	HAVANT	1,400	19.12.39	} June	Sunk by A/C, bombs, off Dunkirk.
	KEITH (Leader) ...	1,400	20. 3.31		
	ACASTA	1,350	11. 2.30	} June	Sunk by SCHARNHORST and GNEISENAU, gunfire, when returning from Norway.
	ARDENT	1,350	14. 4.30		
	KHARTOUM	1,710	6.11.39	23 June	Beached after damage by internal explosion caused by burst torpedo air vessel off Perim Harbour.
	WHIRLWIND	1,100	28. 3.18	5 July	Sunk by U/B, torpedo, S.W. of Ireland.
	ESCORT	1,375	30.10.34	11 July	Sunk by U/B, torpedo, W. Mediterranean.
	IMOGEN	1,370	2. 6.37	16 July	Damaged in collision, caught fire and abandoned off Duncansby Head, N. Scotland.
	BRAZEN	1,360	8. 4.31	20 July	Sunk by A/C off Dover.
	CODRINGTON (Leader) ...	1,540	4. 6.30	27 July	Bombed and sunk in Dover Harbour.
	WREN	1,120	27. 1.23	27 July	Bombed and sunk off Aldeburgh, Suffolk.
	DELIGHT	1,375	31. 1.33	29 July	Bombed and sunk off Portland.
	HOSTILE	1,340	10. 9.36	23 Aug.	Mined and sunk off Cape Bon, Mediterranean.
	ESK	1,375	28. 9.34	} 1 Sept.	Sunk by mine, North Sea.
	IVANHOE	1,370	24. 8.37		
	VENETIA	1,090	27.12.17	19 Oct.	Sunk by mine, Thames Estuary.
	STURDY	905	15.10.19	30 Oct.	Wrecked, Tiree Is. W. Scotland.
	ACHERON	1,350	13.10.31	17 Dec.	Sunk by mine off Isle of Wight.
	HYPERION	1,340	3.12.36	22 Dec.	Sunk by mine off Pantellaria, Mediterranean.

Class	Name	Tonnage	Date of Completion	Date of Loss	How Lost and Where
SUBMARINES	SEAHORSE	640	2.10.33	1940 10 Jan.	Lost in Heligoland Bight.
	UNDINE	540	21. 8.38	15 Jan.	Lost in Heligoland Bight D/C., S.C. Formally paid off.
	STARFISH	640	27.10.33	20 Jan.	Lost in Heligoland Bight D/C., S.C. Formally paid off.
	THISTLE	1,090	4. 7.39	14 Apr.	Lost off Skudesnes, Norway, probably torpedoed, U/B.
	TARPON	1,090	8. 2.40	22 Apr.	Lost North Sea, probably mine.
	STERLET	670	6. 4.38	27 Apr.	Lost, Skagerrak, cause unknown.
	UNITY	540	15.10.38	29 Apr.	Lost, in collision, Tyne area.
	GRAMPUS	1,520	10. 3.37	24 June	Lost in Mediterranean off Augusta, Sicily, cause unknown.
	ODIN	1,475	21.12.29	27 June	Lost in Gulf of Taranto, Mediterranean, cause unknown.
	ORPHEUS...	1,475	23. 9.30	27 June	Lost, probably torpedoed by Italian S/M, between Malta and Alexandria.
	SHARK	670	31.12.34	6 July	Lost, A/C, off Skudesnes, Norway.
	SALMON	670	8. 3.35	14 July	Lost, probably mined, S.W. Norway.
	PHOENIX	1,475	3. 2.31	17 July	Lost, off Sicily, cause unknown.
	NARWHAL	1,520	28. 2.36	1 Aug.	Lost, probably off Trondheim, Norway, cause unknown. Formally paid off.
	OSWALD	1,475	1. 5.29	1 Aug.	Rammed and sunk, 10 miles S.E. Spartevento Bay, by Italian destroyer.
	SPEARFISH	670	11.12.36	2 Aug.	Lost, probably by U/B, torpedo, off Norway. Formally paid off.
	THAMES	1,805	14. 9.32	3 Aug.	Lost, off Norway, probably mined.
	RAINBOW	1,475	18. 1.32	19 Oct.	Sunk off Calabria, S. Italy, by gunfire, Italian S/M. Formally paid off.
	TRIAD	1,090	16. 9.39	20 Oct.	Lost off Calabria, S. Italy, cause unknown.
	H. 49	410	25.10.19	27 Oct.	Lost, D/C, off Dutch Coast, German A/S, S.C. Formally paid off.
	SWORDFISH	640	28.11.32	16 Nov.	Lost, off Ushant, cause unknown.
	REGULUS	1,475	7.12.30	6 Dec.	Lost, Otranto Strait, S. Italy, cause unknown. Formally paid off.
	TRITON	1,095	9.11.38	18 Dec.	Lost in S. Adriatic, probably mined.
ARMED MERCHANT CRUISERS.	CARINTHIA (R)	20,277	1925 As A.M.C. 1.40	7 June	Sunk by U/B, torpedo, West of Ireland.
	SCOTSTOUN (R) ...	17,046	1925 As A.M.C. 9.39	13 June	Sunk by U/B, torpedo, N.W. Approaches.
	ANDANIA (R)	13,950	1922 As A.M.C. 11.39	16 June	Sunk by U/B, torpedo, S.E. of Iceland.
	TRANSYLVANIA (R) ...	16,923	1925 As A.M.C. 10.39	10 Aug.	Sunk by U/B, torpedo, North of Ireland.
	DUNVEGAN CASTLE (R)...	15,007	1936 As A.M.C. 12.39	28 Aug.	Sunk by U/B, torpedo, West of Ireland.
	LAURENTIC (R)	18,724	1927 As A.M.C. 10.39	3 Nov.	Sunk by U/B, torpedo, N.W. Approaches.
	PATROCLUS (R)	11,314	1923 As A.M.C. 1.40	4 Nov.	Attacked by U/B (3rd). Sank West of Ireland.
	JERVIS BAY (R)... ...	14,164	1922 As A.M.C. 10.39	5 Nov.	Sunk by ADMIRAL SHEER, N. Atlantic.

Class	Name	Tonnage	Date of Completion	Date of Loss	How Lost and Where
ARMED MERCHANT CRUISERS (cont).	FORFAR (R)	16,402	1922 As A.M.C. 11.39	1940 2 Dec.	Sunk by U/B, torpedo, West of Ireland.
ARMED BOARDING VESSELS ...	KING ORRY (R) ... VAN DYCK (R)	1,877 13,241	1913 1921	30 May 10 June	Sunk by A/C at Dunkirk. Lost in convoy, probably by air attack, Narvik area.
ANTI-AIRCRAFT SHIP	CURLEW	4,290	20.12.17	26 May	Sunk by A/C, bombs, off Ofot Fiord, Norway.
AUXILIARY ANTI-AIRCRAFT SHIPS SLOOPS	CRESTED EAGLE (R) ... FOYLE BANK (R) ... BITTERN	1,110 5,582 1,190	1925 1930 15. 3.38	29 May 4 July 30 Apr.	Sunk by A/C off Dunkirk. Sunk by A/C at Portland. Sunk by A/C, bombs, off Namsos, Norway.
CORVETTE ...	PENZANCE ... ... DUNDEE ... ... GODETIA	1,025 1,060 940	15. 1.31 31. 3.33 15. 7.40	24 Aug. 15 Sept. 6 Sept.	Sunk by U/B, torpedo, N. Atlantic. Sunk in collision off N. Ireland.
RIVER GUN BOAT	MOSQUITO	585	19. 4.40	1 June	Sunk by A/C during withdrawal from Dunkirk.
MINELAYERS ...	PRINCESS VICTORIA (R) PORT NAPIER (R) ...	2,197 9,600	1939 1940	18–19 May 27 Nov.	Mined, entrance to Humber. Lost by fire, Loch Alsh, W. Scotland.
NETLAYER ...	KYLEMORE (R) ...	319	1897	21 Aug.	Sunk by A/C, Harwich.
MINE DESTRUCTOR VESSEL.	CORBURN	3,060	1936	21 May	Sunk by mine off Le Havre.
MINESWEEPERS ...	SPHINX	875	27. 7.39	3 Feb.	Sunk by A/C, bombs, off N.E. Scotland.
	DUNOON	710	19. 6.19	30 Apr.	Sunk by mine off Great Yarmouth.
	BRIGHTON BELLE (R) ...	396	1900	28 May	Sunk in collision with submerged wreck in Downs.
	GRACIE FIELDS (R) ... WAVERLEY (R) ... ... DEVONIA (R) ...	393 537 622	1936 1899 1905	29 May 31 May	Sunk by A/C, bombs, off Dunkirk. Beached and abandoned after damage by A/C, bombs, off Dunkirk.
	BRIGHTON QUEEN (R)... SKIPJACK	807 815	1905 3. 5.34	1 June 1 June	Lost by gunfire off Dunkirk. Sunk by A/C, bombs, off Dunkirk.
	DUNDALK ... ... MERCURY (R) ...	710 621	2. 5.19 1934	16 Oct. 25 Dec.	Sunk by mine off Harwich. Sank after damage by own mine, South of Ireland.
DEGAUSSING SHIP	BALMORE (R) ...	1,925	1920	11 Nov.	War Cause.
MOTOR TORPEDO BOATS.	No. 15 ... ... 106	18 —	17. 2.39 6.40	24 Sept. 16 Oct.	Sunk by mine, Thames Estuary
	17	18	13. 3.39	21 Oct.	Sunk by explosion, probably mine, off Ostend.
	16	18	3. 3.39	31 Oct.	Sunk by mine, Thames Estuary
MOTOR ATTENDANT CRAFT.	No. 5	—	12.10.36	26 Dec.	Presumed sunk by mine off N.E. Gunfleet.
MOTOR LAUNCHES	No. 109 ... ... 127 ... ... 111	57 65 57	1. 8.40 7.11.40 27. 7.40	30 Oct. 22 Nov. 25 Nov.	Sunk by mine off Humber. Sunk by mine, Thames Estuary Sunk, presumed mined, off Humber.
TRAWLERS ...	KINGSTON CORNELIAN ...	550	1934	5 Jan.	Sunk in collision, East of Gibraltar Straits.
	VALDORA (R)	251	1916	12 Jan.	Believed sunk by A/C, Cromer area.
	FORT ROYAL ... ROBERT BOWEN (R) ... FIFESHIRE (R) ...	550 290 540	1931 1918 1938	9 Feb. 20 Feb.	Sunk by A/C, off Aberdeen. Sunk by A/C, East of Copinsay Orkneys.
	BENVOLIO (R) ... ... PERIDOT ... LOCH ASSATER (R) ...	352 550 210	1930 1933 1910	23 Feb. 15 Mar. 22 Mar.	Sunk by mine off Humber. Sunk by mine off Dover. Sunk by British mine, East Coast of Scotland.
	RUTLANDSHIRE (R) ...	458	1936	20 Apr.	Attacked by A/C, grounded, Namsos, Norway.

Class	Name	Tonnage	Date of Completion	Date of Loss	How Lost and Where
				1940	
TRAWLERS *(cont.)*	BRADMAN (R)	452	1937	25 Apr.	Sunk by A/C, West Coast of Norway.
	HAMMOND (R)	452	1936	25 Apr.*	Sunk by A/C, Aandalsnes, Norway.
	LARWOOD (R)	452	1936	25 Apr.* ⎫	Sunk by A/C, West Coast of Norway.
	CAPE SIRETOKO (R) ...	590	1939	28 Apr. ⎬	Norway.
	CAPE CHELYUSKIN ...	550	1936	29 Apr.	Sunk by A/C, bombs, off Norway.
	JARDINE (R)	452	1936	30 Apr.	Sunk by own forces after damage by A/C, West Coast of Norway.
	WARWICKSHIRE (R) ...	466	1936	30 Apr.	Sunk by A/C, Trondheim area, Norway.
	ASTON VILLA (R) ...	546	1937 ⎫	3 May	Sunk by A/C off Norway.
	GAUL	550	1936 ⎬		
	ST. GORAN (R) ...	565	1936	3 May	Sunk by A/C, Namsos, Norway.
	LOCH NAVER (R) ...	278	1919	6 May	Sunk in collision off Hartlepool.
	RIFSNES (R)	431	1932	20 May	Sunk by A/C off Ostend.
	CAPE PASSARO (R) ...	590	1939	21 May ⎫	Sunk by A/C, Narvik area, Norway.
	MELBOURNE (R) ...	466	1936	22 May ⎬	
	CHARLES BOYES (R) ...	290	1918	25 May	Sunk by mine, East Coast of England.
	THOMAS BARTLETT (R)	290	1918	28 May	Sunk by British mine off Calais.
	THURINGIA	550	1933	28 May	Sunk by mine, North Sea.
	CALVI (R)	363	1930 ⎫	29 May	Sunk by A/C, bombs, off Dunkirk.
	POLLY JOHNSON (R) ...	290	1918 ⎬		
	ST. ACHILLEUS (R) ...	484	1934	31 May	Sunk by mine, Dunkirk area.
	ARGYLLSHIRE (R) ...	540	1938 ⎫	1 June	Sunk by E/B, during evacuation from Dunkirk.
	STELLA DORADO ...	550	1935 ⎬		
	BLACKBURN ROVERS (R)	422	1934	2 June	Sunk by U/B or mine, North Sea.
	WESTELLA	550	1934	2 June	Torpedoed or mined off Dunkirk.
	JUNIPER	505	9.3.40	8 June	Sunk by ADMIRAL HIPPER, gunfire, off Norway.
	SISAPON (R)	326	1928	12 June	Mined off Harwich.
	MYRTLE	550	1928	14 June	Sunk by mine, Thames Estuary.
	MURMANSK (R) ...	348	1929	17 June	Grounded at Brest and abandoned.
	CAYTON WYKE	550	1932	8 July	Sunk by S.C., torpedo, off Dover.
	CRESTFLOWER	550	1930	19 July	Foundered after damage by A/C off Portsmouth.
	CAMPINA (R)	289	1913	22 July	Mined off Holyhead.
	FLEMING (R)	356	1929	24 July	Sunk by A/C, Thames Estuary.
	KINGSTON GALENA ...	550	1934 ⎫	24 July	Sunk by A/C off Dover.
	RODINO (R)	230	1913 ⎬		
	STAUNTON (R) ...	283	1908	28 July	Presumed blown up by magnetic mine, Thames Estuary.
	CAPE FINISTERRE (R) ...	590	1939	2 Aug.	Sunk by A/C off Harwich.
	DRUMMER (R)	297	1915	4 Aug.	Mined off Brightlingsea, Essex.
	MARSONA (R)	276	1918	4 Aug.	Sunk by mine off Cromarty.
	OSWALDIAN (R) ...	260	1917	4 Aug.	Mined, Bristol Channel.
	RIVER CLYDE (R) ...	276	1919	5 Aug.	Sunk by mine off Aldeburgh, Suffolk.
	PYROPE (R)	295	1932	12 Aug.	Sunk by A/C, Thames Estuary.
	TAMARISK	545	1925	12 Aug.	Sunk by A/C, bombs, Thames Estuary.
	ELIZABETH ANGELA (R)	253	1928	13 Aug.	Sunk by A/C in Downs.
	RESPARKO (R)	248	1916	20 Aug.	Sunk by A/C at Falmouth.
	ROYALO (R)	248	1916	1 Sept.	Sunk by mine off S. Cornwall.
	DERVISH (R)	346	1911	9 Sept.	Mined off Humber.
	HARVEST MOON ...	72	1904	9 Sept.	Sunk as blockship.
	LOCH INVER (R) ...	356	1930	24 Sept.	Probably mined, Harwich area.
	STELLA SIRIUS	550	1934	25 Sept.	Sunk by bombs during air raid on Gibraltar.
	RECOIL (R)	344	1938	28 Sept.	Lost on patrol, presumed mined, English Channel.
	COMET (R)	301	1924	30 Sept.	Sunk by mine off Falmouth.
	KINGSTON SAPPHIRE (R)	356	1929	5 Oct.	Sunk by U/B, torpedo, Straits of Dover.
	SEA KING (R)	321	1916	9 Oct.	Sunk by underwater explosion in Grimsby Roads.
	RESOLVO (R)	231	1913	12 Oct.	Sunk by mine, Thames Estuary.
	WARWICK DEEPING ...	550	1934	12 Oct.	Sunk by S.C., torpedo, English Channel.
	LORD STAMP (R) ...	448	1935	14 Oct.	Sunk by mine, English Channel.
	KINGSTON CAIRNGORM (R)	448	1935	18 Oct.	Sunk by mine, English Channel.

* Subsequently salved.

Class	Name	Tonnage	Date of Completion	Date of Loss	How Lost and Where
				1940	
TRAWLERS (cont.)	VELIA (R)	290	1914	19 Oct.	Sunk, presumed mined, Harwich Area.
	WAVEFLOWER	550	1929	21 Oct.	Sunk by mine off Aldeburgh, Suffolk.
	HICKORY...	505	19. 4.40	22 Oct.	Sunk by mine, English Channel.
	JOSEPH BUTTON (R) ...	290	1918	22 Oct.	Sunk by mine off Aldeburgh, Suffolk.
	LORD INCHCAPE (R) ...	338	1924	25 Oct.*	Sunk by mine off Plymouth.
	TILBURY NESS (R) ...	279	1918	1 Nov.	Sunk by A/C, Thames Estuary.
	RINOVA (R)	429	1931	2 Nov.	Sunk by mine off Falmouth.
	WILLIAM WESNEY (R) ...	364	1930	7 Nov.	Sunk by mine off Orfordness.
	KINGSTON ALALITE ...	550	1933	10 Nov.	Sunk by mine off Plymouth.
	STELLA ORION (R) ...	417	1935	11 Nov.	Mined, Thames Estuary.
	DUNGENESS (R) ...	263	1914	15 Nov.	Bombed and total loss off Haisborough, Norfolk.
	ARSENAL	550	1933	16 Nov.	Sunk in collision off Clyde.
	FONTENOY (R)	276	1918	19 Nov.	Sunk by A/C off Lowestoft.
	ETHEL TAYLOR (R) ...	276	1917	22 Nov.	Mined off Tyne.
	AMETHYST	627	1934	24 Nov.	Sunk by mine, Thames Estuary
	CONQUISTADOR (R) ...	224	1915	25 Nov.	Sunk in collision, Thames Estuary.
	KENNYMORE (R) ...	225	1914	25 Nov.	Mined, Thames Estuary.
	ELK (R)	181	1902	27 Nov.	Mined at Plymouth.
	MANX PRINCE (R) ...	221	1910	28 Nov.	} Mined, entrance to Humber.
	CALVERTON (R) ...	214	1913	29 Nov.	
	CHESTNUT	505	21. 5.40	30 Nov.	Sunk by mine off N. Foreland, Kent.
	CAPRICORNUS (R) ...	219	1917	7 Dec.	Sunk by mine off S.E. England.
	CORTINA (R)	213	1913	7 Dec.	Sunk in collision off Humber.
	REFUNDO (R)	258	1917	18 Dec.	Sunk by mine off Harwich.
	PELTON (R)	358	1925	24 Dec.	Sunk by E/B off Yarmouth.
	BANDOLERO	913	1935	30 Dec.	Sunk in collision, Gulf of Sollum, Egypt.
WHALERS ...	SEVRA (R)	253	1929	6 Nov.	} Mined off Falmouth.
	A.N. 2 (R)	221	1926	8 Nov.	
YACHTS	PRINCESS (R)	730	1924	11 Jan.	Sunk in collision, Bristol Channel.
	AMULREE (R)	89	1938	1 June	Sunk in collision, Dover Straits.
	GRIVE (R)	687	1905	1 June	Sunk by A/C during withdrawal from Dunkirk.
	BOOMERANG VI (R) ...	19	1938	8 June	Lost by fire.
	PELLAG II (R)	44	1937	10 June	Presumed lost at Dunkirk.
	CAMPEADOR V (R) ...	195	1938	22 June	Sunk by mine off Portsmouth
	WARRIOR II (R) ...	1,124	1904	11 July	Sunk by A/C off Portland.
	GULZAR (R)	197	1934	29 July	Sunk in air attack, Dover Harbour.
	WHITE FOX II (R) ...	23	1933	27 Aug.	Lost by fire.
	EMELLE (R)	43	1916	31 Aug.	Cause and place not known.
	RHODORA (R)	687	1929	7 Sept.	Lost in collision, Bristol Channel.
	SHASHI III (R) ...	155	—	7 Sept.	Lost by fire.
	SAPPHO (R)	387	—	30 Sept.	Presumed torpedoed, Falmouth area.
	AISHA (R)	117	1934	11 Oct.	Sunk, believed mined, Thames Approaches.
	GAEL (R)	101	1904	24 Nov.	Mined, entrance to Humber.
BOOM DEFENCE VESSELS	LOCH SHIN (R) ...	255	1930	26 May	Capsized at Harstad, Norway, after being damaged by A/C and beached.
	CAMBRIAN (R)	338	1924	30 May	Mined in Spithead.
	MARCELLE (R)	64	1925	10 Nov.	Mined, Bristol Channel.
	RISTANGO (R)	178	1913	14 Nov.	Fouled Medway boom, Sheerness.
	THOMAS CONNOLLY (R)	290	1918	17 Dec.	Sunk by mine, Sheerness.
GATE VESSEL ...	PLACIDAS FAROULT (R)	136	1927	30–31 Oct.	Cause and place unknown.
GUARDSHIP	LORMONT (R)	1,561	1927	7 Dec.	Sunk in collision off Humber.
TUGS	FAIRPLAY TWO (R) ...	282	1921	2 Mar.	Wrecked on Yorkshire Coast.
	ST. ABBS	550	5. 3.19	1 June	} Sunk by A/C, at Dunkirk.
	ST. FAGAN	550	7. 7.19		
	TWENTE (R)	239	1937	12 June	Lost through enemy action.
	CORINGA (R)	294	1914	23 June	Lost in Atlantic, cause unknown.
	SAUCY (R)	597	1918	4 Sept.	Mined, Firth of Forth.
	SALVAGE KING (R) ...	1164	1925	12 Sept.	Grounded West of Duncansby Head, N.E. Scotland.
	DANUBE III (R) ...	234	1924	13 Oct.	Mined off Sheerness.

* Subsequently salved.

Class	Name	Tonnage	Date of Completion	Date of Loss	How Lost and Where
				1940	
Tugs (*cont.*)	Seagem (R)	92	1939	30 Oct. (approx.)	Missing, presumed lost.
	Muria (R)	192	1914	8 Nov.	Sunk by mine off N. Foreland.
	Guardsman (R) ...	102	1905	15 Nov.	Sunk by mine off N. Foreland.
Mooring Vessel	Steady	758 (deep)	18. 4.16	17 July	Sunk by mine off Newhaven.
Drifters ...	Riant (R)	95	1919	25 Jan.	Lost in bad weather off West Coast, Scotland.
	Maida (R)	107	1914	16 Mar.	Sunk by mine off East Coast, England.
	Golden Dawn (R) ...	80	1913	4 Apr.	Sunk at Ardrossan, W. Scotland.
	Boy Roy (R)	95	1911	28 May	Bombed, beached and abandoned in Dunkirk Harbour.
	Ocean Reward (R) ...	95	1912	28 May	Sunk in collision off Dover.
	Paxton (R)	92	1911	28 May	Damaged by A/C, and beached at Dunkirk.
	Comfort (R)	60 (Net)	—	29 May	Rammed and sunk by accident off Dover.
	Girl Pamela (R) ...	93	1912	29 May	Sunk in collision off Dunkirk.
	Nautilus (R) ...	64 (Net)	1929	29 May	Sunk at Dunkirk.
	Fair Breeze (R) ...	92	1925	1 June	Struck wreck off Dunkirk.
	Lord Cavan (R) ...	96	1915	1–2 June	Sunk by gunfire off Dunkirk.
	Ocean Lassie (R) ...	96	1919	4 June	Sunk by mine off Harwich.
	Dewey Eve (R) ...	109	1916	9 June	Sunk in collision, Scapa, Orkneys.
	Ocean Sunlight (R) ...	131	1929	13 June	Mined off Newhaven.
	Charde (R)	99	1919	21 June	Sunk in collision at Portsmouth.
	Embrace (R)	94	1907	2 Aug.	Grounded, total loss, at Loch Alsh, W. Scotland.
	Young Sid (R) ...	100	1912	10 Aug.	Sunk in collision, Moray Firth, E. Scotland.
	Manx Lad (R) ...	24	1937	16 Aug.	Sunk by mine off Holyhead.
	Alfred Colebrook ...	56	1912	9 Sept.	Sunk as blockship, Richborough Channel, S.E. England.
	White Daisy (R) ...	79	1910	25 Sept.	Sunk.
	Scotch Thistle (R) ...	84	1913	6–7 Oct.	Grounded, total loss, Thames Estuary.
	Summer Rose (R) ...	96	1919	13 Oct.	Sunk by mine off Sunderland.
	Apple Tree (R) ...	84	1907	15 Oct.	Sunk in collision, Oban Harbour.
	Duthies (R)	89	1914	25 Oct.	Sunk by A/C, at Montrose.
	Persevere (R) ...	19.8	1937	27 Oct.	Mined, Firth of Forth.
	Harvest Gleaner (R)...	96	1918	28 Oct.	Sunk by A/C, East Coast, England.
	Torbay II (R) ...	83	1910	1 Nov	Sunk by A/C off Dover.
	Goodwill (R)	28 (Net)	—	2 Nov.	Sunk.
	Reed (R)	99	1911	7 Nov.	Mined, Thames Estuary.
	Shipmates (R)	82	1911	14 Nov.	Sunk by A/C, Dover Harbour.
	The Boys (R)	92	1914	14 Nov.	Sunk in heavy weather in Downs, S.E. England.
	Go Ahead (R)	100	1919	18 Nov.	Sunk in collision, Sheerness.
	Xmas Rose (R) ...	96	1918	21 Nov.	Sunk by mine, Thames Estuary.
	Young Fisherman (R)	95	1914	29 Nov.	Grounded, total loss, Oban, W. Scotland.
	Carry On (R)	93	1919	17 Dec.	Sunk by mine, Sheerness.
	Proficient (R) ...	57	—	19 Dec.	Grounded, total loss, Whitby, Yorkshire.
	Lord Howard (R) ...	98	1917	24 Dec.	Sunk in collision, Dover Harbour.
	True Accord (R) ...	92	1921	26 Dec.	Sunk in collision, Yarmouth Area.
Tankers & Oilers	Boardale	8,406(E)	7. 7.37	30 Apr.	Sunk after grounding Narvik, Norway.
	Oleander	7,048	—	8 June	Sunk in Harstead Bay, Norway, after being damaged and beached (26th May).
	War Sepoy	5,574	6. 2.19	19 July	Damaged beyond repair by A/C, off Dover.
Freighters ...	Cape Howe (R) ...	4,443	1930	21 June	} Sunk by U/B, S.W. Approaches
	Willamette Valley (R)	4,702	1928	29 June	
Colliers	Maindy Hill (R) ...	1,918	1911	9 Mar.	Sunk in collision off Hartlepool.
	King City (R) ...	4,744	1928	15 Aug. (approx.)	Sunk by German Raider, Indian Ocean.
	Glynwen (R)	1,076	1923	14 Oct.	Sunk by enemy action.

Class	Name	Tonnage	Date of Completion	Date of Loss	How Lost and Where
				1940	
MOTOR CANAL BOATS.	AMBLEVE	—	—	} 30 May	Ran aground Dunkirk.
	YSER	—	—		
	ESCAUT	—	—	}	Lost at Dunkirk.
	SEMOIS	—	—		
EXAMINATION VESSEL.	LADY SLATER (R)	273	1934	30 July	Caught fire and became total loss.
BALLOON BARRAGE VESSEL.	BOREALIS (R)	451	1930	10 Aug.	Sunk.
SPECIAL SERVICE VESSELS.	DURHAM CASTLE	8,240	1904	26 Jan.	Sunk by mine off Cromarty on way to Scapa.
	BRANKSEA	214	1890	10 Feb.	Sunk off Girdleness on way to Scapa. Cause unknown.
	ILSENSTEIN	8,216	1904	18 Feb.	Sunk as blockship at Scapa.
	BUSK	367	1906	19 Feb.	Sunk as blockship.
	CARRON	1,017	1894	3 Mar.	Sunk as blockship at Scapa.
	GONDOLIER	250	1886	18–25 Mar.	Sunk as blockship.
	REDSTONE	3,110	1918	2 May	Sunk as blockship at Scapa.
	FLORENTINO	1,822	1921	25 May	Sunk as blockship at Zeebrugge, Belgium.
	MASHOBRA (R)	8,324	1920	25 May	Damaged by A/C, and beached at Narvik.
	TRANSEAS	1,499	1924	25 May	} Sunk as blockships at Zeebrugge, Belgium.
	ATLANTIC GUIDE	1,943	1924	27 May	
	BORODINO	2,004	1911	27 May	
	EDV. NISSEN (R)	2,062	1921	} 3 June	Sunk as blockships.
	HOLLAND (R)	1,251	1919		
	WESTCOVE	2,735	1912	3 June	Sunk as blockship at Dunkirk.
	GOURKO	1,975	1911	4 June	Mined off Dunkirk.
	PACIFICO	687	1905	4 June	Sunk as blockship at Dunkirk.
	JACOBUS	1,262	1920	10 June	Sunk as blockship at Dieppe.
	KAUPO (R)	2,420	1888	10 June	Sunk as blockship.
	RIVER TYNE	1,525	1920	10 June	Sunk as blockship at Dieppe.
	TWEEDLEDEE	163	1925	} 1 July	Sunk as blockships.
	TWEEDLEDUM	163	1925		
	JAMES 83	397	1926	3 July*	Sunk as blockship.
	EMERALD WINGS	2,139	1920	5 July (date of arrival)	Sunk as blockship at Scapa.
	JAMES 9	85	1924	8 July	} Sunk as blockships.
	UMVOTI (R)	5,183	1903	29 July	
	MOREA	1,968	–	16 Aug.	
	MINNIE DE LARINAGA	5,046	1914	7–9 Sept.*	Total loss from A/C, London Docks.
	EMPIRE SEAMAN	1,927	1922	4 Dec.	Sunk, cause unknown.
	GAMBHIRA	5,257	1919		} Sunk as blockships, presumed during 1940.
	JUNIATA	1,139	1918		
	LAKE NEUCHATEL	3,859	1907		
	LYCEA	2,338	1924		
	MARTIS	2,483	1894		
	MOYLE	1,761	1907		
				1941	
BATTLESHIPS	BARHAM	31,100	4.10.15	25 Nov.	Sunk by U/B, torpedoes, off Sollum, Egypt.
	PRINCE OF WALES	35,000	31. 3.41	10 Dec.	Sunk by Japanese torpedo-carrying A/C, E. Coast of Malaya.
BATTLE CRUISERS	HOOD	42,100	15. 5.20	24 May	Sunk in action with BISMARCK, N. Atlantic.
	REPULSE	33,250	7. 8.16	10 Dec.	Sunk by Japanese torpedo-carrying A/C, E. Coast of Malaya.
MONITOR	TERROR	7,200	2. 8.16	23 Feb.	Bombed (22nd) and sunk off Derna, Libya.
AIRCRAFT CARRIER	ARK ROYAL	22,000	16.11.38	14 Nov.	Torpedoed (13th) by U/B and sunk, W. Mediterranean.
AUXILIARY AIRCRAFT CARRIER.	AUDACITY (ex HANNOVER) (German prize Vessel).	11,000 (deep)	1939 As A/C Carrier 9.41	21 Dec.	Sunk by U/B, torpedo, N. Atlantic.
CRUISERS	SOUTHAMPTON	9,100	6. 3.37	11 Jan.	Sunk by dive bombers, East of Malta.

* Subsequently salved.

Class	Name	Tonnage	Date of Completion	Date of Loss	How Lost and Where
				1941	
CRUISERS (contd)...	BONAVENTURE	5,450	24. 5.40	31 Mar.	Sunk by U/B, torpedoes, South of Crete.
	FIJI	8,000	17. 5.40	22 May	Sunk by A/C, bombs, during evacuation of Crete.
	GLOUCESTER	9,600	31. 1.39	22 May	Sunk by A/C, bombs, during evacuation of Crete.
	YORK	8,250	1. 5.30	22 May	Lost at Suda Bay, Crete after damage on various dates by E.M.B. and A/C.
	DUNEDIN	4,850	10.19	24 Nov.	Sunk by U/B, torpedo, between W. Africa and Brazil.
	GALATEA	5,220	14. 8.35	14 Dec.	Sunk by U/B, torpedo, off Alexandria.
	NEPTUNE	7,175	23. 2.34	19 Dec.	Sunk by mine off Tripoli, Libya.
DESTROYERS ...	GALLANT	1,335	25. 2.36	20 Jan.	Damaged by mine (10th) and taken in tow. Later bombed and sunk in Malta Harbour.
	DAINTY	1,375	22.12.32	24 Feb.	Sunk by A/C, off Tobruk, Libya.
	EXMOOR	1,000	1.11.40	25 Feb.	Sunk by explosion presumed E/B, torpedo, off Lowestoft.
	MOHAWK	1,870	7. 9.38	16 Apr.	Torpedoed by destroyer, East of Tunisia. Sunk by own Forces.
	DIAMOND	1,375	3.11.32	} 27 Apr.	Sunk by A/C, bombs, during evacuation of Greece.
	WRYNECK	1,100	9.11.18		
	JERSEY	1,760	28. 4.39	2 May	Mined in entrance to Grand Harbour, Malta.
	JUNO	1,760	25. 8.39	21 May	
	GREYHOUND	1,335	1. 2.36	22 May	} Sunk by A/C, bombs, during battle of Crete.
	KASHMIR	1,760	26.10.39	22 May	
	KELLY (Leader) ...	1,760	23. 8.39	23 May	
	MASHONA	1,870	30. 3.39	28 May	Sunk by A/C, bombs, N. Atlantic.
	HEREWARD	1,340	9.12.36	29 May	Sunk by A/C, bombs, off Crete.
	IMPERIAL	1,370	30. 6.37	29 May	Sunk by own forces after being bombed, off Crete.
	WATERHEN (On loan to R.A.N.).	1,100	17. 7.18	29 June	Sunk by A/C, bombs, off Sollum, Egypt.
	DEFENDER	1,375	31.10.32	11 July	Sunk by A/C, bombs, off Sidi Barrani, Egypt.
	FEARLESS	1,375	19.12.34	23 July	Sunk during air attack on convoy, Central Mediterranean.
	BATH (On loan to R.NOR. N.).	1,060	21. 3.19	19 Aug.	Sunk by U/B, torpedo, S.W. of Ireland.
	BROADWATER	1,190	28. 2.20	18 Oct.	Sunk by U/B, torpedo, N. Atlantic.
	COSSACK	1,870	10. 6.38	27 Oct.	Foundered after being torpedoed by U/B (23rd), West of Gibraltar.
	KANDAHAR	1,760	10.10.39	19 Dec.	Mined off Tripoli, Libya, and subsequently sunk by own forces.
	STANLEY	1,190	19. 5.19	19 Dec.	Sunk by U/B, torpedo, N Atlantic.
SUBMARINES ...	SNAPPER	670	14. 6.35	12 Feb.	Lost, Bay of Biscay. Formally paid off.
	USK	540	11.10.40	3 May	Presumed mined, off Cape Bon, Tunisia.
	UNDAUNTED	540	30.12.40	13 May	Presumed Sunk by D/C, S.C. off Tripoli, Libya.
	UMPIRE	540	10. 7.41	19 July	Rammed and sunk by trawler North Sea, off the Wash.
	UNION	540	22. 2.41	22 July	Presumed lost between Tunisia and Pantellaria.
	CACHALOT	1,520	15. 8.38	4 Aug.	Rammed by Italian destroyer off Cyrenaica. Formally Paid off.
	P. 33	540	30. 5.41	20 Aug.	} Presumed mined off Tripoli, Libya.
	P. 32	540	3. 5.41	23 Aug.	Formally paid off.
	TETRARCH	1,093	15. 2.40	2 Nov.	Lost W. Mediterranean, on passage Malta to Gibraltar.
	PERSEUS	1,475	15. 4.30	1 Dec.	Mined off Zante, W. Greece.
	H. 31	410	21. 2.19	24 Dec.	Presumed mined, Bay of Biscay.
ARMED MERCHANT CRUISERS.	VOLTAIRE (R)	13,301	1923 As AMC 1.40	4 Apr. (Approx.)	Sunk by surface raider, mid-Atlantic.

Class	Name	Tonnage	Date of Completion	Date of Loss	How Lost and Where
ARMED MERCHANT CRUISERS (*cont.*)	COMORIN (R)	*15,241*	1925 As AMC 1.40	**1941** 6 Apr.	Destroyed by fire, N. Atlantic.
	RAJPUTANA (R) ...	*16,644*	1926 As AMC 12.39	13 Apr.	Sunk by U/B, torpedo, West of Iceland.
	SALOPIAN (R)	*10,549*	1926 As AMC 10·39	13 May	Sunk by U/B, torpedo, N. Atlantic.
ARMED BOARDING VESSELS	ROSAURA (R)	*1,552*	1905	18 Mar.	Sunk by mine off Tobruk, Libya.
	CHAKDINA (R)	*3,033*	1914	5 Dec.	Sunk by A/C, E. Mediterranean
	CHANTALA (R)	*3,129*	1920	7 Dec.	Sunk by mine, Tobruk Harbour
OCEAN BOARDING VESSELS.	CRISPIN (R)	*5,051*	1935	3 Feb. ⎫	Sunk by U/B, torpedo, N. Atlantic.
	MANISTEE (R)	*5,368*	1920	24 Feb. ⎬	
	CAMITO (R)	*6,833*	1915	6 May	Sunk by U/B, torpedo, N. Atlantic.
	LADY SOMERS (R) ...	*8,194*	1929	15 July ⎭	
	MALVERNIAN (R) ...	*3,133*	1937	19 July	Abandoned after being bombed
AUXILIARY FIGHTER CATAPULT SHIPS.	PATIA (R)	*5,355*	1922	27 Apr.	Sunk by A/C, off Northumberland.
	SPRINGBANK (R) ...	*5,155*	1926	27 Sept.	Sunk by U/B, torpedo, N. Atlantic.
ANTI-AIRCRAFT SHIP.	CALCUTTA	*4,200*	21. 8.19	1 June	Sunk by A/C, bombs, during evacuation of Crete.
AUXILIARY ANTI-AIRCRAFT SHIP.	HELVELLYN (R) ...	*642*	1937	20 Mar.	Sunk by A/C, London Docks,
SLOOPS	GRIMSBY	990	17. 5.34	25 May	Sunk by A/C, off Tobruk Libya.
	AUCKLAND	*1,250*	16.11.38	24 June	Sunk by A/C, bombs, off Tobruk, Libya.
CORVETTES ...	PINTAIL	580	28.11.39	10 June	Sunk by mines off Humber.
	PICOTEE	900	5. 9.40	12 Aug.	Presumed lost, probably torpedoed by U/B, off Iceland.
	ZINNIA	900	30. 3.41	23 Aug.	Sunk by U/B, torpedo, N. Atlantic.
	FLEUR DE LYS	900	26. 8.40	14 Oct.	Sunk by U/B, torpedo, West of Gibraltar.
	GLADIOLUS	965	6. 4.40	16 Oct.	Presumed torpedoed by U/B, N. Atlantic.
	WINDFLOWER (On loan to R.C.N.).	900	4. 2.41	7 Dec.	Sunk by collision in fog, W. Atlantic.
	SALVIA	955	20. 9.40	24 Dec.	Sunk by U/B, torpedo, off Egypt.
AUXILIARY A / S VESSEL.	KAMPAR (R)	*971*	1915	13 Dec.	Destroyed by A/C at Penang after damage (12th.)
RIVER GUN BOATS	LADYBIRD	625	5.16	12 May	Dive bombed and sunk, Tobruk Libya
	GNAT	625	12.15	21 Oct.	Torpedoed by U/B off Bardia, Libya. Total loss.
	PETEREL	310	29.11.27	8 Dec.	Sunk by Japanese Forces at Shanghai.
	MOTH	625	1.16	12 Dec. ⎫	Scuttled at Hong Kong.
	TERN	262	15.11.27	19 Dec. ⎬	
	CICALA	625	2.16	21 Dec. ⎭	Sunk by A/C, bombs, Hong Kong.
	ROBIN	226	23. 7.34	25 Dec.	Scuttled at Hong Kong.
CONVOY SERVICE SHIPS.	FIONA (R)	*2,190*	1927	18 Apr.	Sunk by A/C off Sidi Barrani, Egypt.
	CHAKLA (R)	*3,081*	1914	29 Apr.	Sunk by A/C, Tobruk Harbour Libya.
MINELAYERS ...	LATONA	*2,650*	4. 5.41	25 Oct.	Attacked by A/C, E. Mediterranean.
	REDSTART	498	28.10.38	19 Dec.	Scuttled at Hong Kong.
NETLAYER ...	TONBRIDGE (R) ...	*683*	1924	22 Aug.	Sunk by A/C off Yarmouth, Norfolk.
MINE DESTRUCTOR VESSELS.	QUEENWORTH	*3,010*	1925	9 May	Sunk by A/C, North Sea.
	CORFIELD	*3,000*	1937	8 Sept.	Sunk by mine explosion **off** Humber.

Class	Name	Tonnage	Date of Completion	Date of Loss	How Lost and Where
				1941	
MINESWEEPERS ...	HUNTLEY	710	22. 5.19	31 Jan.	Sunk by A/C, E. Mediterranean
	SOUTHSEA (R)	825	1930	16 Feb.	Mined and beached off Tyne. Constructive total loss.
	MARMION (R)	409	1906	9 Apr.	Sunk by A/C at Harwich. Salved but constructive total loss.
	FERMOY	710	23. 7.19	4 May	Sunk by A/C, bombs, in dock at Malta.
	STOKE	710	30.10.18	7 May	Sunk by A/C at Tobruk.
	CITY OF ROCHESTER ...	194	1904	19 May	Sunk by aerial mine.
	WIDNES	710	17. 9.18	20 May	Bombed and beached in Suda Bay, Crete.
	SNAEFELL (R)	466	1907	5 July	Sunk by A/C, Tyne Area.
	BANKA (R)	623	1914	10 Dec.	Sunk by mine or A/C, E. Coast of Malaya.
MOTOR MINESWEEPER.	No. 39	226	26. 4.41	7 Aug.	Mined and sunk, Thames Estuary.
MOTOR TORPEDO BOATS.	No. 41	33	7.11.40	14 Feb.	Sunk by mine, North Sea.
	28	37	10. 7.40	7 March	Lost by fire.
	67	17	19. 4.40		
	213	17	24.10.40	23 May–	Sunk by A/C, destroyed or
	214	17	10.40	2 June	beached, in Suda Bay, Crete.
	216	17	3. 1.41		
	217	17	7. 1.41		
	68	17	19. 4.40	14 Dec.	Sunk in collision off Libya.
	8	18	3. 9.37	16 Dec.	Destroyed by fire during raid on Hong-Kong.
	12	18	3. 8.38	20 Dec.	Sunk in action with Japanese
	26	13·8	10. 9.38		Landing Craft, Hong-Kong.
	7	18	31. 8.38	26 Dec.	Scuttled at Hong-Kong.
	9	18	8.10.37		
	10	18	11. 7.38		
	11	18	26. 7.38	26 Dec.	Scuttled at Hong-Kong.
	27	13·8	10. 9.38		
MOTOR A/S BOATS	No. 3	19	13. 6.39	28 Feb.	Beached after damage by mine, Suez Canal.
	30	23	18. 8.41	14 Dec.	Fouled boom and sank, Humber.
MOTOR GUN BOATS	No. 12	31	10. 8.40	3 Feb. (approx.)	Sunk by mine, Milford Haven.
	98	—	—	June (approx.)	Lost in air raid on HORNET.
	90	33	—	16 July	Destroyed by fire, Portland
	92	33	—		Harbour.
	62	28	31.12.40	9 Aug.	Lost in collision, North Sea.
MOTOR LAUNCHES	No. 1003...	40	3. 1.41	20 Apr.	Lost in torpedoed ship in
	1037...	40	3. 1.41		Atlantic.
	1011...	40	16.11.40	10 May	Bombed and sunk on passage from Suda Bay to Sphakia, Crete.
	1030...	40	11.11.40	28 May	Lost on passage from Suda Bay, Crete.
	144...	73	12.11.40	22 Sept.	Sunk by mine, English Channel.
	288...	73	19. 8.41	11 Oct.	Lost through stress of weather, off Hartlepool.
	219...	73	17. 5.41	21 Nov.	Grounded off Stornoway, N.W. Scotland. Constructive total loss.
TRAWLERS ...	DESIREE (R)	213	1912	16 Jan.	Mined, Thames Estuary.
	RELONZO (R)	245	1914	20 Jan.	Mined, Crosby Channel, Liverpool.
	LUDA LADY (R) ...	234	1914	22 Jan.	Mined, Humber area.
	DAROGAH (R)	221	1914	27 Jan.	Mined, Thames Estuary.
	ALMOND	505	20. 8.40	2 Feb.	Sunk by mine off Falmouth.
	ARCTIC TRAPPER (R) ...	352	1928	3 Feb.	Sunk by A/C off Ramsgate.
	TOURMALINE	641	1935	5 Feb.	Sunk by A/C, off N. Foreland, Kent.
	RUBENS (R)	320	1937	13 Feb.	Sunk by A/C, Western Approaches.
	ORMONDE (R)	250	1906	16 Feb.	Sunk by A/C off E. Coast of Scotland.
	OUSE	462	8.17	20 Feb.	Sunk by mine, Tobruk, Libya.
	LINCOLN CITY (R) ...	398	1933	21 Feb.	Sunk by A/C, Faroe Islands.
	REMILLO (R)	266	1917	27 Feb.	Sunk by mine, Humber.
	ST. DONATS (R) ...	349	1924	1 Mar.	Sunk in collision off Humber.
	COBBERS (R)	275	1919	3 Mar.	Sunk by A/C, North Sea.

Class	Name	Tonnage	Date of Completion	Date of Loss	How Lost and Where
TRAWLERS (cont.) ...	KERYADO (R)	252	1920	1941 6 Mar.	} Sunk by mine, English Channel.
	GULLFOSS	730	1929	9 Mar.	
	LADY LILIAN (R) ...	581	1939	16 Mar.	Sunk by A/C, West of Ireland.
	DOX (R)	35	1931	20 Mar.	Sunk by enemy action.
	ASAMA (R)	303	1929	21 Mar.	Sunk by A/C in attack on Plymouth.
	LORD SELBORNE (R) ...	247	1917	31 Mar.	Sunk by mine, Humber.
	CRAMOND ISLAND (R) ...	180	1910	2 Apr.	} Sunk by A/C off St. Abb's Head E. Scotland.
	FORTUNA (R)	259	1906	2–3 Apr.	
	ROCHE BONNE (R) ...	258	1913	7 Apr.	Sunk by A/C off the Lizard, Cornwall.
	KOPANES (R)	351	1915	19 Apr.	Sunk by A/C off Tyne.
	TOPAZE	608	1935	20 Apr.	Lost in collision off Clyde.
	CAROLINE (R)	253	1930	28 Apr.	Sunk by mine off Milford Haven.
	JEAN FREDERIC (R) ...	329	1919	1 May	Sunk by A/C off Start Point, English Channel.
	ALBERIC (R)	286	1910	3 May	Sunk in collision off Scapa, Orkneys.
	BEN GAIRN (R) ...	234	1916	4 May	Sunk by parachute mine, Lowestoft.
	SUSARION (R)	260	1917	7 May	Sunk by A/C off Humber.
	SILICIA (R)	250	1913	8 May	Mined off Humber.
	VAN ORLEY (R) ...	352	1927	May	Declared a constructive total loss.
	EVESHAM (R) ...	239	1915	27 May	Sunk by A/C off Yarmouth, Norfolk.
	SINDONIS	913 (deep)	1934	29 May	Sunk by A/C at Tobruk.
	ASH	505	6. 5.40	5 June	Sunk by mine, Thames Estuary.
	RESMILO (R)	258	1917	20 June	Sunk by A/C at Peterhead, E. Scotland.
	BEECH	540	1929	22 June	Sunk by A/C in Scrabster, N. Scotland.
	NOGI (R)	299	1923	23 June	Sunk by A/C off Norfolk.
	TRANIO (R)	275	1918	26 June	Sunk by A/C bombs, whilst in tow, North Sea.
	FORCE (R)	324	1917	27 June	Sunk by A/C off Yarmouth, Norfolk.
	AKRANES (R)	358	1929	4 July	Sunk by A/C, Bridlington Bay, Yorkshire.
	AGATE	627	1934	6 Aug.	Grounded, total loss, off Cromer Norfolk.
	LORINDA (R)	348	1928	20 Aug.	Sank through engine trouble and fires off Freetown, W. Africa.
	BRORA	530	4. 6.41	6 Sept.	Grounded, total loss, Hebrides, W. Scotland.
	STRATHBORVE (R) ...	216	1930	6 Sept.	Mined off Humber.
	MARCONI (R)	322	1916	20 Sept.	Lost in collision off Harwich.
	EILEEN DUNCAN (R) ...	223	1910	30 Sept.	} Sunk by A/C, N. Shields.
	STAR OF DEVERON (R)	220	1915		
	ALDER	560	1929	22 Oct.	Grounded, total loss, E. Scotland.
	EMILION (R)	201	1914	24 Oct.	Mined, Thames Estuary.
	FLOTTA	530	11. 6.41	6 Nov.	Foundered after grounding (29 Oct.) off Buchan Ness, E. Scotland.
	FRANCOLIN (R) ...	322	1916	12 Nov.	Sunk by A/C off Cromer, Norfolk.
	ST. APOLLO (R) ...	580	1940	22 Nov.	Sunk in collision off Hebrides, W. Scotland.
	MILFORD EARL (R) ...	290	1919	8 Dec.	} Sunk by A/C off East Coast Scotland.
	PHINEAS BEARD (R) ...	278	1918		
	LADY SHIRLEY (R) ...	477	1937	11 Dec.	Sunk by U/B, Gibraltar Straits.
	HENRIETTE (R) ...	261	1906	26 Dec.	Sunk by mine off Humber.
WHALERS ...	SOUTHERN FLOE (R) ...	344	1936	11 Feb.	Sunk by mine off Tobruk, Libya.
	SARNA (R)	268	1930	25 Feb.	Sunk by mine, Suez Canal.
	KOS XXIII (R) ...	353	1937	23 May (approx.)	Total loss in Suda Bay, Crete.
	SYVERN (R)	307	1937	27 May	Sunk by enemy action on passage from Crete area.
	KOS XXII (R) ...	353	1937	2 June (date reported)	Sunk on passage from Crete area.
	THORBRYN (R)	305	1936	19 Aug.	Sunk by A/C off Tobruk, Libya.
	KOS XVI (R)	258	1932	24 Aug.	Sunk in collision, North Sea.
	SKUDD 3 (R)	245	1929	27 Aug.	Sunk by A/C, Tobruk, Libya.
	WHIPPET (R)	353	1937	4 Oct.	Bombed and sunk.
	EGELAND (R)	153	1912	29 Nov.	Grounded, Palestine Coast, total loss.

Class	Name	Tonnage	Date of Completion	Date of Loss	How Lost and Where
				1941	
YACHTS	MOLLUSC (R)	597	1906	17 Mar.	Sunk by A/C off Blyth, Northumberland.
	WILNA (R)	461	1939	24 Mar.	Abandoned after A/C attack, Portsmouth.
	SURF (R)	496	1902	6 Apr.	Sunk by A/C at Piraeus.
	TORRENT (R)	336	1930	6 Apr.	Mined and sunk off Falmouth.
	YORKSHIRE BELLE (R)	56	1938	11 Apr.	Sunk by mine, Humber entrance.
	CALANTHE (R)	370	1898	24 Apr.	Sunk by A/C off Milos, Greece.
	NYULA (R)	48	1936	2 May	Sunk in collision off Tyne.
	VIVA II (R)	521	1929	8 May	Sunk by A/C off N. Coast of Cornwall.
	SEA ANGLER (R) ...	23	—	19 May	Destroyed by fire.
	HANYARDS (R)	16·5	1931	21 May	Cause and place unknown.
	ROSABELLE ...	525	1901	11 Dec.	Sunk by explosion, probably torpedoed by U/B, Straits of Gibraltar.
BOOM DEFENCE VESSELS.	OTHELLO (R)	201	1907	11 Apr.	Sunk by mine, Humber.
	ALDGATE	290	23. 6.34		
	BARLIGHT	730	12.12.38	19 Dec.	Scuttled at Hong Kong.
	WATERGATE	290	23. 6.34		
GATE VESSEL ...	KING HENRY (R) ...	162	1900	13 June	Sunk by A/C off Lowestoft.
ACCOMMODATION SHIP.	GYPSY (R)	261	—	11 May	Sunk at Tower Pier during air raid on London.
TUGS	ST. CYRUS	810	5. 4.19	22 Jan.	Sunk by mine off Humber.
	PEUPLIER (R)	—	—	29–30 Apr.	Sunk.
	IRENE VERNICOS (R) ...	250	—	June (approx.)	Constructive total loss.
	ASSURANCE	675	28. 9.40	18 Oct.	Grounded, total loss, Lough Foyle, N. Ireland.
	HELEN BARBARA ...	—	—	21 Oct.	Abandoned in sinking condition, due to heavy weather.
	LETTIE (R)	89	1914	9 Nov.	Sunk, cause unknown, off St. Abb's Head, E. Scotland.
	INDIRA (R)	637	1918	15 Dec.	Sunk during air attack on Hong Kong.
SALVAGE VESSEL...	VIKING (R)	—	—	6 Apr.	Sunk by A/C, Piraeus, Greece.
SCHOONERS ...	KEPHALLINIA (R) ...	1,267	1893	13 Aug.	Foundered off Alexandria.
	KANTARA (R)	—	—	26 Sept.	Cause and place unknown.
	MARIA DI GIOVANNI (R)	—	—	22 Nov.	Grounded, West of Tobruk, Libya.
DRIFTERS ...	NEW SPRAY (R) ...	70	1912	3 Jan.	Lost in gale off Sheerness.
	DUSKY QUEEN (R) ...	40	1920	9 Jan.	Grounded, constructive total loss, Dover Straits.
	UBEROUS (R)	92	1918	11 Jan.	Grounded off Londonderry.
	MIDAS (R)	89	1910	3 Feb.	Sunk in collision off Dungeness.
	IMBAT (R)	92	1918	4 Feb.	Sunk in collision, Scapa, Orkneys.
	BOY ALAN (R)	109	1914	10 Feb.	Sunk in collision, Thames Estuary.
	GLOAMING (R)	21 (Net)	1928	20 Mar.	Mined off Humber.
	SOIZIK (R)	—	—	20 Mar.	Lost by enemy action.
	BAHRAM (R)	72	1924	3 Apr.	Mined in Humber Estuary.
	D'ARCY COOPER (R) ...	126	1928	9 Apr.	Sunk by A/C, Harwich.
	RYPA (R)	31	—	12 Apr.	
	YOUNG ERNIE (R) ...	88	1924	18 Apr.	Sunk in collision off Tyne.
	GOWAN HILL (R) ...	96	1920	7 May	Sunk by A/C, Greenock.
	THISTLE (R)	79	1904	8 May	Mined off Lowestoft.
	UBERTY (R)	93	1912	8 May	Sunk by A/C off Lowestoft.
	M.A. WEST (R) ...	96	1919	14 May	Sunk by A/C off Norfolk Coast.
	JEWEL (R)	84	1908	18 May	Sunk by mine off Belfast Lough.
	AURORA II (R) ...	—	—	24 May	Sunk by A/C at Tobruk, Libya.
	COR JESU (R)	97	1931	8 June	Sunk in air attack off Alnmouth, Northumberland.
	DEVON COUNTY (R) ...	86	1910	1 July	
	RECEPTIVE (R)	86	1913	3 July	Sunk by mine, Thames Estuary.
	LORD ST. VINCENT (R)	115	1929	7 July	
	FERTILE VALE (R) ...	91	1917	17 July	Sunk in collision off River Tay, E. Scotland.
	CHRISTINE ROSE (R) ...	—	—	10 Sept.	Grounded, Knap Rock, Argyll, W. Scotland.
	FORERUNNER (R) ...	92	1911	14 Oct.	Sunk in collision, Thames Estuary. Constructive total loss.
	MONARDA (R)	109	1916	8 Nov.	Foundered, Thames Estuary.

Class	Name	Tonnage	Date of Completion	Date of Loss	How Lost and Where
DRIFTERS (*cont.*)	BOY ANDREW (R) ...	97	1918	1941 9 Nov.	Lost in collision, Firth of Forth, E. Scotland.
	BLIA (R)	—	1936	11 Nov.	Presumed lost.
	HARMONY (R)	24 (Net)	—	15 Nov.	Lost in collision off Invergordon, N.E. Scotland.
	ROWAN TREE (R) ...	91	1917	21 Nov.	Grounded and capsized, entrance to Lowestoft Harbour
	FISHER GIRL (R) ...	85	1914	25 Nov.	Sunk by A/C, Falmouth Harbour.
	FISKAREN (R)	—	—	23 Dec.	Sunk in collision, Belfast, N. Ireland.
	TOKEN (R)	89	1914	23 Dec.	Grounded, broke up in gale, Skerry Sound, Orkneys.
TENDER	CHABOOK (R) ... ... (Tender to SHEBA)	—	—	22 Mar.	Formally paid off.
TANKERS & OILERS.	PERICLES (R)	8,324	1936	14 Apr.	Lost in heavy weather on passage to Alexandria.
	OLNA	12,667	20.10.21	18 May	Bombed and set on fire, Crete.
	JOHN P. PEDERSEN (R)	6,128	1930	20 May	Sunk by U/B, N. Atlantic.
	CAIRNDALE	8,129	26. 1.39	30 May	Sunk by U/B, torpedo, West of Gibraltar Straits.
	SILDRA (R)	7,313	1927	19 Aug.	Sunk by U/B off W. Africa.
	DARKDALE	8,145	15.11.40	22 Oct.	Sunk by explosion, believed torpedoed by U/B, St. Helena.
	WAR MEHTAR	5,502	2. 3.20	20 Nov.	Torpedoed and sunk off Yarmouth.
STORE CARRIERS	ULSTER PRINCE (R) ...	3,791	1930	25 Apr.	Grounded off Nauplia and attacked by A/C during evacuation from Greece.
	TUNA (R)	662	1907	Sept. date (reported)	Constructive total loss after fire at Aden.
	TIBERIO (R)	237	1902	23 Dec.	Foundered off Mersa Matruh, Egypt.
ARMAMENT STORE CARRIER.	ESCAUT (R)	1,087	1938	3–4 Aug.	Sunk by A/C off Suez.
COLLIERS	BOTUSK (R)	3,092	1919	31 Jan.	War Cause.
	BELHAVEN (R)	1,498	1921	13–14 Mar.*	Sunk by bombs during air raid on Clyde.
EXAMINATION VESSELS.	No. 4 (R)	—	—	Feb. (approx.)	Sunk by enemy action.
	10 (R)	281	—	7 June	Mined off entrance to Milford Haven.
	TUNG WO (R)	1,337	1914	13 Dec.	Abandoned as result of enemy action.
BALLOON BARRAGE VESSEL.	SATURNUS (R)	200	1935	1 May	Constructive total loss.
SPECIAL SERVICE VESSELS.	MINNIE DE LARINAGA ...	5,046	1914	5 Feb.	Sunk as blockship at Dover.
	FIDELIA	147	1891	5 May	Sunk by A/C, Lowestoft Harbour.
	VITA (R)	—	—	22 Sept.	Cause and place unknown.
	NORSJOEN (R)	—	—	19 Nov.	Wrecked on enemy coast.
	KANTUNG (R)	—	—	} 9 Dec.	Sunk as blockships in Anking Harbour.
	MACAO (R)	—	—		
	NORSEMANN (R) ...	—	—	Dec.	Cause and place unknown.
SMALL MISCELLANEOUS CRAFT.	AGHIOS PANTALEIMON (R)	105	—	30 May	Presumed lost.
	DANEHILL	14	1933	1 Dec.	Formally paid off.
ARMED TRADER ...	KUDAT (R)	1,725	1914	30 Dec.	Sunk by A/C at Port Swettenham, Malaya.
AIRCRAFT CARRIERS	HERMES	10,850	18. 2.24	1942 9 Apr.	Sunk by Japanese A/C off Ceylon.
	EAGLE	22,600	20. 2.24	11 Aug.	Sunk by U/B, torpedo, W. Mediterranean.
(AUXILIARY AIRCRAFT CARRIER).	AVENGER	13,785 (deep)	2. 3.42	15 Nov.	Sunk by U/B, torpedo, West of Gibraltar Straits.
CRUISERS	EXETER	8,390	23. 7.31	1 Mar.	Sunk in action with Japanese S.C., Java Seas.
	NAIAD	5,450	24. 7.40	11 Mar.	Sunk by U/B, torpedo, E. Mediterranean.

* Subsequently Salved.

Class	Name	Tonnage	Date of Completion	Date of Loss	How Lost and Where
CRUISERS—(cont.)	CORNWALL	10,000	8. 5.28 ⎫	1942.	Sunk by Japanese dive bombers,
	DORSETSHIRE	9,975	30 9.30 ⎬ 5 Apr.		Indian Ocean.
	EDINBURGH	10,000	6. 7.39	2 May	Sunk by destroyer, torpedoes, after U/B damage (30th Apr.), Barent's Sea, Arctic.
	TRINIDAD	8,000	14.10.41	15 May	Sunk by own forces after damage by torpedo carrying A/C, Barent's Sea, Arctic.
	HERMIONE	5,450	25. 3.41	16 June	Sunk by U/B, torpedo, E. Mediterranean.
	MANCHESTER	9,400	4. 8.38	13 Aug.	Sunk by E/B, torpedo, off Kelibia Roads, Tunisia.
DESTROYERS	VIMIERA	1,090	19. 9.17	9 Jan.	Sunk by mine, Thames Estuary.
	GURKHA (ex LARNE) ...	1,920	18. 2.41	17 Jan.	Sunk by U/B, torpedo, E. Mediterranean.
	MATABELE	1,870	25. 1.39	17 Jan.	Sunk by U/B, torpedo, Barent's Sea, Arctic.
	THANET	1,000	30. 8.19	27 Jan.	Sunk in action with Japanese S.C., off Malaya.
	BELMONT	1,190	22.12.19	31 Jan.	Sunk by U/B, torpedo, W. Atlantic.
	MAORI	1,870	30.11.38	11/12 Feb.	Sunk during air raid on Grand Harbour, Malta.
	ELECTRA	1,375	13. 9.34	27 Feb.	Sunk by S.C., gunfire, Java Sea.
	JUPITER	1,760	25. 6.39	27 Feb.	Sunk by torpedo, Java Sea.
	ENCOUNTER	1,375	2.11.34	1 Mar.	Sunk in action, S.C., Java Sea.
	STRONGHOLD	905	2. 7.19	2 Mar.	Sunk in action, S.C., South of Java.
	VORTIGERN	1,090	25. 1.18	15 Mar.	Sunk by E/B, torpedo, off Cromer.
	HEYTHROP	1,050	21. 6.41	20 Mar.	Sunk by U/B, torpedo, E. Mediterranean.
	SOUTHWOLD	1,050	9.10.41	24 Mar.	Sunk by mine off Malta.
	JAGUAR	1,760	12. 9.39	26 Mar.	Sunk by U/B, torpedo, E. Mediterranean.
	LEGION	1,920	19.12.40	26 Mar.	Sunk by A/C, Malta Harbour.
	CAMPELTOWN ...	1,090	20. 1.19	28 Mar.	Sunk as explosion vessel at St. Nazaire.
	TENEDOS	1,000	11. 6.19	5 Apr.	Sunk by A/C, during attack on Colombo.
	HAVOCK	1,340	16. 1.37	6 Apr.	Grounded, total loss, off Kelibia, Tunisia.
	LANCE	1,920	13. 5.41	9 Apr.*	Sunk by A/C, bombs, at Malta.
	VAMPIRE (On loan to R.A.N.).	1,090	22. 9.17	9 Apr.	Sunk by A/C, bombs, East of Ceylon.
	KINGSTON	1,760	14. 9.39	11 Apr.	Sunk by A/C, bombs, at Malta.
	PUNJABI	1,870	29. 3.39	1 May	Sunk after collision, N. Atlantic.
	KIPLING	1,760	22.12.39	11 May ⎫	
	LIVELY	1,920	20. 7.41	11 May ⎬ Sunk by A/C, E. Mediterranean.	
	JACKAL	1,760	13. 4.39	12 May ⎭	
	GROVE	1,050	5. 2.42	12 June	Sunk by U/B, torpedo, E. Mediterranean.
	AIREDALE	1,050	8. 1.42	15 June	Sunk by A/C, during attack on convoy, E. Mediterranean.
	BEDOUIN	1,870	15. 3.39	15 June	Sunk by A/C, torpedo, Central Mediterranean.
	HASTY	1,340	11.11.36	15 June	Sunk by U/B, torpedo, E. Mediterranean.
	NESTOR (on loan to R.A.N.).	1,760	12. 2.41	15 June	Sunk by A/C, bombs, E. Mediterranean.
	KUJAWIAK (ex OAKLEY) (on loan to Polish Navy).	1,050	17. 6.41	16 June	Sunk by mine off Malta.
	WILD SWAN	1,120	14.11.19	17 June	Sunk by A/C, bombs, Western Approaches.
	FORESIGHT	1,350	15. 5.35	13 Aug.	Sunk by A/C, torpedo, Central Mediterranean.
	BERKELEY	1,000	6. 6.40	19 Aug.	Sunk by A/C during operations at Dieppe.
	SIKH	1,870	12.10.38	14 Sept.	Sunk by gunfire, shore batteries, Tobruk.
	ZULU	1,870	6. 9.38	14 Sept.	Sunk by A/C, bombs, E. Mediterranean.
	SOMALI (Leader) ...	1,870	7.12.38	24 Sept.	Sunk in tow, after U/B, torpedo (20th), off Iceland.
	VETERAN	1,120	13.11.19	26 Sept.	Sunk by U/B, torpedo, N. Atlantic.
	BROKE (Leader)... ...	1,480	20. 1.25	8 Nov.	Sunk by gunfire, shore batteries, Algiers.

* Subsequently Salved.

B

Class	Name	Tonnage	Date of Completion	Date of Loss	How Lost and Where
				1942	
DESTROYERS (cont.)	MARTIN	1,920	4. 4.42	10 Nov.	Sunk by U/B, torpedo, W. Mediterranean.
	QUENTIN	1,705	15. 4.42	2 Dec.	Sunk by A.C, torpedo, W. Mediterranean.
	PENYLAN	1,050	31. 8.42	3 Dec.	Sunk by E/B, torpedo, English Channel.
	BLEAN	1,050	23.8.42	11 Dec.	Sunk by U/B, torpedo, West of Oran, Algeria.
	FIREDRAKE	1,350	30. 5.35	16 Dec.	Sunk by U/B, torpedo, N. Atlantic.
	PARTRIDGE	1,540	22. 2.42	18 Dec.	Sunk by U/B, torpedo, W. Mediterranean.
	ACHATES	1,350	27. 3.30	31 Dec.	Sunk by S.C. gunfire, when escorting convoy, Barent's Sea, Arctic.
SUBMARINES ...	TRIUMPH	1,090	2. 5.39	20 Jan.	Lost, possibly mined, Aegean Sea. Formally Paid Off.
	TEMPEST	1,090	6.12.41	13 Feb. Approx.	Sunk by D/C, Italian S.C., Gulf of Taranto.
	P.38	540	17.10.41	25 Feb.	Lost, possibly mined, Gulf of Hammamet, Tunisia.
	P.39	540	16.11.41	26 Mar.	Sunk by A/C, bombs, at Malta.
	P.36	540	24. 9.41	1 Apr.	Sunk by A/C during raid on Malta Harbour.
	PANDORA	1,475	30. 6.30		
	UPHOLDER	540	31.10.40	14 Apr.	Lost, Probably S.C., D/C, off Tripoli.
	JASTRZAB (ex P.551) (on loan to Polish Navy).	800	9. 7.23	2 May	Sunk by gunfire, own forces, N. Norway, Arctic Ocean, after accidental damage.
	URGE	540	12.12.40	6 May	Lost, possibly mined, E. Mediterranean.
	OLYMPUS	1,475	14. 6.30	8 May	Sunk by mine off Grand Harbour, Malta.
	P.514 ... ... ' ...	530	7.10.18	21 June	Rammed and Sunk by own Forces, W. Atlantic.
	THORN	1,090	26. 8.41	11 Aug.	Lost, probably mined, Libya, E. Mediterranean. Formally Paid Off.
	TALISMAN	1,093	29. 6.40	18 Sept.	Lost, in Sicilian Channel. Formally Paid Off.
	UNIQUE	540	27. 9.40	24 Oct.	Lost, cause unknown, West of Gibraltar Straits.
	UNBEATEN	540	20.11.40	11 Nov.	Lost, possibly by own forces, Bay of Biscay.
	UTMOST	540	17. 8.40	24 Nov.	Lost, probably by S.C., D/C, off Cape Marittimo, West of Sicily.
	P.222	715	4. 5.42	12 Dec.	Lost, probably by S.C, D/C, off Naples.
	TRAVELLER	1,090	10. 4.42	12 Dec.	Lost, probably by D/C from Italian T.B., Gulf of Taranto. Formally paid off.
CHARIOTS ...	No. VI	1·2*	8. 9.42	31 Oct.	Lost in Operation TITLE (projected attack on TIRPITZ in Ofot Fiord, Norway),
	No. VIII	1·2*	11. 9.42		
ARMED MERCHANT CRUISER.	HECTOR (R)	11,198	1924	5 Apr.	Bombed and set on fire during air raid on Colombo.
ANTI-AIRCRAFT SHIPS.	CAIRO	4,200	14.10.19	12 Aug.	Sunk by U/B, torpedo, off Bizerta, Tunisia.
	COVENTRY	4,290	21. 2.18	14 Sept.	Sunk by dive bombers, E. Mediterranean.
	CURAÇOA	4,290	18. 2.18	2 Oct.	Lost in collision, N.W. Approaches.
AUXILIARY ANTI-AIRCRAFT SHIP.	TYNWALD	3,650 (deep)	1.10.41	12 Nov.	Sunk by mine, off Bougie, Algeria.
SLOOP	IBIS	1,300	30. 8.41	10 Nov.	Sunk by A/C, W. Mediterranean
CORVETTES ...	ARBUTUS	900	12.10.40	5 Feb.	Sunk by U/B, torpedo, N. Atlantic.
	ALYSSE (ex ALYSSUM) (On loan to Free French Force).	950	17. 6.41	8 Feb.	Sunk by U/B, torpedo, W. Atlantic.
	SPIKENARD (On loan R.C.N.).	900	7. 4.41	11 Feb.	Sunk by U/B, torpedo, N. Atlantic.

* Submerged.

Class	Name	Tonnage	Date of Completion	Date of Loss	How Lost and Where
				1942	
CORVETTES (*cont.*)	HOLLYHOCK	1,010	19.11.40	9 Apr.	Sunk by A/C, bombs, East of Ceylon.
	AURICULA	915	5. 3.41	5 May	Mined in Courrier Bay, Madagascar.
	MIMOSA (On loan to Free French Force).	1,015	11. 5.41	9 June	Sunk by U/B, torpedo, W. Atlantic.
	GARDENIA	1,015	24. 5.40	9 Nov.	Sunk in collision with own Forces, off Oran, Algeria.
	MONTBRETIA (On loan to R. Nor. N.).	1,015	29. 9.41	18 Nov.	Sunk by U/B, torpedo, N. Atlantic.
	MARIGOLD	1,015	28. 2.41	9 Dec.	Sunk by A/C, torpedo, West of Gibraltar Straits.
	SNAPDRAGON	955	28.10.40	19 Dec.	Sunk by A/C, bombs, Central Mediterranean.
CUTTERS	CULVER	1,546	1929	31 Jan.	Sunk by U/B, torpedo, N. Atlantic.
	HARTLAND	1,546	1928 ⎫	8 Nov.	Sunk by gunfire, Oran Harbour.
	WALNEY	1,546	1930 ⎭		
AUXILIARY A/S VESSELS.	SHU KWANG (R) ...	788	1924	13 Feb.	Sunk by A/C, Dutch East Indies.
	SIANG WO (R) ...	2,595	1926	13 Feb.	Bombed and beached, Dutch East Indies.
	KUALA (R)	954	1911	14 Feb.	Sunk by A/C, Dutch East Indies.
	TIEN KWANG (R) ...	787	1925	Feb.	Lost or destroyed to prevent falling into enemy hands, Singapore Area.
	MATA HARI (R) ...	1,020	1915	28 Feb.	Sunk by A/C in Sunda Strait, Java Sea.
PATROL VESSEL ...	GIANG BEE (R) ...	1,646	1908	Feb.	Lost or destroyed to prevent falling into enemy hands, Singapore Area.
RIVER GUN BOATS	SCORPION	700	14.12.38	13 Feb.	Sunk by gunfire from Japanese S.C., Banka Straits, Sumatra, after attack by A/C (9th).
	DRAGONFLY	625	5. 6.39	14 Feb. ⎫	Sunk by A/C, bombs, after leaving Singapore.
	GRASSHOPPER	625	13. 6.39	14 Feb. ⎭	
MINELAYER ...	KUNG WO (R)	4,636	1921	14 Feb.	Sunk by A/C, bombs, near Lingga Archipelago, Singapore Area.
MINESWEEPERS ...	HUA TONG (R) ...	280	1927	13 Feb. (approx.)	Sunk by A/C in Palembang River, Sumatra.
	CHANGTEH (R)	244	—	14 Feb.	Sunk by A/C, bombs, Singapore Area.
	KLIAS (R)	207	1927	15 Feb.	Scuttled at Palembang, Sumatra.
	JARAK (R)	208	—	17 Feb.	Sunk by A/C, bombs, Singapore Area.
	MALACCA (R)	210	1927	18 Feb.	Scuttled in Tjemako River, Sumatra.
	FUH WO (R)	953	1922 ⎫		Lost by enemy action or destroyed to prevent falling into enemy hands at Singapore.
	LI WO (R)	707	1938 ⎪	Feb.-Mar.	
	SIN AIK LEE (R) ...	198	1928 ⎬		
	TAPAH (R)	208	1926 ⎭		
	SCOTT HARLEY (R) ...	620	1913	3 Mar.	Sunk, probably by S.C., Indian Ocean.
	ABINGDON	710	6.11.18	5 Apr.	Sunk by A/C, bombs, during raid on Malta.
	FITZROY	800	1. 7.19	27 May	Sunk by mine off Great Yarmouth.
	GOSSAMER	815	31. 3.38	24 June	Sunk by A/C, bombs, in Kola Inlet, N. Russia.
	NIGER	815	4. 6.36	6 July	Sunk by mine off Iceland.
	LEDA	815	19. 5.38	20 Sept.	Sunk by U/B, torpedo, Greenland Sea.
	CROMER	656	4. 4.41	9 Nov.	Sunk by mine, E. Mediterranean.
	ALGERINE	940	23. 3.42	15 Nov.	Sunk by U/B, torpedo, off Bougie, Algeria.
	BRAMBLE	815	22. 6.39	31 Dec.	Sunk by S.C, gunfire, Barents Sea, Arctic.
MOTOR MINE-SWEEPERS.	No. 180	226	29. 1.42	13 Feb.	Rammed in convoy, sank off Tyne.
	51	226	29.11.41	4 Mar.	Scuttled, South of Java, to prevent falling into enemy hands.

Class	Name	Tonnage	Date of Completion	Date of Loss	How Lost and Where
				1942	
MOTOR MINE-SWEEPERS (cont.)	No. 174	226	6. 7.42	12 July* ·	Sunk in A/C. attack, Brixham, Devon.
DEGAUSSING SHIP	DAISY (R)	50	1902	25 Apr.	Lost through heavy weather at Greenock.
STEAM GUN BOAT	No. 7	135	11. 3.42	19 June	Sunk in action with S.C. English Channel.
MOTOR TORPEDO BOATS.	No. 47	33	8. 7.41	17 Jan.	Sunk in action by S.C., off Gris Nez, N.E. France.
	74	33	17.12.41	28 Mar. (approx.)	Lost after leaving St. Nazaire.
	215	17	6.12.40	29 Mar.	Paid off, presumed lost.
	220	35	30. 7.41	13 May	Sunk in action with E/B. off Ambleteuse, N.E. France.
	338	—	—	16 May	Wrecked by fire and explosion, Trinidad.
	259	32	—	June	Lost in tow in Mediterranean.
	201	38·6	27.11.41	15 June }	Sank after action with S.C. Dover Straits.
	44	33	1. 4.41	7 Aug. }	
	237	38·6	18. 6.42	7 Aug.	Sank after action with S.C., off Barfleur, France.
	43	33	13. 1.41	18 Aug.	Sunk by S.C. off Gravelines, N.E. France.
	218	35	9. 6.41	18 Aug.	Sunk by S.C. and mine, Dover Straits.
	308	34·4	31. 1.42 }		Lost probably by A/C. attack, Tobruk.
	310	38	10. 2.42 } 14 Sept.		
	312	34·4	21. 2.42 }		
	314	34·4	2. 3.42 }		
	29	34	2. 6.40	6 Oct.	Sank after collision when in action with E/B's. North Sea.
	87	38·6	12. 6.42	31 Oct. }	Sunk by mine, North Sea.
	30	34	11. 7.40	18 Dec. }	
MOTOR GUN BOATS	No. 314	67	26. 6.41	28 Mar.	Sunk by own forces at St. Nazaire, as no longer serviceable.
	328	67	13.10.41	21 July	Lost during attack on enemy convoy, Dover Straits.
	601	85	9. 3.42	24 July	Sunk by enemy action, Dover Straits.
	501	—	19. 5.42	27 July	Sunk after internal explosion, off Lands End, Cornwall.
	335	67	3.10.41	10/11 Sept.	Seriously damaged, set on fire in action with S.C., North Sea.
	18	30	22. 5.41	30 Sept.	Sunk by gunfire, S.C., off Terschelling, Holland.
	78	33	8. 6.42	2/3 Oct.	Attacked by S.C., gunfire, off Holland, beached and abandoned.
	76	33	14. 5.42	6 Oct.	Sunk by E/B, North Sea.
	19	30	28. 7.41	6 Nov.	Bombed and wrecked on slipway.
MOTOR LAUNCHES	KELANA (R)	88	—	16 Jan	Sunk by A/C. Malaya
	PENGHAMBAT	—	— }	Feb.	Lost or destroyed to prevent falling into enemy hands at Singapore.
	PENINGAT (R)	—	— }		
	No. 311	73	29.11.41	14 Feb.	Sunk by Japanese gunfire, Banka Straits, Sumatra.
	169	73	27.11.40	15 Feb.	Destroyed by fire and explosion, Gibraltar Harbour.
	310	73	29.11.41	15 Feb.	Lost by enemy action, S.C., Tjebia Island.
	1062	40	1.42	16 Feb.	Sunk by gunfire, Banka Straits, Sumatra.
	1063	40	1.42	1 Mar.	Sunk in action, Tanjong Priok, Java.
	129	73	14.10.40	22 Mar.	Sunk by A.C. bombs, off Algeria.
	457	73	21.11.41	28 Mar.	Sunk in action, St. Nazaire.
	156	73	18.12.40 }		Sunk by own forces at St. Nazaire as no longer serviceable.
	270	73	26. 6.41 } 28 Mar.		
	446	73	21.11.41 }		
	177	73	12.40 }		
	No. 192 (On loan to Free French Force).	73	1. 8.41 }	28 Mar.	Missing, presumed sunk, at St. Nazaire.
	No. 262 (On loan to Free French Force).	73	18. 6.41 }		

* Subsequently salved.

Class	Name	Tonnage	Date of Completion	Date of Loss	How Lost and Where
MOTOR LAUNCHES (*cont.*)	No. 267 (On loan to Free French Force).	73	25. 7.41	**1942**	
	No. 268 (On loan to Free French Force).	73	17. 7.41	28 Mar.	Missing, presumed sunk, at St Nazaire.
	No. 298	73	21.11.41		
	306	73	18.12.41		
	447	73	8. 1.42	28 Mar.	Sunk in action, St. Nazaire.
	160	73	27.12.40	6 May	Sunk by A/C. bombs, Brixham, S. Devon.
	130	73	9.10.40	7 May	Sunk by gunfire during engagement off Malta.
	301	73	2.12.41	9 Aug.	Sunk by explosion, Freetown Area.
	103	57	28. 6.40	24 Aug.	Sunk by mine, Dover Straits.
	352	73	9. 6.42	14 Sept.	Sunk by A/C, Tobruk, Libya.
	353	73	26. 5.42		
	1153	40	18. 8.42	Sept.	Destroyed by enemy action en route for Turkey.
	339	73	16.10.41	7 Oct.	Sunk by S.C., torpedo, North Sea.
	242	73	28. 5.41	29 Nov.	Gutted by fire.
TRAWLERS ...	IRVANA (R)	276	1917	16 Jan.	Sunk by A/C off Yarmouth, Norfolk.
	ERIN (R)	394	1933	18 Jan.	Sunk by explosion, Gibraltar Harbour.
	HONJO (R)	308	1928		
	ROSEMONDE (R) ...	364	1910	22 Jan.	Probably torpedoed by U/B, Atlantic.
	LOCH ALSH (R) ...	358	1926	30 Jan.	Sunk by A/C, Humber Area.
	CAPE SPARTEL (R) ...	346	1929	2 Feb.	
	CLOUGHTON WYKE (R)	324	1918	2 Feb.	
	BOTANIC	670 (deep)	1928	18 Feb.	Sunk by A/C, bombs, North Sea.
	WARLAND	406 (deep)	—		
	NORTHERN PRINCESS (R) (On loan to U.S.N.).	655	1936	7 Mar.	Sunk, cause unknown, W. Atlantic.
	NOTTS COUNTY (R) ...	541	1937	8 Mar.	Sunk by mine or U/B, South of Iceland.
	STELLA CAPELLA ...	815 (deep)	1937	19 Mar.	Missing, Iceland Area.
	SOLOMON (R)	357	1928	1 Apr.	Mined and sunk, North of Cromer.
	ST. CATHAN (R) (On loan to U.S.N.).	565	1936	11 Apr.	Sunk in collision off S. Carolina, U.S.A.
	LORD SNOWDON (R) ...	444	1934	13 Apr.	Sunk in collision off Falmouth.
	CORAL	705	1935	Apr.	Sunk by A/C during raid on Malta.
	JADE	630	1933	21 Apr.	
	SENATEUR DUHAMEL (On loan to U.S.N.) (R) ...	913	1927	6 May	Sunk in collision off Wilmington, U.S.A.
	BEDFORDSHIRE (On loan to U.S.N.).	913 (deep)	1935	11 May	Sunk by U/B off Cape Lookout, N. Carolina.
	BEN ARDNA (R) ...	226	1917	12 May	Sunk in collision, Tyne Area.
	AGHIOS GEORGIOS IV (R)	164	—	8 June	Sunk in Mozambique Channel.
	KINGSTON CEYLONITE (On loan to U.S.N.).	940	1935	15 June	Sunk by mine off Chesapeake Bay, U.S.A.
	TRANQUIL (R)	294	1912	16 June	Sunk in collision off Deal.
	SWORD DANCE	530	20. 1.41	5 July	Sunk in collision, Moray Firth, E. Scotland.
	MANOR (R)	314	1913	9 July	Sunk during E/B attack, English Channel.
	LAERTES	530	9. 4.41	25 July	Sunk by U/B, torpedo, Freetown Area.
	PIERRE DESCELLIERS (R)	153	1933	13 Aug.	Sunk by A/C, bombs, off Salcombe.
	WATERFLY (R)	387	1931	17 Sept.	Sunk by A/C off Dungeness.
	ALOUETTE (R)	520	1939	19 Sept.	Sunk by U/B, torpedo, off Portugal.
	PENTLAND FIRTH (On loan to U.S.N.).	900 (deep)	1934	19 Sept.	Sunk in collision off New York.
	LORD STONEHAVEN (R)	444	1934	2 Oct.	Sunk during E/B attack off Eddystone, English Channel.
	INVERCLYDE (R) ...	215	1914	16 Oct.	Sank in tow off Beachy Head.
	ULLSWATER	555	15.11.39	19 Nov.	Sunk by E/B, probably torpedoed, English Channel.
	LEYLAND	857 (deep)	1936	25 Nov.	Sunk in collision, Gibraltar Bay.
	BEN ROSSAL (R) ...	260	1929	29 Nov.*	Sank at moorings.

* Subsequently salved.

Class	Name	Tonnage	Date of Completion	Date of Loss	How Lost and Where
				1942	
TRAWLERS (cont.)	JASPER	596	1932	1 Dec.	Sunk by E/B., torpedo, English Channel.
	BENGALI	880 (deep)	1937		
	CANNA	545	7. 4.41	5 Dec.	Sunk by explosion at Lagos, Nigeria.
	SPANIARD	880 (deep)	1937		
WHALERS ...	SOTRA (R)	313	1925	29 Jan.	Sunk by A/C., off Bardia, Libya.
	TRANG (R)	205	1912	14 Feb.	Set on fire and abandoned Cooper Channel, Singapore.
	RAHMAN (R)	209	1926	1 Mar.	Lost or destroyed, Batavia.
	GEMAS (R)	207	1925	2 Mar.	Scuttled, Tjilatjap, Java.
	JERANTUT (R)	217	1927	8 Mar.	Scuttled, Palembang, Sumatra.
	SHERA (R)	253	1929	9 Mar.	Capsized in heavy swell and pack ice, Barents Sea.
	JERAM (R)	210	1927	Mar.	Presumed lost, Singapore Area.
	SULLA (R)	251	1928	25 Mar.	Sunk, probably by S.C., Barents Sea. Formally paid off.
	SVANA (R)	268	1930	8 Apr.	Sunk by A/C. at Alexandria.
	THORGRIM (R)	305	1936		
	SAMBHUR (R)	223	1926	5 May	Stranded off Colombo.
	COCKER (R)	305	1936	3 June	Sunk by U/B. off Bardia, Libya.
	PARKTOWN (R) ...	250	1929	21 June	Sunk by E/B.'s off Tobruk, Libya.
YACHTS ...	SILVIA (R)	—	—	15 Feb.	Constructive total loss.
	SURPRISE	1,144	1896	28 Feb.	Caught fire and capsized at Lagos, West Africa.
	SONA	519	1922	4 Jan.	Sunk by A/C. during attack on Poole, Dorset.
	THALIA	161	1904	11 Oct.	Sunk in collision Lymn of Lorne, West Scotland.
BOOM DEFENCE VESSELS.	DOWGATE	290	18.11.35	Feb.	Lost or destroyed to prevent falling into enemy hands at Singapore.
	LUDGATE	290	18.11.35		
	CHORLEY (R)	284	1914	25 Apr.	Foundered off Start Point, Devon.
	TUNISIAN (R)	238	1930	9 July	Mined and sunk, Harwich Area.
	PANORAMA	548	1919	30 Oct.*	Overdue at Bathurst, W. Africa. Formally paid off.
NAVAL SERVICING BOAT.	No. 9 (On loan to U.S. Authorities).	20	–.12.40	14 Sept.	Sunk.
DESTROYER DEPÔT SHIP.	HECLA	10,850	6. 1.41	12 Nov.	Sunk by U/B., Torpedo, West of Gibraltar Straits.
SUBMARINE DEPÔT SHIP	MEDWAY	14,650	6. 7.29	30 June	Sunk by U/B., torpedo, off Alexandria.
BOOM ACCOMMODATION SHIP.	SUI WO (R)	2,672	1896	Feb.	Lost or destroyed to prevent falling into enemy hands at Singapore.
BASE SHIP ...	ANKING (R)	3,472	1925	3 Mar.	Sunk by gunfire from Japanese S.C., South of Java, Indian Ocean.
TUGS	DAISY (R)	—	—	2 Jan.	Foundered on passage from Alexandria to Tobruk.
	PENGAWAL	—	—	14 Feb.	Sunk by A/C., Durian Straits, Singapore.
	ST. BREOCK	810	—	14 Feb.	Sunk by A/C., bombs, off Sumatra.
	ST. JUST	810	1919	14 Feb.	Sunk by A/C., Durian Straits, Singapore.
	WO KWANG (R) ...	350	1927	Feb.	Assumed lost at Singapore.
	VAILLANT (R)	58	—	15 Feb.	Formally paid off.
	YIN PING (R)	—	1914	15 Feb.	Sunk by gunfire.
	ST. SAMPSON (R) ...	451	1919	7 Mar.	Foundered in Red Sea.
	ADEPT	700	–.3.42	17 Mar.	Grounded, total loss, Hebrides, W. Scotland.
	WEST COCKER ...	229	30.8.19	6 Apr.	Sunk by A/C. during raid on Malta.
	EMILY (R)	—	—	7 Apr.	
	HELLESPONT	690	—	Apr.	
	J.T.A. 6 (R)	—	—	Apr.*	Constructive total loss.

* Subsequently salved.

Class	Name	Tonnage	Date of Completion	Date of Loss	How Lost and Where
TUGS (cont.)	ANDROMEDA (R) ...	—	—	1942 18 Apr.	Sunk by A/C during raid on Malta.
	C. 308	154	—	11 May ⎫	Sunk by mine off Malta
	ST. ANGELO	150 (deep)	1935	30 May ⎭	
	VISION ...	—	—	18 Jun.	Sunk at Mersa Matruh, Egypt.
	ALAISIA (R)	72	1929	20 Jun.	Lost by enemy action at Tobruk, Libya.
	J.T.A. 1 (R)	—	⎫		
	J.T.A. 7 (R)	—	— ⎬	20 Jun.	Lost at Tobruk, Libya.
	J.T.A. 14 (R)	—	⎭		
	ST. OLAVES (R)	468	1919	21 Sept.	Grounded, total loss, off Duncansby Head, N.E. Scotland.
	CAROLINE MOLLER (R)	444	1919	7 Oct.	Torpedoed and sunk by E/B's, North Sea.
	BAIA (R)	—		3 Nov.	Lost in tow between Mogadishu and Mombasa.
	ST. ISSEY	810	28.12.18	28 Dec.	Sunk, probably by U/B, off Benghazi, Libya.
MOORING VESSEL	MOOR	767	15.8.19	Apr.	Blown up and Sunk by enemy action at Malta.
DRIFTERS ...	UNICITY (R)	96	1919	31 Jan.	Capsized and sank while on sweeping duties of Blyth.
	BOY ROY (R)	20	—	11 Feb.	Cause and place unknown.
	VICTORIA I (R)	—	—	25 Mar.	Sunk by enemy action.
	CATHERINE (R)	78	1914	8 Jun.	Foundered in Scapa area, Orkneys.
	TRUSTY STAR	96	1920	10 June ⎫	Mined off Malta.
	JUSTIFIED	93	1925	16 June ⎭	
	HIGHLAND QUEEN (R)	—	—	20–21 June	Scuttled during fall of Tobruk, Libya.
	INTREPEDE (R)	—	—	13 Aug.	Sunk by A/C off Salcombe.
	GOLDEN SUNBEAM (R)	84	1920	19 Aug.	Sunk in Collision off Dungeness, English Channel.
	WINSOME (R)	46	1902	18 Nov.	Sunk at Fairlie, total loss.
	LEGEND (R)	—	—	28 Dec.	Cause and place unknown.
TANKERS AND OILERS.	NYHOLT (R)	8,087	1931	17 Jan.	Sunk by U/B, W. Atlantic.
	CIRCE SHELL (R) ...	8,207	1931	21 Feb.	Sunk by U/B off Venezuela.
	FINNANGER (R) ...	9,551	1928	24 Feb.	Sunk by U/B, N. Atlantic.
	WAR SIRDAR	5,518	–. 2.20	1 Mar.	Lost on reef, N.W. Batavia.
	FRANCOL	2,623 (E)	18.12.17	3 Mar.	Sunk by gunfire, Japanese S.C., South of Java.
	SLAVOL	2,623	1.11.17	26 Mar.	Sunk by U/B, torpedo, en route for Tobruk, Libya.
	SVENOR (R)	7,616	1931	27 Mar.	Sunk by U/B, W. Atlantic.
	PLUMLEAF	5,916	11. 3.17	4 Apr.	Sunk by A/C, bombs, at Malta.
	SANDAR (R)	7,624	1928	2 May	Sunk by U/B off Tobago, W. Indies.
	BETH (R)	6,852	1930	18 May	Sunk by U/B, off Barbados, W. Indies.
	MONTENOL	2,646	20.11.17	21 May	Torpedoed by U/B, N. Atlantic. Sunk by own forces.
	ALDERSDALE	8,402	17. 9.37	26 May	Sunk, Cause unknown, Barents Sea, Arctic.
	DINSDALE	8,250	11. 4.42	31 May	Sunk by U/B, torpedo, S. Atlantic.
	SLEMDAL (R)	7,374	1931	15 Jun.	Sunk by U/B, N. Atlantic.
	ANDREA BROVIG (R) ...	10,173	1940	23 Jun. ⎫	Sunk by U/B, W. Indies.
	LEIV EIRIKSSON (R) ...	9,952	1936	27 Jun. ⎭	
	TANKEXPRESS (R) ...	10,095	1937	25 Jul.	Sunk by U/B, off W. Africa.
	HAVSTEN (R)	6,161	1930	3 Aug.	Sunk by U/B, W. Atlantic.
	MALMANGER (R) ...	7,078	1920	9 Aug.	Sunk by U/B. off W. Africa.
	MIRLO (R)	7,455	1922	11 Aug.	Sunk by U/B, off W. Africa.
	THELMA (R)	8,297	1937	26 Aug.	Cause and place unknown.
	VARDAAS (R)	8,176	1931	30 Aug.	Sunk by U/B, off Tobago, W. Indies.
	SVEVE (R)	6,313	1930	10 Sept.	Sunk by U/B, N. Atlantic.
	THORSHAVET (R) ...	11,015	1938	3 Nov.	Sunk by U/B, Caribbean Sea.
	BELITA (R)	6,323	1933	3 Dec.	Sunk by U/B, off Socotra, Arabian Sea.
DISTILLING SHIP	STAGHOUND (R) ...	468	1894	27 Mar.*	Sunk by A/C, bombs, at Torquay.
WATER CARRIER	KALGAH (R)	—	—	24 Sept.	Cause and place unknown.
COLLIERS ...	ZANNIS L. CAMBANIS (R)	5,317	1920	21 Jan.	Mined off Singapore.
	FERNWOOD (R) ...	1,892	1923	18 Sept.*	Sunk by A/C, at Dartmouth.

* Subsequently salved.

Class	Name	Tonnage	Date of Completion	Date of Loss	How Lost and Where
FLEET AIR ARM TARGET VESSEL.	ST. BRIAC (R)	2,312	1924	1942 12 Mar.	Sunk by mine off Aberdeen, E. Scotland.
EXAMINATION VESSEL.	SOLEN (R)	—	—	Feb.	Presumed lost at Singapore.
BALLOON BARRAGE VESSEL.	REIDAR (R)	—	1915	28 Dec.	Constructive total loss.
SPECIAL SERVICE VESSELS.	COLLINGDOC	1,780	1925	Mar.	Sunk as Blockship.
	MARS (R)	—	1938	May (date reported)	⎫ Cause and place unknown.
	FREYA I (R)	—	1934	2 May	⎬
	JOKER (R)	—	—	16 July	Lost in tow in heavy weather.
	SJO (R)	—	1938	Dec. (Date reported)	⎫ Cause and place unknown.
	ARTHUR (R)	—	—	1 Dec.	⎬
	ASEL I (R)	10	1919	11 Dec.	
	FIDELITY (R)	2,456	—	30 Dec.	Probably torpedoed by U/B, N. Atlantic.
SMALL MISCELLANEOUS CRAFT.	BOY PETER	14	—	5 Feb.	Lost by fire·
	SHUN AN (R)	—	—	Feb.	Lost or destroyed to prevent falling into enemy hands at Singapore.
	MATCHLOCK	70	—	—	Sunk by mine at Canton. Date unknown.
TRANSPORT VESSELS.	ZOODOCHOS PIGHI (R) ...	170	—	13 March.	Sunk by enemy action, E. Mediterranean.
	TERPSITHEA (R) ...	157	1919	29 Apr.	Mined at Famagusta, Cyprus
	FAROUK (R)	91	—	13 June	Cause and place unknown.
ARMED TRADERS	LARUT (R)	894	1927 ⎫	22 Jan.	Sunk by A/C off East Coast, Sumatra.
	RAUB (R)	1,161	1926 ⎬		
	VYNER BROOKE (R) ...	1,670	1928	14 Feb.	Sunk by A/C off Banka Straits, Sumatra.
	LIPIS (R)	845	1927	Feb.	Believed lost off Singapore by enemy action.
HARBOUR DUTY VESSELS.	NYKEN (R)	111	—	Jan. (date reported)	Constructive total loss.
	CHRYSOLITE (R) ...	—	1934	15 July	Cause and place unknown.
	VASSILIKI (R)	—	—	23 July	Sunk by U/B on passage from Beirut to Famagusta.
	RUBY (R)	46 Net.	1902	9 Oct.	Wrecked in gale, Scapa Flow, Orkneys.
	BRODRENE (R)	—	1922	26 Dec.	Sunk in collision, Hvalfiord, Iceland.
FERRY SERVICE VESSEL.	SANDOY (R)	49	1940	11 Dec.	Cause and place unknown.
DUMB BARGES ...	CELT				
	COOLIE				
	COSSACK				
	DERVISH				
	MAORI				
	MATABELE			⎫	Sunk for boom defence purposes, presumed in 1942.
	ODESSA			⎬	
	PARTISAN				
	PHILISTINE				
	REDRESS				
	RESPITE				
	REVENGE				
	VALENCIA				
	DARTMOUTH (R) ...	226 (deep) (E)	1923	2 Oct.	Sunk as blockship.
AIRCRAFT CARRIER (ESCORT CARRIER).	DASHER	13,785 (deep)	2.7.42	1943 27 Mar.	Sunk, probably due to petrol explosion, South of Cumbrae Island, W. Scotland.
CRUISER	CHARYBDIS	5,450	3.12.41	23 Oct.	Sunk by E/B, torpedoes, English Channel.
DESTROYERS ...	HARVESTER	1,400	25.3.40	11 Mar.	Sunk by U/B, torpedo, N. Atlantic.
	LIGHTNING	1,920	28.5.41	12 Mar.	Sunk by E/B, torpedo, Central Mediterranean.

Class	Name	Tonnage	Date of Completion	Date of Loss	How Lost and Where
				1943	
DESTROYERS (*cont.*)	BEVERLEY	1,190	3. 4.20	11 Apr.	Sunk by U/B, torpedo, N. Atlantic.
	ESKDALE (on loan to R. Nor. N.).	1,050	31. 7.42	14 Apr.	Sunk by E/B, torpedo, off Lizard Head, Cornwall.
	PAKENHAM (Leader) ...	1,550	4. 2.42	16 Apr.	Sunk by own forces after damage in action with destroyers off Sicily.
	PUCKERIDGE	1,050	30. 7.41	6 Sept.	Sunk by U/B, torpedo, W. Mediterranean.
	INTREPID	1,370	29. 7.37	27 Sept.	Sunk by A/C, in Leros Harbour Dodecanese.
	ORKAN (ex MYRMIDON) (On loan to Polish Navy).	1,920	5.12.42	8 Oct.	Sunk by U/B, torpedo, N. Atlantic.
	PANTHER	1,540	12.12.41	9 Oct.	Sunk by A/C, bombs, Scarpanto Strait, Dodecanese.
	HURWORTH	1,050	5.10.41	22 Oct.	Sunk by mine off Kalimno, Dodecanese.
	LIMBOURNE	1,050	24.10.42	23 Oct.	Sunk by own forces after damage by E/B, torpedoes, English Channel.
	ECLIPSE ...	1,375	29.11.34	24 Oct.	Sunk by mine off Kalimno, Dodecanese.
	DULVERTON	1,050	27. 9.41	13 Nov.	Sunk by A/C, glider bomb, off Kos, Dodecanese.
	HOLCOMBE	1,050	16. 9.42	12 Dec.	Sunk by U/B., torpedo, West Mediterranean.
	TYNEDALE	1,000	2.12.40	12 Dec.	Sunk by U/B., torpedo, West Mediterranean.
	HURRICANE	1,400	21.6.40	24 Dec.	Sunk by U/B., torpedo, N. Atlantic.
SUBMARINES ...	P. 48 ...	540	18. 6.42	4 Jan.	Lost, possibly mined, Gulf of Tunis.
	P. 311 ...	1,090	7. 8.42	8 Jan.	Lost, possibly mined, off Maddalena, Sardinia.
	VANDAL ...	540	20. 2.43	24 Feb.	Lost by accident, Firth of Clyde, W. Scotland.
	UREDD (ex P. 41) (On loan to R. Nor. N.).	540	12.12.41	24 Feb. (approx.)	Lost, probably mined, Bodo area, Norway.
	TIGRIS ...	1,093	20. 6.40	10 Mar.	Lost, cause unknown, Gulf of Naples.
	THUNDERBOLT ...	1,090	1.11.40	13 Mar.	Sunk by S.C., D/C, off Cape Milazzo, Sicily.
	TURBULENT ...	1,090	2.12.41	23 Mar. (approx.)	Lost, probably mined, off Sardinia.
	REGENT ...	1,475	11.11.30	16 Apr.	Sunk by S.C., Straits of Otranto.
	SPLENDID	715	8. 8.42	21 Apr.	Scuttled after D/C attack, W. Coast of Corsica.
	SAHIB	715	13. 5.42	24 Apr.	Scuttled after D/C attack off Cape Milazzo, Sicily.
	UNTAMED	540	14. 4.43	30 May†	Failed to surface during exercises off Campbeltown.
	PARTHIAN	1,475	13. 1.31	11 Aug.	Lost, possibly mined, S. Adriatic.
	SARACEN	715	27. 6.42	18 Aug.	Sunk by S.C., D/C, off Bastia, Corsica.
	USURPER...	540	2. 2.43	11 Oct. (approx.)	Lost, probably mined, Gulf of Genoa.
	TROOPER	1,090	29. 8.42	17 Oct.	Lost, possibly mined, Aegean Sea.
	SIMOOM ...	715	30.12.42	19 Nov. (approx.)	Lost, Dardanelles Approach.
X CRAFT ...	X 8	29·8*	21. 1.43	17 Sept.	
	X 5	29·8*	29.12.42		Lost in attack on Tirpitz, Kaa Fiord, Alten Fiord, Norway.
	X 6	29·8*	21. 1.43	22 Sept.	Lost in attack on Tirpitz, Kaa Fiord, Alten Fiord, Norway.
	X 7	29·8*	14. 1.43		Lost in attack on Tirpitz, Kaa Fiord, Alten Fiord, Norway.
	X 10	29·8*	8. 2.43	3 Oct.	Lost in attack on Tirpitz, Kaa Fiord, Alten Fiord, Norway.
	X 9	29·8*	29. 1.43	15 Oct.	Lost in attack on Tirpitz, Kaa Fiord, Alten Fiord, Norway.
CHARIOTS ...	No. XV ...	1·2*	6.10.42		Lost in Operation PRINCIPAL (Palermo, Italy).
	XVI...	1·2*	10.10.42		Lost in Operation PRINCIPAL (Palermo, Italy).
	XIX	1·2*	16.10.42	2 Jan.	Lost in Operation PRINCIPAL (Palermo, Italy).
	XXII	1·2*	29.10.42		Lost in Operation PRINCIPAL (Palermo, Italy).
	XXIII	1·2*	23.10.42		Lost in Operation PRINCIPAL (Palermo, Italy).
	X ...	1·2*	15. 9.42	8 Jan.	Lost in Operation PRINCIPAL (Maddalena, Sardinia).
	XVIII	1·2*	14.10.42	8 Jan.	Lost in Operation PRINCIPAL (Maddalena, Sardinia).
	XII ...	1·2*	30. 9.42	19 Jan.	Lost in Operation WELCOME (Tripoli).
	XIII	1·2*	30. 9.42	19 Jan.	Lost in Operation WELCOME (Tripoli).

* Submerged.
† Subsequently salved and renamed VITALITY.

Class	Name	Tonnage	Date of Completion	Date of Loss	How Lost and Where
				1943	
CHARIOTS (cont.).	No. LII ... ... LVII	1·2* 1·2*	14. 5.43 29. 6.43 }	22 Nov.	Jettisoned in heavy weather in attack on German shipping in Norwegian Fiords.
WELMAN CRAFT ...	No. 10	2·4*	12. 5.43	9 Sept.	Accidently lost during exercises.
	45 ... ... 46 ... ... 47 ... ... 48	2·4* 2·4* 2·4* 2·4*	2. 9.43 7. 9.43 2. 9.43 13. 9.43 }	22 Nov.	Lost during attack on Bergen Harbour, Norway.
AUXILIARY ANTI-AIRCRAFT SHIP.	POZARICA	4,540	7. 3.41	13 Feb.	Capsized after torpedo attack by A/C off Bougie, Algeria (29 Jan.).
SLOOP	EGRET	1,250	10.11.38	27 Aug.	Sunk by A/C, glider bomb, off N.W. Spain.
FRIGATE	ITCHEN	1,325	28.12.42	23 Sept.	Sunk by U/B, torpedo, N. Atlantic.
CORVETTES ...	SAMPHIRE	1,015	30. 6.41	30 Jan.	Sunk by U/B, torpedo, W. Mediterranean.
	ERICA	955	7. 8.40	9 Feb.	Sunk by mine, N.E. of Benghazi, Libya.
	POLYANTHUS	1,015	23. 4.41	20 Sept.	Sunk by U/B, torpedo, N. Atlantic.
MINELAYERS ...	CORNCRAKE	700	7.12.42	25 Jan.	Foundered in bad weather, N. Atlantic.
	WELSHMAN	2,650	25. 8.41	1 Feb.	Sunk by U/B, torpedo, off Libya.
	ABDIEL	2,650	15. 4.41	10 Sept.	Sunk by mine in Taranto Bay, S. Italy.
MINESWEEPERS ...	HYTHE	605	5. 3.42	11 Oct.	Sunk by U/B, torpedo, off Bougie, Algeria.
	CROMARTY	605	13.12.41	23 Oct.	Sunk by mine, Western Approaches to Straits of Bonifacio, Mediterranean.
	HEBE	815	23.10.37	22 Nov.	Sunk by mine off Bari, E. Italy.
	FELIXSTOWE	656	11. 7.41	18 Dec.	Sunk by mine off Sardinia.
	CLACTON	605	4. 6.42	31 Dec.	Sunk by mine off Corsica.
B.Y.M.S. MINE-SWEEPER.	No. 2019... ...	290	15. 8.42	19 Sept.	Mined and beached off Cotrone, Italy.
MOTOR MINESWEEPERS.	No. 89	240	5. 1.42	12 May	Sunk by mine off Bizerta, Tunisia.
	70 ...	240	18. 5.42	24 Sept.	Sunk, believed by mine, in Gulf of Taranto, S. Italy.
MOTOR TORPEDO BOATS.	No. 105	9	– 8.40	1 Jan.	Taken in tow and sunk by own forces.
	262 ... ... 622	32 95	— –.10.42	24 Feb. 10 March	Formally paid off. Sunk by S.C. when attacking convoy off Terschelling, Holland.
	631 ... ... (On loan to R.Nor.N.)	95	–. 8.42	14 March	Grounded during attack on ships in Norwegian Fiords.
	63 ... ... 64	35 35	18. 2.42 23. 2.42 }	2 April	Sunk in collision off Benghazi.
	267	32	—	2 April	Damaged in rough weather on passage, Benghazi to Malta. Sunk by own forces.
	639	95	22. 1.43	28 April	Sunk by A/C, Central Mediterranean.
	311	34·4	17. 2.42	2 May	Sunk by mine, Central Mediterranean.
	61	35	9. 1.42	9 May	Lost by stranding in attack on Motor Barges at Kelibia, Tunisia.
	264	32	—	10 May	Sunk by mine off Sousse, Tunisia.
	316	34·4	12. 3.42	17 July	Sunk by torpedo from Italian cruiser off Reggio, S. Italy.
	288 ... ... 665	40 95	26. 3.43 5.43	21/22 July 15 Aug.	Sunk by A/C, Augusta, Sicily. Sunk by gunfire, shore batteries, Messina, Sicily.
	77	38·6	28. 5.42	8 Sept.	Sunk by A/C off Vibo Valencia, S.W. Italy.

* Submerged.

Class	Name	Tonnage	Date of Completion	Date of Loss	How Lost and Where
				1943	
MOTOR TORPEDO BOATS (*cont.*).	No. 636	95	1.43	15 Oct.	Sunk by S.C. off Elba, W. Italy.
	356	37	1. 7.43	16 Oct.	Sunk by S.C. off Holland.
	669	95	29. 4.43	26 Oct.	Sunk by S.C. off Norwegian coast.
	606	90	7. 7.42	3/4 Nov.	Sunk by S.C. off Hook of Holland.
	222 ... ... (On loan to R. Neth. N.).	38·6	15. 2.42	9/10 Nov.	Sunk by mine, North Sea.
	230	38·6	5. 5.42	9/10 Nov.	Rammed by M.T.B.222 in action, North Sea.
	626 ... ... (On loan to R. Nor. N.).	95	8.42 ⎫		
			⎬	22 Nov.	Lost by fire, Lerwick, Shetland.
	686	95	9. 6.43 ⎭		
	73	38·6	3.10.41	24 Nov.	Sunk by A/C, Maddalena, Sardinia.
	357	37	25. 8.43	24 Dec.	Sunk by accident after damage by S.C. (23rd).
MOTOR GUN BOATS	No. 109	37	30. 9.42	25 Feb.	Mined and severely damaged (7th). Formally paid off.
	79	37	24. 7.42	28 Feb.	Sunk in action with S.C., Hook of Holland area.
	110	37	14.11.42	29 May	Sunk in action with S.C. in vicinity of Dunkirk.
	648	90	1.43	14 June	Sunk by A/C, Pantellaria, Central Mediterranean.
	644	90	12.42	26 June	Mined between Marsala and Mazzara, Sicily. Sunk by own forces.
	641	90	29.12.42	14/15 July	Sunk by gunfire from battery on Italian mainland, Straits of Messina.
	64	28	11. 2.41	8 Aug.*	Foundered on patrol in heavy weather between Ostend and U.K.
MOTOR LAUNCHES	No. 251	75·5	7.41	6 Mar.	Rammed and sunk by accident, Atlantic.
	1157	40	30.12.42 ⎫		
	1212	40	11.12.42 ⎬	Apr.	Lost in shipment.
	133	75·5	12.12.40	11 May	Destroyed by fire and explosion W. Scotland.
	1154	40	30. 1.43	14 May	Sunk by mine at Bizerta, Tunisia.
	108	66	4. 7.40	5 Sept.	Sunk by mine, English Channel.
	1015	40	24. 2.41	Oct.	Lost due to heavy gales, E. Mediterranean.
	835	75·5	8. 8.43	12 Oct. ⎫	Sunk by A/C, Leros, Dodecanese.
	579	75·5	3. 6.43	26 Oct. ⎭	
	1054	40	6.11.41	Nov.	Total loss.
	1244	40	20. 8.43	Nov. ⎫	Lost on passage.
	1289	40	2. 7.43	Nov. ⎭	
	358	75·5	9.42	12 Nov.	Lost off Leros, Dodecanese.
	126	75·5	19. 9.40	27 Nov.	Lost after damage by U/B, torpedo, W. Italy.
	1388	40	25.11.43	24 Dec.	Grounded off Hartlepool.
	1121	40	10. 7.42	31 Dec.	Formally paid off.
TRAWLERS ...	HORATIO	545	27. 1.41	7 Jan.	Sunk by E/B, torpedo, W. Mediterranean.
	JURA	545	12. 6.42	7 Jan.	Sunk by torpedo, U/B, or A/C, W. Mediterranean.
	KINGSTON JACINTH (R)	356	1929	12 Jan.	Mined off Portsmouth.
	STRONSAY	545	24. 4.42	5 Feb.	Sunk by explosion, probably mine, off Philippeville, W. Mediterranean.
	TERVANI (R) ...	409	1930	7 Feb.	Probably sunk by U/B off Cape Bougaroni, Algeria.
	BREDON	750	29. 4.42	8 Feb.	Sunk by U/B, torpedo, N. Atlantic.
	LORD HAILSHAM ...	891 (deep)	1934	27 Feb.	Attacked by E/Bs, probably torpedoed, English Channel.
	MORAVIA (R)	306	1917	14 Mar.	Sunk by mine, North Sea.
	CAMPOBELLO	545	21.10.42	16 Mar.	Foundered on passage to U.K. after being badly damaged at Quebec.
	CAULONIA (R)	296	1912	31 Mar.	Ran aground and foundered, Rye Bay, Sussex.
	ADONIS	1,004	1915	15 Apr.	Sunk by E/B, torpedo, off Lowestoft.

* Subsequently salved.

Class	Name	Tonnage	Date of Completion	Date of Loss	How Lost and Where
TRAWLERS (cont.)	HERRING...	590	15. 4.43	1943 22 Apr.	Sunk in collision, North Sea.
	DANEMAN	1,050 (deep)	1937	8 May	Believed to have struck submerged ice. Abandoned after being taken in tow, N. Atlantic.
	HONG LAM (R)... ...	104	—	26 May	Foundered off Adam's Bridge, between India and Ceylon. Formally paid off.
	RED GAUNTLET (R) ...	338	1930	5 Aug.	Sunk by E/Bs, North Sea.
	ZEE MEEUW (R) ...	—	—	21 Sept.	Sunk in collision, Gravesend Reach, Thames.
	DONNA NOOK (R) ...	307	1916	25 Sept.	Sunk in collision, North Sea.
	FRANC TIREUR (R) ...	314	1916	25 Sept.	Sunk by E/B off Harwich.
	ARACARI (R)	245	1908	3 Oct.	Grounded, total loss, Filicudi Island, North of Sicily.
	MEROR (R)	250	1905	3 Oct.	Mined, Humber area.
	ORFASY	545	14. 7.42	22 Oct.	Lost, probably by U/B torpedo, off W. Africa.
	WILLIAM STEPHEN (R)...	235	1917	25 Oct.	Sunk by E/B off Cromer.
	AVANTURINE (R) ...	296	1930	1 Dec.	Sunk by E/Bs off Beachy Head.
	RYSA	545	13. 8.41	8 Dec.	Sunk by mine off Maddalena, Sardinia.
	KINGSTON BERYL (R)...	356	1928	25 Dec.	Mined, N.W. Approaches.
WHALERS... ...	BODO (R)	351	—	4 Jan.	Mined off E. Coast of Scotland.
	HARSTAD (R)	258	—	27 Feb.	Sunk by E/B, English Channel.
	SANTA (R)	355	1936	23 Nov.	Mined, West of Maddalena, Sardinia.
YACHTS	SARGASSO (R)	223	1926	6 June	Mined off Isle of Wight.
	ATTENDANT (R) ...	357	1913	Nov. (date reported)	Cause and place unknown.
BOOM DEFENCE VESSELS.	FABIOUS (R)	230 (deep)	—	16 Jan.	Sunk.
	BARFLAKE	750	23. 9.42	22 Nov.	Sunk by mine, Naples.
BARRAGE VESSELS	B.V.42	270	9.12.18	22 Dec.	Lost by explosion, Leith Docks, E. Scotland.
NAVAL SERVICING BOAT.	No. 30	8	5. 3.41	8 Nov.	Sunk.
NAVAL AUXILIARY BOAT.	LILY	—	—	24–25 Dec.	Sunk in collision off Portland.
TUGS	HORSA	700	21.12.42	16 Mar.	Grounded, total loss, Osfles Rock, E. Iceland.
	CORY BROS (R)... ...	38	—	9 Aug.	Constructive, total loss.
	TIENTSIN (R)	—	—	26 Oct.	Foundered, Red Sea, on passage to Massawa.
RESCUE SHIP ...	ST. SUNNIVA (R) ...	1,368	1931	22 Jan.	Marine cause.
DRIFTERS ...	PREMIER (R)	14	1918	3 Feb.	Collided with No. 10 Holme Hook Buoy, Humber, and sank.
	UT PROSIM (R)	91	1925	2 Mar.	Sunk by gunfire in Dover Harbour.
	GOLDEN GIFT (R) ...	89	1910	6 Apr.	Sunk in collision in Oban Bay, W. Scotland.
	THORA (R)	37	1930	26 Apr.	Fouled boom in bad weather, Grimsby.
	NORNES (R)	—	1902	14 Aug.	⎫
	NOSS HEAD	22 Net	—	9 Sept.	
	ROSA (R)	83	1908	11 Sept.	⎬ Cause and place unknown.
	NISR (R)	—	—	16 Sept.	
	BRAE FLETT (R) ...	54 Net	1902	22 Sept.	⎭
	OCEAN RETRIEVER (R)	95	1912	22 Sept.	Mined, Thames Estuary.
	GOLDEN EFFORT (R) ...	86	1914	23 Sept.	Sunk, cause unknown, off Greenock.
	CHANCELLOR (R) ...	24	1916	30 Oct.	Sunk in tow.
	ROSE VALLEY (R) ...	100	1918	16 Dec.	Sunk in collision.
TANKERS AND OILERS.	ALBERT L. ELLSWORTH (R).	8,309	1937	8 Jan. (approx.)	⎫ Sunk by U/B off W. Africa.
	MINISTER WEDEL (R) ...	6,833	1930	9 Jan.	⎭
	ROSEWOOD (R)	5,989	1931	9 Mar.	Torpedoed and presumed sunk.
	HALLANGER (R)... ...	9,551	1928	30 Mar.	Sunk by U/B, W. Mediterranean.
	ALCIDES (R)	7,634	1930	2 Aug. (approx.)	Sunk by Japanese Raider, Indian Ocean.

Class	Name	Tonnage	Date of Completion	Date of Loss	How Lost and Where
TANKERS AND OILERS (*cont.*)	THORSHOVDI (R)	9,944	1937	1943 4 Aug.	War cause.
	MARIT (R)	5,542	1918	4 Oct.	Sunk by U/B, off Benghazi, Libya.
	LITIOPA (R)	5,356	1917	22 Oct.	Sunk by U/B off W. Africa.
VICTUALLING STORE SHIP.	MORAY (R)	206	1918	13 Mar.	Foundered off Milford Haven.
WATER CARRIER	EMPIRE ARTHUR (R)	760	1942	22 Nov.	Capsized and sank, Freetown, W. Africa.
COLLIER ...	NEVA (R)	1,456	1928	22 Jan.	Presumed sunk by U/B, N. Atlantic.
WATER BOATS ...	ISBJORN (R)	—	—	13 May	Sunk.
	CECIL (R)	—	—	18 Dec.	Constructive total loss.
SPECIAL SERVICE VESSELS.	FEIOY (R)	—	—	Jan.	⎫
	GULDBORG (R)	—	—	22 Jan.	⎬ Cause and place unknown.
	BERGHOLM (R)	50	1935	23 Mar.	
	BRATTHOLM (R)	50	1937	30 Mar.	⎭
	DAH PU (R)	1,974	1922	28 June	Torpedoed by U/B, Muscat Harbour, E. Coast of Arabia.
	EVANGELISTRIA (CHIOS 345) (R).	—	—	23 Sept.	Sunk by enemy action.
	BILLDORA (R)	—	—	⎫	
	SQUALLY (R)	—	—	⎬ 11 Nov.	Sunk by enemy action.
	WESTWICK (R)	18	1935	⎭	
SMALL MISCELLANEOUS CRAFT.	NAIEM ...	—	—	Jan.	Sunk at Tobruk.
	FOLIOT ...	33	1905	17 Nov.	Sunk in Collision.
HARBOUR DUTY VESSEL.	ST. ANNE (R)	37	—	Dec.	Cause and place unknown.
DUMB BARGES ...	NELL JESS	96	1902	May	Wrecked, English Channel.
	CLACTON	196 (deep) (E).	—	Nov.* (approx.)	⎫
	FOUR	204 (deep) (E).		Nov. (approx.)	
	GREENFINCH	218 (deep) (E).	—	Nov.* (approx.)	⎬ Cause and place unknown.
	MONICA ...	233 (deep) (E).	—	Nov.* (approx.)	
	SAN FRANCISCO	241 (deep) (E).	—	Nov. (approx.)	
	UTOPIA ...	226 (deep) (E).	—	Nov. (approx.)	⎭
CRUISERS ...	SPARTAN	5,770	10. 8.43	1944 29 Jan.	Sunk by A/C, Glider Bomb, off Anzio, W. Italy.
	PENELOPE	5,270	13.11.36	18 Feb.	Sunk by U/B, torpedo, Anzio area, W. Italy.
	DURBAN ...	4,850	31.10.21	9 June	Sunk as blockship for Mulberry Harbour, Normandy.
	DRAGON ... (on loan to Polish Navy)	4,850	16. 8.18	8 July	Damaged by human torpedo off Normandy. Constructive total loss.
DESTROYERS ...	JANUS ...	1,760	5. 8.39	23 Jan.	Sunk by A/C, torpedo, off Anzio, W. Italy.
	HARDY (Leader)	1,730	14. 8.43	30 Jan.	Sunk by U/B, torpedo, Barents Sea, Arctic.
	WARWICK	1,100	20. 3.18	20 Feb.	Sunk by U/B, torpedo, off N. Cornwall.
	INGLEFIELD (Leader) ...	1,530	25. 6.37	25 Feb.	Sunk by A/C, glider bomb, off Anzio, W. Italy.
	MAHRATTA	1,920	8. 4.43	25 Feb.	Sunk by U/B, torpedo, Barents Sea, Arctic.
	LAFOREY (Leader)	1,935	26. 8.41	30 Mar.	Sunk by U/B, torpedo, North of Sicily.
	SVENNER (ex SHARK) ... (On loan to R. Nor. N.)	1,710	18. 3.44	6 June	Sunk by S.C., torpedo, off Normandy.

* Subsequently Salved.

Class	Name	Tonnage	Date of Completion	Date of Loss	How Lost and Where
				1944	
DESTROYERS (*cont.*)	WRESTLER	1,100	15. 5.18	6 June	Damaged beyond repair by mine off Normandy.
	BOADICEA	1,360	7. 4.31	13 June	Sunk by A/C, torpedo, off Portland, English Channel.
	QUAIL	1,705	7. 1.43	18 June	Sank in tow, Bari to Taranto, after damage by mine (15th Nov. 1943).
	FURY	1,350	18. 5.35	21 June	Damaged beyond repair by mine off Normandy.
	SWIFT	1,710	6.12.43	24 June	Sunk by mine off Normandy.
	ISIS	1,370	2. 6.37	20 July	} Sunk by human torpedo, or
	QUORN	1,000	21. 9.40	3 Aug.	} mine off Normandy.
	ROCKINGHAM	1,190	31. 7.19	27 Sept.	Sunk by mine, E. Scotland.
	ALDENHAM	1,050	5. 2.42	14 Dec.	Sunk by mine, N.E. Adriatic.
SUBMARINES ...	P. 715 (*ex* GRAPH) (German Prize vessel)	880 (submerged)	—	20 Mar.	Dismantled, broke adrift and lost on West Coast of Islay, W. Scotland.
	STONEHENGE	715	15. 6.43	22 Mar. (approx.)	Lost on patrol, probably off Nicobar Islands, Indian Oc.
	SYRTIS	715	23. 4.43	28 Mar.	Sunk by mine off Bodo, Norway.
	SICKLE	715	1.12.42	18 June (approx.)	Sunk, probably mined, Anti-Kithera Channel, Greece.
	B.1 (*ex* SUNFISH) ... (On loan to Soviet Navy)	670	2. 7.37	27 July	Lost on passage to U.S.S.R. with Soviet crew.
	STRATAGEM	715	9.10.43	22 Nov.	Sunk by S.C., D/C, off Malacca, East Indies.
X CRAFT	X. 22	29·8*	31.10.43	7 Feb.	Lost in collision, Pentland Firth, N. Scotland.
CHARIOTS ...	No. LVIII	1·2*	11. 6.43	} 22 June	Lost in attack on Spezia.
	LX	1·2*	17. 8.43		
	LXXIX	1·94*	17. 4.44	} 28 Oct.	Lost in operation, Puket Harbour.
	LXXX	1·94*	15. 5.44		
AUXILIARY ANTI-AIRCRAFT SHIP.	GLEN AVON (R) ...	678 (deep)	1912	2 Sept.	Foundered in gale, Seine Bay, Normandy.
SLOOPS	WOODPECKER	1,350	14.12.42	27 Feb.	Stern blown off (20th) by torpedo. Capsized and sank in tow, N. Atlantic.
	KITE	1,350	1. 3.43	21 Aug.	Sunk by U/B, torpedo, Greenland Sea.
FRIGATES ...	TWEED	1,375	28. 4.43	7 Jan.	} Sunk by U/B, torpedo, N.
	GOULD	1,600	18. 9.43	1 Mar.	} Atlantic.
	LAWFORD	1,150	3.11.43	8 June	Bombed and sunk on service as H.Q. ship, Normandy.
	BLACKWOOD	1,150	29. 3.43	} 15 June	Sunk by U/B, torpedo, English
	MOURNE	1,365	30. 4.43		Channel.
	BICKERTON	1,300	17.10.43	22 Aug.	Sunk by U/B, torpedo, Barents Sea, Arctic.
	BULLEN	1,300	25.10.43	6 Dec.	Sunk by U/B, torpedo, N.W. Scotland.
	CAPEL	1,150	16. 8.43	26 Dec.	Sunk by U/B, torpedo, off Cherbourg.
CORVETTES ...	ASPHODEL	1,015	11. 9.40	9 Mar.	Sunk by U/B, torpedo, N. Atlantic.
	HURST CASTLE	1,060	9. 6.44	1 Sept.	Sunk by U/B, torpedo, off N.W. Ireland.
	ROSE ... ... (On loan to R. Nor. N.)	1,060	31.10.41	26 Oct.	Sunk in collision, W. Atlantic.
	TUNSBERG CASTLE ... (*ex* SHREWSBURY CASTLE) (On loan to R. Nor. N.)	1,060	29. 4.44	12 Dec.	Sunk by mine off N. Russia.
NETLAYER ...	MINSTER (R)	707	1924	8 June	Sunk by mine, Seine Bay, Normandy.
MINESWEEPERS ...	CATO	1,110	29. 7.43	6 July	} Sunk by human torpedo, off
	MAGIC	1,110	28.10.43	6 July	} Normandy.
	PYLADES	1,110	27.11.43	8 July	
	LOYALTY	940	22.4.43	22 Aug.	Sunk by mine, or U/B, torpedo, English Channel.
	BRITOMART	815	24. 8.39	} 27 Aug.	Sunk by accident in attack by
	HUSSAR	815	16. 1.35		friendly aircraft off Normandy

* Submerged.

Class	Name	Tonnage	Date of Completion	Date of Loss	How Lost and Where
				1944	
B.Y.M.S. MINE-SWEEPERS.	No. 2022	290	12. 9.42	16 Aug.	Lost, after damage by mine, Frejus Gulf, S. France.
	2255	290	30.11.43	5 Oct.	Sunk by mine, Boulogne.
	2030	290	30. 7.42	8 Oct.	Sunk by mine off Le Havre.
	2077	290	7. 7.43	25 Oct.	Sunk by mine, Gulf of Corinth, Greece.
MOTOR MINE-SWEEPERS.	No. 229	255	25.10.42	13 June }	Sunk by mine off Normandy.
	8	255	8. 1.41	24 June }	
	1019	360	23. 8.43	2 July	Sunk by mine off Cherbourg.
	55	255	3. 9.41	10 July	Sunk by mine off Normandy.
	117	255	7. 4.42	1 Sept.	Sunk by mine, Civita Vecchia, W. Italy.
	278	255	8. 3.43	14 Sept.	Stranded on rocks in Le Rance River, St. Malo, N. France.
	170	255	7. 9.42	12 Oct.	Sunk by mine off Gorgona Island, W. Italy.
	101	255	6. 2.43	29 Nov.	Sunk by mine off Salonika, Greece.
	257	255	9.10.43	11 Dec.	Sunk by mine, River Schelde, Holland.
MOTOR TORPEDO BOATS.	No. 417	37	8. 9.42	15/16 Mar.	Sunk by S.C., whilst attacking convoy between Calais and Boulogne.
	352	37	31. 5.43	25/26 Mar.	Sunk in collision, North Sea.
	241	38·6	30. 3.42	31 Mar.	Sunk by enemy action off Ijmuiden and Helder.
	707	95	11.43	18 Apr.	Cut in two in collision off N. Ireland.
	671	95	16. 5.43	24 Apr.	Sunk in torpedo attack on destroyers off Barfleur, N. France.
	708	95	11.43	5 May	Damaged by friendly A/C English Channel, and subsequently sunk by own forces.
	732	97	17. 4.44	28 May	Sunk by accident, English Channel.
	248	41	4. 3.43	6 June	Sunk in collision, English Channel.
	681	95	7.43	9/10 June	Sunk when attacking convoy off Holland.
	448	37	23. 9.43	11 June	Sunk by accident in torpedo attack by friendly aircraft off Normandy.
	734	97	30. 5.44	26 June	Damaged by Beaufighters and eventually sunk by own forces, North Sea.
	640	85	1.11.42	26/27 June	Sunk by mine, Leghorn-Spezia area.
	460 (On loan to R.C.N.).	41	22. 3.44	3 July	Sunk by mine off Normandy.
	666	95	10. 6.43	4/5 July	Sunk by S.C. off Holland.
	463 (On loan to R.C.N.).	41	25. 3.44	8 July	Sunk by mine off Normandy.
	434	37	25. 1.43	9 July	Sunk by S.C. off Normandy.
	372	47	7.10.43	23/24 July	Sunk by S.C., gunfire, when patrolling off Cape Loviste, Adriatic.
	412	37	14. 2.42	26/27 July	Sunk in collision off Normandy.
	430	37	16.11.42	26/27 July	Rammed by E/B off Normandy.
	93	38·6	10. 9.42	18 Aug.	Lost in collision off Harwich.
	360	37	30. 6.43 }	1 Oct.	Sunk by S.C. off Ymuiden, Holland.
	347	37	18. 3.43 }		
	287	36·5	12. 3.43 }	24 Nov.	Grounded on Levron Island, Adriatic, and subsequently destroyed by own forces.
	371	—	4.10.43 }		
	782	108	25.10.44	29 Dec.	Sunk by mine off River Schelde, Holland.
MOTOR GUN BOATS	No. 17	30	19.12.40	11 June	Sunk, possibly mined, off Normandy.
	326	67	18. 8.41	28 June	Sunk by mine off Normandy.
	313	67	12. 6.41	16 Aug.	Sunk by mine or torpedo off Normandy.
	663	90	8. 3.43	10 Oct.	Sunk by mine off Maestra Point, N.E. Adriatic.
MOTOR LAUNCHES	No. 210 (On loan to R. Nor. N.).	75·5	7. 4.41	15 Feb.	Sunk by mine off Dieppe.

Class	Name	Tonnage	Date of Completion	Date of Loss	How Lost and Where
MOTOR LAUNCHES (*cont.*).	1083	40	23.10.41	1944 20 Feb.	Lost through grounding in Gulf of Kos, Aegean.
	387	75·5	1. 6.43	5 Mar.	Destroyed by internal explosion, Beirut Harbour, Syria.
	1380	40	16. 9.43	May	Missing in Aegean.
	265	75·5	30. 5.41 ⎫	1 July	Destroyed by petrol fire and explosion, Freetown, W. Africa.
	287	75·5	23. 8.41 ⎭		
	443	75·5	11.41	12 July	Mined off Vada, W. Italy. Fore part blown off.
	563	75·5	3. 3.43	16 Aug.	Sunk by mine off Frejus, S. France.
	1179	40	4. 3.43	21 Aug.	Sunk off Rio Bueno, Jamaica, in hurricane.
	216	75·5	28. 5.41	28 Sept.	Foundered in heavy weather after being mined (19th), North Sea.
	1227	44	24.11.42	5 Oct.	Sunk by S.C. off Piraeus, Greece.
	1057	40	30. 9.41	13 Oct.	Lost through detonation of demolition charges off Kilindini, E. Africa.
	870	75·5	2. 8.44	15 Oct.	Sunk by mine off Piraeus, Greece.
	916	75·5	16. 9.44	8 Nov.	Sunk by mine at Walsoorden, Holland.
TRAWLERS ...	WALLASEA	545	31. 7.43	6 Jan.	Sunk by S.C., torpedo, off Mounts Bay, Cornwall.
	PINE	545	3. 7.40	31 Jan.	Sunk by E/B, torpedo, off Selsey Bill, Sussex.
	CAP D'ANTIFER (R)	—	—	13 Feb.	Sunk by E/Bs off Humber.
	WYOMING (R)	302	1915	20 May	Mined and sunk off Harwich.
	BIRDLIP	750	23.12.41	13 June	Sunk by U/B, torpedo, off W. Africa.
	LORD AUSTIN (R) ...	473	1937	24 June	Mined and sunk, Seine Bay, Normandy.
	GANILLY	545	3. 9.43	5 July	Sunk by mine, English Channel.
	TEXAS	301	—	19 July	Sunk in collision, Jamaica Area.
	LORD WAKEFIELD ...	825 (deep)	1933	29 July	Sunk by A/C off Normandy.
	GAIRSAY	545	30. 4.43	3 Aug.	Sunk by human torpedo off Normandy.
	CHOICE (R)	197	—	25 Aug.	Foundered, total wreck, Arromanches, Normandy.
	MIRABELLE (R)	203	1918	17 Sept.	Rammed and sunk by accident.
	VIDONIA (R)	276	—	6 Oct.	Sunk in collision, English Channel.
	COLSAY	554	4. 3.44	2 Nov.	Sunk by human torpedo off Ostend.
	TRANSVAAL (R)	250	—	18 Nov.	Foundered in gale, English Channel.
	NORTHCOATES (R) ...	277	—	2 Dec.	Sank in tow, through stress of weather, English Channel.
MOTOR FISHING VESSELS.	No. 70	43·5	1. 5.43	27 Feb.	Lost after striking submerged object en route for Casteloriso, Dodecanese.
	1032	93	−. 2.44	13 Sept.	Sunk in tow.
	117	50	30.12.43	14 Oct.	Sunk by explosion, probably mine, off Pasha Island, N. Aegean.
WHALERS	MAALØY (R)	249	—	27 Mar.	Sunk by U/B off Ceylon.
	FIRMAMENT (R)	248	1930	30 May	Grounded, total loss, off Alexandria.
	SOUTHERN PRIDE (R) ...	582	1936	16 June	Stranded, total loss, off Sierra Leone.
	BEVER (R)	252	1930	30 Nov.	Sunk by mine off Pireaus, Greece.
YACHTS	ORACLE	745	—	29 Jan.	Destroyed by fire off Liverpool.
	BREDA	1,207	—	18 Feb.	Sank after collision, Campbeltown Loch.
NAVAL AUXILIARY BOAT.	SPIDER BOY	14	—	14 Jan.	Cause and place unknown.
TRAINING SHIP (Ex BATTLESHIP)	CENTURION.	25,500	−. 5.13	9 June	Sunk as blockship for Mulberry Harbour, Normandy.

Class	Name	Tonnage	Date of Completion	Date of Loss	How Lost and Where
				1944	
TUGS	ADHERENT	700	30. 3.42	14 Jan.	Foundered, N. Atlantic.
	ROODE ZEE (R) ...	468	—	24 Apl.	Sunk by E/B, torpedo, off Dungeness.
	SESAME	700	18. 1.44	11 June	Sunk by E/B, torpedo, off Normandy.
	SOLITAIRE	91	1904	20 June	Capsized and sank off Normandy.
SALVAGE VESSEL	SÀLVIKING	1,490	27. 1.43	14 Feb.	Sunk by U/B, torpedo, Indian Ocean.
DRIFTERS... ...	NOT MANN (R)... ...	—	—	11 Jan. }	Cause and place unknown.
	LE DUE PAOLE (R) ...	—	—	21 Feb. }	
	FORECAST (R)	96	1925	10 Apr.	Sunk at Greenock.
	GLEAM (R)	57	1922	15 June	Sunk in collision.
	FAIRHAVEN (R)... ...	96	1919	5 Sept.	Foundered, N.E. Atlantic.
	SUPPORTER (R)	88	1914	4–5 Nov.	Grounded off Newhaven. Total loss.
HARBOUR TENDER	SENGA (R)	—	—	21 Jan.*	Sunk in collision off Londonderry.
OILER	WAR DIWAN	5,551	22. 8.19	16 Dec.	Sunk by mine, River Schelde, Holland.
WATER CARRIER...	GENERAAL VAN DER HEIJDEN (R).	1,213	1929	14 Apr.	Marine cause.
COLLIERS	OLGA E. EMBIRICOS (R)	4,677	1922	29 Jan.	Sunk by U/B, Gulf of Aden.
	IOANNIS FAFALIOS (R)...	5,670	1919	5 Sept.	War cause.
	YEWDALE (R)	823	1929	3 Oct.	Marine cause.
	P.L.M. 21 (R)	5,400	1921	3 Dec.	Grounded off Milford Haven. Subsequently sank.
WATER BOATS ...	GENERAAL VAN SWIETEN	1,300	1928	14 Apr.	Marine cause.
	CHANT 69 (R)	400	1944	14 June	Capsized off Normandy.
	PETRONELLA (R) ...	2,770	1927	15 Oct.	Mined off Pireaus, Greece.
EXAMINATION VESSEL.	FRATTON (R)	757	1925	18 Aug.	Sunk at anchor by underwater explosion, probably torpedoed by S.C., Seine Bay, Normandy.
SPECIAL SERVICE VESSELS.	DOVER HILL	5,815	1918	7 Feb.	
	FLOWERGATE	5,200	1911	7 Feb.	
	BECHEVILLE	4,200	1924	8 Feb.	
	PANOS	4,900	1920	8 Feb.	
	ELSWICK PARK	4,200	1920	10 Feb.	
	SALTERSGATE	3,900	1924	11 Feb.	
	ALYNBANK (R)	5,157	1925	Feb.	
	EMPIRE BUNTING ...	6,448	1919	Feb.	
	EMPIRE DEFIANCE ...	4,632	1909	Feb.	
	EMPIRE FLAMINGO ...	5,200	1920	Feb.	
	EMPIRE MOORHEN ...	5,617	1919	Feb.	
	EMPIRE TAMAR	6,581	1907	Feb.	
	EMPIRE WATERHEN ...	6,004	1920	Feb.	
	INGMAN (R)	3,169	1907	Feb.	
	MODLIN	3,569	1906	Feb.	
	VINLAKE...	3,938	1913	21 Feb.	
	LYNGHAUG	2,839	1919	26 Feb.	
	SIREHEI	3,888	1907	26 Feb.	
	EMPIRE TANA	6,148	1923	Mar.	} Sunk as blockships.
	GEORGIOS P.	4,052	1903	Mar.	
	NJEGOS (R)	4,393	1908	Mar.	
	WINHA	3,391	1904	Mar.	
	MANCHESTER SPINNER...	4,767	1918	25 Mar.	
	MARIPOSA	3,800	1914	27 Mar.	
	BENDORAN	5,600	1919	28 Mar.	
	VERA RADCLIFFE ...	5,600	1925	30 Mar.	
	FORBIN (R)	7,291	1922	Apr.	
	INNERTON	5,300	1919	16 Apr.	
	BELGIQUE	4,606	1902	June	
	EMPIRE BITTERN ...	8,500	1902	June	
	PARKHAVEN	4,803	1920	June	
	PARKLAAN	3,807	1911	June	
	NORFALK...	5,672	1919	24 June	
	NORJERV...	5,600	1919	26 June	
	STANWELL	5,800	1914	29 June	
	MAYCREST	5,900	1913	30 June	
	BOSWORTH	6,672	1919	4 Sept.	

* Subsequently salved.

Class	Name	Tonnage	Date of Completion	Date of Loss	How Lost and Where
				1944	
SPECIAL SERVICE VESSELS (*cont.*)	SYLVIA (R)	—	—	20 Sept.	Lost by enemy action.
	DUPLEX (R)	—	—	4 Oct.	Cause and place unknown.
	GRETHE MORTENSEN (R)	35	1943	7 Nov.	Abandoned in sinking condition off N. Foreland, Kent.
SMALL MISCELLANEOUS CRAFT.	AYIOS IOANNIS (CHIOS 466) (R).	—	—	15 Dec.	Cause and place unknown.
	EUSTATHIOS GHIOKIS (R)	—	—	16 Dec.	Constructive total loss.
TRANSPORT VESSELS.	EVANGELISTRIA (SAMOS 82) (R).	—	—	25 Jan.	Constructive total loss.
	TRIUMPH VI (R) ...	46	1903	15 Dec.	Sunk in collision, Rosyth area.
HARBOUR DEFENCE VESSEL.	MANORA (R)	—	1936	17 Dec.	Lost through fouling boom.
HARBOUR DUTY VESSEL.	ISMINI (R)	—	—	16 Oct.	Cause and place unknown.
FERRY SERVICE VESSEL.	SANDVIKHORN (R) ...	78 (Net)	1917	Jan.	Sunk in collision, Londonderry.
SAILING BARGES...	DELTA	—	1898	Nov.	Sank at Harty Point, Sheppey.
	DUNDONALD	50	1897	29 Nov.	Foundered when moored off Chatham.
	E.F.Q.	32	1900	Dec.	Sank at Sheerness.
				1945	
DESTROYERS ...	DEIATELNYI (ex CHURCHILL) (On loan to Soviet Navy).	1,190	17. 4.20	16 Jan.	Sunk by U/B, torpedo, Arctic Ocean.
	LA COMBATTANTE (ex HALDON) (On loan to French Navy).	1,050	30.12.42	23 Feb.	Sunk by mine, North Sea.
SUBMARINE ...	PORPOISE	1,500	11. 3.33	19 Jan. (Approx.)	Sunk, probably by A/C, Malacca Strait, E. Indies.
CHARIOTS ...	No. V	1·2*	1. 9.42	June (date reported)	Lost, W. Scotland.
	XI	1·2*	19. 9.42 ⎫		
	XIV	1·2*	5.10.42		
	XVII	1·2*	3.10.42	June	
	XX	1·2*	16.10.42 ⎬	(date	Lost at Malta.
	XXI	1·2*	19.10.42	reported)	
	XXIV	1·2*	17.11.42		
	XXV	1·2*	23.11.42 ⎭		
	XXIX	1·2*	18. 1.43 ⎫	June	
	XXXI	1·2*	19. 1.43 ⎬	(date	Lost, W. Scotland.
	XXXIV	1·2*	8. 2.43 ⎭	reported)	
SLOOPS	LARK	1,350	10. 4.44	17 Feb.	Damaged beyond repair by torpedo.
	LAPWING	1,460	21. 3.44	20 Mar.	Sunk by U/B, torpedo, off Kola Inlet, N. Russia.
FRIGATE	GOODALL	1,150	4.10.43	29 Apr.	Torpedoed by U/B, off Kola Inlet, N. Russia. Sunk by own forces.
CORVETTES ...	DENBIGH CASTLE ...	1,060	30.12.44	13 Feb.	Damaged by mine or U/B torpedo, grounded, total loss, N. Russia.
	BLUEBELL	1,060	19. 7.40	17 Feb.	Sunk by U/B, torpedo, Barents Sea, Arctic.
	VERVAIN	1,020	9. 6.41	20 Feb.	Sunk by U/B, torpedo, off S. Ireland.
MINESWEEPERS ...	REGULUS	1,010	20. 5.44	12 Jan.	Sunk by mine, Corfu Channel, Greece.
	GUYSBOROUGH (On loan to R.C.N.).	672	22. 4.42	17 Mar.	Sunk by U/B, torpedo, Bay of Biscay.
	SQUIRREL	940	16. 8.44	24 July	Damaged by mine off Puket, Siam, sunk by own forces.
	VESTAL	940	10. 9.43	26 July	Sunk by A/C, off Puket, Siam.
B.Y.M.S. MINESWEEPER.	No. 2053	290	11. 6.43	28 Apr.	Sunk by mine off Porto Corsini, N.E. Italy.
MOTOR MINESWEEPERS.	No. 248	255	11. 9.43	30 Jan.	Sunk by mine off River Schelde, Holland.

* Submerged.

Class	Name	Tonnage	Date of Completion	Date of Loss	How Lost and Where
				1945	
MOTOR MINE-SWEEPERS (cont.)	No. 68	255	28.12.41	4 Feb.	Sunk by mine off Cephalonia, Greece.
	168	255	5. 7.42	25 June	Sunk by mine in Genoa Harbour, Italy.
MOTOR TORPEDO BOATS.	No. 690	102	15. 9.43	18 Jan.	Lost after striking wreck.
	255	36	30. 7.43		
	438	37	31. 3.43		
	444	37	21. 7.43		
	459 (On loan to R.C.N.).	41	2. 3.44		
	461 (On loan to R.C.N.).	41	15. 3.44		
	462 (On loan to R.C.N.).	41	25. 3.44	14 Feb.	Lost by fire and explosion, Ostend Harbour.
	465 (On loan to R.C.N.).	41	31. 3.44		
	466 (On loan to R.C.N.).	41	18. 4.44		
	776	108	8.44		
	789	108	17.10.44		
	791	108	4.11.44		
	798	.108	16.10.44		
	605	102	16. 6.42	17 Feb.	Foundered after striking submerged obstruction on passage Ostend to Dover.
	655	102	− 1.43	21 Mar.	Sunk by mine, Quarnero Gulf, N.E. Adriatic.
	705	102	7. 8.43	23 Mar.	Sunk by mine, Maknare Channel, N.E. Adriatic.
	494	44	9.11.44	7 Apr.	Rammed and sunk by E/Bs, North Sea.
	5001...	108	18.12.44	7 Apr.	Sunk by E/Bs, North Sea.
	710	102	18. 9.43	10 Apr.	Sunk by mine near Zara, N.E. Adriatic.
	697	102	−. 7.43	17 Apr.	Sunk by mine off Krk Island, N.E. Adriatic.
	715 ... ... (On loan to R. Nor. N.)	102	9.12.43	19 May	Sunk by explosion at Fosnavaag, Norway.
	243	40	18.11.42	July (date reported)	Sunk as targets.
	635	102	−.11.42		
	242	40.	23.10.42	July	Sunk whilst being towed to Malta.
	712	102	10. 2.44	19 July	Formally paid off.
	261	32·4	—	26 Aug.	Sunk at Alexandria.
MOTOR GUN BOATS	No. 99	—	—	Apr.	Constructive total loss.
	2002...	93	5. 7.43	12 May	Sunk by mine on passage Aberdeen to Gothenburg, Sweden.
	2007...	93	28. 8.43	24 May	Broke in two off Aberdeen after grounding (22nd).
MOTOR LAUNCHES	No. 1163...	46	31.12.42	5 Jan.	Sunk by torpedo, probably S.C., Mulat Island, N.E. Adriatic.
	891	75·5	28. 3.44	24 Jan.	Sunk by mine, Kyauk Pyu, North of Ramree Island, Burma.
	183	75·5	10. 2.41	11 Feb.	Sunk after collision with East Pier, Dieppe, N. France.
	1417...	46	28. 3.44	15 Feb.	Sunk by mine, in tow, off Flushing.
	466	75·5	31. 3.42	25 Mar.	Sunk by mine off Walcheren, Holland.
	558	75·5	12. 2.43	5 May	Mined, N. Adriatic, total loss.
	591	75·5	18. 4.44	9 May	Foundered in tidal wave, Sittang River estuary, Burma.
	905	75·5	10. 5.44		
	230	75·5	28. 3.41	17 Aug.	Sunk in collision.
TRAWLERS ...	HAYBURN WYKE (R) ...	324	1917	2 Jan.	Torpedoed by U/B at anchor off Ostend, Belgium.
	NORTHERN ISLES (R) ...	655	1936	19 Jan.	Ran aground while on loop patrol off Durban, S. Africa. Total loss.
	COMPUTATOR (R) ...	286	1919	21 Jan.	Sunk in collision, Seine Bay, Normandy.
	ARLEY (R)	304	1914	3 Feb.	Damaged by mine. Sank in tow, North Sea.
	ELLESMERE	580	12.10.39	24 Feb.	Sunk by U/B, torpedo, English Channel.

C 2

Class	Name	Tonnage	Date of Completion	Date of Loss	How Lost and Where
				1945	
TRAWLERS (cont.)	EBOR WYKE (R) ...	348	1929	2 May	Presumed torpedoed by U/B off E. Coast of Iceland.
	CORIOLANUS	545	6. 2.41	5 May	Sunk by mine, N. Adriatic.
	HILDASAY	545	30. 9.41	21 June	Grounded on reef near Kilindini, total loss.
	ELIZABETH THERESE (R)	156	1934	4 July	Sunk.
	LA NANTAISE (R) ...	359	—	8 July	Sunk in collision off S.E. England.
	KURD (R)	352	1930	10 July	Sunk by mine off Lizard Head, Cornwall.
WHALERS... ...	TREERN (R) ... ... (On loan to S.A.N.F.)	247	1929	12 Jan.	Sunk by mine off E. Coast of Greece.
	SOUTHERN FLOWER (R)	328	1928	3 Mar.	Torpedoed by U/B off Reykjavik, Iceland.
	SPERCHEIOS (ex NOBLE NORA) (R). (On loan to R.H.N.)	160	—	3 Apr.	Capsized and sank off Greece.
NAVAL SERVICING BOAT.	No. 38	20	—	9 Feb.	Capsized and sank after damage.
NAVAL AUXILIARY BOATS.	No. 47	—	—		
	48	—	—	Jan.	
	49	—	—	(date	Cause and place unknown.
	58	—	—	reported)	
	59	—	—		
TUGS	HESPERIA	1,118	21. 5.43	9 Feb.	Grounded off Libya.
	ALLIGATOR	395	6. 2.41	Mar. (date reported)	Cause and place unknown.
	ATHLETE...	570	15.11.43	17 July	Sunk by mine off Leghorn, Italy.
DRIFTERS... ...	GOLDEN WEST (R) ...	—	—	15 Jan.	Foundered in Aberdeen Harbour, E. Scotland.
	HIGH TIDE (R)... ...	106	1919	30 Mar.	Foundered off N. Wales.
	BROADLAND (R) ...	76	1913	6 June	Lost in heavy weather, N. Atlantic.
FUELLING SHIP ...	ILTON CASTLE (R) ...	—	—	1 Aug.	Cause and place unknown.
COLLIER	ROLFSBORG (R)... ...	1,831	1915	13 July	Sunk in collision, Firth of Forth, E. Scotland.
BALLOON BARRAGE VESSELS.	SVERRE (R)	—	1938	2 Jan.	Foundered off E. Coast, England.
	TANEVIK (R)	—	—	19 Jan.	Foundered in tow from Methil to Buckie, E. Scotland.
SPECIAL SERVICE VESSEL.	ARMENIER (R)	914	—	Apr.	Scuttled.
TRANSPORT VESSEL	MARY VI (R)	13	—	2 Mar.	Destroyed by fire.
HARBOUR DUTY VESSEL.	AYIOS IOANNIS (CHIOS 116) (R).	—	—	13 Apr.	Cause and place unknown.
TRAIN FERRY ...	DAFFODIL	2,500	—	18 Mar.	Sank after being mined off Dieppe (17th).

II. SUMMARY OF LOSSES—BY YEAR AND CLASS

Class	3rd Sept., 1939 to 31st Dec., 1939	1940	1941	1942	1943	1944	1st Jan., 1945 to 15th Aug., 1945	Total Number Lost	Total Displacement Tonnage lost
	No.	No.	No.	No.	No.	No.	No.	No.	Tons
BATTLESHIPS	1	—	2	—	—	—	—	3	95,250
BATTLE CRUISERS	—	—	2	—	—	—	—	2	75,350
MONITOR	—	—	1	—	—	—	—	1	7,200
AIRCRAFT CARRIERS	1	1	1	2	—	—	—	5	100,450
AUXILIARY AIRCRAFT CARRIERS	—	—	1	1	1	—	—	3	38,570 (deep)
CRUISERS	—	2	8	8	6	4	—	28	164,230
DESTROYERS	3	34	22	46	16	16	2	139	195,130
SUBMARINES	1	23	11	18	16	6	1	76	67,673
X CRAFT	—	—	—	—	6	1	—	7	880
CHARIOTS	—	—	—	2	11	4	11	28	208·6 (Sub.)
WELMAN CRAFT	—	—	—	—	5	—	—	5	35·08 (Sub.) / 12 (Sub.)
ARMED MERCHANT CRUISERS	1	9	4	1	—	—	—	15	227,437
ARMED BOARDING VESSELS	—	2	3	—	—	—	—	5	22,832
OCEAN BOARDING VESSELS	—	—	5	—	—	—	—	5	28,579
AUXILIARY FIGHTER CATAPULT SHIPS	—	—	2	—	—	—	—	2	10,510
ANTI-AIRCRAFT SHIPS	—	1	1	3	—	—	—	5	21,270
AUXILIARY ANTI-AIRCRAFT SHIPS	—	2	1	1	1	1	—	6	4,540 (deep) / 4,328
SLOOPS	—	3	2	1	1	2	2	11	7,334
FRIGATES	—	—	—	—	1	8	1	10	13,575
CORVETTES	—	1	7	10	3	4	3	28	12,865
CUTTERS	—	—	—	3	—	—	—	3	27,050
AUX. A/S VESSELS	—	—	1	5	—	—	—	6	4,638
PATROL VESSEL	—	—	—	1	—	—	—	1	7,115
RIVER GUNBOATS	—	1	7	3	—	—	—	11	1,646
CONVOY SERVICE SHIPS	—	—	2	—	—	—	—	2	5,833
MINELAYERS	—	2	2	1	3	—	—	8	5,271
NETLAYERS	—	1	1	—	—	1	—	3	9,148
MINE DESTRUCTOR VESSEL	—	1	2	—	—	—	—	3	16,433 / 1,709 / 9,070
MINESWEEPERS	—	10	9	18	5	6	4	52	25,064 / 9,728
B.Y.M.S. MINESWEEPERS	—	—	—	—	1	4	1	6	1,740
MOTOR MINESWEEPERS	—	—	1	3	2	9	3	18	4,549
DEGAUSSING SHIPS	—	1	—	1	—	—	—	2	1,975
STEAM GUN BOAT	—	—	—	1	—	—	—	1	135
MOTOR TORPEDO BOATS	1	4	16	18	25	25	26	115	5,723·9 (a)
MOTOR ATTENDANT CRAFT	—	1	—	—	—	—	—	1	(b)
MOTOR A/S BOATS	—	—	2	—	—	—	—	2	42
MOTOR GUN BOATS	—	—	5	9	7	4	3	28	1,386 (c)

II. SUMMARY OF LOSSES—BY YEAR AND CLASS—continued

CLASS	3rd Sept, 1939 to 31st Dec, 1939	1940	1941	1942	1943	1944	1st Jan, 1945 to 15th Aug, 1945	Total Numbers Lost	Total Displacement Tonnage lost
	No.	No.	No.	No.	No.	No.	No.	No.	Tons
Motor Launches	—	3	7	30	16	14	9	79	4,819·4 (d) / 88
Trawlers	11	92	57	39	25	16	11	251	36,314 (deep) / 10,000 / 57,435 / 186·5
Motor Fishing Vessels	—	—	—	—	—	3	—	3	9,659
Whalers	—	2	10	13	3	4	3	35	12,403·5 (c)
Yachts	—	15	11	4	2	2	—	34	3,793
Boom Defence Vessels	1	5	4	5	2	—	—	17	230 (deep) / 1,848
Barrage Vessels	—	—	1	—	—	—	—	1	270
Gate Vessels	—	1	—	1	1	—	1	2	268
Naval Servicing Boats	—	—	—	1	1	—	5	3	48
Naval Auxiliary Boats	—	—	—	1	—	1	—	7	14 (e)
Destroyer Depôt Ship	—	—	1	—	—	—	—	1	10,850
Submarine Depôt Ship	—	—	—	—	—	—	—	1	14,650
Accommodation Ship	—	—	1	—	—	—	—	1	261
Boom Accommodation Ship	—	1	—	—	—	—	—	1	2,672
Training Ship	—	—	—	1	—	—	—	1	25,500
Base Ship	—	—	—	—	—	1	—	1	1,561
Guardship	—	1	—	1	—	1	—	1	3,472
Tugs	1	11	7	25	3	4	3	54	6,658 / 150 (deep)
Salvage Vessels	—	—	1	—	—	1	—	2	11,080 (f)
Rescue Ship	—	—	—	—	1	—	—	1	1,490 (c)
Mooring Vessels	—	1	—	1	—	—	—	2	1,368 / 767 (deep)
Schooners	3	—	3	—	—	—	—	3	758
Drifters	3	38	33	11	13	6	3	107	1,267 (d) / 7292·9 (net) (g)
Tenders	1	—	1	—	—	—	—	2	273 (b)
Tankers and Oilers	—	3	7	25	8	1	1	45	331,496
Fuelling Ship	—	—	—	1	—	1	—	1	—
Oil Distilling Ship	—	—	—	—	—	—	—	—	
Store Carriers	—	—	3	1	—	—	—	1	468 (b)
Victualling Store Ship	—	—	—	1	—	—	—	3	4,690
Water Carriers	—	—	1	1	—	—	—	1	206
Armament Store Carrier	—	—	1	1	1	1	—	3	1,973 (c)
Ammunition Hulks	5	2	—	—	—	—	—	3	1,087
Freighters	—	3	1	—	—	—	—	5	9,171
Colliers	—	3	2	2	—	—	1	13	9,145 / 39,394

								Total No.	Total Tonnage
Water Boats								5	4,470 (d)
Fleet Air Arm Target Ship				1				1	2,312 (b)
Motor Canal Boats		4	3	1		3		4	— (d)
Examination Vessels		1	7	8				6	2,648 (d)
Balloon Barrage Vessels			2	3		1	2	5	651 (h)
Special Service Vessels		35		3	9	40	1	100	280,444 (i)
Small Misc. Craft					2	2		9	866 (i)
Transport Vessels			1	4		2	1	6	477 (c)
Armed Traders						1		5	6,295 (b)
Harbour Defence Vessels					1			1	—
Harbour Duty Vessels				5		1	1	8	148 46 (net) (j)
Train Ferry							1	1	2,500
Ferry Service Vessels				1		1		2	49 78 (net)
Sailing Barges								3	123
Dumb Barges				14	7	3		21	1,544 (deep) 96 (k)
Total Nos.	30	317	284	359	205	208	100	1,503	—
Total Tonnage — Standard Displacement	—	135,828 (e)	305,771·6 (h)	254,910 (l)	70,561·2 (k)	109,475·7 (m)	24,488·3 (m)		959,757·8 (n)
Deep Displacement	58,723	758	11,913	24,132	17,274	1,503	—		55,580
Submerged Displacement	—	—	—	2·4	204	916·08	13·2		1,135·68
Gross Registered Tonnage	—	344,331·8	209,630·5	239,756	87,871	228,711	6,459		1,147,497·3
Net Registered Tonnage	30,738	152	45	46	76	78	—		397

(a) Excludes tonnage of 3 vessels which is unknown.
(b) Tonnage unknown.
(c) Excludes tonnage of 1 vessel which is unknown.
(d) Excludes tonnage of 2 vessels which is unknown.
(e) Excludes tonnage of 6 vessels which is unknown.
(f) Excludes tonnage of 14 vessels which is unknown.
(g) Excludes tonnage of 15 vessels which is unknown.
(h) Excludes tonnage of 17 vessels which is unknown.
(i) Excludes tonnage of 4 vessels which is unknown.
(j) Excludes tonnage of 5 vessels which is unknown.
(k) Excludes tonnage of 13 vessels which is unknown.
(l) Excludes tonnage of 46 vessels which is unknown.
(m) Excludes tonnage of 12 vessels which is unknown.
(n) Excludes tonnage of 106 vessels which is unknown.

III. ANALYSIS OF CAUSES OF LOSS BY CLASSES

Class	Cause of Loss (Enemy)							Cause of Loss (other)							Total
	Mine	Aircraft	Sub-marine	Surface Craft	Rammed	Shore Batteries	Action with the Enemy. Cause unknown	Wrecked	Used as Blockship	Collision	Accident	Fire	Own Forces	Unknown	
Battleships		1	2												3
Battle Cruisers		1		1											2
Monitor		1													1
Aircraft Carriers			3					1	1						5
Auxiliary Aircraft Carriers			2					1							3
Cruisers	1	7	8 (a)	5 (b)		2									23
Destroyers	23 (e)	50 (d)	35 (c)	20 (d)			2	2	1	3	1		2		139
Submarines	23 (e)	5 (d)	4 (f)	13 (g)	2		6	1	1	1	5	1	2	20	76
X Craft							6							1	7
Chariots							15						2	11	28
Welman Craft							4								5
Armed Merchant Cruisers	2	1	10	3				2			1	1	2		15
Armed Boarding Vessels		3 (e)													5
Ocean Boarding Vessels		1	4												5
Aux. Fighter Catapult Ships		1	1												5
Anti-Aircraft Ships		3													2
Auxiliary Anti-Aircraft Ships	1	4					2								5
Sloops	1	5	4 (d)				2	1		1		1	3		6
Frigates		1	9										1		11
Corvettes	5 (h)	3	16 (i)				2	1		4					10
Cutters	1		1				1								28
Auxiliary A/S Vessels		5					1								3
Patrol Vessel			1	1											6
River Gun Boats		5	1									1			1
Convoy Service Ships		2	1										3		11
Minelayers	2	2						1					1		2
Netlayers	1	1													8
Mine Destructor Vessels	1	17		2 (d)							3	1			3
Minesweepers	15 (j)	1	7 (k)				5	1					2		3
B.Y.M.S. Minesweepers	6												1		52
Motor Minesweepers	14 (d)	1		1	1		1	1							6
Degaussing Ship								1							18
Steam Gun Boat															2
Motor Torpedo Boats	18 (d)	9 (l)	7 (k)	21 (m)	2	1	11	8		8	7	16	8	6	1
Motor Attendant Craft	1 (n)	1									1				115
Motor A/S Boats		3		6		1	2	2		1	1	2	1	1	1
Motor Gun Boats	8 (o)	8 (c)	18 (q)	4 (d)		1	18	9		27	5	5	3	9	2
Motor Launches	16 (d)	71 (c)		20			2	14	1	1	8	1		10	28
Trawlers	79 (p)	6	3				4	1		1		1	2	1	79
Motor Fishing Vessels	1 (n)	9	1 (n)	3 (d)			2	6		6		6		5	251
Whalers	8 (d)	1					2	1			1		3	2	3
Yachts	5 (d)														35
Boom Defence Vessels	7														34
															17

Vessel	1	2	3	4	5	6	7	8	9	10	11	12	13	14	Total
Barrage Vessel														1	1
Gate Vessels		1												1	2
Naval Servicing Boats		1												2	3
Naval Auxiliary Boats			1											6	7
Destroyer Depot Ship				1											1
Submarine Depot Ship			1												1
Accommodation Ship				1											1
Boom Accommodation Ship								1							1
Training Ship				1											1
Base Ship		1													1
Guardship									1						1
Tugs	9 (d)	10	1	3			13	8						10	54
Salvage Vessels		1												1	2
Rescue Ships								1							1
Mooring Vessels	1													1	2
Schooners							1	1						1	3
Drifters	22	14	2				21	5	22			3		18 (d)	107
Tenders	1													1	2
Tankers and Oilers	1	3	29 (d)	2			5	3						2	45
Fuelling Ship														1	1
Oil and Distilling Ship		1													1
Store Carriers				1							1			1	3
Victualling Store Ship											1				1
Water Carriers	1						2								3
Armament Store Carrier			1				1	1				2			5
Ammunition Hulks		1							5						13
Freighters	1			1											2
Colliers	2		2	2			2	3	2						13
Water Boats	1						2	2							5
F.A.A. Target Ship	1														1
Motor Canal Boats	1			1 (n)			2								4
Examination Vessels	1							3						2	6
Balloon Barrage Vessels			2 (d)											3	5
Special Service Vessels	2	3		1 (m)			70	5	5				1	14	100
Small Miscellaneous Craft	1	1	2 (d)					2						4	9
Transport Vessels	1						1	1	1					2	6
Armed Traders		4							1						5
Harbour Defence Vessels								1							1
Harbour Duty Vessels				1			1	1	1					5	8
Train Ferry	1														1
Ferry Service Vessels							1							1	2
Sailing Barges							1							2	3
Dumb Barges							14 (r)							6	21
Total	281	271	172	109	5	4	116	114	89	85	38	37	28	154	1,503

(a) Includes 1 sunk by human torpedo.
(b) Includes 1 partly caused by aircraft.
(c) Includes 1 unconfirmed and 2 sunk by human torpedoes or mine.
(d) Includes 1 unconfirmed.
(e) Includes 20 unconfirmed.
(f) Includes 3 unconfirmed.
(g) Includes 5 unconfirmed.
(h) Includes 1 unconfirmed, possibly sunk by submarine.
(i) Includes 2 unconfirmed.
(j) Includes 1 sunk by aerial mine, 2 unconfirmed, 1 possibly sunk by aircraft and 1 by submarine.
(k) Includes 3 sunk by human torpedoes.
(l) Includes 4 unconfirmed.
(m) Includes 1 also mined.
(n) Unconfirmed.
(o) Includes 2 unconfirmed, 1 possibly torpedoed.
(p) Includes 6 unconfirmed, 1 possibly sunk by submarine.
(q) Includes 2 sunk by human torpedoes, and 6 unconfirmed as torpedoed ; 1 possibly mined and 1 possibly sunk by aircraft.
(r) Includes 13 sunk for boom defence purposes.

IV. SUMMARY OF LOSSES BY YEAR AND CAUSE

Year	Cause of Loss (Enemy)							Cause of Loss (other)						Unknown	Total
	Mine	Aircraft	Sub-marine	Surface Craft	Rammed	Shore Batteries	Action with the Enemy Cause unknown	Wrecked	Used as Blockship	Collision	Accident	Fire	Own Forces		
1939	15	—	3	1	—	—	—	2	—	2	1	—	—	6	30
1940	86	75	23	18	1	—	12	17	31	23	6	5	—	20	317
1941	50	95	29	6	1	—	18	22	3	19	2	7	12	20	284
1942	28	81	56	42	1	2	48	14	16	14	9	6	10	32	359
1943	36	12	24	25	—	2	27	19	—	9	8	3	3	37	205
1944	43	6	27	15	1	—	10	25	39	14	10	3	—	15	208
1945	23	2	10	2	1	—	1	15	—	4	2	13	3	24	100
Total	281	271	172	109	5	4	116	114	89	85	38	37	28	154	1,503

V. CLASSIFIED NOMINAL LIST OF LOSSES

BATTLESHIPS

BARHAM
PRINCE OF WALES
ROYAL OAK

Total   3

BATTLE CRUISERS

HOOD
REPULSE

Total   2

MONITOR

TERROR

Total   1

AIRCRAFT CARRIERS

ARK ROYAL
COURAGEOUS
EAGLE
GLORIOUS
HERMES

Total   5

AUXILIARY AIR-CRAFT CARRIERS

AUDACITY
AVENGER
DASHER

Total   3

CRUISERS

BONAVENTURE
CALYPSO
CHARYBDIS
CORNWALL
DORSETSHIRE
DRAGON
DUNEDIN
DURBAN
EDINBURGH
EFFINGHAM
EXETER
FIJI
GALATEA
GLOUCESTER
HERMIONE
MANCHESTER
NAIAD
NEPTUNE
PENELOPE
SOUTHAMPTON
SPARTAN
TRINIDAD
YORK

Total   23

DESTROYERS

ACASTA
ACHATES
ACHERON
AFRIDI
AIREDALE
ALDENHAM
ARDENT
BASILISK
BATH

DESTROYERS (cont.)

BEDOUIN
BELMONT
BERKELEY
BEVERLEY
BLANCHE
BLEAN
BOADICEA
BRAZEN
BROADWATER
BROKE
CAMPBELTOWN
CODRINGTON
COSSACK
DAINTY
DARING
DEFENDER
DEITELNYI
   (ex CHURCHILL)
DELIGHT
DIAMOND
DUCHESS
DULVERTON
ECLIPSE
ELECTRA
ENCOUNTER
ESCORT
ESK
ESKDALE
EXMOOR
EXMOUTH
FEARLESS
FIREDRAKE
FORESIGHT
FURY
GALLANT
GIPSY
GLOWWORM
GRAFTON
GRENADE
GRENVILLE
GREYHOUND
GROVE
GURKHA (1)
GURKHA (ex LARNE)
HARDY (1)
HARDY (2)
HARVESTER
HASTY
HAVANT
HAVOCK
HEREWARD
HEYTHROP
HOLCOMBE
HOSTILE
HUNTER
HURRICANE
HURWORTH
HYPERION
IMOGEN
IMPERIAL
INGLEFIELD
INTREPID
ISIS
IVANHOE
JACKAL
JAGUAR
JANUS
JERSEY
JUNO
JUPITER
KANDAHAR
KASHMIR
KEITH
KELLY
KHARTOUM
KINGSTON
KIPLING
KUJAWIAK
   (ex OAKLEY)
LA COMBATTANTE
   (ex HALDON)
LAFOREY
LANCE
LEGION

DESTROYERS (cont.)

LIGHTNING
LIMBOURNE
LIVELY
MAHRATTA
MAORI
MARTIN
MASHONA
MATABELE
MOHAWK
NESTOR
ORKAN (ex MYRMIDON)
PAKENHAM
PANTHER
PARTRIDGE
PENYLAN
PUCKERIDGE
PUNJABI
QUAIL
QUENTIN
QUORN
ROCKINGHAM
SIKH
SOMALI
SOUTHWOLD
STANLEY
STRONGHOLD
STURDY
SVENNER (ex SHARK)
SWIFT
TENEDOS
THANET
TYNEDALE
VALENTINE
VAMPIRE
VENETIA
VETERAN
VIMIERA
VORTIGERN
WAKEFUL
WARWICK
WATERHEN
WESSEX
WHIRLWIND
WHITLEY
WILD SWAN
WREN
WRESTLER
WRYNECK
ZULU

Total   139

SUBMARINES

B. 1 (ex SUNFISH)
CACHALOT
GRAMPUS
H. 31
H. 49
JASTRZAB
   (ex P. 551)
NARWHAL
ODIN
OLYMPUS
ORPHEUS
OSWALD
OXLEY
P. 32
P. 33
P. 36
P. 38
P. 39
P. 48
P. 222
P. 311
P. 514
P. 715 (ex GRAPH)
PANDORA
PARTHIAN
PERSEUS
PHOENIX
PORPOISE

SUBMARINES (cont.)

RAINBOW
REGENT
REGULUS
SAHIB
SALMON
SARACEN
SEA HORSE
SHARK
SICKLE
SIMOOM
SNAPPER
SPEARFISH
SPLENDID
STARFISH
STERLET
STONEHENGE
STRATAGEM
SWORDFISH
SYRTIS
TALISMAN
TARPON
TEMPEST
TETRARCH
THAMES
THISTLE
THORN
THUNDERBOLT
TIGRIS
TRAVELLER
TRIAD
TRITON
TRIUMPH
TROOPER
TURBULENT
UMPIRE
UNBEATEN
UNDAUNTED
UNDINE
UNION
UNIQUE
UNITY
*UNTAMED
UPHOLDER
UREDD (ex P. 41)
URGE
USK
USURPER
UTMOST
VANDAL

Total   76

X CRAFT

X 5
X 6
X 7
X 8
X 9
X 10
X 22

Total   7

CHARIOTS

No. V
VI
VIII
X
XI
XII
XIII
XIV
XV
XVI
XVII
XVIII
XIX
XX
XXI

* Subsequently salved and renamed VITALITY

CHARIOTS (*cont.*)

No. XXII
XXIII
XXIV
XXV
XXIX
XXXI
XXXIV
LII
LVII
LVIII
LX
LXXIX
LXXX

Total 28

WELMAN CRAFT

No. 10
45
46
47
48

Total 5

ARMED MERCHANT CRUISERS

ANDANIA (R)
CARINTHIA (R)
COMORIN (R)
DUNVEGAN CASTLE (R)
FORFAR (R)
HECTOR (R)
JERVIS BAY (R)
LAURENTIC (R)
PATROCLUS (R)
RAJPUTANA (R)
RAWALPINDI (R)
SALOPIAN (R)
SCOTSTOUN (R)
TRANSYLVANIA (R)
VOLTAIRE (R)

Total 15

ARMED BOARDING VESSELS

CHAKDINA (R)
CHANTALA (R)
KING ORRY (R)
ROSAURA (R)
VAN DYCK (R)

Total 5

OCEAN BOARDING VESSELS

CAMITO (R)
CRISPIN (R)
LADY SOMERS (R)
MALVERNIAN (R)
MANISTEE (R)

Total 5

AUXILIARY FIGHTER CATAPULT SHIPS

PATIA (R)
SPRINGBANK (R)

Total 2

ANTI-AIRCRAFT SHIPS

CAIRO
CALCUTTA
COVENTRY
CURACOA
CURLEW

Total 5

AUXILIARY ANTI-AIRCRAFT SHIPS

CRESTED EAGLE (R)
FOYLEBANK (R)
GLEN AVON (R)
HELVELLYN (R)
POZARICA
TYNWALD

Total 6

SLOOPS

AUCKLAND
BITTERN
DUNDEE
EGRET
GRIMSBY
IBIS
KITE
LAPWING
LARK
PENZANCE
WOODPECKER

Total 11

FRIGATES

BICKERTON
BLACKWOOD
BULLEN
CAPEL
GOODALL
GOULD
ITCHEN
LAWFORD
MOURNE
TWEED

Total 10

CORVETTES

ALYSSE (*ex* ALYSSUM)
ARBUTUS
ASPHODEL
AURICULA
BLUEBELL
DENBIGH CASTLE
ERICA
FLEUR DE LYS
GARDENIA
GLADIOLUS
GODETIA
HOLLYHOCK
HURST CASTLE
MARIGOLD
MIMOSA
MONTBRETIA
PICOTEE
PINTAIL
POLYANTHUS
ROSE
SALVIA
SAMPHIRE
SNAPDRAGON
SPIKENARD
TUNSBERG CASTLE (*ex* SHREWSBURY CASTLE)
VERVAIN
WINDFLOWER
ZINNIA

Total 28

CUTTERS

CULVER
HARTLAND
WALNEY

Total 3

AUXILIARY A/S VESSELS

KAMPAR (R)
KUALA (R)
MATA HARI (R)
SHU KWANG (R)
SIANG WO (R)
TIEN KWANG (R)

Total 6

PATROL VESSEL

GIANG BEE (R)

Total 1

RIVER GUNBOATS

CICALA
DRAGONFLY
GNAT
GRASSHOPPER
LADYBIRD
MOSQUITO
MOTH
PETEREL
ROBIN
SCORPION
TERN

Total 11

CONVOY SERVICE SHIPS

CHAKLA (R)
FIONA (R)

Total 2

MINELAYERS

ABDIEL
CORNCRAKE
KUNG WO (R)
LATONA
PORT NAPIER (R)
PRINCESS VICTORIA (R)
REDSTART
WELSHMAN

Total 8

NETLAYERS

KYLEMORE (R)
MINSTER (R)
TONBRIDGE (R)

Total 3

MINE DESTRUCTOR VESSELS

CORBURN
CORFIELD
QUEENWORTH

Total 3

MINESWEEPERS

ABINGDON
ALGERINE
BANKA (R)
BRAMBLE
BRIGHTON BELLE (R)
BRIGHTON QUEEN (R)
BRITOMART
CATO
CHANGTEH (R)
CITY OF ROCHESTER
CLACTON
CROMARTY
CROMER
DEVONIA (R)
DUNDALK
DUNOON
FELIXSTOWE
FERMOY
FITZROY
FUHWO (R)
GOSSAMER
GRACIE FIELDS
GUYSBOROUGH
HEBE
HUA TONG (R)
HUNTLEY
HUSSAR
HYTHE
JARAK (R)
KLIAS (R)
LEDA
LI WO (R)
LOYALTY
MAGIC
MALACCA (R)
MARMION (R)
MERCURY (R)
NIGER
PYLADES
REGULUS
SCOTT HARLEY (R)
SIN AIK LEE (R)
SKIPJACK
SNAEFELL (R)
SOUTHSEA (R)
SPHINX
SQUIRREL
STOKE
TAPAH (R)
VESTAL
WAVERLEY (R)
WIDNES

Total 52

B.Y.M.S. MINE-SWEEPERS

No. 2019
2022
2030
2053
2077
2255

Total 6

MOTOR MINESWEEPERS

No. 8
39
51
55
68
70
89
101
117
168
170
174*
180
229
248

* Subsequently Salved.

MOTOR MINESWEEPERS (cont.)	MOTOR TORPEDO BOATS (cont.)	MOTOR GUN BOATS (cont.)	MOTOR LAUNCHES (cont.)
	No. 316	No. 76	No. 1015
No. 257	338	78	1030
278	347	79	1037
1019	352	90	1054
	356	92	1057
Total 18	357	98	1062
	360	99	1063
	371	109	1083
DEGAUSSING SHIPS	372	110	1121
	412	313	1153
BALMORE (R)	417	314	1154
DAISY (R)	430	326	1157
	434	328	1163
Total 2	438	335	1179
	444	501	1212
	448	601	1227
STEAM GUN BOAT	459	641	1244
	460	644	1289
No. 7	461	648	1380
	462	663	1388
Total 1	463	2002	1417
	465	2007	
	466		Total 79
	494	Total 28	
MOTOR TORPEDO BOATS	605		
	606		
	622	MOTOR LAUNCHES	TRAWLERS
No. 6	626		
7	631	KELANA (R)	ADONIS
8	635	PENGHAMBAT	AGATE
9	636	PENINGAT (R)	AGHIOS GEORGIOS (IV)
10	639	No. 103	(R)
11	640	108	AKRANES (R)
12	655	109	ALBERIC (R)
15	665	111	ALDER
16	666	126	ALMOND
17	669	127	ALOUETTE (R)
26	671	129	AMETHYST
27	681	130	ARACARI (R)
28	686	133	ARAGONITE (R)
29	690	144	ARCTIC TRAPPER (R)
30	697	156	ARGYLLSHIRE (R)
41	705	160	ARLEY (R)
43	707	169	ARSENAL
44	708	177	ASAMA (R)
47	710	183	ASH
61	712	192	ASTON VILLA (R)
63	715	210	AVANTURINE (R)
64	732	216	BANDOLERO
67	734	219	BARBARA ROBERTSON
68	776	230	(R)
73	782	242	BEDFORDSHIRE
74	789	251	BEECH
77	791	262	BEN ARDNA (R)
87	798	265	BEN GAIRN (R)
93	5001	267	BENGALI
105		268	*BEN ROSSAL (R)
106	Total 115	270	BENVOLIO (R)
201		287	BIRDLIP
213		288	BLACKBURN ROVERS
214		298	(R)
215	MOTOR ATTENDANT CRAFT	301	BOTANIC
216		306	BRADMAN (R)
217		310	BREDON
218	No. 5	311	BRORA
220		339	CALVERTON (R)
222	Total 1	352	CALVI (R)
230		353	CAMPINA (R)
237		358	CAMPOBELLO
241	MOTOR A/S BOATS	387	CANNA
242		443	CAP D'ANTIFER (R)
243	No. 3	446	CAPE CHELYUSKIN
248	30	447	CAPE FINISTERRE (R)
255		457	CAPE PASSARO (R)
259	Total 2	466	CAPE SIRETOKO (R)
261		558	CAPE SPARTEL (R)
262		563	CAPRICORNUS (R)
264		579	CAROLINE (R)
267	MOTOR GUN BOATS	591	CAULONIA (R)
287		835	CAYTON WYKE
288	No. 12	870	CHARLES BOYES (R)
308	17	891	CHESTNUT
310	18	905	CHOICE (R)
311	19	916	CLOUGHTON WYKE (R)
312	62	1003	COBBERS (R)
314	64	1011	COLSAY

* Subsequently Salved.

TRAWLERS (cont.)

COMET (R)
COMPUTATOR (R)
CONQUISTADOR (R)
CORAL
CORIOLANUS
CORTINA (R)
CRAMOND ISLAND (R)
CRESTFLOWER
DANEMAN
DAROGAH (R)
DERVISH (R)
DESIRÉE (R)
DONNA NOOK (R)
DOX (R)
DROMIO (R)
DRUMMER (R)
DUNGENESS (R)
EBOR WYKE (R)
EILEEN DUNCAN (R)
ELIZABETH
  ANGELA (R)
ELIZABETH THERESE (R)
ELK (R)
ELLESMERE
EMILION (R)
ERIN
ETHEL TAYLOR
EVELINA (R)
EVESHAM (R)
FIFESHIRE (R)
FLEMING (R)
FLOTTA
FONTENOY (R)
FORCE (R)
FORT ROYAL
FORTUNA (R)
FRANCOLIN (R)
FRANC TIREUR (R)
GAIRSAY
GANILLY
GAUL
GULLFOSS
*HAMMOND (R)
HARVEST MOON
HAYBURN WYKE (R)
HENRIETTE (R)
HERRING
HICKORY
HILDASAY
HONG LAM (R)
HONJO (R)
HORATIO
INVERCLYDE (R)
IRVANA (R)
JADE
JAMES LUDFORD
JARDINE (R)
JASPER
JEAN FREDERICK (R)
JOSEPH BUTTON (R)
JUNIPER
JURA
KENNYMORE (R)
KERYADO (R)
KINGSTON ALALITE
KINGSTON BERYL (R)
KINGSTON CAIRNGORM (R)
KINGSTON CEYLONITE
KINGSTON CORNELIAN
KINGSTON GALENA
KINGSTON JACINTH (R)
KINGSTON SAPPHIRE (R)
KOPANES (R)
KURD (R)
LADY LILIAN (R)
LADY SHIRLEY (R)
LAERTES
LA NANTAISE (R)
*LARWOOD (R)
LEYLAND
LINCOLN CITY (R)
LOCH ALSH (R)
LOCH ASSATER (R)
LOCH DOON (R)
LOCH INVER (R)
LOCH NAVER (R)

TRAWLERS (cont.)

LORD AUSTIN (R)
LORD HAILSHAM
*LORD INCHCAPE (R)
LORD SELBORNE (R)
LORD SNOWDEN (R)
LORD STAMP (R)
LORD STONEHAVEN (R)
LORD WAKEFIELD
LORINDA (R)
LUDA LADY (R)
MANOR (R)
MANX PRINCE (R)
MARCONI (R)
MARSONA (R)
MASTIFF
MELBOURNE (R)
MEROR (R)
MILFORD EARL (R)
MIRABELLE (R)
MORAVIA (R)
MURMANSK (R)
MYRTLE
NOGI (R)
NORTHCOATES (R)
NORTHERN ISLES (R)
NORTHERN PRINCESS (R)
NORTHERN ROVER (R)
NOTTS COUNTY (R)
ORFASY
ORMONDE (R)
OSWALDIAN (R)
OUSE
PELTON (R)
PENTLAND FIRTH
PERIDOT
PHINEAS BEARD (R)
PIERRE DESCELLIERS (R)
PINE
POLLY JOHNSON (R)
PYROPE (R)
RECOIL (R)
RED GAUNTLET (R)
REFUNDO (R)
RELONZO (R)
REMILLO (R)
RESMILO (R)
RESOLVO (R)
RESPARKO (R)
RIFSNES (R)
RINOVA (R)
RIVER CLYDE (R)
ROBERT BOWEN (R)
ROCHE BONNE (R)
RODINO (R)
ROSEMONDE (R)
ROYALO
RUBENS (R)
RUTLANDSHIRE (R)
RYSA
ST. ACHILLEUS (R)
ST. APOLLO (R)
ST. CATHAN (R)
ST. DONATS (R)
ST. GORAN (R)
SEA KING (R)
SEDGEFLY (R)
SENATEUR DUHAMEL (R)
SILICIA (R)
SINDONIS
SISAPON (R)
SOLOMON (R)
SPANIARD
STAR OF DEVERON (R)
STAUNTON (R)
STELLA CAPELLA
STELLA DORADA
STELLA ORION (R)
STELLA SIRIUS
STRATHBORVE (R)
STRONSAY
SUSARION (R)
SWORD DANCE
TAMARISK
TERVANI (R)
TEXAS
THOMAS BARTLETT (R)
THURINGIA

TRAWLERS (cont.)

TILBURY NESS (R)
TOPAZE
TOURMALINE
TRANIO (R)
TRANQUIL (R)
TRANSVAAL (R)
ULLSWATER
VALDORA (R)
VAN ORLEY (R)
VELIA (R)
VIDONIA (R)
WALLASEA
WARLAND
WARWICK DEEPING
WARWICKSHIRE (R)
WASHINGTON (R)
WATERFLY (R)
WAVE FLOWER
WESTELLA
WILLIAM HALLETT (R)
WILLIAM STEPHEN (R)
WILLIAM WESNEY (R)
WYOMING (R)
ZEE MEEUW (R)

Total 251

MOTOR FISHING VESSELS

No. 70
117
1032

Total 3

WHALERS

A.N. 2 (R)
BEVER (R)
BODÖ (R)
COCKER (R)
EGELAND (R)
FIRMAMENT (R)
GEMAS (R)
HARSTAD (R)
JERAM (R)
JERANTUT (R)
KOS XVI (R)
KOS XXII (R)
KOS XXIII (R)
MAALØY (R)
PARKTOWN (R)
RAHMAN (R)
SAMBHUR (R)
SANTA (R)
SARNA (R)
SEVRA (R)
SHERA (R)
SKUDD 3 (R)
SOTRA (R)
SOUTHERN FLOE (R)
SOUTHERN FLOWER (R)
SOUTHERN PRIDE (R)
SPERCHEIOS (ex NOBLE NORA) (R)
SULLA (R)
SVANA (R)
SYVERN (R)
THORBRYN (R)
THORGRIM (R)
TRANG (R)
TREERN (R)
WHIPPET (R)

Total 35

YACHTS

AISHA (R)
AMULREE (R)
ATTENDANT (R)
BOOMERANG VI (R)
BREDA

YACHTS (cont.)

CALANTHE (R)
CAMPEADOR V (R)
EMELLE (R)
GAEL (R)
GRIVE (R)
GULZAR (R)
HANYARDS (R)
MOLLUSC (R)
NYULA (R)
ORACLE
PELLAG II (R)
PRINCESS (R)
RHODORA (R)
ROSABELLE
SAPPHO (R)
SARGASSO (R)
SEA ANGLER (R)
SHASHI III (R)
SILVIA (R)
SONA
SURF (R)
SURPRISE
THALIA
TORRENT (R)
VIVA II (R)
WARRIOR II (R)
WHITE FOX II (R)
WILNA (R)
YORKSHIRE BELLE (R)

Total 34

BOOM DEFENCE VESSELS

ALDGATE
BARFLAKE
BARLIGHT
BAYONET
CAMBRIAN (R)
CHORLEY (R)
DOWGATE
FABIOUS (R)
LOCH SHIN (R)
LUDGATE
MARCELLE (R)
OTHELLO (R)
*PANORAMA
RISTANGO (R)
THOMAS CONNOLLY (R)
TUNISIAN (R)
WATERGATE

Total 17

BARRAGE VESSEL

No. 42

Total 1

GATE VESSELS

KING HENRY (R)
PLACIDAS FAROULT (R)

Total 2

NAVAL SERVICING BOATS

No. 9
30
38

Total 3

* Subsequently salved.

NAVAL AUXILIARY BOATS

LILY
SPIDER BOY
No. 47
   48
   49
   58
   59

Total 7

DESTROYER DEPÔT SHIP

HECLA

Total 1

SUBMARINE DEPÔT SHIP

MEDWAY

Total 1

ACCOMMODATION SHIP

GYPSY (R)

Total 1

BOOM ACCOMMODATION SHIP

SUI WO (R)

Total 1

TRAINING SHIP (ex BATTLESHIP)

CENTURION

Total 1

BASE SHIP

ANKING (R)

Total 1

GUARDSHIP

LORMONT (R)

Total 1

TUGS

ADEPT
ADHERENT
ALAISIA (R)
ALLIGATOR
ANDROMEDA (R)
ASSURANCE
ATHLETE
BAIA (R)
C. 308
CAROLINE MOLLER (R)
CORINGA (R)
CORY BROS (R)
DAISY (R)
DANUBE III (R)
EMILY (R)
FAIRPLAY TWO (R)
GUARDSMAN (R)
HELEN BARBARA
HELLESPONT
HESPERIA
HORSA
INDIRA (R)

TUGS (cont.)

IRENE VERNICOS (R)
J.T.A. 1 (R)
*J.T.A. 6 (R)
J.T.A. 7 (R)
J.T.A. 14 (R)
LETTIE (R)
MURIA (R)
NAPIA (R)
PENGAWAL
PEUPLIER (R)
ROODE ZEE (R)
ST. ABBS
ST. ANGELO
ST. BREOCK
ST. CYRUS
ST. FAGAN
ST. ISSEY
ST. JUST
ST. OLAVES (R)
ST. SAMPSON (R)
SALVAGE KING (R)
SAUCY (R)
SEAGEM (R)
SESAME
SOLITAIRE
TIENTSIN (R)
TWENTE (R)
VAILLANT (R)
VISION
WEST COCKER
WO KWANG (R)
YIN PING (R)

Total 54

SALVAGE VESSELS

SALVIKING
VIKING (R)

Total 2

RESCUE SHIP

ST. SUNNIVA (R)

Total 1

MOORING VESSELS

MOOR
STEADY

Total 2

SCHOONERS

KANTARA (R)
KEPHALLINIA (R)
MARIA D. GIOVANNI (R)

Total 3

DRIFTERS

ALFRED COLEBROOK
APPLE TREE (R)
AURORA II (R)
BAHRAM (R)
BLIA (R)
BOY ALAN (R)
BOY ANDREW (R)
BOY ROY (R) (1)
BOY ROY (R) (2)
BRAE FLETT (R)
BROADLAND (R)
CARRY ON (R)
CATHERINE (R)
CHANCELLOR (R)
CHARDE (R)
CHRISTINE ROSE (R)
COMFORT (R)
COR JESU (R)
D'ARCY COOPER (R)
DEVON COUNTY (R)

DRIFTERS (cont.)

DEWEY EVE (R)
DUSKY QUEEN (R)
DUTHIES (R)
EMBRACE (R)
FAIR BREEZE (R)
FAIRHAVEN (R)
FERTILE VALE (R)
FISHERGIRL (R)
FISKAREN (R)
FORECAST (R)
FORERUNNER (R)
GIRL PAMELA (R)
GLEAM
GLEN ALBYN (R)
GLOAMING (R)
GO AHEAD (R)
GOLDEN DAWN (R)
GOLDEN EFFORT (R)
GOLDEN GIFT
GOLDEN SUNBEAM (R)
GOLDEN WEST (R)
GOODWILL (R)
GOWAN HILL (R)
HARMONY (R)
HARVEST GLEANER (R)
HIGHLAND QUEEN (R)
HIGHTIDE (R)
IMBAT (R)
INTREPEDE (R)
JEWEL (R)
JUSTIFIED
LE DUE PAOLE (R)
LEGEND (R)
LORD CAVAN (R)
LORD HOWARD (R)
LORD ST. VINCENT (R)
MAIDA (R)
MANX LAD (R)
M. A. WEST (R)
MIDAS (R)
MONARDA (R)
NAUTILUS (R)
NEW SPRAY (R)
NISR (R)
NORNES (R)
NOSS HEAD
NOT MANN (R)
OCEAN LASSIE (R)
OCEAN RETRIEVER (R)
OCEAN REWARD (R)
OCEAN SUNLIGHT (R)
PAXTON (R)
PERSEVERE (R)
PREMIER
PROFICIENT (R)
PROMOTIVE (R)
RAY OF HOPE (R)
RECEPTIVE (R)
REED (R)
RIANT (R)
ROSA (R)
ROSE VALLEY (R)
ROWAN TREE (R)
RYPA (R)
SCOTCH THISTLE (R)
SHIPMATES (R)
SOIZIK (R)
SUMMER ROSE (R)
SUPPORTER (R)
THE BOYS (R)
THISTLE (R)
THORA
TOKEN (R)
TORBAY II (R)
TRUE ACCORD (R)
TRUSTY STAR
UBEROUS (R)
UBERTY (R)
UNICITY (R)
UT PROSIM (R)
VICTORIA I (R)
WHITE DAISY (R)
WINSOME (R)
XMAS ROSE (R)
YOUNG ERNIE (R)
YOUNG FISHERMAN (R)
YOUNG SID (R)

Total 107

TENDERS

CHABOOK (R)
*SENGA (R)

Total 2

TANKERS AND OILERS

ALBERT L. ELLSWORTH (R)
ALCIDES (R)
ALDERSDALE
ANDREA BROVIG (R)
BELITA (R)
BETH (R)
BIRCHOL
BOARDALE
CAIRNDALE
CIRCE SHELL (R)
DARKDALE
DINSDALE
FINNANGER (R)
FRANCOL
HALLANGER (R)
HAVSTEN (R)
JOHN P. PEDERSON (R)
LEIV EIRIKSSON (R)
LITIOPA (R)
MALMANGER (R)
MARIT (R)
MINISTER WEDEL (R)
MIRLO (R)
MONTENOL
NYHOLT (R)
OLEANDER
OLNA
PERICLES (R)
PLUMLEAF
ROSEWOOD (R)
SANDAR (R)
SILDRA (R)
SLAVOL
SLEMDAL (R)
SVENOR (R)
SVEVE (R)
TANK EXPRESS (R)
THELMA (R)
THORSHAVET (R)
THORSHOVDI (R)
VARDAAS (R)
WAR DIWAN
WAR MEHTAR
WAR SEPOY
WAR SIRDAR

Total 45

FUELLING SHIP

ILTON CASTLE (R)

Total 1

DISTILLING SHIP

*STAGHOUND (R)

Total 1

STORE CARRIERS

TIBERIO (R)
TUNA (R)
ULSTER PRINCE (R)

Total 3

VICTUALLING STORE SHIP

MORAY (R)

Total 1

* Subsequently salved.

WATER CARRIERS

EMPIRE ARTHUR (R)
GENERAL VAN DER
  HEIJDEN (R)
KALGAH (R)

Total 3

ARMANENT STORE CARRIER

ESCAUT (R)

Total 1

AMMUNITION HULKS

CARLO
DUNMORE
LUCY BORCHARDT
MOURINO
STANLARD

Total 5

FREIGHTERS

CAPE HOWE (R)
WILL AMETTE VALLEY
  (R)

Total 2

COLLIERS

*BELHAVEN (R)
BOTUSK (R)
FERNWOOD (R)
GLYNWEN (R)
IOANNIS FAFALIOS (R)
KING CITY (R)
MAINDY HILL (R)
NEVA (R)
OLGA E.
EMBIRICOS (R)
P.L.M. 21 (R)
ROLFSBORG (R)
YEWDALE (R)
ZANNIS L.
CAMBANIS (R)

Total 13

WATER BOATS

CECIL (R)
CHANT. 69 (R)
GENERAL VAN
  SWIETEN (R)
ISBJORN (R)
PETRONELLA (R)

Total 5

FLEET AIR ARM TARGET SHIP

ST. BRIAC (R)

Total 1

MOTOR CANAL BOATS

AMBLEVE
ESCAUT
SEMOIS
YSER

Total 4

EXAMINATION VESSELS

NO. 4 (R)
NO. 10 (R)
FRATTON (R)
LADY SLATER (R)
SOLEN (R)
TUNG WO (R)

Total 6

BALLOON BARRAGE VESSELS

BOREALIS (R)
REIDAR (R)
SATURNUS (R)
SVERRE (R)
TANEVIK (R)

Total 5

SPECIAL SERVICE VESSELS

AKSEL I (R)
ALYNBANK (R)
ARMENIER (R)
ARTHUR (R)
ATLANTIC GUIDE
BECHEVILLE
BELGIQUE
BENDORAN
BERGHOLM (R)
BILLDORA (R)
BORODINO (R)
BOSWORTH
BRANKSEA
BRATTHOLM (R)
BUSK
CARRON
COLLINGDOC
DAH PU (R)
DOVER HILL
DUPLEX (R)
DURHAM CASTLE
EDV. NISSEN (R)
ELSWICK PARK
EMERALD WINGS
EMPIRE BITTERN
EMPIRE BUNTING
EMPIRE DEFIANCE
EMPIRE FLAMINGO
EMPIRE MOORHEN
EMPIRE SEAMAN
EMPIRE TAMAR
EMPIRE TANA
EMPIRE WATERHEN
EVANGELISTRIA
  (CHIOS 345) (R)
FEIOY (R)
FIDELIA
FIDELITY (R)
FLORENTINO
FLOWERGATE
FORBIN (R)
FREYA 1 (R)
GAMBHIRA
GEORGIOS P.
GONDOLIER
GOURKO
GRETHE MORTENSEN (R)
GULDBORG (R)
HOLLAND (R)
ILSENSTEIN
INGMAN (R)
INNERTON
JACOBUS
JAMES 9
JAMES 83

SPECIAL SERVICE VESSELS (cont.)

JOKER (R)
JUNIATA
KANTUNG (R)
KAUPO (R)
LAKE NEUCHATEL
LYCEA
LYN CHAUG
MACAO
MANCHESTER SPINNER
MARIPOSA
MARS (R)
MARTIS
MASHOBRA (R)
MAYCREST
†MINNIE DE LARINAGA
MODLIN
MOREA
MOYLE
NJEGOS (R)
NORFALK
NORJERV
NORSEMAN (R)
NORSJOEN (R)
PACIFICO
PANOS
PARKHAVEN
PARKLAAN
REDSTONE
RIVER TYNE
SALTERSGATE
SIREHEI
SJO (R)
SQUALLY (R)
STANWELL
SYLVIA (R)
TRANSEAS
TWEEDLE DEE
TWEEDLE DUM
UMVOTI
VERA RADCLIFFE
VINLAKE
VITA (R)
WESTCOVE
WESTWICK (R)
WINHA

Total 99‡

SMALL MISCELLANEOUS CRAFT

AGHIOS PANTALEIMON
  (R)
AYIOS IOANNIS
  (CHIOS 466) (R)
ROY PETER
DANEHILL
EUSTATHIOS GHIOKIS
  (R)
FOLIOT
MATCHLOCK
NAIEM
SHUN AN (R)

Total 9

TRANSPORT VESSELS

EVANGELISTRIA
  (SAMOS 82) (R)
FAROUK (R)
MARY VI (R)
TERPSITHEA (R)
TRIUMPH VI (R)
ZOODOCHOS PIGHI (R)

Total 6

ARMED TRADERS

KUDAT (R)
LARUT (R)
LIPIS (R)
RAUB (R)
VYNER BROOKE (R)

Total 5

HARBOUR DEFENCE VESSEL

MANORA (R)

Total 1

HARBOUR DUTY VESSELS

AYIOS IOANNIS
  (CHIOS 116) (R)
BRODRENE (R)
CHRYSOLITE (R)
ISMINI (R)
NYKEN (R)
RUBY (R)
ST. ANNE (R)
VASSILIKI (R)

Total 8

TRAIN FERRY

DAFFODIL

Total 1

FERRY SERVICE VESSELS

SANDOY (R)
SANDVIKHORN (R)

Total 2

SAILING BARGES

DELTA
DUNDONALD
E.F.Q.

Total 3

DUMB BARGES

CELT
*CLACTON
COOLIE
COSSACK
DARTMOUTH (R)
DERVISH
FOUR
*GREENFINCH
MAORI
MATABELE
*MONICA
NELL JESS
ODESSA
PARTISAN
PHILISTINE
REDRESS
RESPITE
REVENGE
SAN FRANCISCO
UTOPIA
VALENCIA

Total 21

* Subsequently salved.   † Reported sunk and salved 1940. Finally sunk 1941.
‡ Includes 1 ship to be counted twice.

PART II

LANDING SHIPS, CRAFT AND BARGES

I—LIST OF LOSSES
ARRANGED ACCORDING TO YEAR AND CLASS

NOTES

(i) (R) Signifies that the vessel was requisitioned for Naval Service.

(ii) Tonnage for Landing Ships is Standard Displacement unless otherwise stated.

(iii) Gross Registered Tonnage is shewn in italics.

(iv) W.L. signifies War Load Displacement.

LIST OF ABBREVIATIONS

A/C Aircraft.
E/B E-Boat.
U/B U/Boat.

Class and Nos.	Date of Loss	How Lost and Where
LANDING CRAFT ASSAULT	1940.	
(W.L. 11–13·5 tons)		
Nos. 4, 18 (total 2)	29 May	Lost in CLAN MACALISTER, sunk by A/C at Dunkirk.
16	29 May	Sunk by A/C at Dunkirk.
8, 15 (total 2)	31 May	Lost at Dunkirk.
11, 14 (total 2)	9 June }	Lost in home waters.
1, 2 (total 2)	14 June }	
6	July (date reported)	Cause and place unknown.
LANDING CRAFT MECHANISED		
(Mark I) (W.L. 30–37 tons)		
Nos. 10, 11, 14, 15, 18–20 (total 7)	6–27 May	Presumed lost during operations at Narvik, Norway.
12, 22 (total 2)	2 June }	Abandoned at Dunkirk.
17	3 June }	
LANDING CRAFT PERSONNEL (Large)		
(W.L. 8–11 tons)		
No. 30	20–21 Dec.	Lost in air raid on Liverpool.

Class	Name	Tonnage	Date of Completion	Date of Loss	How Lost and Where
RAIDING CRAFT CARRIER.*	PRINCE PHILIPPE (R) ...	2,938	1939	1941 15 July	Sunk in collision off W. Scotland.

Class and Nos.	Date of Loss	How Lost and Where
LANDING CRAFT ASSAULT	1941	
(W.L. 11–13·5 tons)		
Nos. 28	May	Lost during evacuation of Crete.
119	July (date reported).	Sunk in home waters.
31, 32, 38, 39, 45, 48, 49, 51, 60, 63, 64, } 75, 79–81, 87, 105, 113 (total 18) }	Aug. (date reported).	Lost in Middle East.
121	24 Dec.	Cause and place unknown.
70	—	Lost in Middle East.
LANDING CRAFT MECHANISED		
(Mark I) (W.L. 30–37 tons)		
Nos. 106	May	Lost at Crete.
32, 55, 67, 95, 96, 103, 107, 108 (total 8) ...	Aug. (date reported). }	Lost in Middle East.
82, 97 (total 2)	Aug.–Sept. }	
1	—	Sunk in home waters.

* Raiding Craft were subsequently redesignated Landing Craft Personnel (Large).

Class and Nos.	Date of Loss	How Lost and Where
	1941	
LANDING CRAFT PERSONNEL (Large) (W.L. 8–11 tons)		
Nos. 107–109 (total 3)	May	Lost in home waters in transit from U.S.A.
63	Aug. (date reported).	Lost in Middle East.
59, 71 (total 2)	2 Sept.	Lost through heavy weather while at anchor, Middle East.
193, 194 (total 2)	Dec.	Lost overboard through heavy weather in Home waters.
24–27, 38, 82 (total 6)	—	Lost in Home waters.
LANDING CRAFT SUPPORT (Medium) (Mark I) (W.L. 9–10·7 tons)		
No. 1	—	Unknown.
LANDING CRAFT TANK (Mark I) (W.L. 372 tons)		
Nos. 16	2 June	Lost in Suda Bay, Crete.
6, 20 (total 2)	June	Lost in Middle East.
10	17 July	Lost by enemy action, Middle East.
8	29 July	
1, 12, 15, 19 (total 4)	Aug. (date reported).	Lost in Middle East.
5	Aug. (date reported).	Lost in Home waters.
14	12 Aug.	
2, 7 (total 2)	12–13 Oct.	Lost after leaving Tobruk.
11	16 Dec.	Lost in Middle East.
LANDING CRAFT TANK (Mark II) (W.L. 450–453 tons)		
Nos. 102, 103 (total 2)	10 Oct.	
105, 109 (total 2)	4 Nov.	Lost in Home Waters.
110, 143 (total 2)	Nov.	

Class	Name	Tonnage	Date of Completion	Date of Loss	How Lost and Where
				1942	
LANDING SHIP INFANTRY (LARGE).	KARANJA (R)	9,890	1931	12 Nov.	Sunk by A/C, Bougie, Algeria.

Class and Nos.	Date of Loss	How Lost and Where
	1942.	
LANDING CRAFT ASSAULT (W.L. 11–13·5 tons)		
Nos. 166	19 Apr.	
211	Apr.	Lost in Home Waters.
138	June	
193	20 June	Lost during fall of Tobruk.
196	July	Lost by enemy action.
37, 52, 92, 94, 97, 102, 192, 209, 214, 215, 237, 247, 251, 262, 284, 314, 317 (total 17)	19 Aug.	Lost in operation JUBILEE (Dieppe).
35, 55, 128, 135, 153, 167, 169, 176, 187–189, 218, 219, 221, 227, 235, 239, 244, 245, 259–261, 266, 269, 271, 286, 287, 301, 307, 309, 310, 321, 375, 423, 436, 447, 451 (total 37).	Nov. (approx.)	Lost in operation TORCH (N. Africa).
LANDING CRAFT FLAK (Mark II) (W.L. 500–540 tons)		
No. 2	19 Aug.	Lost in operation JUBILEE (Dieppe).
LANDING CRAFT MECHANISED (Mark I) (W.L. 30–37 tons)		
Nos. 51, 53 (total 2)	Mar.	Lost in Middle East.
38	Apr. (date reported).	Lost in Mediterranean.
46	5 May	Capsized and sank, E. Indies.
84, 90, 93, 119, 122, 135, 137 (total 7) ...	June	Lost in Middle East.
110, 113, 145, 146, 148 (total 5)	20 June	Lost during fall of Tobruk.
140	July	
23–25, 34, 45 (total 5)	Aug.	Lost in Middle East.
56	19 Aug.	Lost in operation JUBILEE (Dieppe).
31	Oct. (date reported).	Lost in Home Waters.
89	22 Oct.	Believed lost in tow en route to Colombo.
63–65, 69, 72, 73, 120, 147, 153, 161, 169, 186 (total 12).	Nov.	Lost in operation TORCH (N. Africa).
139	20 Nov.	Lost through heavy weather in Middle East.
98	6 Dec.	Lost by enemy action in Benghazi area.

Class and Nos.	Date of Loss	How Lost and Where
LANDING CRAFT MECHANISED	1942	
(Mark III) (W.L. 52 tons)		
Nos. 501, 510, 516 (total 3)	Aug.	Lost in Middle East.
508, 509, 519, 522, 523, 532, 537, 547, 620 (total 9).	13 Oct.	Lost in SOUTHERN EMPRESS, torpedoed in convoy, N. Atlantic.
611, 613, 632–634, 636 (total 6)	14 Oct.	Lost in EMPIRE TARPON, off N.W. Scotland.
518, 520, 528, 539, 543, 551, 555, 556, 558, 564, 567, 569, 571, 572, 574, 581, 584, 590, 592, 593, 595, 596, 606, 609, 624, 635 (total 26).	Nov.	Lost in operation TORCH (N. Africa).
LANDING CRAFT PERSONNEL (Large)		
(W.L. 8–11 tons)		
Nos. 180–185 (total 6)	Feb.	Lost at Singapore.
57	Mar.	Bombed at Tobruk.
117	Mar.	Lost in Home Waters.
64	20 June	Lost during fall of Tobruk.
65	30 June	Lost in bad weather off Alexandria.
93	10 July	Destroyed by fire at Shoreham.
42, 45, 81, 157, 164, 174, 210, 212 (total 8)	19 Aug.	Lost in operation JUBILEE (Dieppe).
83	2 Sept.	Lost by fire at Newhaven.
29	15 Sept.	Lost by fire in Middle East.
209	6 Nov.	Lost in Seaford Bay.
138, 507, 543, 544, 550, 560, 562, 565, 566, 568, 573, 575, 576, 759 (total 14).	Nov.	Lost in operation TORCH (N. Africa).
36	24–25 Dec.	Lost by fire at Chittagong, India.
LANDING CRAFT PERSONNEL (Ramped)		
(W.L. 9–11 tons)		
Nos. 1008	Aug.	Damaged and sunk in heavy weather in Home Waters.
1012	Aug.	Sunk in collision in Home Waters.
617	15 Sept.	Sunk in Home Waters.
622	24 Sept.	
603, 620, 629, 721, 783, 794, 837, 850, 858, 901, 909, 1009, 1029, 1036 (total 14).	Nov. (approx.)	Lost in operation TORCH (N. Africa).
578	13 Dec.	Lost at Inveraray, W. Scotland.
LANDING CRAFT SUPPORT (Medium)		
(Mark I) (W.L. 9–10·7 tons)		
Nos. 4, 6, 15, 18, 19, 22 (total 6)	20 June	Lost during fall of Tobruk.
9	19 Aug.	Lost in operation JUBILEE (Dieppe).
11, 14 (total 2)	Nov.	Lost in operation TORCH (N. Africa).
LANDING CRAFT SUPPORT (Medium)		
(Mark II) (W.L. 12·5 tons)		
No. 28	Nov.	Lost in operation TORCH (N. Africa).
LANDING CRAFT TANK		
(Mark II) (W.L. 450–453 tons)		
Nos. 155	Mar.	Lost on passage to Gibraltar.
119, 150 (total 2)	20 June	Lost at Tobruk.
121, 124, 126, 145, 159 (total 5)	19 Aug.	Lost in operation JUBILEE (Dieppe).
120	20 Nov.	Lost in heavy weather.
LANDING CRAFT TANK		
(Mark V) (W.L. 291–311 tons)		
Nos. 2006	13 Oct.	
2281	27 Oct.	
2190, 2192, 2284 (total 3)	28 Oct.	Lost in transit from U.S.A
2187	Nov.	
2054, 2312 (total 2)...	Dec.	
LANDING CRAFT VEHICLE		
(W.L. 10–11 tons)		
Nos. 597	12 Sept.	Lost in Home Waters.
798	25 Sept.	
579	13 Dec.	Lost at Inveraray, W. Scotland.
752, 754 (total 2)	30 Dec.	Lost in FIDELITY, sunk N. Atlantic.
LANDING BARGES		
(B.B.) (150 ton type)		
Nos. 332, 362 (total 2)	19 Sept.	Sunk by A/C near Salcombe.
(C.C.) (200 ton type)		
No. 382	Sept.	Cause and place unknown.

Class	Number	Tonnage	Date of Completion	Date of Loss	How Lost and Where
Landing Ships Tank (Class II).	429	2,750	21. 2.43	1943 3 July	Lost by fire, Mediterranean.
	414	2,750	20. 1.43	15 Aug.	Torpedoed by A/C. off Cani Rocks, Tunisia. Beached off Bizerta.
	79	2,750	17. 7.43	30 Sept.	Sunk by A/C. off Corsica.

Class and Nos.	Date of Loss	How Lost and Where
LANDING CRAFT ASSAULT (W.L. 11–13·5 tons)	1943	
Nos. 272	Apr.	Lost in Mediterranean.
78	June (date reported).	Lost in tow from Algiers to Djedjelli.
222, 312 (total 2)	June (date reported).	Lost in Mediterranean.
446	29 Aug.	Lost in heavy weather in Mediterranean.
675	24 Sept.	Lost during gale at Salerno.
212, 316, 505, 545 (total 4)	Nov. (date reported).	Lost in Mediterranean.
813	29 Nov.	Lost during exercises in Home Waters.
553	2 Dec.	Sunk in collision off Southampton.
645, 646 (total 2)	21 Dec.	Lost in heavy weather, English Channel.
723	Dec. (approx.)	Broke adrift from Hopetoun II, Port Edgar.
LANDING CRAFT EMERGENCY REPAIR (W.L. 10 tons)		
Nos. 1, 9 (total 2)	Oct.	Lost in Mediterranean.
LANDING CRAFT FLAK (Mark III) (W.L. 550 tons)		
No. 13	12 June	Bombed off Pantellaria, Central Mediterranean. Total wreck.
LANDING CRAFT GUN (Large) (Mark III) (W.L. 627 tons)		
Nos. 15	25 Apr. }	Lost off Milford Haven in heavy weather.
16	26 Apr.	
LANDING CRAFT INFANTRY (Large) (W.L. 380–384 tons)		
Nos. 162	7 Feb.	Exploded and sank en route for Algiers.
7	21 Apr.	Sunk by A/C. off Algiers.
107	2 Sept.	Wrecked off Reggio, Italy.
309	23 Oct.	Sunk by A/C. in Biscay area.
LANDING CRAFT MECHANISED (Mark I) (W.L. 30–37 tons)		
Nos. 26	2 Jan. }	Sunk in Mediterranean, off Libya.
58	25 Jan.	
80	6 Feb.	Stranded off Benghazi. Total loss.
61	8 Feb.	Sunk in Benghazi Harbour through heavy weather.
232	Oct. (approx.)	Lost in Mediterranean.
181	Nov. (date reported).	Lost in Azores.
33	20 Dec.	Damaged beyond repair in Home Waters.
LANDING CRAFT MECHANISED (Mark III) (W.L. 52 tons)		
Nos. 545, 938, 1044 (total 3)	Oct. (approx.).	Lost in Mediterranean.
1165, 1182 (total 2)	Oct. (approx.).	Lost in Home Waters.
583	Nov. (date reported).	Lost in Mediterranean.

Class and Nos.	Date of Loss	How Lost and Where
	1943	
LANDING CRAFT PERSONNEL (Large)		
(W.L. 8–11 tons)		
Nos. 17	3 Jan.	Lost by fire at Chittagong, India.
80	15 Jan.	Broke adrift during gale in Home Waters.
203–206 (total 4)	Jan.	Lost at Sourabaya, Java.
87	25 Feb.	Lost in Home Waters.
106	4 Mar.	Wrecked off Tobruk.
276, 277 (total 2)	Mar.	Lost in transit.
126	Aug.	Burnt out.
325	4 Sept. ⎫	Sunk at Bombay.
316	12 Sept. ⎬	
136	8 Dec.	Caught fire and blew up during exercises off Southampton.
LANDING CRAFT PERSONNEL (Ramped)		
(W.L. 9–11 tons)		
Nos. 673, 680, 684, 685, 689, 692, 693, 727 (total 8).	4 Mar.	Lost in MARIETTA E., sunk by U/B. in Convoy, Indian Ocean.
780, 782 (total 2)	17 April	Lost in SEMBILAN. Sunk by U/B, Indian Ocean.
769	June (date reported).	Lost in Mediterranean.
879	12 Sept.	Wrecked at Bombay.
1019	28 Sept.	Sunk during heavy weather in Salerno Bay, Italy.
753, 771, 795 (total 3)	19 Dec.	Lost during beaching exercises in Home Waters.
613, 661, 1035 (total 3)	22 Dec.	Lost overboard from HILARY.
LANDING CRAFT PERSONNEL (Medium)		
(W.L. 7·5 tons)		
Nos. 17	5 Jan.	Lost off Isle of Wight.
14	Nov. (date reported).	—
LANDING CRAFT PERSONNEL (Small)		
(W.L. 6 tons)		
No. 116	22 Dec.	Lost during exercises in Home Waters.
LANDING CRAFT SUPPORT (Large)		
(Mark I) (W.L. 23 tons)		
No. 201	Sept.	Lost in collision, English Channel.
LANDING CRAFT SUPPORT (Medium)		
(Mark I) (W.L. 9–13·5 tons)		
Nos. 23	Mar.	Lost on patrol, Mayu River, Burma.
17	25 Apr.	Sunk by enemy action, Mayu River, Burma.
16	29 Aug.	Lost in India.
LANDING CRAFT TANK		
(Mark I) (W.L. 372 tons)		
No. 3	11 Oct.*	Presumed lost in attack on Kos, Dodecanese. Formally paid off.
LANDING CRAFT TANK		
(Mark II) (W.L. 450–453 tons)		
Nos. 106, 107 (total 2)	6 Jan.	Sunk in Benghazi Harbour as result of heavy weather.
115	28 Oct.	Sunk by A/C. off Casteloriso, Aegean.
LANDING CRAFT TANK		
(Mark III) (W.L. 625–640 tons)		
Nos. 326	2 Feb.	Lost by weather or mine off Isle of Man.
403	24 Feb.	Lost through stress of weather off Barra Head, outer Hebrides.
381	27 Feb.	Missing from Convoy after attack by E/Bs, English Channel.
358	18 June	Lost in Mediterranean.
395	18 June	Mined and grounded in Mediterranean.
353	27 July	Sunk by A/C. at Syracuse, Sicily.
391	1 Oct. (approx.).	Formally paid off.

* Later recovered and redesignated N.S.C.(L) 94.

Class and Nos.						Date of Loss	How Lost and Where
						1943	
LANDING CRAFT TANK							
(Mark III) (W.L. 625–640 tons)—*cont.*							
Nos. 333, 343, 385 (total 3)	...	...	...	...	...	14 Nov.	Sunk in gale off Land's End.
332	...	...	...	...	...	16 Nov.	Lost off Gijon, Spain, after engine failure.
418	...	...	...	...	...	16 Nov.	Lost in gale off N.W. France.
329	...	...	...	...	...	23 Nov.	Damaged beyond economical repair.
LANDING CRAFT TANK							
(Mark IV) (W.L. 611–640 tons)							
Nos. 547	...	...	...	...	...	8 July	Foundered off Malta.
624	...	...	...	...	...	8 Sept.	Formally paid off.
572, 626 (total 2)	...	...	...	...	9 Sept.	
553	...	...	...	...	...	1 Oct.	
618	...	...	...	...	...	2 Oct.	} Lost in Mediterranean.
621	...	...	...	...	...	7 Oct.	
583	...	...	...	...	...	4 Nov.	
LANDING CRAFT TANK							
(Mark V) (W.L. 291–311 tons)							
Nos. 2239, 2267, 2344 (total 3)	...	...	...	17 Jan.	Lost in VESTFOLD, torpedoed in convoy, N. Atlantic.
2335	...	...	...	...	...	7 Feb.	Lost in DAGHILD, torpedoed in convoy, N. Atlantic.
2480	...	...	...	...	...	8 Mar.	Lost in FORT LAMY, torpedoed in convoy, N. Atlantic.
2341	...	...	...	...	...	10 Mar.	Lost in BONNEVILLE, torpedoed in convoy, N. Atlantic.
2398	...	...	...	...	...	Mar.	Lost in GORGAS.
2231	...	...	...	...	...	30 Sept.	Lost in L.S.T. 79, sunk off Corsica.
LANDING CRAFT VEHICLE							
(W.L. 10–11 tons)							
Nos. 584	...	...	...	...	...	15 Mar.	Sunk off Inellan, W. Scotland.
825	...	...	...	...	...	21–22 May	Blew up during exercises off W. Scotland.
LANDING CRAFT VEHICLE (Personnel)							
(W.L. 10·5–13·5 tons)							
No. 1040	...	...	...	...	...	1 Nov.	Capsized off Newhaven after engine room flooding.

Class	Name or Number	Tonnage	Date of Completion	Date of Loss	How Lost and Where
				1944	
LANDING SHIPS INFANTRY (LARGE).	EL HIND (R)	5,319	—	14 Apr.	Destroyed by fire in Bombay Docks.
	EMPIRE BROADSWORD ...	4,285 (Light)	—	2 July	Sunk by mine off Normandy.
	EMPIRE JAVELIN ...	4,285 (Light)	—	28 Dec.	Lost on passage from Portsmouth to Le Havre, believed torpedoed by U/B.
LANDING SHIP INFANTRY (SMALL).	PRINCE LEOPOLD (R) ...	2,938	1930	29 July	Torpedoed by U/B, capsized and sank, English Channel.
LANDING SHIPS TANK (CLASS II).	No. 411	2,750	8. 1.43	1 Jan.	Mined or torpedoed (31 Dec., 1943) on passage from Maddalena to Bastia. Abandoned owing to heavy weather.
	No. 422	2,750	5. 2.43	26 Jan.	Mined and sunk in Operation SHINGLE (Anzio).
	No. 418	2,750	1. 2.43	16 Feb.	Sunk after 2 underwater explosions, Operation SHINGLE (Anzio).
	No. 305	2,750	7.12.42	20 Feb.	Sunk by U/B, torpedo, during Operation SHINGLE (Anzio).
	No. 362	2,750	23.11.42	2 Mar.	Sunk by U/B, torpedo, Biscay area.
	No. 407	2,750	31.12.42	24 Apr.	Damaged beyond repair by weather in Mediterranean.
	No. 420	2,750	16. 2.43	7 Nov.	Sunk by mine off Ostend.
FIGHTER DIRECTION TENDER.	No. 216	2,750	4. 8.43	7 July	Sunk by A/C, torpedo, off Barfleur, N. France.

Class and Nos.	Date of Loss	How Lost and Where
LANDING CRAFT ASSAULT (W.L. 11—13·5 tons)	**1944**	
Nos. 783, 790, 865 (total 3)	19 Jan. (date reported)	Lost in Home Waters off E. Scotland.
845	29 Jan.	Became waterlogged and sank during exercises off Leith, E. Scotland.
323, 394, 428, 697 (total 4)	Jan. (approx.)	Lost in Operation SHINGLE (Anzio).
552	9 Feb.	Wrecked during exercises off E. Scotland.
726, 908 (total 2)	1 March	Lost in Home Waters.
130	May (date reported)	Destroyed by fire at Marve.
364, 382, 398, 417, 433, 459, 492, 526, 573, 761 (total 10)	May (date reported)	Cause and place unknown.
33, 56, 146 (total 3)	June (date reported)	Lost in E. Indies.
182	June (date reported)	Cause and place unknown.
107	6 June	Sunk.
59, 69 (total 2)	15 June	Lost, Bombay area.
171, 208, 279, 289, 303, 320, 337, 339, 341, 349, 350, 352, 360, 367, 383, 387, 401, 409, 418, 424, 431, 434, 442, 458, 462, 463, 476, 485, 494, 496, 503, 509, 518–520, 522, 525, 530, 535, 540, 566, 579, 581, 584, 586, 588–590, 592–594, 611, 613, 623, 637, 642, 649–652, 655, 661, 664, 665, 673, 683, 691, 692, 704, 705, 710, 717, 721, 722, 729, 731, 738, 748, 750, 768, 775, 779, 780, 788, 791, 792, 795–797, 803, 808–810, 812, 814, 815, 821, 825, 827, 835, 849, 853, 857, 859, 860, 867, 869–871, 879, 881, 886, 900, 903, 911, 913, 914, 918–920, 929, 933, 946, 949, 958, 978, 984, 998–1000, 1005, 1008, 1013, 1016, 1021, 1024, 1026–1028, 1034, 1050, 1057–1059, 1063, 1068, 1069, 1074, 1082, 1086, 1088, 1091, 1093, 1096, 1129, 1131, 1132, 1137, 1138, 1143, 1144, 1146, 1149–1151, 1155, 1156, 1213, 1215, 1216, 1251–1253, 1256, 1338–1341, 1343, 1372, 1379, 1381–1383 (total 184).	June–July	Lost in Operation NEPTUNE (Normandy).
54	July (date reported)	Lost in E. Indies.
248, 400 (total 2)	1 July	Lost in Mediterranean.
1393	3 July	Lost in Operation OVERLORD (Normandy).
1304	14 July	Lost in heavy weather in Home Waters.
577, 625 (total 2)	Sept. (date reported)	Lost in Mediterranean.
848, 1378 (total 2)	26 Sept.	Lost in heavy weather in Home Waters.
713, 725, 817, 831, 843, 1018, 1030, 1079, 1125, 1260 (total 10)	2–5 Nov.	Lost in Operation INFATUATE (Walcheren).
551	7 Nov.	Lost in heavy weather, River Blackwater, Essex.
149	16 Nov.	Lost in India.
614	29 Nov.	Lost in heavy weather, English Channel.
1188	Dec.	Lost in Solomon Islands.
326	—	Lost in Mediterranean.
226, 254, 347, 440, 487, 696, 753 (total 7)	—	Cause and place unknown.
LANDING CRAFT ASSAULT (Hedgerow) (W.L. 12 tons)		
689	13 Mar.	Sank in Home Waters.
672, 811 (total 2)	2 Apr.	Foundered during exercises off E. Scotland.
671, 690, 965, 1072 (total 4)	June–July	Lost in Operation NEPTUNE (Normandy).
183, 258, 802 (total 3)	1 July	Lost in Mediterranean.
LANDING CRAFT EMERGENCY REPAIR (W.L. 10 tons)		
Nos. 5, 14, 21 (total 3)	May (date reported)	} Cause and place unknown.
15	13 July.	
LANDING CRAFT FLAK (Mark II) (W.L. 500–540 tons)		
No. 1	17 Aug.	Blew up and sank, Operation NEPTUNE (Normandy).
LANDING CRAFT FLAK (Mark III) (W.L. 515–550 tons)		
No. 15	16–17 June	Mined in Convoy, Operation BRASSARD (Elba).

F

Class and Nos.	Date of Loss	How Lost and Where
LANDING CRAFT FLAK (Mark IV,) (W.L. 500–510 tons) Nos. 31	1944 5 Sept. (date reported)	Lost in Operation NEPTUNE (Normandy).
37, 38 (total 2)	1 Nov.	Lost in Operation INFATUATE (Walcheren).
LANDING CRAFT GUN (Large) (Mark III) (W.L. 500 tons) Nos. 1, 2 (total 2)	2 Nov.	Lost in Operation INFATUATE (Walcheren).
LANDING CRAFT GUN (Large) (Mark IV) (W.L. 530 tons) Nos. 764, 831, 1062 (total 3)	July-Aug.	Lost in Operation NEPTUNE (Normandy).
LANDING CRAFT GUN (Medium) (Mark I) (W.L. 381 tons) Nos. 101, 102 (total 2)	1 Nov.	Los. in Operation INFATUATE (Walcheren).
LANDING CRAFT HEADQUARTERS (W.L. 384 tons) No. 185	25 June	Sunk by mine, Operation NEPTUNE (Normandy).
LANDING CRAFT INFANTRY (Large) (W.L. 380–384 tons) No. 273	17 Mar.	Sunk by A/C, Anzio.
105	8 June	Torpedoed, Operation NEPTUNE (Normandy).
132	17 June	Lost and formally paid off.
99	14 Aug.	Sunk in Convoy, presumed by U/B, Operation NEPTUNE (Normandy).
102	11 Nov.	Damaged by gales and abandoned, Vis, Adriatic.
LANDING CRAFT INFANTRY (Small) (W.L. 110 tons) Nos. 511	2 Feb.	Beached at Portslade, Sussex. Total loss.
512, 517, 524, 531, 540 (total 5)	June	Lost in Operation NEPTUNE (Normandy).
537	June	Damaged beyond economical repair.
532	1 Nov.	Lost in Operation INFATUATE (Walcheren).
LANDING CRAFT MECHANISED (Mark I) (W.L. 30–37 tons) Nos. 192, 234, 254, 279, 282, 327, 329, 367 (total 8)	Feb. (date reported)	Lost in Home Waters.
76	Mar. (date reported)	
131, 182, 183, 207, 209 (total 5) ...	May (date reported)	Lost in E. Indies.
212, 215, 218, 219, 243, 272, 277, 285, 288, 324 (total 10)	May (date reported)	Lost overseas.
91	June (date reported)	Lost in E. Indies.
295	June (date reported)	Lost overseas.
127, 128, 165, 168, 180, 191, 203, 216, 226, 229, 231, 241, 251, 281, 316, 319, 330, 335, 337, 338, 345, 346, 348, 355, 357, 377, 382, 383, 408, 409, 419, 421, 425, 443, 444, 466 (total 36).	June–July	Lost in Operation NEPTUNE (Normandy).
138	7 July	Lost, English Channel.
263	11 Sept.	Wrecked on beach, Operation NEPTUNE (Normandy).
340, 424 (total 2)	19 Nov.	Lost overboard from JOHN L. MANSON in Mount's Bay.
LANDING CRAFT MECHANISED (Mark III) (W.L. 52 tons) Nos. 623, 910, 930, 1022, 1064, 1173, 1204 (total 7).	Jan. (approx.)	Lost in Operation SHINGLE (Anzio).
1313, 1314, 1373, 1378 (total 4)	Apr. (date reported)	Lost on passage from U.S.A. to India.
527, 534, 540, 588, 1029, 1045, 1071, 1083, 1123, 1171, 1205 (total 11).	May (date reported)	Lost overseas.
1380, 1381 (total 2)...	May (date reported)	
1115, 1130 (total 2)...	June (date reported)	Lost in Mediterranean.
577	June	Lost in Operation OVERLORD (Normandy).

Class and Nos.	Date of Loss	How Lost and Where
LANDING CRAFT MECHANISED (Mark III) (W.L. 52 tons)—*cont.*	1944	
531, 535, 568, 587, 627, 628, 631, 641, 908, 929, 1053, 1059, 1062, 1088, 1098, 1108, 1120, 1127, 1128, 1139, 1145, 1146, 1161, 1175, 1189, 1197, 1200, 1207, 1208, 1212, 1220, 1221, 1227, 1232, 1233, 1240, 1244, 1278, 1282, 1293, 1297, 1397 (total 42).	June–July	Lost in Operation NEPTUNE (Normandy).
618, 640 (total 2)	9 Aug.	Lost in Mediterranean.
1101	15 Nov.	Wrecked near Aden, en route to India.
525, 559, 591, 650, 907 (total 5)	—	Lost overseas, presumed during 1944.
LANDING CRAFT PERSONNEL (Large) (W.L. 8–11 tons)		
Nos. 66, 356, 373 (total 3)	Jan. (approx.)	Lost in Operation SHINGLE (Anzio).
152	24 Feb.	Wrecked during exercises in Home Waters.
541	28–29 Feb.	Lost off Isle of Wight.
360, 367 (total 2)	Apr. (date reported)	Lost during exercises at Mandapam.
323	14 Apr.	Destroyed in explosion at Bombay.
8, 263, 287, 577 (total 4)	May (date reported)	Lost overseas.
13, 14, 21–23, 40, 51, 121, 132, 139, 170, 175, 176, 187, 189, 197, 199, 208, 272, 280, 282, 285, 286, 289, 309, 312, 528, 556 (total 28).	June—July	Lost in Operation NEPTUNE (Normandy).
267	8 July	Sunk by mine off Cherbourg.
229, 298–300, 303–305, 308, 310 (total 9)	July	Lost in Home Waters.
84, 85, 88, 97, 98, 110, 118, 128, 137, 145, 146, 149, 162, 163, 198, 200, 230–233, 235, 238, 239, 241, 242, 246, 247, 269, 293, 294 (total 30)	Aug.–Sept.	Lost in Operation NEPTUNE (Normandy) while on loan to U.S. Navy.
348	15 Sept.	Destroyed by fire in India.
7, 18 (total 2)	6 Oct.	Lost in Home Waters.
52	11 Oct.	Lost by fire, Portsmouth Area.
133	5 Nov.	Lost in Schelde Area.
302	5 Nov.	Wrecked East of Ostend.
127, 134 (total 2)	Dec. (date reported)	Lost in Operation INFATUATE (Walcheren).
540, 760 (total 2)	—	Lost overseas, presumed during 1944.
LANDING CRAFT PERSONNEL (Ramped) (W.L. 9–11 tons)		
Nos. 616	22 Jan.	Broke adrift and badly holed in Home Waters.
781	14 Feb.	Lost in collision, Home Waters.
1026	23 Mar.	Sunk in Mediterranean.
866	14 Apr.	Destroyed by fire at Bombay.
614, 634, 663, 824, 844, 912, 913, 995 (total 8)	May (date reported)	Lost overseas.
584	May	Sunk in Home Waters.
643	May (approx.)	Lost at Naples.
723	June (date reported)	Lost in Mediterranean.
854	June (date reported)	Cause and place unknown.
966	June (date reported)	Damaged en route to Anzio.
970	June (date reported)	Lost in Home Waters.
867	June	Wrecked at Mandapam, Ceylon.
894, 896 (total 2)	June	Lost in Operation NEPTUNE (Normandy).
895	June	Damaged and sunk, Portsmouth area.
905	19 June	Lost in bad weather in Home Waters.
683	July (date reported)	Lost in action off coast of France.
971	28 July	Lost in collision in Home Waters.
999	26 Sept.	Sunk in gale in Home Waters.
1011	21 Oct.	Lost in collision in Home Waters.
805, 806 (total 2)	Nov (date reported)	Cause and place unknown.
652, 669 (total 2)	—	Lost in Home Waters, presumed during 1944.
640, 735, 978, 982, 987, 989, 991, 993, 1023 (total 9)	—	Lost overseas, presumed during 1944.
LANDING CRAFT PERSONNEL (Survey) (W.L. 9 tons)		
No. 154	July (date reported)	Cause and place unknown.

Class and Nos.	Date of Loss	How Lost and Where
LANDING CRAFT PERSONNEL .(Small) (W.L. 6 tons)	1944	
Nos. 60	25 Jan.	Wrecked in Azores.
76	13 Mar.	Lost on passage.
9	6 Apr.	Driven ashore at Weymouth.
74	May (date reported)	Lost overboard at Messina.
25, 50, 61, 73, 101, 135, 137 (total 7) ...	May (date reported)	Cause and place unknown.
136	June	Lost in Operation NEPTUNE (Normandy).
183	July (date reported)	Wrecked in Mediterranean.
129	10 Nov.	Lost by fire at Hythe.
1	—	Cause and place unknown.
LANDING CRAFT SUPPORT (Large) (Mark II) (W.L. 112 tons)		
Nos. 252, 256, 258 (total 3)	1 Nov.	Lost in Operation INFATUATE (Walcheren).
LANDING CRAFT SUPPORT (Medium) (Mark III) (W.L. 13·5 tons)		
Nos. 46	Jan. (approx.)	Lost in Operation SHINGLE (Anzio).
69	3 Mar.	Sunk during exercises off E. Scotland.
59	May (date reported)	Cause and place unknown.
75, 76, 80, 81, 83, 91, 99, 101, 103, 108, 114 (total 11)	June	Lost in Operation NEPTUNE (Normandy).
47	June	
54	1 July	
42	25 Aug.	Cause and place unknown.
49	—	
LANDING CRAFT TANK (Mark II) (W.L. 450–453 tons)		
No. 129	Nov. (date reported)	Cause and place unknown.
LANDING CRAFT TANK (Mark III) (W.L. 625–640 tons)		
Nos. 375	Feb. (date reported)	Sunk in Mediterranean.
390	9 July	
7057, 7064 (total 2)	16 July	Cause and place unknown.
387	17 July	Mined off W. Italy.
427	Aug.	Cause and place unknown.
377	Oct.	Lost, probably mined, on passage Marseilles to Maddalena.
480, 488, 491, 494, 7014, 7015 (total 6) ...	18—19 Oct.	Lost through stress of weather off Land's End.
7011	2 Nov.	Lost in Operation INFATUATE (Walcheren).
328	5 Dec.	Mined off W. Greece.
7089	6 Dec.	Hit obstruction in Boulogne Harbour. Total loss.
LANDING CRAFT TANK (Mark IV) (W.L. 611–640 tons)		
Nos. 1029	16 Jan.	Blew up, possibly mined, while at anchor off Skegness.
875	8 June	Sunk by enemy action.
967	13 June	Mined.
524, 715, 750, 809, 886, 947 (total 6) ...	June	Lost in Operation NEPTUNE (Normandy).
589	16 June	Destroyed to avoid capture, Mediterranean.
511	9 July	Broke back while in tow.
757	10 July	Formally paid off.
689	20 July	Destroyed by explosion.
1023	23 July	Damaged beyond economical repair.
901	24 July	
1039	5 Aug.	Broke backs.
1076	5 Aug.	Broke in two.
1092	10 Aug.	Broke back while in tow.
631	17 Aug.	Broke back.
1074	25 Aug.	Mined, English Channel.
943	Oct.	Sunk.
1045	25 Oct.	Broke in two while in tow, English Channel.
936	30 Oct.	Broke back through stress of weather off Lowestoft.
1171	23 Oct.	Sunk off N. European Coast.
789, 839, 1133 (total 3)	2 Nov.	Lost in Operation INFATUATE (Walcheren).
609	6 Nov.	Abandoned after damage by weather off Ostend.
976	7 Nov.	Abandoned with broken back, Schelde area.
1022	17 Nov.	Wrecked through stress of weather off Dungeness.

Class and Nos.	Date of Loss	How Lost and Where
LANDING CRAFT TANK	1944	
(Mark V) (W.L. 291–311 tons)		
Nos. 2498	June	Lost in Operation NEPTUNE (Normandy).
2049, 2229, 2307 (total 3)	6 June	Lost in Operation NEPTUNE (Normandy) while on loan to U.S. Navy.
2331 ... ,...	July	Broken back.
2461	Nov.	Capsized and sunk by gunfire, Bay of Bengal.
LANDING CRAFT TANK (Armoured)		
(Mark V) (W.L. 290–295 tons)		
Nos. 2039	June	Cause and place unknown.
2273, 2301, 2402 (total 3)	June	Lost in Operation NEPTUNE (Normandy) while on loan to U.S. Navy.
2428	June	Lost in Operation NEPTUNE (Normandy).
2263	15 July	Cause and place unknown.
2454	13 Oct.	Ran ashore in Lyme Bay, English Channel, in heavy gale. Wrecked.
LANDING CRAFT TANK (Rocket)		
(W.L. 600 tons)		
No. 457	5 Nov.	Mined off Ostend.
LANDING CRAFT VEHICLE		
(W.L. 10–11 tons)		
Nos. 894	Feb. (date reported)	Lost on service with R.A.S.C., C.T.C., Rothesay.
719	June	Cause and place unknown.
801	18 Oct.	Broke adrift and holed, Portsmouth area.
LANDING CRAFT VEHICLE (Personnel)		
(W.L. 10·5–13·5 tons)		
Nos. 1066	Feb.	Lost during exercises, Richborough area, Kent.
1016, 1029, 1031, 1033, 1044–1046, 1049, 1054, 1056, 1062, 1065, 1084, 1088, 1093, 1098, 1101, 1102, 1104, 1106, 1111, 1114, 1117, 1120–1122, 1124, 1129, 1132, 1133, 1139, 1146, 1153, 1155, 1157, 1159, 1165, 1170–1172, 1184, 1188, 1201, 1204, 1211, 1216, 1218, 1242, 1245, 1246, 1248, 1249, 1251, 1255, 1260, 1262, 1264 (total 57).	June (approx.)	Lost in Operation NEPTUNE (Normandy).
1288	13 July	Lost in Home Waters.
1103	20 Nov.	Abandoned at Chichester.
1199	25 Nov.	Sank, Portsmouth area.
1228	27 Nov.	Lost in Home Waters.
LANDING BARGES, EMERGENCY REPAIR		
(200 ton type)		
Nos. 8, 17, 25–27, 57, 60 (total 7)	19–25 June	Written off charge as result of damage caused in assault area during gale.
LANDING BARGES, OILER (200 ton type)		
Nos. 50	June	Cause and place unknown.
46, 56, 84 (total 3)	19–25 June	Written off charge as result of damage caused in assault area during gale.
87	11th July }	Cause and place unknown.
53	9 Aug. }	
(150 ton type)		
10	19–25 June	Written off charge as result of damage caused in assault area during gale.
73	9 Aug. }	Cause and place unknown.
4	17 Aug. }	
30	31 Aug. }	
LANDING BARGES, VEHICLE		
(Mark I) (150 ton type)		
Nos. 367	17 Jan.	Wrecked on passage Dartmouth to Portland.
136, 149, 497 (total 3)	Feb. }	
229, 266 (total 2)	Mar. (date reported) }	Cause and place unknown.
52	7 June }	
16, 51 (total 2)	12 June	Lost through stress of weather.
84	26 June }	Cause and place unknown.
121, 175 (total 2)	1 July }	
154	14 Aug.	Sank at moorings off Portsmouth.
83	19 Aug.	Sank in tow.

Class and Nos.	Date of Loss	How Lost and Where
LANDING BARGES, VEHICLE	1944.	
(Mark II) (200 ton type)		
Nos. 172, 176, 206, 232 (total 4)	19–25 June	Written off charge as result of damage caused in assault area during gale.
(150 ton type)		
16, 20, 51 (total 3)	June	Cause and place unknown.
3, 27, 49, 61, 67, 94, 95, 103, 209, 214 (total 10).	19–25 June	Written off charge as result of damage caused in assault area during gale.
19, 28, 116, 122 (total 4)	29 July	Cause and place unknown.
LANDING BARGES, WATER		
(200 ton type)		
Nos. 15	19–25 June	Written off charge as result of damage caused in assault area during gale.
(150 ton type)		
7	19–25 June	Written off charge as result of damage caused in assault area during dale.
14	29 Aug. }	Cause and place unknown.
11	12 Sept. }	
RAMPED DUMB BARGES		
(100 ton type)		
Nos. 83	23 May	Sank on passage to Sheerness.
43, 65 (total 2)	1 July	Cause and place unknown.

Class	Name	Tonnage	Date of Completion	Date of Loss	How Lost and Where
				1945	
LANDING SHIPS TANK (Class II)	No. 364	2,750	7.12.42	22 Feb.	Torpedoed by U/B. off Ramsgate.
	178	2,750		24 Feb.	Mined on passage to Corfu, grounded and became total wreck.
	80	2,750	19.7.43	20 Mar.	Mined in English Channel and sank off Ostend.

Class and Nos.	Date of Loss	How Lost and Where
LANDING CRAFT ASSAULT	1945	
(W.L. 11–13·5 tons)		
Nos. 1161	26 Feb.	Lost through heavy weather at Leyte, Pacific.
1112, 1153 (total 2)	Mar. (date reported)	Presumed lost during 1945.
1472	27 Mar.	Lost at Leyte, Pacific.
1433	30 Mar.	Smashed by heavy seas. Admiralty Islands, S.W. Pacific.
1346, 1396 (total 2)	Apr. (date reported)	Lost in Mediterranean ; presumed during 1945.
841	22 Apr.	Sunk in operations off Holland.
1329, 1591 (total 2)	17 Aug.	Lost overboard from L.S.I. off India.
LANDING CRAFT ASSAULT		
(Obstruction Clearance)		
(W.L. 13·5 tons)		
1211	May (date reported)	Lost in Home Waters, presumed during 1945.
LANDING CRAFT MECHANISED		
(Mark I) (W.L. 30–37 tons)		
Nos. 136	Feb. (date reported)	Cause and place unknown.
270, 339, 359, 422 (total 4)	Feb. (date reported)	Lost from ASA LOTHROP.
354, 493 (total 2)	June (date reported)	Lost in operations on Arakan Coast, Burma.
LANDING CRAFT MECHANISED		
(Mark III) (W.L. 52 tons)		
Nos. 1131	23 Jan.	Lost in Arromanches Area, Normandy.
1011	Mar. (date reported)	Lost in Mediterranean.
1319, 1327 (total 2)	Apr.	Lost on Arakan Coast, Burma.
1092	June (date reported)	Cause and place unknown.

Class and Nos.	Date of Loss	How Lost and Where
LANDING CRAFT MECHANISED (Mark III) (W.L. 52 tons)—*cont.*	1945	
1185	July (date reported)	Lost, presumed during 1945.
LANDING CRAFT PERSONNEL (Large) (W.L. 8–11 tons)		
Nos. 11	18 Jan.	Lost on Passage from Brest to Cherbourg.
764	18 Mar.	Lost in Home Waters.
344, 378 (total 2)	29 May	Sunk at Akyab, Burma.
LANDING CRAFT PERSONNEL (Ramped) (W.L. 9–11 tons)		
Nos. 1018	26 Jan.	Lost in Scheldt area.
707	22 Feb.	Lost by enemy action in Home Waters.
979	5 Mar.	Lost when in use as ship's boat in Eastern Theatre.
840	28 Mar.	Lost by enemy action in Home Waters.
738	9 Apr.	Lost during storm in Mediterranean.
832	June (date reported)	Lost in tow in Mediterranean.
965	July (date reported)	
LANDING CRAFT PERSONNEL (Mark II) (W.L. 3·8 tons)		
Nos. 1110, 1121 (total 2)	May	Lost in Aegean Operations.
1113	June (date reported)	Damaged in gale at Maddalena and written off.
LANDING CRAFT SUPPORT (Medium) (Mark II) (W.L. 12·5 tons)		
No. 30	June (date reported)	Lost in operations on Arakan Coast, Burma.
LANDING CRAFT SUPPORT (Medium) (Mark III) (W.L. 13·5 tons)		
No. 148	June (date reported)	Lost in operations on Arakan Coast, Burma.
LANDING CRAFT TANK (Mark III) (W.L. 625–640 tons)		
Nos. 492	6 Mar.	Capsized and sank, Red Sea.
357	29 May	Lost in Suda Bay, Crete, as result of explosion.
LANDING CRAFT TANK (Mark IV) (W.L. 611–640 tons)		
No. 1238	2 May	Mined in Rangoon River.
LANDING CRAFT VEHICLE (W.L. 10–11 tons)		
No. 814	30 Jan.	Lost in Home Waters.
802	2 Aug.	Lost in tow in Home Waters.
LANDING CRAFT VEHICLE (Personnel) (W.L. 10·5–13·5 tons)		
1191	Jan.	Cause and place unknown.
LANDING CRAFT VEHICLE (Personnel) (W.L. 10·5–13·5 tons)		
1358	Apr.	Lost by stranding, E. Mediterranean.
1167	15 July	Lost, Channel Islands.
LANDING BARGE, EMERGENCY REPAIR (200 ton type)		
Nos. 12, 30, 32–34 (total 5)	June (date reported)	Written off.
LANDING BARGE, KITCHEN		
No. 8	31 July	Sank in tow, English Channel
LANDING BARGES, OILER (200 ton type)		
Nos. 13, 37, 63, 69, 88, 96 (total 6)	June (date reported)	Written off.
(150 ton type)		
Nos. 17	20 Jan.	Swamped and sank in Arromanches Harbour during gale.
11, 21, 24, 26, 77, 82, 92, 95 (total 8) ...	June (date reported)	Written off.

Class and Nos.	Date and Loss	How Lost and Where
LANDING BARGE, VEHICLE	1945	
(Mark II) (200 ton type)		
Nos. 152	May (date reported)	⎫
137, 140, 157, 170 (total 4)	June (date reported)	⎬ Written off.
132	29 July	⎭
(150 ton type)		
Nos. 1, 5, 9, 11, 31, 35, 42, 65, 72, 73, 75, 76, 99, 118, 211, 212 (total 16)	June (date reported)	Written off.
LANDING BARGE, WATER		
(150 ton type)		
Nos. 1, 6 (total 2)	June (date reported)	Written off.
RAMPED DUMB BARGES		
(150 ton type)		
No. 114	June (date reported)	Written off.
59	26 Nov.	Sank in Edinburgh Channel.

II. SUMMARY OF LOSSES BY YEAR AND CLASS

LANDING SHIPS

Class	3 Sept., 1939 to 31 Dec. 1939	1940	1941	1942	1943	1944	1 Jan. 1945 to 15 Aug. 1945	Total	Total Displacement Tonnage lost
LANDING SHIPS INFANTRY— (LARGE)	—	—	—	1	—	3	—	4	8,570 (Light) 15,209
(SMALL)	—	—	—	—	—	1	—	1	2,938
LANDING SHIPS TANK— (MARK II)	—	—	—	—	3	7	3	13	35,750
FIGHTER DIRECTION TENDER	—	—	—	—	—	1	—	1	2,750
RAIDING CRAFT CARRIER ...	—	—	1	—	—	←	—	1	2,938
TOTAL NUMBERS	—	—	1	1	3	12	3	20	—
TOTAL TONNAGE : STANDARD DISPLACEMENT	—	—	—	—	8,250	22,000	8,250	—	38,500
LIGHT DISPLACEMENT ...	—	—	—	—	—	8,570	—	—	8,570
GROSS REGISTERED TONNAGE	—	—	2,938	9,890	—	8,257	—	—	21,085

LANDING CRAFT

Class	3 Sept., 1939 to 31 Dec., 1939	1940	1941	1942	1943	1944	1 Jan., 1945 to 15 Aug., 1945	Total
LANDING CRAFT—								
ASSAULT	—	10	22	59	15	244	10	360
(HEDGEROW)	—	—	—	—	—	10	—	10
(OBSTRUCTION CLEARANCE)	—	—	—	—	—	—	1	1
LANDING CRAFT EMERGENCY REPAIR	—	—	—	—	2	4	—	6
LANDING CRAFT FLAK—								
(MARK II)	—	—	—	1	—	1	—	2
(MARK III)	—	—	—	—	1	1	—	2
LANDING CRAFT GUN—								
(LARGE) (MARK III)	—	—	—	—	2	2	—	4
(LARGE) (MARK IV)	—	—	—	—	—	3	—	3
(MEDIUM)	—	—	—	—	—	2	—	2
LANDING CRAFT HEADQUARTERS	—	—	—	—	—	1	—	1
LANDING CRAFT INFANTRY—								
(LARGE)	—	—	—	—	4	5	—	9
(SMALL)	—	—	—	—	—	8	—	8
LANDING CRAFT MECHANISED—								
(MARK I)	—	10	12	39	7	66	7	141
(MARK III)	—	—	—	44	6	77	6	133
LANDING CRAFT PERSONNEL								
(LARGE)	—	1	14	37	14	90	4	160
(RAMPED)	—	—	—	19	19	40	7	85
(SURVEY)	—	—	—	—	—	1	—	1
(MEDIUM)	—	—	—	—	2	—	—	2
(SMALL)	—	—	—	—	1	15	—	16
(MARK II)	—	—	—	—	—	—	3	3
LANDING CRAFT SUPPORT—								
(LARGE) (MARK I)	—	—	—	—	1	—	—	1
(LARGE) (MARK II)	—	—	—	—	—	3	—	3
(MEDIUM) (MARK I)	—	—	1	9	3	—	—	13
(MEDIUM) (MARK II)	—	—	—	1	—	—	1	2
(MEDIUM) (MARK III)	—	—	—	—	—	18	1	19
LANDING CRAFT TANK—								
(MARK I)	—	—	14	—	1	—	—	15
(MARK II)	—	—	6	9	3	1	—	19
(MARK III)	—	—	—	—	13	16	2	31
(MARK IV)	—	—	—	—	8	30	1	39
(MARK V)	—	—	—	8	8	6	—	22
(ARMOURED) (MARK V)	—	—	—	—	—	7	—	7
(ROCKET)	—	—	—	—	—	1	—	1
LANDING CRAFT VEHICLE	—	—	—	5	2	3	2	12
(PERSONNEL)	—	—	—	—	1	62	3	66
TOTAL	—	21	69	231	113	717	48	1,199
LANDING BARGES—								
(UNCLASSIFIED)	—	—	—	3	—	—	—	3
LANDING BARGES, EMERGENCY REPAIR	—	—	—	—	—	7	5	12
LANDING BARGE, KITCHEN	—	—	—	—	—	—	1	1
LANDING BARGES, OILER	—	—	—	—	—	10	15	25
LANDING BARGES, VEHICLE—								
(MARK I)	—	—	—	—	—	14	—	14
(MARK II)	—	—	—	—	—	21	22	43
LANDING BARGES, WATER	—	—	—	—	—	4	2	6
RAMPED DUMB BARGES	—	—	—	—	—	3	2	5
TOTAL	—	—	—	3	—	59	47	109
GRAND TOTAL LANDING CRAFT AND LANDING BARGES	—	21	69	234	113	776	95	1,308

INDEX

BRITISH MERCHANT VESSELS LOST OR DAMAGED BY ENEMY ACTION DURING SECOND WORLD WAR

3rd SEPTEMBER, 1939 TO 2nd SEPTEMBER, 1945

FOREWORD

This volume contains a list of all British Merchant and Fishing vessels lost or damaged by enemy action. The dates and positions given are, as a rule, those on which the vessels were attacked. In the case of ships lost other than on the actual date of attack, the fact has been noted in the remarks column together with any other relevant particulars.

The detailed information is as recorded in the Admiralty at 15th September, 1945.

British merchant ships commissioned for naval service or used as Royal Fleet Auxiliaries, are not included. Merchant vessels on charter to or requisitioned by the Admiralty are included, being distinguished by a * after their names in the name column.

Cases of minor or superficial damage to vessels have been omitted.

A table has also been included showing the monthly total of all non-enemy merchant shipping tonnage sunk correct to the nearest 1,000 tons, together with an analysis by cause ; and also a statement of casualties to personnel.

The following definition and abbreviations have been adopted :—

DEFINITION

British Merchant Vessels

Merchant vessels under the British Flag (i.e. those on United Kingdom, Dominion, Indian or Colonial Registers, and vessels on Bareboat Charter or on Requisition from other Flags).

ABBREVIATIONS

TYPE		
S. ....Steamship	M.T......Motor Trawler
M. ....Motor Vessel	F.V. ......Fishing Vessel
T-E. ......Turbo Electric	Aux. ......Sailing Vessel with auxiliary motor
S.B..........Sailing Barge	Tank .....Tanker
S.V. ......Sailing Vessel	O.R. ......Oil Refinery
S.T..........Steam Trawler	Sch. ......Schooner

CAUSE OF LOSS		
S.M. ......Submarine	C.U. ......Cause unknown or uncertain
A.C. ......Aircraft	

OTHER		
Lt. ....Light	B. ....Bomb
L.H. ......Lighthouse	G...........Gunfire
L.V. ......Light Vessel	Nr. ....Near
Pt. ....Point	Est. ....Estimated
m. ....Miles	Approx..Approximate
T. ....Torpedo	* ....Presumed

* After a Vessel's name in the *name* column indicates that she was on charter to or requisitioned by the Admiralty.

CONTENTS

LIST I

BRITISH MERCHANT VESSELS LOST BY ENEMY ACTION

Date	Name	Type	Gross tons	Position	Cause of loss	How lost	Remarks
SEPTEMBER, 1939							
3	ATHENIA	S.	13,581	56°44′N. 14°05′W.	S.M.	T.	
5	BOSNIA	S.	2,407	45°29′N. 09°45′W.	S.M.	T. & G.	
5	ROYAL SCEPTRE	S.	4,853	46°23′N. 14°59′W.	S.M.	T. & G.	
6	RIO CLARO	S.	4,086	46°30′N. 12°00′W.	S.M.	T. & G.	
6	MANAAR	S.	7,242	38°28′N. 10°50′W.	S.M.	T. & G.	
7	PUKKASTAN	S.	5,809	49°23′N. 07°49′W.	S.M.	T. & G.	
7	OLIVEGROVE	S.	4,060	49°05′N. 15°58′W.	S.M.	T.	
7	GARTAVON	S.	1,777	47°04′N. 11°32′W.	S.M.	G.	
8	WINKLEIGH	S.	5,055	48°06′N. 18°12′W.	S.M.	T.	
8	REGENT TIGER	M. Tank	10,177	49°57′N. 15°34′W.	S.M.	T.	
8	KENNEBEC	S. Tank	5,548	49°18′N. 08°13′W.	S.M.	T. & G.	Wreckage sunk by H.M.S. on 9th Sept.
10	GOODWOOD	S.	2,796	1m. S.E. of Flamboro' Head (Approx.)	Mine	—	
10	MAGDAPUR	S.	8,641	52°11′N. 01°43′E.	Mine	—	
11	BLAIRLOGIE	S.	4,425	54°58′N. 15°14′W.	S.M.	T. & G.	Abandoned and sunk in position 54°59′N. 15°09′W.
11	FIRBY	S.	4,869	59°40′N. 13°50′W.	S.M.	T. & G.	
11	INVERLIFFEY	M. Tank	9,456	48°14′N. 11°48′W.	S.M.	T. & G.	
13	NEPTUNIA*	Tug	798	49°20′N. 14°40′W.	S.M.	T. & G.	
14	VANCOUVER CITY	M.	4,955	51°23′N. 07°03′W.	S.M.	T.	
14	FANAD HEAD	S.	5,200	56°43′N. 15°21′W.	S.M.	T. & G.	
14	BRITISH INFLUENCE	M. Tank	8,431	49°43′N. 12°49′W.	S.M.	T. & G.	
15	CHEYENNE	M. Tank	8,826	50°20′N. 13°30′W.	S.M.	T. & G.	
15	TRURO	S.	974	58°20′N. 02°00′E.	S.M.	T. & G.	
16	AVIEMORE	S.	4,060	49°11′N. 13°38′W.	S.M.	T.	
16	ARKLESIDE	S.	1,567	48°00′N. 09°30′W.	S.M.	G.	
16	BRAMDEN	S.	1,594	51°22′N. 02°31′E.	Mine	—	
17	KAFIRISTAN	S.	5,193	50°16′N. 16°55′W.	S.M.	T.	
18	KENSINGTON COURT	S.	4,863	50°31′N. 08°27′W.	S.M.	G.	
22	AKENSIDE	S.	2,694	60°07′N. 04°37′E.	S.M.	T.	
24	HAZELSIDE	S.	4,646	51°17′N. 09°22′W.	S.M.	T. & G.	
30	CLEMENT	S.	5,051	09°05′S. 34°05′W.	Raider	—	" Admiral Graf Spee "
	Total...	30	153,634				
OCTOBER, 1939							
4	GLEN FARG	S.	876	58°52′N. 01°31′W.	S.M.	T. & G.	
5	STONEGATE	S.	5,044	31°10′N. 54°00′W.	Raider	—	" Deutschland "
5	NEWTON BEECH	S.	4,651	09°35′S. 06°30′W.	Raider	—	" Admiral Graf Spee "
7	ASHLEA	S.	4,222	09°S. 03°W. (Approx.)	Raider	—	" Admiral Graf Spee "
10	HUNTSMAN	S.	8,196	08°30′S. 05°15′W.	Raider	—	" Admiral Graf Spee "
13	HERONSPOOL	S.	5,202	50°13′N. 14°48′W.	S.M.	T.	
14	LOCHAVON	M.	9,205	50°25′N. 13°10′W.	S.M.	T.	
14	SNEATON	S.	3,678	49°05′N. 13°05′W.	S.M.	T. & G.	
17	YORKSHIRE	S.	10,184	44°52′N. 14°31′W.	S.M.	T.	
17	CITY OF MANDALAY	S.	7,028	44°57′N. 13°36′W.	S.M.	T.	
17	CLAN CHISHOLM	S.	7,256	45°N. 15°W. (Approx.)	S.M.	T.	
20	SEA VENTURE	S.	2,327	60°50′N. 00°15′E.	S.M.	T. & G.	
21	ORSA	S.	1,478	150° 15m. from Flamboro' Head	Mine	—	

Date	Name	Type	Gross tons	Position	Cause of loss	How lost	Remarks
OCTOBER, 1939—(Contd.)							
22	WHITEMANTLE ...	S.	1,692	5 to 6m. E. of Withernsea Lt.	Mine	—	
22	TREVANION... ...	M.	5,299	19°40′S. 04°02′E.	Raider	—	" Admiral Graf Spee "
24	LEDBURY	S.	3,528	36°01′N. 07°22′W.	S.M.	G.	
24	MENIN RIDGE ...	S.	2,474	36°01′N. 07°22′W.	S.M.	T.	
24	TAFNA	S.	4,413	35°44′N. 07°23′W.	S.M.	T.	
27	BRONTE	S.	5,317	49°30′N. 12°15′W.	S.M.	T.	Sunk by H.M.S. on 30th October
29	MALABAR	S.	7,976	49°57′N. 07°37′W.	S.M.	T.	
30	CAIRNMONA ⁻...	S.	4,666	57°38′N. 01°45′W.	S.M.	T.	
	Total ... 21		104,712				
NOVEMBER, 1939							
9	CARMARTHEN COAST	S.	961	3m. off Seaham Harbour	Mine	—	
13	PONZANO	M.	1,346	51°29′N. 01°25′E.	Mine	—	
13	MATRA	S.	8,003	1m. E. of Tongue L.V.	Mine	—	
15	WOODTOWN ...	S.	794	¾m. N.E. of N.E. Spit Buoy, near Margate	Mine	—	
15	AFRICA SHELL ...	M. Tank	706	10½m. S.W. × S. of Cape Zavora L.H.	Raider	—	" Admiral Graf Spee "
16	ARLINGTON COURT	S.	4,915	248° 320m. from Start Pt.	S.M.	T.	
About 17	PARKHILL	S.	500	North Sea	C.U.	—	
18	BLACKHILL ...	S.	2,492	145° 7½ cables from Longsand Head Buoy	Mine	—	
19	TORCHBEARER ...	S.	1,267	025° 2m. from Shipwash L.V.	Mine	—	
19	PENSILVA	S.	4,258	46°51′N. 11°36′W.	S.M.	T.	
19	DARINO	S.	1,351	44°12′N. 11°07′W.	S.M.	T.	
About 20	STANBROOK ...	S.	1,383	North Sea	C.U.	—	
About 20	BOWLING	S.	793	North Sea	C.U.	—	
21	GERALDUS	S.	2,495	3m. W.N.W. of Sunk L.V.	Mine	—	
22	LOWLAND	S.	974	2m. E.N.E. of N.E. Gunfleet Buoy	Mine	—	
23	HOOKWOOD ...	S.	1,537	3½m. E.N.E. of Tongue L.V.	Mine	—	
24	MANGALORE ...	S.	8,886	288° 1¼m. from Spurn L.H.	Mine	—	
25	ROYSTON GRANGE...	S.	5,144	49°15′N. 09°00′W. (Approx.)	S.M.	T.	
25	USKMOUTH	S.	2,483	43°22′N. 11°27′W.	S.M.	T. & G.	
28	RUBISLAW ...	S.	1,041	1-1½m. E.N.E. of Tongue L.V.	Mine	—	
29	IONIAN	S.	3,114	132° 1½m. from Newarp L.V.	Mine	—	Abandoned in position 340° 4m. from Newarp L.V.
30	SHEAF CREST ...	S.	2,730	51°32′N. 01°26′E.	Mine	—	
	Total ... 22		57,173				
DECEMBER, 1939							
1	DALRYAN	S.	4,558	2 to 2½m. S.W. of Tongue L.V.	Mine	—	
2	SAN CALISTO ...	M. Tank	8,010	2½m. N.N.E. of Tongue L.V.	Mine	—	
2	DORIC STAR ...	S.	10,086	19°15′S. 05°05′E.	Raider	—	" Admiral Graf Spee "
3	TAIROA	S.	7,983	20°20′S. 03°05′E.	Raider	—	" Admiral Graf Spee "

3

Date	Name	Type	Gross tons	Position	Cause of loss	How lost	Remarks
DECEMBER, 1939—(Contd.)							
3	MOORTOFT	S.	875	North Sea	C.U.	—	
4	HORSTED	S.	1,670	53°48′N. 00°16′E.	S.M.	T.	
5	NAVASOTA ..: ...	S.	8,795	50°43′N. 10°16′W.	S.M.	T.	
7	THOMAS WALTON ...	S.	4,460	67°52′N. 14°28′E.	S.M.	T.	
7	STREONSHALH ...	S.	3,895	25°00′S. 27°50′W.	Raider	—	" Admiral Graf Spee "
8	MEREL	S.	1,088	Nr. Gull- L.V. off Ramsgate	Mine	—	
8	BRANDON	S.	6,668	50°28′N. 08°26′W.	S.M.	T.	
8	COREA	S.	751	2½m. N.E. ½ N. of Cromer Lt.	Mine	—	
9	SAN ALBERTO* ...	M. Tank	7,397	49°20′N. 09°45′W.	S.M.	T.	Sunk on 11th by H.M.S.
10	WILLOWPOOL ...	S.	4,815	3m. E. of Newarp L.V.	Mine	—	
12	MARWICK HEAD ...	S.	496	½m. S. of N. Caister Buoy	Mine	—	
12	KING EGBERT ...	M.	4,535	4m. S.W. of Haisboro' L.V.	Mine	—	
13	DEPTFORD ...	S.	4,101	½m. N.N.W. of Honningsvaag	S.M.	T.	
14	INVERLANE ...	M. Tank	9,141	55°05′N. 01°07′W.	Mine	—	
16	AMBLE	S.	1,162	54°55′N. 01°03′W.	Mine	—	
17	SERENITY	M.	487	8m. E.N.E. of Whitby	A.C.	B.	
19	CITY OF KOBE ...	S.	4,373	52°35′N. 01°59′E.	Mine	—	
25	STANHOLME ...	S.	2,473	51°20′N. 03°39′W.	Mine	—	
31	BOX HILL ...	S.	5,677	53°32′N. 00°24′E.	Mine	—	
	Total ... 23		103,496				
JANUARY, 1940							
7	CEDRINGTON COURT	S.	5,160	2m. N.E. of North Goodwin L.V.	Mine	—	
7	TOWNELEY ...	S.	2,888	1m. E.N.E. of N.E. Spit Buoy, nr. Margate	Mine	—	
9	DUNBAR CASTLE ...	M.	10,002	51°23′N. 01°34′E.	Mine	—	
9	OAKGROVE	S.	1,985	12 to 15m. S.E. of Cromer Knoll L.V.	A.C.	B.	
9	GOWRIE	S.	689	4m. E. of Stonehaven	A.C.	B.	
10	UPMINSTER ...	S.	1,013	53°03′N. 01°29′E.	A.C.	B.	
11	EL OSO	S. Tank	7,267	280° 6m. from Bar L.V., Mersey	Mine	—	
11	KEYNES	S.	1,706	53°47′N. 00°46′E.	A.C.	B.	Previously attacked in position 53°03′N. 01°40′E.
12	GRANTA	S.	2,719	53°13′N. 01°21′E.	Mine	—	
16	INVERDARGLE ...	M. Tank	9,456	51°16′N. 03°43′W.	Mine	—	
17	CAIRNROSS	S.	5,494	276° 7 to 8m. from Bar L.V., Mersey	Mine	—	
17	POLZELLA	S.	4,751	Off Muckle Flugga, Shetlands	C.U.	—	
20	CARONI RIVER ...	M. Tank	7,807	50°06′N. 05°01′W.	Mine	—	
21	FERRYHILL ...	S.	1,086	005° 1½m. from St. Mary's L.V., off Tyne	Mine	—	
21	PROTESILAUS ...	S.	9,577	51°31′N. 04°04′W.	Mine	—	
23	BALTANGLIA ...	S.	1,523	55°35′N. 01°27′W.	S.M.	T.	
28	ESTON	S.	1,487	Off Blyth	Mine	—	
29	STANBURN	S.	2,881	10m. S.E. × E.½ S. of Flamboro' Head	A.C.	B.	
29	LEO DAWSON ...	S.	4,330	North Sea	C.U.	—	
30	GIRALDA*	S.	2,178	3m. S.E. of Grimness, S. Ronaldsay, Orkneys	A.C.	B.	
30	VACLITE	S. Tank	5,026	49°20′N. 07°04′W.	S.M.	T.	
30	BANCREST	S.	4,450	58°53′N. 01°52′W.	A.C.	B.	

Date	Name	Type	Gross tons	Position	Cause of loss	How lost	Remarks
JANUARY, 1940—(Contd.)							
30	VOREDA	S. Tank	7,216	52°59′N. 01°59′E.	A.C.	B.	
30	HIGHWAVE	S.	1,178	1m. N.N.E. of Kentish Knock	A.C.	B.	
	Total ... 24		101,869				
FEBRUARY, 1940							
1	CREOFIELD	S. Tank	838	North Sea	C.U.	—	
2	ELLEN M.	M.	498	North Sea	C.U.	—	
2	PORTELET	S.	1,064	3 to 4m. S.W. × W. of New Smiths Knoll	Mine	—	
2	BRITISH COUNCILLOR	S. Tank	7,048	53°48′N. 00°34′E.	S.M.	T.	Sank on 3rd
3	ARMANISTAN ...	S.	6,805	38°15′N. 11°15′W.	S.M.	T.	
5	BEAVERBURN ...	S.	9,874	49°20′N. 10°07′W.	S.M.	T.	
7	MUNSTER	M.	4,305	53°36′N. 03°24′W.	Mine	—	
9	CHAGRES	S.	5,406	270° 5½m. from Bar L.V., Mersey	Mine	—	
9	AGNES ELLEN ...	S.	293	On voyage Holyhead to Workington	Mine	—	
13	BRITISH TRIUMPH...	M. Tank	8,501	53°06′N. 01°25′E.	Mine	—	
14	GRETAFIELD* ...	S. Tank	10,191	58°27′N. 02°33′W.	S.M.	T.	Beached, later total loss
14	TIBERTON	S.	5,225	North Sea	C.U.	—	
14	SULTAN STAR ...	S.	12,306	48°54′N. 10°03′W.	S.M.	T.	
14	LANGLEEFORD ...	S.	4,622	70m. N.W. of Fastnet	S.M.	T.	
17	BARON AILSA ...	S.	3,656	53°17′N. 01°12′E.	Mine	—	
17	PYRRHUS	S.	7,418	44°02′N. 10°18′W.	S.M.	T.	
21	LOCH MADDY ...	S.	4,996	070° 20m from Copinsay L.H., Orkneys	S.M.	T.	
22	BRITISH ENDEAVOUR	S. Tank	4,580	42°11′N. 11°35′W.	S.M.	T.	
24	ROYAL ARCHER ...	S.	2,266	56°06′N. 02°55′W.	Mine	—	
24	CLAN MORRISON* ...	S.	5,936	53°07′N. 01°22′E.	Mine	—	
24	JEVINGTON COURT...	S.	4,544	53°08′N. 01°22′E.	Mine	—	
	Total ... 21		110,372				
MARCH, 1940							
2	ALBANO	S.	1,176	128¼° 7.6m. from Coquet Lt.	Mine	—	
3	CATO	S.	710	51°24′N. 03°33′W.	Mine	—	
4	PACIFIC RELIANCE	M.	6,717	50°23′N. 05°49′W.	S.M.	T.	
4	THURSTON	S.	3,072	32m. W. by N. of Trevose Head	S.M.*	T.*	
8	COUNSELLOR ...	S.	5,068	280° 6m. from Bar L.V., Mersey. (Approx.)	Mine	—	Sank in position 53°38′N. 03°23′W.
9	CHEVYCHASE ...	S.	2,719	53°18′N. 01°13′E.	Mine	—	
9	BORTHWICK ...	S.	1,097	51°44′N. 03°22′E.	Mine	—	
9 About	AKELD	S.	643	51°44′N. 03°22′E.	Mine	—	
11	ABBOTSFORD ...	S.	1,585	North Sea	C.U.	—	
12	GARDENIA	S.	3,745	53°04′N. 01°33′E.	Mine	—	
15	MELROSE	S.	1,589	51°21′N. 02°13′E.	Mine	—	
20	BARN HILL ...	S.	5,439	3m. S.S.W. of Beachy Head	A.C.	B.	
25	DAGHESTAN* ...	S. Tank	5,742	212° 9m. from Copinsay, Orkneys	S.M.	T.	
	Total ... 13		39,302				
APRIL, 1940							
9	THISTLEBRAE ...	S.	4,747	Trondheim	Seized	—	Taken in prize
10	BLYTHMOOR ...	S.	6,582	Narvik	C.U.	—	Sunk or seized

Date	Name	Type	Gross tons	Position	Cause of loss	How lost	Remarks
APRIL, 1940—*(Contd.)*							
12	THORLAND	S.	5,208	Sandefjord	Seized	—	Taken in prize
12	STANCLIFFE ...	S.	4,511	45m. N.E. of Unst Is., Shetlands	S.M.	T.	
15	SALERNO	S.	870	Sauda Fjord	Seized	—	Taken in prize
15	SALMON POOL ...	S.	4,803	Sauda Fjord	Seized	—	Taken in prize
15	MERSINGTON COURT	S.	5,141	Narvik	C.U.	—	Sunk or seized
15	NORTH CORNWALL	S.	4,304	Narvik	C.U.	—	Sunk or seized
17	SWAINBY	S.	4,935	065° 25m. from Muckle Flugga, Shetlands	S.M.	T.	
20	HAWNBY	S.	5,380	51°32′N. 01°13′E.	Mine	—	
20	MERSEY	S.	1,037	Nr. Midbrake Buoy, The Downs	Mine	—	
21	CEDARBANK ...	M.	5,159	62°49′N. 04°10′E.	S.M.	T.	
22	ROMANBY	S.	4,887	Narvik	C.U.	—	Sunk or seized
22	RIVERTON	S.	5,378	Narvik	C.U.	—	Sunk or seized
23	LOLWORTH* ...	S.	1,969	½m. N.W. of Elbow Buoy, off North Foreland	Mine	—	
24	STOKESLEY ...	S.	1,149	51°32′N. 01°16′E.	Mine	—	
24	RYDAL FORCE ...	S.	1,101	400 yds. S. of Gull L.V., Thames Estuary	Mine	—	
24	HAXBY	S.	5,207	31°30′N. 51°30′W.	Raider	—	
25	MARGAM ABBEY ...	S.	2,470	000° 9 cables from East Knob Buoy, Thames Estuary	Mine	—	
	Total ... 19		74,838				
MAY, 1940							
3	SCIENTIST	S.	6,199	20°00′S. 04°30′E. (Approx.)	Raider	—	
4	SAN TIBURCIO* ...	S. Tank	5,995	330° 4m. from Tarbet Ness	Mine	—	
6	BRIGHTON	S.	5,359	51°03′N. 02°09′E.	Mine	—	
10	HENRY WOODALL...	S.	625	3m. E. of Withernsea	Mine	—	
11	TRINGA	S.	1,930	50°21′N. 02°55′E.	Mine	—	
12	ROEK	S.	1,041	51°54′N. 04°21′E.	Mine	—	
12	ST. DENIS	S.	2,435	Rotterdam	Scuttled	—	
13	CITY OF BRUSSELS...	S.	629	Brussels	Seized	—	
20	PEMBROKE COAST ...	M.	625	Harstad Harbour, Norway	A.C.	B.	
20	MAVIS	S.	935	Off No. 4 Green Buoy, Calais Roads	A.C.	B.	
21	FIRTH FISHER ...	S.	574	½m. E. of Boulogne Pier	Mine	—	
21	BAWTRY	S.	835	Off Dunkirk	A.C.	B.	Salved by Germans and taken in prize
21	HUBBASTONE ...	S.	873	Dieppe Harbour	A.C.	B.	Salved by Germans
21	MAID OF KENT ...	S.	2,693	Dieppe Harbour	A.C.	B.	
24	BRIGHTON	S.	2,391	Dieppe Quay	A.C.	B.	
25	SPINEL	M.	650	Dunkirk	A.C.	B.	Salved by Germans and taken in prize
27	SEQUACITY	M.	870	1½m. from No. 2 Buoy to E. of Calais	Shelled by shore battery	—	
27	WORTHTOWN ...	S.	868	Dunkirk	A.C.	B.	Salved by Germans and taken in prize
27	SHEAF MEAD ...	S.	5,008	43°48′N. 12°32′W.	S.M.	T.	
28	QUEEN OF THE CHANNEL	M.	1,162	51°15′N. 02°40′E.	A.C.	B.	
28	CARARE	S.	6,878	51°18′N. 03°45′W.	Mine	—	
28	ABUKIR	S.	694	51°20′N. 02°16′E.	E-Boat	T.	
28	MARJORY H. ...	M.	84	Dunkirk	Seized	—	Taken in prize
29	MONA'S QUEEN ...	S.	2,756	Off Dunkirk	Mine	—	
29	LORINA	S.	1,578	Dunkirk Roads	A.C.	B.	
29	CLAN MACALISTER	S.	6,787	Off Dunkirk	A.C.	B.	
29	FENELLA	S.	2,376	Dunkirk	A.C.	B.	
29	TELENA	M. Tank	7,406	42°25′N. 09°08′W.	S.M.	G.	

A*

Date	Name	Type	Gross tons	Position	Cause of loss	How lost	Remarks
MAY, 1940—(Contd.)							
30	NORMANNIA ...	S.	1,567	Off Dunkirk	A.C.	B.	
30	STANHALL	S.	4,831	48°59′N. 05°17′W.	S.M.	T.	
31	ORANGEMOOR ...	S.	5,775	49°43′N. 03°23′W.	S.M.	T.	
	Total ... 31		82,429				
JUNE, 1940							
1	SCOTIA	S.	3,454	51°07′N. 02°10′E.	A.C.	B.	
1	ORFORD	S.	20,043	Marseilles	A.C.	B.	
1	LARK	S.B.	67	Dunkirk	Abandoned	—	
1	ROYALTY	S.B.	101	Malo-les-Bains (Dunkirk)	Beached & abandoned	—	
1	DUCHESS	S.B.	91	Dunkirk	Beached & abandoned	—	
1	LADY ROSEBERY ...	S.B.	109	3m. E. of Dunkirk	Mine	—	
1	DORIS	S.B.	83	3m. E. of Dunkirk	Mine	—	
1	BARBARA JEAN ...	S.B.	144	Dunkirk	Blown up & abandoned	—	
1	AIDIE	S.B.	144	Dunkirk	Beached & set on fire	—	
1	ETHEL EVERARD ...	S.B.	190	Dunkirk	Beached & abandoned	—	
2	FOSSA*	Tug	105	Dunkirk	Stranded & abandoned	—	
2	ASTRONOMER* ...	S.	8,401	58°04′N. 02°12′W.	S.M.	T.	
2	PARIS	S.	1,790	51°11′N. 02°07′E.	A.C.	B.	
2	POLYCARP	S.	3,577	49°19′N. 05°35′W.	S.M.	T.	
5	SWEEP II	Sludge Vessel	145	138° 1.4m. from Landguard Pt., Felixstowe	Mine	—	
5	CAPABLE	M.	216	131° 2.8m. from Horsesand Fort, Spithead	Mine	—	
5	STANCOR	S.	798	58°48′N. 08°45′W.	S.M.	G.	
6	FRANCES MASSEY ...	S.	4,212	55°33′N. 08°26′W.	S.M.	T.	
6	HARCALO	S.	5,081	51°19′N. 01°32′E.	Mine	—	
8	HARDINGHAM ...	S.	5,415	51°34′N. 01°37′E.	Mine	—	
8	OILPIONEER* ...	M. Tank	5,666	67°44′N. 03°52′E.	Warship	—	" Admiral Hipper "
8	ORAMA	S.	19,840	67°44′N. 03°52′E.	Warship	—	" Admiral Hipper "
9	EMPIRE COMMERCE	S.	3,857	4 cables W. of N.E. Spit Buoy, nr. Margate	Mine	—	
9	DULWICH	S.	4,102	Off Villequier, River Seine	Beached & set on fire	—	Salved by Germans and taken in prize
11	ST. RONAIG ...	M.	509	132° 1m. from West Breakwater Lt., Newhaven	Mine	—	
11	BRUGES	S.	2,949	Off Le Havre	A.C.	B.	
12	BARON SALTOUN ...	S.	3,404	Outer Roads, Cherbourg	Mine	—	
12	WILLOWBANK ...	M.	5,041	44°16′N. 13°54′W.	S.M.	T.	
12	EARLSPARK	S.	5,250	42°26′N. 11°33′W.	S.M.	T.	
12	BARBARA MARIE ...	S.	4,223	44°16′N. 13°54′W.	S.M.	T.	
12	TRAIN FERRY No. 2	S.	2,678	Le Havre	Beached & abandoned	—	
12	SWALLOW	M.	209	Paris	Damaged & abandoned	—	Taken in prize
12	INNISULVA	M.	264	Paris	Damaged & abandoned	—	
13	BRITISH INVENTOR	S. Tank	7,101	230° 5m. from St. Alban's Head	Mine	—	
14	BRITISH PETROL* ...	M. Tank	6,891	20°N. 50°W. (Approx.)	Raider	—	
14	BALMORALWOOD ...	S.	5,834	50°19′N. 10°28′W.	S.M.	T.	
15	ERIK BOYE ...	S.	2,238	50°37′N. 08°44′W.	S.M.	T.	
16	WELLINGTON STAR	M.	13,212	42°39′N. 17°01′W.	S.M.	T.	
17	TEIRESIAS	S.	7,405	47°07′N. 02°23′W.	A.C.	B.	
17	LANCASTRIA ...	S.	16,243	St. Nazaire	A.C.	B.	

Date	Name	Type	Gross tons	Position	Cause of loss	How lost	Remarks
JUNE, 1940—(Contd.)							
18	NIAGARA	S.	13,415	35°53′S. 174°54′E.	Mine	—	
18	RONWYN	S.	1,766	Rochefort	Damaged & abandoned	—	
18	HESTER	S.	1,199	Rochefort	Damaged & abandoned	—	
18	DIDO	S.	3,554	Brest	Abandoned & seized	—	
19	ROSEBURN	S.	3,103	Off Dungeness	E-Boat	T. & G.	
19	BARON LOUDOUN ...	S.	3,164	45°00′N. 11°21′W.	S.M.	T.	
19	BRITISH MONARCH	S.	5,661	45°00′N. 11°21′W.	S.M.	T.	
19	THE MONARCH ...	S.	824	47°20′N. 04°40′W.	S.M.	T.	
20	STESSO	S.	2,290	Cardiff	A.C.	B.	
20	EMPIRE CONVEYOR	S.	5,911	56°16′N. 08°10′W.	S.M.	T.	
20	OTTERPOOL ...	S.	4,876	48°47′N. 07°50′W.	S.M.	T.	
21	LUFFWORTH ...	S.	279	Brest	Abandoned	—	Taken in prize
21	YARRAVILLE ...	S. Tank	8,627	39°40′N. 11°34′W.	S.M.	T.	
21	SAN FERNANDO ...	S. Tank	13,056	50°20′N. 10°24′W.	S.M.	T.	
24	ALBUERA	S.	3,477	2m. S.W. of Lydd Light Float	E-Boat	T.	
24	KINGFISHER ...	M.	276	50°30′N. 00°28′E.	E-Boat	T.	
25	WINDSORWOOD ...	S.	5,395	48°31′N. 14°50′W.	S.M.	T.	
25	SARANAC	S. Tank	12,049	48°24′N. 15°05′W.	S.M.	T. & G.	
27	LLANARTH ...	S.	5,053	47°30′N. 10°30′W.	S.M.	T.	
29	EMPIRE TOUCAN ...	S.	4,127	49°20′N. 13°52′W.	S.M.	T. & G.	
30	AVELONA STAR ...	S.	13,376	46°46′N. 12°17′W.	S.M.	T.	Sank 1st July
	Total ... 61		282,560				
JULY, 1940							
1	BEIGNON	M.	5,218	47°20′N. 10°30′W. (Approx.)	S.M.	T.	
1	CLEARTON	S.	5,219	47°53′N. 09°30′W.	S.M.	T.	
2	AENEAS	S.	10,058	21m. S.E. of Start Pt.	A.C.	B.	
2	ARANDORA STAR ...	S.	15,501	55°20′N. 10°33′W.	S.M.	T.	
2	ATHELLAIRD ...	M. Tank	8,999	47°24′N. 16°49′W.	S.M.	T.	
3	BIJOU	S.B.	98	Mistley Quay, nr. Harwich	A.C.	B.	
4	ELMCREST	S.	4,343	13m. S. of Portland	E-Boat	T.	
4	DALLAS CITY ...	M.	4,952	50°09′N. 02°01′W.	A.C.	B.	
4	SILVERDIAL ...	Tug	55	Portland Harbour	A.C.	B. & G.	
4	COQUET MOUTH ...	Dredger	477	Off Amble, N. of Blyth	Mine	—	
5	DELAMBRE	S.	7,032	04°S. 26°W. (Approx.)	Raider	—	
5	MAGOG	S.	2,053	50°31′N. 11°05′W.	S.M.	T. & G.	
8	HUMBER ARM ...	S.	5,758	50°36′N. 09°24′W.	S.M.	T.	
9	AYLESBURY ...	S.	3,944	48°39′N. 13°33′W.	S.M.	T.	
10	TASCALUSA* ...	S. Tank	6,499	Falmouth Harbour	A.C.	B.	
10	WATERLOO	S.	1,905	2½m. N.E. of Smith's Knoll Buoy	A.C.	B.	
10	DAVISIAN ...	S.	6,433	18°00′N. 54°30′W. (Approx.)	Raider	—	
11	SEA GLORY ...	S.	1,964	North Atlantic	S.M.	T.	
11	CITY OF BAGDAD ...	S.	7,506	00°16′S. 90°00′E.	Raider	—	
11	MALLARD	S.	352	Between St. Catherine's Pt. and Beachy Head	E-Boat	T.	
12	HORNCHURCH ...	S.	2,162	Off Aldeburgh L.V.	A.C.	B.	
13	KING JOHN ...	M.	5,228	20°N. 60°W. (Approx.)	Raider	—	
13	KEMMENDINE ...	S.	7,769	04°S. 82°E. (Approx.)	Raider	—	
14	ISLAND QUEEN ...	S.	779	4 cables off A Buoy, Dover	A.C.	B. & G.	

Date	Name	Type	Gross tons	Position	Cause of loss	How lost	Remarks
JULY, 1940—(*Contd.*)							
About 14	GRACEFIELD ...	S.	4,631	13°S. 31°W. (Approx.)	Raider	—	
15	BELLEROCK ...	S.	1,199	51°20′N. 03°47′W.	Mine	—	
15	HEWORTH	S.	2,855	10m. S. of Aldeburgh L.V.	A.C.	B.	
15	CITY OF LIMERICK...	S.	1,359	48°39′N. 07°12′W.	A.C.	B.	
16	WENDOVER... ...	S.	5,487	23°S. 35°W. (Approx.)	Raider	—	
16	SCOTTISH MINSTREL	M. Tank	6,998	56°10′N. 10°20′W.	S.M.	T.	Sank on the 17th
17	MANIPUR	S.	8,652	58°41′N. 05°14′W.	S.M.	T.	
17	WOODBURY	S.	4,434	50°46′N. 13°56′W.	S.M.	T.	
17	FELLSIDE	S.	3,509	56°09′N. 12°30′W.	S.M.	T.	
19	PEARLMOOR	S.	4,581	55°23′N. 09°18′W.	S.M.	T.	
20	TROUTPOOL... ...	S.	4,886	54°40′N. 05°40′W.	Mine	—	
20	PULBOROUGH ...	S.	960	2½m. S.E. × S. of Dover Pier	A.C.	B.	
21	TERLINGS	S.	2,318	10m. S.W. of St. Catherine's Point, I.O.W.	A.C.	B.	
21	ELLAROY	S.	712	42°30′N. 12°36′W.	S.M.	G.	
23	THE LADY MOSTYN	M.	305	079° 1½m. from Formby L.V.	Mine	—	
25	CORHAVEN	S.	991	Off Dover	A.C.	B.	
25	POLGRANGE ...	S.	804	Off Dover	A.C.	B.	
25	LEO	S.	1,140	Off Dover	A.C.	B.	
25	HENRY MOON ...	S.	1,091	Off Sandgate	A.C.	B.	
25	PORTSLADE ...	S.	1,091	Off Sandgate	A.C.	B.	
26	LULONGA	S.	821	10m. S. of Shoreham	E-Boat	T.	
26	HAYTOR	S.	1,189	51°47′N. 01°48′E.	Mine	—	
26	BROADHURST ...	S.	1,013	14m. S. × W. of Shoreham	E-Boat	T.	
26	LONDON TRADER ...	S.	646	13m. S. × W. of Shoreham	E-Boat	T.	
26	ACCRA	M.	9,337	55°40′N. 16°28′W.	S.M.	T.	
26	VINEMOOR	M.	4,359	55°43′N. 16°25′W.	S.M.	T.	
27	DURDHAM	Sand Dredger	477	140½° 1.54m. from Lavernock, Bristol Channel	Mine	—	
27	SALVESTRIA ...	S. Tank	11,938	042° 2.8 m. from Inchkeith L.H.	Mine	—	
27	SAMBRE	S.	5,260	56°37′N. 17°53′W.	S.M.	T.	
27	THIARA	M. Tank	10,364	56°37′N. 17°56′W.	S.M.	T.	
28	ORLOCK HEAD ...	S.	1,563	58°44′N. 04°21′W.	A.C.	B. & G.	Sank 320° 6.7 m. from Strathie Pt.
28	AUCKLAND STAR ...	M.	13,212	52°17′N. 12°32′W.	S.M.	T.	
29	GRONLAND	S.	1,264	Dover Harbour	A.C.	B.	Previously damaged by aircraft on 25th
29	OUSEBRIDGE ...	S.	5,601	Queen's Channel, Liverpool	Mine	—	
29	MOIDART	S.	1,262	51°59′N. 01°49′E.	Mine	—	
29	CLAN MONROE ...	S.	5,952	51°52′N. 01°48′E.	Mine	—	
29	CLAN MENZIES ...	S.	7,336	54°10′N. 12°00′W.	S.M.	T.	
30	JAMAICA PROGRESS	S.	5,475	56°26′N. 08°30′W.	S.M.	T.	
31	JERSEY CITY ...	S.	6,322	55°47′N. 09°18′W.	S.M.	T.	
31	DOMINGO DE LARRINAGA	S.	5,358	05°26′S. 18°06′W.	Raider	—	
	Total ... 64		271,056				
AUGUST, 1940							
2	CITY OF BRISBANE...	S.	8,006	Off S. Longsand Buoy, Thames Estuary	A.C.	B.	
3	STATIRA	M.	4,852	38m. N. of Stornaway	A.C.	B.	
3	WYCHWOOD ...	S.	2,794	52°00′N. 01°48′E.	Mine	—	
4	GERALDINE MARY...	S.	7,244	56°58′N. 15°55′W.	S.M.	T.	
4	KING ALFRED ...	S.	5,272	56°59′N. 17°38′W.	S.M.	T.	

Date	Name	Type	Gross tons	Position	Cause of loss	How lost	Remarks
AUGUST, 1940—(*Contd.*)							
4	GOGOVALE	S.	4,586	57°08′N. 16°26′W.	S.M.	T.	
5	BOMA	S.	5,408	55°44′N. 08°04′W.	S.M.	T.	
7	MOHAMED ALI el-KEBIR	S.	7,527	55°22′N. 13°18′W.	S.M.	T.	
8	UPWEY GRANGE ...	M.	9,130	54°20′N. 15°28′W.	S.M.	T.	
8	HOLME FORCE* ...	S.	1,216	Off Newhaven	E-Boat	T.	
8	FIFE COAST ...	M.	367	10 to 15m. W. of Beachy Head	E-Boat	T.	
8	COQUETDALE* ...	S.	1,597	15m. W. of St. Catherine's Pt., I.O.W.	A.C.	B. & G.	
8	EMPIRE CRUSADER	S.	1,042	15m. W. of St. Catherine's Pt., I.O.W.	A.C.	B.	
8	OUSE	S.	1,004	Off Newhaven	Collision	—	In avoiding torpedo from E-Boat
11	LLANFAIR	S.	4,966	54°48′N. 13°46′W.	S.M.	T.	
12	BRITISH FAME ...	M. Tank	8,406	37°44′N. 22°56′W.	S.M.	T.	
14	BETTY	S.	2,339	260° 35m. from Tory Island	S.M.	T.	
15	SYLVAFIELD* ...	M. Tank	5,709	56°39′N. 11°16′W.	S.M.	T.	
15	BRIXTON	S.	1,557	52°06′N. 01°49′E.	Mine	—	
16	CLAN MACPHEE ...	S.	6,628	57°30′N. 17°14′W.	S.M.	T.	
16	EMPIRE MERCHANT	M.	4,864	55°23′N. 13°24′W.	S.M.	T.	
16	CITY OF BIRMINGHAM	S.	5,309	115° 5½m. from Spurn Pt.	Mine	—	
16	MEATH	S.	1,598	6 to 7 cables N.E. of Breakwater Lt., Holyhead	Mine	—	
18	AMPLEFORTH ...	S.	4,576	56°10′N. 10°40′W.	S.M.	T.	
20	TURAKINA	S.	9,691	38°27′S. 167°35′E.	Raider	—	
21	ANGLO SAXON ...	S.	5,596	26°10′N. 34°09′W.	Raider	—	
21	JAMES No. 70 ...	Hopper Barge	182	Southampton	A.C.	B.	
22	THOROLD	S.	1,689	2¼m. S. of Smalls	A.C.	B. & G.	
23	CUMBERLAND ...	S.	10,939	55°43′N. 07°33′W.	S.M.	T.	
23	MAKALLA	S.	6,677	58°17′N. 02°27′W.	A.C.	B.	
23	LLANISHEN ...	S.	5,053	58°17′N. 02°27′W.	A.C.	B.	
23	SEVERN LEIGH ...	S.	5,242	54°31′N. 25°41′W.	S.M.	T.	
23	ST. DUNSTAN ...	S.	5,681	55°43′N. 08°10′W.	S.M.	T.	Taken in tow but sank on 27th
23	BROOKWOOD ...	S.	5,100	54°40′N. 27°57′W.	S.M.	T. & G.	
24	BLAIRMORE... ...	S.	4,141	56°00′N. 27°30′W.	S.M.	T.	
24	LA BREA	S. Tank	6,666	57°24′N. 11°21′W.	S.M.	T.	
24	KING CITY ...	S.	4,744	17°S. 66°E. (Approx.)	Raider	—	
25	YEWCREST	S.	3,774	55°10′N. 25°02′W.	S.M.	G.	
25	JAMAICA PIONEER	S.	5,471	57°05′N. 11°02′W.	S.M.	T.	
25	PECTEN*	M. Tank	7,468	56°22′N. 07°55′W.	S.M.	T.	
25	EMPIRE MERLIN ...	S.	5,763	58°30′N. 10°15′W.	S.M.	T.	
25	ATHELCREST ...	M. Tank	6,825	58°24′N. 11°25′W.	S.M.	T.	
25	HARPALYCE ...	S.	5,169	58°52′N. 06°34′W.	S.M.	T.	
25	GOATHLAND ...	S.	3,821	50°21′N. 15°08′W.	A.C.	B. & G.	
25	FIRCREST	S.	5,394	58°52′N. 06°34′W.	S.M.	T.	
26	ILVINGTON COURT...	S.	5,187	37°14′N. 21°52′W.	S.M.	T.	
26	REMUERA ...	S.	11,445	57°50′N. 01°54′W.	A.C.	T.	
26	CAPE YORK ...	M.	5,027	45° 10m. from Kinnaird Head	A.C.	T.	
26	BRITISH COMMANDER	S. Tank	6,901	29°37′S. 45°50′E.	Raider	—	
28	KYNO	S.	3,946	58°06′N. 13°26′W.	S.M.	T.	
28	DALBLAIR	S.	4,608	56°06′N. 13°33′W.	S.M.	T.	
29	EMPIRE MOOSE ...	S.	6,103	56°06′N. 14°00′W.	S.M.	T.	
29	ASTRA II	S.	2,393	56°09′N. 12°14′W.	S.M.	T.	
30	CHELSEA	S.	4,804	59°45′N. 04°00′W.	S.M.	T.	
30	MILL HILL	S.	4,318	58°48′N. 06°49′W.	S.M.	T.	
31	HAR ZION	S.	2,508	56°20′N. 10°00′W. (Approx.)	S.M.	T.	
	Total ... 56		278,323				

Date	Name	Type	Gross tons	Position	Cause of loss	How lost	Remarks
SEPTEMBER, 1940							
2	Thornlea	S.	4,261	55°14′N. 16°40′W.	S.M.	T.	
2	Cymbeline*	S. Tank	6,317	28°N. 35°W. (Approx.)	Raider	—	
3	Ulva	S.	1,401	55°45′N. 11°45′W.	S.M.	T.	
4	Titan	S.	9,035	58°14′N. 15°50′W.	S.M.	T.	
4	Luimneach	S.	1,074	47°50′N. 09°12′W.	S.M.	G.	
4	Corbrook	S.	1,729	52°50′N. 02°09′E.	E-Boat	T.	
4	New Lambton	S.	2,709	52°50′N. 02°09′E.	E-Boat	T.	
4	Joseph Swan	S.	1,571	52°50′N. 02°09′E.	E-Boat	T.	
4	Fulham V	S.	1,562	52°50′N. 02°09′E.	E-Boat	T. & G.	
6	St. Glen	S.	4,647	57°25′N. 01°38′W.	A.C.	B.	
7	Beckton	Tug	45	Beckton Gas Works, London River	A.C.	B.	
7	Jose de Larrinaga	S.	5,303	58°30′N. 16°10′W.	S.M.	T.	
7	Neptunian	S.	5,155	58°27′N. 17°27′W.	S.M.	T.	
9	Athelking...	M. Tank	9,557	21°48′S. 67°40′E.	Raider	—	
9	Mardinian...	S.	2,434	56°37′N. 09°00′W.	S.M.	T.	
9	Minnie de Larrinaga	S.	5,049	Port of London	A.C.	B.	
10	Benarty	S.	5,800	18°40′S. 70°54′E.	Raider	—	
11	Albionic	S.	2,468	North Atlantic	Raider*	—	
12	Benavon	S.	5,872	26°S. 51°E. (Approx.)	Raider	—	
12	Gothic	S. Tank	2,444	130° 7,500 yds. from Spurn Pt.	Mine	—	
14	St. Agnes	S.	5,199	41°27′N. 21°50′W.	S.M.	T. & G.	
15	Empire Volunteer	S.	5,319	56°43′N. 15°17′W. (Approx.)	S.M.	T.	
15	Kenordoc...	S.	1,780	57°42′N. 15°02′W.	S.M.	G.	
15	Halland	S.	1,264	070° 8m. from Dunbar	A.C.	B.	
15	Nailsea River	S.	5,548	4m. E. of Montrose	A.C.	T.	
16	Aska	S.	8,323	55°15′N. 05°55′W.	A.C.	B.	
16	Bibury	S.	4,616	12°N. 25°W. (Approx.)	Raider	—	
16	City of Mobile	S.	6,614	54°18′N. 05°16′W.	A.C.	B.	
17	Crown Arun	S.	2,372	58°02′N. 14°18′W.	S.M.	T.	
17	City of Benares	S.	11,081	56°43′N. 21°15′W.	S.M.	T.	
17	Tregenna	S.	5,242	58°22′N. 15°42′W.	S.M.	T.	
17	Marina	S.	5,088	56°46′N. 21°15′W.	S.M.	T.	
17	Commissaire Ramel	S.	10,061	28°25′S. 74°27′E.	Raider	—	
18	Magdalena	S.	3,118	57°20′N. 20°16′W.	S.M.	T.	
19	Shelbrit I	M. Tank	1,025	57°39′N. 03°56′W.	Mine	—	
20	Invershannon*	M. Tank	9,154	55°40′N. 22°04′W. (Approx.)	S.M.	T.	Sank on 21st
20	Empire Adventure	S.	5,145	Off Islay	S.M.	T.	
20	New Sevilla*	S. Tank	13,801	55°48′N. 07°22′W.	S.M.	T.	
20	Baron Blythswood	S.	3,668	56°N. 23°W. (Approx.)	S.M.	T.	
21	Frederick S. Fales*	M. Tank	10,525	55°30′N. 13°40′W.	S.M.	T.	
21	City of Simla	S.	10,138	55°55′N. 08°20′W.	S.M.	T.	
21	Torinia*	M. Tank	10,364	55°N. 19°W. (Approx.)	S.M.	T.	
21	Canonesa	S.	8,286	54°55′N. 18°25′W.	S.M.	T.	
21	Scholar	S.	3,940	55°11′N. 17°58′W.	S.M.	T.	Abandoned 54°38′N 16°40′W. on 24th
21	Empire Airman	S.	6,586	54°N. 18°W. (Approx.)	S.M.	T.	
21	Blairangus	S.	4,409	55°18′N. 22°21′W.	S.M.	T.	
21	Elmbank	M.	5,156	55°20′N. 22°30′W.	S.M.	T.	
21	Dalcairn	S.	4,608	55°N. 19°W. (Approx.)	S.M.	T.	
24	Continental Coaster	S.	555	52°59′N. 02°10′E.	E-Boat	T.	
25	Mabriton	S.	6,694	56°12′N. 23°00′W.	S.M.	T.	
25	Eurymedon	M.	6,223	53°34′N. 20°23′W.	S.M.	T.	Sank on 27th
25	Sulairia	S.	5,802	53°43′N. 20°10′W.	S.M.	T.	

Date	Name	Type	Gross tons	Position	Cause of loss	How lost	Remarks
SEPTEMBER, 1940—(*Contd.*)							
26	STRATFORD	S. Tank	4,753	54°50′N. 10°40′W.	S.M.	T.	
26	CORRIENTES	S.	6,863	53°49′N. 24°19′W.	S.M.	T.	
26	PORT DENISON	S.	8,043	6m. N.E. of Peterhead	A.C.	T.	Sank on 27th
26	MANCHESTER BRIGADE	S.	6,042	54°53′N. 10°22′W.	S.M.	T.	
28	EMPIRE OCELOT	S.	5,759	54°37N. 21°30′W.	S.M.	T.	Sank in position 54°55′N. 22°06′W.
28	DARCOILA	S.	4,084	North Atlantic	S.M.	T.	
28	DALVEEN	S.	5,193	58°10′N. 02°19′W.	A.C.	B.	
29	BASSA	S.	5,267	54°N. 21°W. (Approx.)	S.M.*	—	
30	HEMINGE	S.	2,499	53°26′N. 18°33′W.	S.M.	T.	
30	SAMALA	S.	5,390	46°N. 33°W. (Approx.)	S.M.*	—	
	Total ... 62		324,030				
OCTOBER, 1940							
1	HIGHLAND PATRIOT	S.	14,172	52°20′N. 19°04′W.	S.M.	T.	
2	KAYESON	S.	4,606	51°12′N. 24°22′W.	S.M.	T.	
2	LATYMER	S.	2,218	51°20′N. 10°30′W.	A.C.	B.	
3	LADY OF THE ISLES*	Cable ship	166	About 3m. E. of St. Anthony Pt., Nr. Falmouth	Mine	—	
4	SIRDAR	Tug	34	Cod's Reach, River Swale	A.C.	B.	
5	ADAPTITY	S.	372	51°44′N. 01°17′E. (Approx.)	Mine	—	
6	BENLAWERS	S.	5,943	53°20′N. 26°10′W.	S.M.	T.	
6	JERSEY QUEEN	S.	910	160° 1½ m. from St. Anthony Pt., Nr. Falmouth	Mine	—	
6	BRITISH GENERAL	S. Tank	6,989	51°42′N. 24°03′W.	S.M.	T.	Sank on 7th.
8	BELLONA II	S.	840	4m. E. of Gourdon, Kincardineshire	A.C.	B.	
8	CONFIELD	S.	4,956	56°48′N. 10°17′W.	S.M.	T.	Sank on 9th
8	NATIA	S.	8,715	00°50′N. 32°24′W.	Raider	—	
9	GRAIGWEN	S.	3,697	58°11′N. 13°57′W.	S.M.	T.	
9	ALDERNEY QUEEN	M.	633	Off Grassholm Island, N. Wales	A.C.	B. & G.	
11	PORT GISBORNE	M.	8,390	56°38′N. 16°40′W.	S.M.	T.	
12	ST. MALO	S.	5,779	57°58′N. 16°32′W.	S.M.	T.	
12	PACIFIC RANGER	M.	6,865	56°20′N. 11°43′W.	S.M.	T.	
13	STANGRANT	S.	5,804	58°27′N. 12°36′W.	S.M.	T.	
14	HURUNUI	S.	9,331	58°58′N. 09°54′W.	S.M.	T.	
14	RECULVER (Trinity House Vessel)	M.	683	195° 1.2m. from Spurn Pt. L.H.	Mine	—	
15	THISTLEGARTH	S.	4,747	58°43′N. 15°00′W.	S.M.	T.	
15	BONHEUR	S.	5,327	57°10′N. 08°36′W.	S.M.	T.	
16	TREVISA	S.	1,813	57°28′N. 20°30′W.	S.M.	T.	
17	USKBRIDGE	S.	2,715	60°40′N. 15°50′W.	S.M.	T.	
17	SCORESBY	S.	3,843	59°14′N. 17°51′W.	S.M.	T.	
17	LANGUEDOC	M. Tank	9,512	59°14′N. 17°51′W.	S.M.	T.	
17	FRANKRIG	S.	1,361	52°03′N. 01°48′E.	Mine	—	
17	HAUXLEY	S.	1,595	6m. N.N.W. of Smith's Knoll	E-Boat	T.	Sank on 18th
18	ASSYRIAN	S.	2,962	57°12′N. 10°43′W.	S.M.	T.	Sank on 19th
18	SANDSEND	S.	3,612	58°15′N. 21°29′W.	S.M.	T.	
18	BEATUS	S.	4,885	57°31′N. 13°10′W.	S.M.	T.	
18	EMPIRE MINIVER	S.	6,055	310° 250m. from Rathlin Head	S.M.	T.	
18	CREEKIRK	S.	3,917	57°30′N. 11°10′W. (Approx.)	S.M.	T.	
18	FISCUS	S.	4,815	57°29′N. 11°10′W. (Approx.)	S.M.	T.	
18	SHEKATIKA	S.	5,458	57°12′N. 11°08′W. (Approx.)	S.M.	T.	

Date	Name	Type	Gross tons	Position	Cause of loss	How lost	Remarks
OCTOBER, 1940—(*Contd.*)							
18	EMPIRE BRIGADE ...	S.	5,154	57°12′N. 10°43′W. (Approx.)	S.M.	T.	
19	WANDBY	S.	4,947	56°45′N. 17°07′W.	S.M.	T.	Sank on 21st
19	ARIDITY	M.	336	40 yds. N.E. of E. Oaze L.V.	Mine	—	
19	MATHERAN	S.	7,653	57°N. 17°W. (Approx.)	S.M.	T.	
19	LA ESTANCIA ...	S.	5,185	57°N. 17°W. (Approx.)	S.M.	T.	
19	CAPRELLA	M. Tank	8,230	56°37′N. 17°15′W.	S.M.	T.	
19	RUPERRA	S.	4,548	57°N. 16°W. (Approx.)	S.M.	T.	
19	SHIRAK	S. Tank	6,023	57°00′N. 16°35′W.	S.M.	T.	
19	SULACO	S.	5,389	57°25′N. 25°00′W.	S.M.	T.	
19	UGANDA	S.	4,966	56°37′N. 17°15′W.	S.M.	T.	
19	SITALA	M. Tank	6,218	150m. S.W. of Rockall	S.M.	T.	
19	CLINTONIA	.S.	3,106	57°10′N. 11°20′W.	S.M.	T. & G.	
19	SEDGEPOOL ...	S.	5,556	57°20′N. 11°22′W.	S.M.	T.	
20	LOCH LOMOND ...	S.	5,452	56°00′N. 14°30′W.	S.M.	T.	
20	WHITFORD POINT ...	S.	5,026	56°38′N. 16°00′W.	S.M.	T.	
21	KERRY HEAD ...	S.	825	5m. due S. of Blackball Head, Eire	A.C.	B.	
21	HOUSTON CITY ...	S.	4,935	225° ½m. from E. Oaze L.V.	Mine	—	
24	MATINA	S.	5,389	57°30′N. 16°31′W. (Approx.)	C.U.	—	
26	DOSINIA	M. Tank	8,053	Near Q.1 Black Buoy, Queens Channel, Mersey	Mine	—	
27	SUAVITY	M.	634	54°44′N. 01°05′W.	Mine	—	
28	DEVONIA	S.	98	51°23′N. 03°15′W.	Mine	—	
28	SHEAF FIELD ...	S.	2,719	2m. S.W. of Sunk L.V.	Mine	—	
28	SAGACITY	S.	490	148° 4,000 yds. from Spurn Main Lt.	Mine	—	
28	WYTHBURN ...	S.	420	51°22′N. 03°15′W.	Mine	—	
28	EMPRESS OF BRITAIN	S.	42,348	55°16′N. 09°50′W.	S.M.	T.	Previously attacked by A.C. and set on fire on 26th in position 54°53′N. 10°49′W. Attacked again by S.M. as shown and sunk
29	G. W. HUMPHREYS	Sludge Vessel	1,500	E. Oaze Buoy, bearing E.S.E. about 2 cables	Mine	—	
30	RUTLAND	S.	1,437	57°14′N. 16°00′W. (Est.)	S.M.*	—	
31	HILLFERN	S.	1,535	35m. N.N.W. of Kinnaird Head	C.U.	—	
	Total ... 63		301,892				
NOVEMBER, 1940							
1	EMPIRE BISON ...	S.	5,612	59°30′N. 17°40′W.	S.M.	T.	
1	LETCHWORTH ...	S.	1,317	W. Oaze Buoy W. × N. 1 cable & Mouse L.V. S.S.W. 1 cable	A.C.	B.	
2	LEA	Tug	168	Tilbury Basin	Mine	—	
2	DEANBROOK ...	Tug	149	Tilbury Basin	Mine	—	
3	CASANARE	S.	5,376	53°58′N. 14°13′W.	S.M.	T.	
3	KILDALE	S.	3,877	57°45′N. 01°45′W.	A.C.	B.	
5	SCOTTISH MAIDEN ...	M. Tank	6,993	54°36′N. 14°23′W.	S.M.	T.	
5	MAIDAN	S.	7,908	52°26′N. 32°34′W. (Approx.)	Raider	—	" Admiral Scheer "
5	TREWELLARD ...	S.	5,201	52°26′N. 32°34′W. (Approx.)	Raider	—	" Admiral Scheer "
5	BEAVERFORD ...	S.	10,042	52°26′N. 32°34′W.	Raider	—	" Admiral Scheer "

Date	Name	Type	Gross tons	Position	Cause of loss	How lost	Remarks
NOVEMBER, 1940—(Contd.)							
5	Haig Rose ...	S.	1,117	Bristol Channel	C.U.	—	
5	Kenbane Head ...	S.	5,225	52°26′N. 32°34′W.	Raider	—	" Admiral Scheer "
5	Mopan	S.	5,389	52°48′N. 32°15′W. (Approx.)	Raider	—	" Admiral Scheer "
5	Fresno City ...	M.	4,955	51°47′N. 33°29′W.	Raider	—	" Admiral Scheer " Sank on 6th
6	Nalon	S.	7,222	53°57′N. 15°03′W.	A.C.	B.	
6	Clan Mackinlay...	S.	6,365	58°33′N. 02°53′W.	A.C.	B.	
7	Herland	S.	2,645	146° 2 cables from Nore L.V.	Mine	—	
7	Cambridge... ...	S.	10,855	6m. E. of Wilson's Promontory Bass Strait, S.W. Pacific	Mine	—	
7	Astrologer ...	S.	1,673	51°32′N. 01°06′E.	A.C.	B.	
9	Baltrader ...	S.	1,699	51°41′N. 01°18′E.	Mine	– –	
11	Automedon ...	S.	7,528	04°18′N. 89°20′E.	Raider	—	
11	Trebartha ...	S.	4,597	4m. S.E. of Aberdeen	A.C.	B. & G.	
11	Skarv	S.	158	Bristol Channel	Mine*	—	
11	Creemuir	S.	3,997	10m. S.E. of Aberdeen	A.C.	T.	
11	Balmore	S.	1,925	52°N. 17°W. (Approx.)	A.C.	B.	
12	Argus (Trinity House Vessel)	S.	661	199° 3 cables from S. Oaze Buoy	Mine	—	
13	Cape St. Andrew...	S.	5,094	55°14′N. 10°29′W.	S.M.	T.	
13	Empire Wind ...	S.	7,459	53°48′N. 15°52′W.	A.C.	B.	
13	Leon Martin ...	M. Tank	1,951	202° 5.2 cables from St. Anthony Pt., nr. Falmouth	Mine	—	
14	St. Catherine ...	S.	1,216	½m. S. of Outer Buoy, Swept Channel, Aberdeen	A.C.	T.	
14	Buoyant	M.	300	Off Skegness*	Mine	—	
15	Kohinur	S.	5,168	04°24′N. 13°46′W.	S.M.	T.	
15	Amenity	M.	297	53°33′N. 00°09′E.	Mine	—	
15	Apapa	M.	9,333	54°34′N. 16°47′W.	A.C.	B.	
15	Blue Galleon ...	S.	712	52°57′N. 01°56′E.	A.C.	B.	
16	Fabian	S.	3,059	02°49′N. 15°29′W.	S.M.	T.	
16	Planter	S.	5,887	55°38′N. 08°28′W.	S.M.	T.	
17	St. Germain ...	M.	1,044	55°40′N. 08°40′W.	S.M.	T.	
18	Lilian Moller ...	S.	4,866	North Atlantic	S.M.	T.	
18	Congonian... ...	M. Tank	5,065	08°21′N. 16°12′W.	S.M.	T.	
18	Ability	Motor Barge	293	51°45′N. 01°11′E.	Mine	—	
18	Nestlea	S.	4,274	50°38′N. 10°00′W.	A.C.	B. & G.	
18	Nowshera ...	S.	7,920	30°S. 90°E. (Approx.)	Raider	—	
20	Maimoa	S.	10,123	31°50′S. 100°21′E.	Raider	—	
21	Daydawn ...	S.	4,768	56°30′N. 14°10′W.	S.M.	T.	
21	Dakotian	S.	6,426	Dale Roads, Milford Haven	Mine	—	
21	Cree	S.	4,791	54°39′N. 18°50′W.	S.M.	T.	
21	Port Brisbane ...	S.	8,739	29°22′S. 95°36′E.	Raider	—	
22	Justitia	S.	4,562	55°00′N. 13°10′W.	S.M.	T.	
22	Bradfyne	S.	4,740	55°04′N. 12°15′W.	S.M.	T.	
22	Hercules	Tug	82	55°01′N. 01°23′W.	Mine	—	
22	Pikepool	S.	3,683	23m.E.S.E. of Smalls Lt.	Mine*	—	
22	Oakcrest	S.	5,407	53°N. 17°W. (Approx.)	S.M.	T.	
23	Bonaparte ...	Tug	38	Southampton	A.C.	B.	
23	Leise Maersk ...	M.	3,136	55°30′N. 11°00′W.	S.M.	T.	
23	King Idwal ...	S.	5,115	56°44′N. 19°13′W.	S.M.	T.	
23	Tymeric	S.	5,228	57°00′N. 20°30′W.	S.M.	T.	
24	Preserver... ...	Salvage Vessel	630	054° 1 cable from No. 1 Buoy, Milford Haven	Mine	—	
24	Ryal	M.	367	51°32′N. 01°04′E.	Mine	—	
24	Behar	S.	6,100	51°42′N. 05°07′W.	Mine	—	Beached, later total loss

Date	Name	Type	Gross tons	Position	Cause of loss	How lost	Remarks
NOVEMBER, 1940—(Contd.)							
24	THOMAS M. ...	M.	310	Approx. 135° 1½m. from Yarmouth Harbour Entrance	Mine	—	
24	ALICE MARIE ...	S.	2,206	255° 8 cables from Knob L.V., Barrow Deep	Mine	—	
24	PORT HOBART ...	S.	7,448	24°44′N. 58°21′W.	Raider	—	" Admiral Scheer "
25	HOLMWOOD ...	S.	546	27m. W. × S. of Durham Pt., Chatham Is., S. Pacific	Raider	—	
25	T. C. C. HOPPER No. 3	Hopper Barge	698	54°40′N. 01°07′W.	Mine	—	
26	RANGITANE ...	M.	16,712	36°58′S. 175°22′W.	Raider	—	
27	DIPLOMAT ...	S.	8,240	55°42′N. 11°37′W.	S.M.	T.	
27	GLENMOOR* ...	M.	4,393	54°35′N. 14°31′W,	S.M.	T.	
28	ST. ELWYN ...	S.	4,940	55°30′N. 19°30′W.	S.M.	T.	
28	IRENE MARIA ...	S.	1,860	North Atlantic	S.M.*	—	
29	AID	Tug	134	8m. off Start Pt.	Warship	—	
29	B.H.C. No. 10 ...	Barge	290	8m. off Start Pt.	Warship	—	
29	ARACATACA... ...	S.	5,378	57°08′N. 20°50′W.	S.M.	T.	
	Total ... 73		303,682				
DECEMBER, 1940							
1	HER MAJESTY ...	Paddle Steamer	235	Southampton	A.C.	B.	
1	BRITISH OFFICER ...	S. Tank	6,990	About ½m. E. of North Pier Lt., Tyne	Mine	—	
1	PORT WELLINGTON	S.	8,301	32°10′S. 75°00′E. (Approx.)	Raider	—	
1	PALMELLA	S.	1,578	40°30′N. 13°30′W.	S.M.	T.	
1	TRIBESMAN ...	S.	6,242	15°N. 35°W. (Approx.)	Raider	—	" Admiral Scheer "
1	APPALACHEE ...	M. Tank	8,826	54°30′N. 20°00′W.	S.M.	T.	
2	CONCH*	M. Tank	8,376	55°40′N. 19°00′W.	S.M.	T.	
2	JEANNE M. ...	S.	2,465	39°19′N. 13°54′W.	S.M.	T.	
2	WILHELMINA ...	S.	7,135	55°55′N. 15°20′W.	S.M.	T.	
2	KAVAK	S.	2,782	55°00′N. 19°30′W.	S.M.	T.	
2	TASSO	S.	1,586	55°03′N. 18°04′W.	S.M.	T.	
2	STIRLINGSHIRE ...	M.	6,022	55°36′N. 16°22′W.	S.M.	T.	
2	GOODLEIGH... ...	S.	5,448	55°02′N. 18°45′W.	S.M.	T.	
2	VICTOR ROSS ...	M. Tank	12,247	56°04′N. 18°30′W.	S.M.	T.	
2	LADY GLANELY ...	M.	5,497	55°N. 20°W. (Approx.)	S.M.	T.	
2	VICTORIA CITY ...	S.	4,739	North Atlantic	S.M.	T.	
2	PACIFIC PRESIDENT	M.	7,113	56°04′N. 18°45′W. (Approx.)	S.M.	T.	
2	JOLLY GIRLS* ...	M.	483	101° 18 cables from North Pier Lt., Tyne	Mine	—	
3	W. HENDRIK ...	S.	4,360	56°26′N. 12°20′W.	A.C.	B.	
5	SILVERPINE ...	M.	5,066	54°14′N. 18°08′W.	S.M.	T.	
5	NIMBIN	M.	1,052	33°15′S. 151°47′E.	Mine	—	
5	EMPIRE STATESMAN	M.	5,306	North Atlantic	S.M.*	—	
6	SUPREMITY ...	M.	554	W.S.W. 3 cables from East Oaze L.V., Thames Estuary	Mine	—	
6	TRIONA	S.	4,413	Nauru	Raider	—	
7	KOMATA	S.	3,900	Nauru	Raider	—	
7	TRIADIC	M.	6,378	Nauru	Raider	—	
7	TRIASTER ...	M.	6,032	Nauru	Raider	—	
8	CALABRIA ...	S.	9,515	52°43′N. 18°07′W.	S.M.	T.	
8	ACTUALITY ...	M.	311	3m. S.W. of Mouse L.V.	Mine	—	
8	EMPIRE JAGUAR ...	S.	5,186	51°34′N. 17°35′W.	S.M.	T.	
9	ROYAL SOVEREIGN*	M.	1,527	51°24′N. 03°08′W.	Mine	—	
11	ROTORUA	S.	10,890	58°56′N. 11°20′W.	S.M.	T.	
14	WESTERN PRINCE...	M.	10,926	59°32′N. 17°47′W.	S.M.	T.	

Date	Name	Type	Gross tons	Position	Cause of loss	How lost	Remarks
DECEMBER, 1940—(*Contd.*)							
14	KYLEGLEN	S.	3,670	58°N. 25°W. (Approx.)	C.U.	—	
14	EUPHORBIA... ...	S.	3,380	North Atlantic	C.U.	—	
15	N. C. MONBERG ...	S.	2,301	52°40′N. 02°10′E.	E-Boat	T.	
17	INVER	S.	1,543	Off Southend	Mine	—	
17	MALRIX	S.	703	Off Southend	Mine	—	
17	BENEFICENT ...	S.	2,944	Off Southend	Mine	—	
17	AQUEITY	M.	370	Off Southend	Mine	—	
17	BELVEDERE ...	S.	869	Off Southend	Mine	—	
18	NAPIER STAR ...	S.	10,116	58°58′N. 23°13′W.	S.M.	T.	
18	DUQUESA	S.	8,651	00°57′N. 22°42′W.	Raider	—	" Admiral Scheer "
18	OSAGE	M. Tank	1,010	4m. N.E. of Arklow L.V., Co. Wicklow	A.C.	B.	
19	AMICUS	S.	3,660	54°10′N. 15°50′W.	S.M.	T.	
19	ARINIA	M. Tank	8,024	8m. E.S.E. of Southend Pier	Mine	—	
19	ISOLDA (L.V. Tender)	M.	734	Vicinity of Barrels Rock L.V., S. Wexford	A.C.	T.	
20	CARLTON	S.	5,162	54°30′N. 18°30′W.	S.M.	T. & G.	
21	SILVIO	S.	1,293	Liverpool	A.C.	B.	
21	INNISFALLEN ...	M.	3,071	Entrance Canada Dock, River Mersey	Mine	—	
21	T.I.C. 12	Barge	118	51°28′N. 00°46′E.	Mine	—	
21	SUN IX* ...	Tug	196	Between 1 and 2 buoys, Yantlet Channel, Thames Estuary	Mine	—	
21	RIVER THAMES* ...	Tug	88	51°28′N. 00°46′E.	Mine	—	
22	POOLGARTH ...	Tug	179	Off Canada Dock, S. Pier Head, Liverpool	Mine	—	
24	BRITISH PREMIER...	S. Tank	5,872	06°20′N. 13°20′W. (Approx.)	S.M.	T.	
25	JUMNA	S.	6,078	43°N. 20°W. (Approx.)	Raider	—	" Admiral Hipper "
26	WAIOTIRA ...	M.	12,823	58°05′N. 17°10′W.	S.M.	T.	Sank on 27th
27	KINNAIRD HEAD ...	S.	449	Off Southend	Mine	—	
27	ARABY	M.	4,936	9 cables W. of Nore L.V.	Mine	—	
27	ARDANBHAN ...	S.	4,980	59°16′N. 20°27′W.	S.M.	T.	
30	CALCIUM	S.	613	53°25′N. 03°45′W.	Mine	—	
	Total ... 61		265,314				
JANUARY, 1941							
2	NALGORA	S.	6,579	22°24′N. 21°11′W.	S.M.	T. & G.	
3	PINEWOOD	S.	2,466	1½m. S. of Pier, Southend	Mine	—	
5	SHAKESPEAR ...	S.	5,029	18°05′N. 21°10′W.	S.M.	G.	
6	LION*	Tug	87	320° 2½ cables from No. 5 Medway Buoy	Mine	—	
7	H. H. PETERSEN ...	S.	975	52°22′N. 02°05′E.	Mine	—	
6	EMPIRE THUNDER...	S.	5,965	59°14′N. 12°43′W.	S.M.	T.	
8	STRATHEARN (Trinity House Tender)	M.	683	51°45′N. 01°10′E.	Mine	—	
8	CLYTONEUS... ...	M.	6,278	56°23′N. 15°28′W.	A.C.	B.	
9	BASSANO	S.	4,843	57°57′N. 17°42′W.	S.M.	T.	
10	MIDDLESEX ...	S.	9,583	198° 0.8m. from Flatholm Is.	Mine	—	
11	BEACHY*	S.	1,600	53°29′N. 16°24′W.	A.C.	B.	
14	EUMAEUS	S.	7,472	08°55′N. 15°03′W.	S.M.	T.	
15	MANCUNIUM ...	Sludge Vessel	1,286	2m. N.E. of Bar L.V., Mersey	Mine	—	
16	OROPESA	S.	14,118	56°28′N. 12°00′W.	S.M.	T.	
16	ZEALANDIC ...	S.	10,578	58°28′N. 20°43′W.	S.M.	T.	
17	ALMEDA STAR ...	S.	14,935	58°16′N. 13°40′W.	S.M.	T.	
18	BRITISH UNION* ...	M. Tank	6,987	26°34′N. 30°58′W.	Raider	—	

Date	Name	Type	Gross tons	Position	Cause of loss	How lost	Remarks

JANUARY, 1941—(Contd.)

Date	Name	Type	Gross tons	Position	Cause of loss	How lost	Remarks
19	BONNINGTON COURT	M.	4,909	275° 9.5 cables from Sunk L.V.	A.C.	B.	
20	FLORIAN	S.	3,174	North Atlantic	S.M.*	—	
20	STANPARK	S.	5,103	09°27'S. 03°00'W.	Raider	--	" Admiral Scheer "
21	TEMPLE MEAD ...	S.	4,427	54°14'N. 14°30'W.	A.C.	B.	
21	ENGLISHMAN* ...	Tug	487	40m. W. of Tory Island	A.C.	B.	
23	LURIGETHAN ...	S.	3,564	53°46'N. 16°00'W.	A.C.	B.	
23	LANGLEEGORSE ...	S.	4,524	53°19'N. 13°11'W.	A.C.	B.	
23	MOSTYN	S.	1,859	54°30'N. 14°52'W.	A.C.	B.	
24	CORHEATH ...	S.	1,096	270° 1m. from Botany Buoy, Thames Estuary	Mine	—	
24	MANDASOR	S.	5,144	04°18'S. 61°00'E.	Raider	---	
26	MERIONES ...	S.	7,557	52°53'N. 01°47'E.	A.C.	B.	
27	RINGWALL	S.	407	Irish Sea, S. of Isle of Man	Mine	—	
28	URLA ...	S.	5,198	54°54'N. 19°00'W.	S.M.	T.	
28	PANDION	S.	1,944	55°34'N. 10°22'W.	A.C.	B.	
28	GRELROSA ...	S.	4,574	55°12'N. 15°41'W.	A.C.	B.	
29	WEST WALES ...	S.	4,354	56°00'N. 15°23'W.	S.M.	T.	
29	RUSHPOOL ...	S.	5,125	56°00'N. 15°42'W.	S.M.	T.	
29	KING ROBERT ...	S.	5,886	56°00'N. 15°23'W.	S.M.	T.	
29	EURYLOCHUS ...	S.	5,723	08°15'N. 25°04'W.	Raider	—	
29	AFRIC STAR ...	S.	11,900	08°N. 25°W. (Approx.)	Raider	---	
29	W.B. WALKER ...	S. Tank	10,468	56°00'N. 15°23'W.	S.M.	T.	
31	PIZARRO	M.	1,367	49°03'N. 19°40'W.	S.M.	T.	
31	ROWANBANK ...	S.	5,159	57°00'N. 16°30'W.	A.C.	—	
31	SPEYBANK	M.	5,154	Indian Ocean	Raider	—	Taken in prize
	Total ... 41		208,567				

FEBRUARY, 1941

Date	Name	Type	Gross tons	Position	Cause of loss	How lost	Remarks
2	EMPIRE ENGINEER	S.	5,358	54°N. 35°W. (Approx.)	S.M.*	—	
2	THE SULTAN ...	S.	824	51°43'N. 01°26'E.	A.C.	B.	
3	EMPIRE CITIZEN ...	S.	4,683	58°12'N. 23°22'W.	S.M.	T.	
4	DIONE II ...	S.	2,660	55°50'N. 10°30'W. (Approx.)	S.M.	G.	Previously attacked by A.C. on 3rd in position 55°40'N. 14°23'W.
4	GWYNWOOD ...	S.	1,177	Convoy anchorage, Humber	Mine	—	
5	RANEE	S.	5,060	Suez Canal	Mine	---	
6	MAPLECOURT ...	S.	3,388	55°39'N. 15°56'W.	S.M.	T.	
6	ANGULARITY ...	M.	501	Off East Coast between Ipswich and Newcastle	E-Boat	—	
7	BAY FISHER* ...	S.	575	3½m. N.E. of Bell Rock	A.C.	B.	
8	CANFORD CHINE ...	S.	3,364	Last seen in position 55°N. 15°W.	C.U.	---	
9	COURLAND ...	S.	1,325	35°53'N. 13°13'W.	S.M.	T.	
9	ESTRELLANO ...	S.	1,983	35°53'N. 13°13'W.	S.M.	T.	
9	VARNA	S.	1,514	35°42'N. 14°38'W.	A.C.	B.	Sank on 16th in position 44°55'N. 22°30'W.
9	BRITANNIC	S.	2,490	35°42'N. 14°38'W.	A.C.	B.	
9	JURA	S.	1,759	35°42'N. 14°38'W.	A.C.	B.	
9	DAGMAR I	S.	2,471	35°42'N. 14°38'W.	A.C.	B.	
10	BRANDENBURGH ...	S.	1,473	36°10'N. 16°38'W.	S.M.	T.	
11	ICELAND ...	S.	1,236	37°03'N. 19°50'W.	Raider	—	" Admiral Hipper "
12	WARLABY ...	S.	4,876	37°12'N. 21°20'W.	Raider	---	" Admiral Hipper "
12	WESTBURY ...	S.	4,712	37°10'N. 21°20'W.	Raider	—	" Admiral Hipper "
12	OSWESTRY GRANGE	S.	4,684	37°10'N. 21°20'W.	Raider	---	" Admiral Hipper "
12	SHREWSBURY ...	S.	4,542	36°46'N. 20°12'W.	Raider	---	" Admiral Hipper "
12	DERRYNANE ...	S.	4,896	37°12'N. 21°20'W.	Raider	--	" Admiral Hipper "

Date	Name	Type	Gross tons	Position	Cause of loss	How lost	Remarks
FEBRUARY, 1941—(*Contd.*)							
13	ARTHUR F. CORWIN	M. Tank	10,516	60°25′N. 17°11′W.	S.M.	T.	
About 13	CLEA*	M. Tank	8,074	North Western Approaches	S.M.	T.	
14	ELISABETH MARIE	S.	616	54°58′N. 12°30′W. (Approx.)	A.C.	B.	
15	ALNMOOR	S.	6,573	55°N. 13°W. (Est.)	C.U.	—	
15	BELCREST	S.	4,517	54°N. 21°W. (Approx.)	S.M.*	—	
15	HOLYSTONE ...	S.	5,462	Mid-North Atlantic	S.M.*	—	
16	GAIRSOPPA	S.	5,237	300m. S.W. of Galway Bay	S.M.	T.	
17	SIAMESE PRINCE ...	M.	8,456	59°53′N. 12°13′W.	S.M.	T.	
17	KYLE RONA ...	S.	307	Irish Sea	C.U.	—	
17	BEN REIN*	S.	156	Off Falmouth	Mine	—	
17	BLACK OSPREY ...	S.	5,680	61°30′N. 18°10′W. (Approx.)	S.M.	T.	
18	EMPIRE BLANDA ...	S.	5,693	North Atlantic	S.M.*	—	
18	SEAFORTH	M.	5,459	58°48′N. 18°17′W.	S.M.	T.	
18	EDWY R. BROWN...	M. Tank	10,455	61°N. 18°W. (Approx.)	S.M.	T.	
19	ALGARVE	S.	1,355	Nr. Sheringham Lt. Float	E-Boat	T.	
19	GRACIA	S.	5,642	59°39′N. 07°24′W. (Approx.)	A.C.	B.	
19	HOUSATONIC* ...	S. Tank	5,559	59°39′N. 07°24′W. (Approx.)	A.C.	B.	
20	BRITISH ADVOCATE	S. Tank	6,994	Indian Ocean (West of Seychelles)	Raider	—	" Admiral Scheer " Taken in prize
20	FORT MEDINE ...	S.	5,261	51°35′N. 03°56′W.	Mine	—	
20	RIGMOR	S.	1,278	49°54′N. 04°51′W.	A.C.	B.	
21	SCOTTISH STANDARD*	M. Tank	6,999	59°20′N. 16°12′W.	S.M.	T.	Previously attacked same day by A.C. in position 59°09′N. 16°18′W.
21	CANADIAN CRUISER	S.	7,178	06°36′S. 47°18′E.	Raider	—	" Admiral Scheer "
22	TRELAWNEY ...	S.	4,689	47°12′N. 40°13′W.	Raider	—	" Scharnhorst " or " Gneisenau "
22	LUSTROUS	S. Tank	6,156	47°12′N. 40°13′W.	Raider	—	" Scharnhorst " or " Gneisenau "
22	HARLESDEN ...	S.	5,483	47°12′N. 40°18′W. (Approx.)	Raider	—	" Scharnhorst " or " Gneisenau "
22	KANTARA	S.	3,237	47°12′N. 40°13′W. (Approx.)	Raider	—	" Scharnhorst " or " Gneisenau "
22	A. D. HUFF ...	S.	6,219	47°12′N. 40°13′W. (Approx.)	Raider	—	" Scharnhorst " or " Gneisenau "
23	ANGLO PERUVIAN ...	S.	5,457	59°30′N. 21°00′W.	S.M.	T.	
23	CAPE NELSON ...	S.	3,807	59°30′N. 21°00′W.	S.M.	T.	
23	MARSLEW	S.	4,542	59°18′N. 21°30′W.	S.M.	T.	
23	SHOAL FISHER ...	M.	698	50°10′N. 04°50′W.	Mine	—	
23	TEMPLE MOAT ...	S.	4,427	59°27′N. 20°20′W.	S.M.	—	
24	JONATHAN HOLT ...	S.	4,973	61°10′N. 11°55′W.	S.M.	T.	
24	LINARIA	S.	3,385	61°N. 5°W. (Approx.)	S.M.*	—	
24	NAILSEA LASS ...	S.	4,289	60m. S.W. of Fastnet	S.M.	T.	
24	SIRIKISHNA ...	S.	5,458	58°N. 21°W. (Approx.)	S.M.	T. & G.	
24	BRITISH GUNNER ...	S. Tank	6,894	61°09′N. 12°04′W.	S.M.	T.	
24	MANSEPOOL ...	S.	4,894	61°01′N. 12°00′W.	S.M.	T.	
24	HUNTINGDON ...	S.	10,946	58°25′N. 20°23′W.	S.M.	T.	
24	WAYNEGATE ...	S.	4,260	58°50′N. 21°47′W.	S.M.	T.	
25	GLOBE	S.B.	54	079° 6,100 yds. from Garrison Pt., Sheerness	Mine	—	
26	MINORCA	S.	1,123	53°04′N. 01°21′E.	E-Boat	T.	
26	MAHANADA ...	S.	7,181	54°07′N. 17°06′W.	A.C.	T.	
26	SWINBURNE ...	S.	4,659	54°00′N. 16°58′W.	A.C.	B.	
26	LLANWERN ...	S.	4,966	54°07′N. 17°06′W.	A.C.	B.	
27	BALTISTAN	S.	6,803	51°52′N. 19°55′W.	S.M.	T.	
27	STANWOLD	S.	1,020	10m. W.S.W. of Selsey	C.U.	—	

Date	Name	Type	Gross tons	Position	Cause of loss	How lost	Remarks
FEBRUARY, 1941—(Contd.)							
27	OLD CHARLTON ...	S.	1,562	51°57′N. 01°40′E.	A.C.	B.	
27	ANCHISES	S.	10,000	55°30′N. 13°17′W.	A.C.	B.	Again attacked by A.C. on the 28th and sunk
27	NOSS HEAD ...	S.	438	Vicinity of Gardens-town, E. Scotland	C.U.	—	
28	HOLMELEA	S.	4,223	54°24′N. 17°25′W.	S.M.	T.	
28	CARENDA	M.	534	51°34′N. 03°54′W.	Mine	—	
	Total ... 75		315,304				
MARCH, 1941							
1	PACIFIC	S.	6,034	180m. W.S.W. of Sydero Is., Faroes	S.M.	T.	
1	CADILLAC	S. Tank	12,062	59°44′N. 11°16′W.	S.M.	T.	
1	EFFNA	S.	6,461	61°30′N. 15°45′W. (Est.)	S.M.*	—	
2	CASTLEHILL ...	S.	690	East of Minehead	A.C.	B.	
3	PORT TOWNSVILLE	M.	8,661	52°05′N. 05°24′W.	A.C.	B.	Sank on 4th
4	ANONITY ...	M.	303	1¼m. S.E. of Skegness Pier	Mine	—	
5	SILVERSTONE ...	Tug	58	3m. above Rochester Bridge, Medway	Mine*	—	
6	SUN VII*	Tug	202	060° 1 to 2m. from North Knob Buoy, Barrow Deep	Mine	—	
7	TERJE VIKEN ...	S. Tank	20,638	60°00′N. 12°50′W.	S.M.	T.	
7	ATHELBEACH ...	M. Tank	6,568	60°30′N. 13°30′W.	S.M.	T.	
7	DOTTEREL	S.	1,385	Off No. 6 Buoy, Southwold	E-Boat	T.	
7	KENTON	S.	1,047	52°57′N. 01°30′E.	E-Boat	T.	
7	CORDUFF	S.	2,345	Off No. 8 Buoy. Nr. Cromer	E-Boat	T.	
7	BOULDERPOOL ...	S.	4,805	52°58′N. 01°28′E. (Approx.)	E-Boat	T.	
7	FLASHLIGHT ...	S.	934	53°34′N. 00°49′E.	A.C.	B.	
7	DUNAFF HEAD ...	S.	5,258	60°33′N. 18°50′W.	S.M.	T.	
7	RYE	S.	1,048	Off Cromer	E-Boat	T.	
8	HINDPOOL	S.	4,897	20°51′N. 20°32′W.	S.M.	T.	
8	LAHORE	S.	5,304	21°03′N. 20°38′W.	S.M.	T.	
8	HARMODIUS ...	S.	5,229	20°35′N. 20°40′W.	S.M.	T.	
8	TIELBANK	S.	5,084	20°51′N. 20°32′W.	S.M.	T.	
8	NARDANA	S.	7,974	20°51′N. 20°32′W.	S.M.	T.	
8	TOGSTON	S.	1,547	305° 2m. from Smith's Knoll. (Approx.)	E-Boat	T.	
8	NORMAN QUEEN ...	S.	957	Off S. Haisboro' Buoy, E. of Cromer	E-Boat	T.	
10	CORINIA	S.	870	50°55′N. 00°35′E.	Mine	—	
10	SPARTA	S.	708	50°55′N. 00°35′E.	Mine	—	
10	WATERLAND ...	S.	1,107	50°55′N. 00°35′E.	Mine	—	
11	MEMNON	M.	7,506	20°41′N. 21°00′W.	S.M.	T.	
11	TREVETHOE ...	M.	5,257	52°46′N. 01°57′E.	E-Boat	T.	
12	EMPIRE FROST ...	S.	7,005	51°36′N. 05°40′W.	A.C.	B.	Attacked again on 13th whilst in tow and sank
13	TACOMA CITY ...	S.	4,738	104° 2½ cables from Rock Ferry Lt., Mersey	Mine	—	
13	ULLAPOOL ...	S.	4,891	Off Princes Stage, Mersey	Mine	—	
13	BULLGER*	Tug	270	Druridge Bay, 16m. N. of Tyne	Mine	—	
14	WESTERN CHIEF ...	S.	5,759	58°52′N. 21°13′W.	S.M.	T.	
14	HERPORT	S.	2,633	53°15′N. 01°05′E.	Mine	—	
14	STANLEIGH* ...	S.	1,802	288° 12m. from Bar L.V., Mersey	A.C.	B.	
14	ARTEMISIA	S.	6,507	52°53′N. 01°39′E.	A.C.	B.	
15	BRITISH STRENGTH	M. Tank	7,139	42°N 43°W. (Approx.)	Raider	—	"Scharnhorst" or "Gneisenau"

Date	Name	Type	Gross tons	Position	Cause of loss	How lost	Remarks
MARCH, 1941—(Contd.)							
15	SIMNIA	M. Tank	6,197	40°28′N. 43°30′W.	Raider	—	" Gneisenau "
15	SAN CASIMIRO ...	M. Tank	8,046	39°58′N. 43°19′W.	Raider	—	" Gneisenau." Captured 15th. Scuttled 20th in position 45°12′N. 19°42′W.
15	ROYAL CROWN ...	S.	4,388	42°N. 43°W. (Approx.)	Raider	—	" Gneisenau "
15	MYSON	S.	4,564	42°N. 43°W. (Approx.)	Raider	—	" Scharnhorst "
15	RIO DORADO ...	S.	4,507	42°N. 43°W. (Approx.)	Raider	—	" Scharnhorst " or " Gneisenau "
15	ATHELFOAM ...	M. Tank	6,554	42°00′N. 43°25′W.	Raider	—	" Scharnhorst "
16	SARDINIAN PRINCE	S.	3,491	44°N. 43°W. (Approx.)	Raider	—	" Scharnhorst "
16	SILVERFIR	M.	4,347	42°N. 43°W. (Approx.)	Raider	—	" Gneisenau "
16	EMPIRE INDUSTRY	S.	3,721	42°N. 43°W. (Approx.)	Raider	—	" Scharnhorst "
16	DEMETERTON ...	S.	5,251	45°58′N. 44°00′W.	Raider	—	" Scharnhorst "
16	CHILEAN REEFER ...	M.	1,739	46°13′N. 44°45′W.	Raider	—	" Gneisenau "
16	VENETIA	S. Tank	5,728	61°00′N. 12°36′W.	S.M.	T.	
17	ANDALUSIAN ...	S.	3,082	14°33′N. 21°06′W.	S.M.	T.	
17	J. B. WHITE ...	S.	7,375	60°57′N. 12°27′W.	S.M.	T.	
17	MEDJERDA	S.	4,380	17°N. 21°W. (Est.)	S.M. *	—	
18	DAPHNE II... ...	S.	1,970	59 Buoy, off Humber	E-Boat	T.	
19	BENVORLICH ...	S.	5,193	54°48′N. 13°10′W.	A.C.		
20	SIR BEVOIS* ...	Tug	338	Plymouth	A.C.	B.	
20	CLAN OGILVY ...	S.	5,802	20°04′N. 25°45′W.	S.M.	T.	
21	BENWYVIS	S.	5,920	20°N. 26°W. (Approx.)	S.M.	T.	
21	JHELUM	S.	4,038	21°N. 25°W. (Approx.)	S.M.	T.	
21	LONDON II... ...	S.	1,260	51°23′N. 04°30′W.	A.C.	B.	
21	MILLISLE	S.	617	2m. E. of Helwick L.B., Bristol Channel	A.C.	—	
22	AGNITA	M. Tank	3,552	02°30′N. 25°00′W.	Raider	—	
22	ST. FINTAN ...	S.	495	7m. N.N.W. of Smalls (Approx.)	A.C.	—	
23	CHAMA	M. Tank	8,077	49°35′N. 19°13′W.	S.M.	T.	
About 24	KORANTON	S.	6,695	59°N. 27°W. (Approx.)	S.M.	—	
24	AGNETE MAERSK ...	S.	2,104	49°00′N. 22°55′W.	S.M.	G.	
25	ROSSMORE	S.	627	12m. N.E. of Godrevy Is.	A.C.	B.	
25	BEAVERBRAE ...	S.	9,956	60°12′N. 09°00′W.	A.C.	B.	
25	BRITANNIA	S.	8,799	07°24′N. 24°03′W.	Raider	—	
26	FARADAY*	Cable ship	5,533	038° 3m. from St. Anne's Head	A.C.	B.	
26	BRIER ROSE ...	S.	503	Irish Sea	C.U.	—	
26	SOMALI	S.	6,809	Off Blyth	A.C.	B.	Sank on 27th 1m. E. of Snoop Head, Sunderland
26	EMPIRE MERMAID	S.	6,381	58°36′N. 10°00′W.	A.C.	B.	Sank on 28th in position 57°33′N. 12°43′W.
27	CANADOLITE ...	M. Tank	11,309	05°N. 33°W. (Approx.)	Raider	—	Taken in prize.
27	MEG MERRILIES ...	S.	642	1m. S. of St. Govan's L.V.	A.C.	B.	
28	OLIVINE	S.	929	In Irish Sea or Bristol Channel	C.U.	—	
29	EMMA	Spritsail Barge	81	Rotherhithe	M.	—	
29	HYLTON	M.	5,197	60°02′N. 18°10′W.	S.M.	T.	
29	GERMANIC	S.	5,352	61°18′N. 22°05′W.	S.M.	T.	
29	OILTRADER ...	S. Tank	5,550	52°34′N. 02°01′E.	A.C.	B.	

Date	Name	Type	Gross tons	Position	Cause of loss	How lost	Remarks
MARCH, 1941—(Contd.)							
30	EASTLEA	S.	4,267	North Atlantic	S.M.*	—	
30	COULTARN	S.	3,759	60°18′N. 29°28′W.	S.M.	T.	
30	UMONA	S.	3,767	About 90m. S.W. of Freetown	S.M.	T.	
	Total ... 83		364,575				
APRIL, 1941							
1	SAN CONRADO ...	M. Tank	7,982	325° 13m. from Smalls	A.C.	B.	
2	BRITISH RELIANCE	M. Tank	7,000	58°21′N. 28°30′W.	S.M.	T.	
2	BEAVERDALE ...	S.	9,957	60°50′N. 29°19′W.	S.M.	T. & G.	
2	HOMEFIELD ...	S.	5,324	Off Gavdo Is., E. Mediterranean	A.C.	B.	
2	FERMAIN	S.	759	50°35′N. 00°52′E.	A.C.	B.	
3	BRITISH VISCOUNT*	S. Tank	6,895	58°15′N. 27°30′W.	S.M.	T.	
3	ALDERPOOL ...	S.	4,313	58°21′N. 27°59′W.	S.M.	T.	
3	WESTPOOL	S.	5,724	58°12′N. 27°40′W.	S.M.	T.	
3	CAIRNIE	S.	250	6 to 8m. S. × W. of Tod Head	A.C.	B.	
3	GREENAWN ...	S.	784	North Sea, nr. Montrose	C.U.	—	
3	NORTHERN PRINCE	M.	10,917	Anti-Kithera Channel, E. Mediterranean	A.C.	B.	
4	ATHENIC	S.	5,351	58°32′N. 20°13′W.	S.M.	T.	
4	HARBLEDOWN ...	S.	5,414	58°30′N. 23°00′W.	S.M.	T.	
4	CONUS*	M. Tank	8,132	56°14′N. 31°19′W.	S.M.	T.	
4	WELCOMBE ...	S.	5,122	59°09′N. 22°00′W.	S.M.	T.	
4	MARLENE	S.	6,507	08°15′N. 14°19′W.	S.M.	T.	
4	SALVUS	S.	4,815	53°05′N. 01°27′E.	A.C.	B.	
5	ENA DE LARRINAGA	S.	5,200	01°10′N. 26°00′W.	S.M.	T.	
5	ST. CLEMENT ...	S.	450	57°19′N. 01°50′W.	A.C.	B.	
5	RATTRAY HEAD ...	S.	496	8m. E.N.E. of Aberdeen	A.C.	B.	
6	DUNSTAN	S.	5,149	59°09′N. 08°22′W.	A.C.	B.	
6	OLGA S.	M.	2,252	55°48′N. 09°45′W.	A.C.	B.	
6	CYPRIAN PRINCE ...	S.	1,988	Piraeus	A.C.	B.	
6	CLAN FRASER ...	S.	7,529	Piraeus	A.C.	B.	
6	CITY OF ROUBAIX	S.	7,108	Piraeus	A.C.	B.	
6	PATRIS	S.	1,706	Piraeus	A.C.	B.	
7	PORTADOC	S.	1,746	07°17′N. 16°53′W. (Approx.)	S.M.	T.	
7	ELISABETH	S.	945	5m. E.S.E. of Porthscatho, S.E. Cornwall	Mine	—	
8	HELENA MARGARETA	S.	3,316	33°00′N. 23°52′W.	S.M.	T.	
8	TWEED	S.	2,697	07°43′N. 15°11′W.	S.M.	T.	
8	HARPATHIAN ...	S.	4,671	32°22′N. 22°53′W.	S.M.	T.	
8	ESKDENE	S.	3,829	34°43′N. 24°21′W.	S.M.	T.	
8	AHAMO*	* S. Tank	8,621	53°22′N. 00°59′E.	Mine	—	
9	DUFFIELD*... ...	M. Tank	8,516	31°13′N. 23°24′W.	S.M.	T.	Previously attacked by S.M. on 8th in position 32°00′N. 23°24′W.
9	LUNULA	S. Tank	6,363	Thames Haven	Mine	—	
9	CRAFTSMAN... ...	S.	8,022	05°S. 20°W. (Approx.)	Raider	—	
9	DUDLEY ROSE* ...	S.	1,600	150° 4m. from Berry Head	A.C.	B.	
11	RETRIEVER ...	Cable Ship	674	264° 1m. from Aliki Rocks, off Phleva Is., Greece	A.C.	B.	
11	DRACO	S.	2,018	Tobruk	A.C.	B.	Again bombed 21st and became total loss
12	ST. HELENA ...	S.	4,313	07°50′N. 14°00′W.	S.M.	T.	

Date	Name	Type	Gross tons	Position	Cause of loss	How lost	Remarks
APRIL, 1941—(*Contd.*)							
12	MARIE MAERSK ...	M. Tank	8,271	Piraeus	A.C.	B.	
13	CORINTHIC ...	S.	4,823	08°10′N. 14°40′W.	S.M.	T.	
13	CITY OF KARACHI ...	S.	7,140	Volo, Greece	A.C.	B.	
14	CLAN CUMMING ...	S.	7,264	Gulf of Athens	Mine	—	
15	AURILLAC	S.	4,733	37°09′N. 18°42′W.	S.M.	T.	
15	GOALPARA	S.	5,314	Eleusis Bay, Piraeus	A.C.	B.	
15	QUILOA	S.	7,765	Eleusis Bay, Piraeus	A.C.	B.	
15	AQUILA	Tug	59	Hull	A.C.	B.	
16	SWEDRU	M.	5,379	55°21′N. 12°50′W.	A.C.	B.	
16	ANGLESEA ROSE ...	S.	1,151	50°25′N. 05°35′W.	A.C.	B.	
16	AMIENS*	S.	1,548	50°25′N. 05°35′W.	A.C.	B.	
17	EFFRA	S.	1,446	Nr. Cross Sand, L.V.	E-Boat	T.	
17	MONTALTO ...	S.	623	Rochester	A.C.	B.	
18	BRITISH SCIENCE ...	M. Tank	7,138	36°06′N. 24°00′E.	A.C.	T.	
20	EMPIRE ENDURANCE	S.	8,570	53°05′N. 23°14′W.	S.M.	T.	
21	BANKURA	S.	3,185	Tobruk	A.C.	B.	Subsequently further damaged by A.C. and became total loss
21	CALCHAS	S.	10,305	23°50′N. 27°00′W.	S.M.	T.	
21	URANIA	S.	1,953	Tobruk	C.U.	—	
22	CORONATION OF LEEDS	Steam Barge	87	Off Thames Haven	Mine	—	
23	SANTA CLARA VALLEY	M.	4,665	Nauplia Bay, Greece	A.C.	B.	
24	CAVALLO	S.	2,269	Nauplia, Greece	A.C.*	—	Sank on 25th
25	EMPIRE LIGHT ...	S.	6,828	02°S. 61°E. (Approx.)	Raider	—	
26	MOUNTPARK ...	S.	4,648	56°17′N. 12°21′W.	A.C.	B.	
27	BEACON GRANGE ...	M.	10,160	62°05′N. 16°26′W.	S.M.	T.	
27	CELTE	S.	943	61°20′N. 11°00′W.	A.C.	B.	
27	HENRI MORY ...	S.	2,564	330m. W.N.W. of Blaskets, nr. Achill Head	S.M.	T.	
28	PORT HARDY ...	S.	8,897	60°14′N. 15°20′W.	S.M.	T.	
28	OILFIELD	M. Tank	8,516	60°05′N. 16°00′W.	S.M.	T.	
28	CAPULET* ...	M. Tank	8,190	60°10′N. 17°00′W.	S.M.	T.	
28	AMBROSE FLEMING	S.	1,555	53°14′N. 01°08′E.	E-Boat	T.	
28	CLAN BUCHANAN ...	S.	7,266	05°24′N. 62°46′E.	Raider	—	
29	CITY OF NAGPUR ...	S.	10,146	52°30′N. 26°00′W.	S.M.*	—	
29	KALUA	S.	722	½m. N.N.E. of T.2 Buoy, Mouth of Tyne	A.C.	B.	
30	NERISSA	S.	5,583	55°57′N. 10°08′W.	S.M.	T.	
30	LASSELL	M.	7,417	12°55′N. 28°56′W.	S.M.	T.	
	Total ... 75		361,578				
MAY, 1941							
1	SAMSO	S.	1,494	08°35′N. 16°17′W.	S.M.	T.	
2	PARRACOMBE ...	S.	4,702	Mediterranean	Mine	—	
3	ARAYBANK... ...	M.	7,258	Suda Bay, Crete	A.C.	B.	Again bombed on 16th and became total loss
3	WRAY CASTLE ...	S.	4,253	06°48′N. 13°55′W.	S.M.	T.	
3	CORBET	S.	468	248° 2 cables from Herculaneum Dock entrance, Liverpool	Mine	—	
3	BARNACLE	S.B.	138	Liverpool	A.C.	B.	
3	BONITA	Tug	65	Liverpool	A.C.	B.	
3	ELSTREE GRANGE	S.	6,598	Liverpool	A.C.	B.	
3	DOMINO	S.	1,453	Liverpool	A.C.	B.	
3	LUCE	Barge	143	Liverpool	A.C.	B.	
3	EUROPA	M.	10,224	Liverpool	A.C.	B.	
3	MALAKAND... ...	S.	7,649	Liverpool	A.C.	B.	

Date	Name	Type	Gross tons	Position	Cause of loss	How lost	Remarks
MAY, 1941—*(Contd.)*							
3	EMILY BURTON ...	Motor Barge	58	Liverpool	A.C.	B.	
3	PIKE	S.B.	168	Liverpool	A.C.	B.	
3	LING	S.B.	164	Liverpool	A.C.	B.	
About							
3	WALTON	Steam Barge	82	Liverpool	A.C.	B.	
3	SILVERDALE ...	S.B.	176	Liverpool	A.C.	B.	
4	ROYSTON ...	S.	2,722	270° from 62C Buoy (Humber)	A.C.	B.	Taken in tow and sank on 5th in position 53°37'N. 00°39'E. (Approx.)
4	TREGOR	M.	222	6m. off Trevose Head	A.C.	B.	
4	PNEUMATIC ELEVATOR No. 11	—	295	Liverpool	A.C.	B.	
5	QUEEN MAUD ...	M.	4,976	07°54'N. 16°41'W.	S.M.	T.	
5	TRAFFIC	Steam Barge	155	Liverpool	A.C.	B.	
5	FAIR HEAD ...	S.	1,719	Belfast	A.C.	B.	
6	SURAT	M.	5,529	08°23'N. 15°13'W.	S.M.	T.	
6	OAKDENE	S.	4,255	06°19'N. 27°55'W.	S.M.	T.	
6	DUNKWA	M.	4,752	08°43'N. 17°13'W.	S.M.	T.	
7	IXION	S.	10,263	61°29'N. 22°40'W.	S.M.	T.	
7	BRITISH EMPEROR	S. Tank	3,663	08°30'N. 56°25'E.	Raider	—	
7	RIL IDA	S.	53	Hull	A.C.	B.	
7	BLUESTONE ...	S.	106	Greenock	A.C.	B.	
7	KILEENAN	Steam Barge	72	Liverpool	Mine	—	
7	IDA BURTON ...	S.B.	46	Liverpool	A.C.	B.	
8	MARTON	S.	4,969	Liverpool	A.C.	B.	
8	ROSE	Steam Barge	143	Liverpool	A.C.	B.	
8	TRENTINO	S.	3,079	Liverpool	A.C.	B.	
8	DELITE	S.B.	89	Hull	A.C.	B.	
8	LADORE	S.B.	91	Hull	A.C.	B.	
8	WHITAKERS No. II	S.B.	48	Hull	A.C.	B.	
8	IRISHMAN ...	Tug	99	Portsmouth Harbour	Mine	—	
8	RAMILLIES	S.	4,553	48°05'N. 32°26'W.	S.M.	T.	
8	RAWNSLEY ...	M.	4,998	34°59'N. 25°46'E.	A.C.	B.	Sank on 12th.
9	CITY OF WINCHESTER	S.	7,120	08°20'N. 26°14'W.	S.M.	T.	
9	GREGALIA	S.	5,802	60°24'N. 32°37'W.	S.M.	T.	
9	BENGORE HEAD ...	S.	2,609	60°45'N. 33°02'W.	S.M.	T.	
9	ESMOND	S.	4,976	60°45'N. 33°02'W.	S.M.	T.	
9	EMPIRE SONG ...	S.	9,228	Off Malta	Mine	—	
10	EMPIRE CARIBOU ...	S.	4,861	59°28'N. 35°44'W.	S.M.	T.	
10	CITY OF SHANGHAI	S.	5,828	06°40'N. 27°50'W.	S.M.	T.	
11	SOMERSET	S.	8,790	54°54'N. 16°20'W.	A.C.	B.	
12	FOWBERRY TOWER	S.	4,484	1m. S.W. × W. of Humber L.V.	A.C.	B.	
12	RICHARD DE LARRINAGA	S.	5,358	4 cables N. of 20 R. Buoy, Tyne	A.C.	B.	
13	BENVRACKIE ...	S.	6,434	00°49'N. 20°15'W.	S.M.	T.	
13	F	Hopper Barge	496	350 yds. S. of Dingle Oil Jetty	Mine	—	
13	SOMERSBY	S.	5,170	60°39'N. 26°13'W.	S.M.	T.	
14	RABAUL	M.	6,809	19°30'S. 04°30'E.	Raider	—	
14	DALESMAN	S.	6,343	Suda Bay, Crete	A.C.	B.	
15	BENVENUE	S.	5,920	04°27'N. 18°25'W.	S.M.	T.	
16	RODNEY STAR ...	S.	11,803	05°03'N. 19°02'W.	S.M.	T.	
16	ARCHANGEL ...	S.	2,448	57°55'N. 02°03'W.	A.C.	B.	
16	ETHEL RADCLIFFE	S.	5,673	Great Yarmouth	A.C.	B.	Previously damaged By E-Boat on 17th April
16	LOGICIAN	S.	5,993	Suda Bay, Crete	A.C.	B.	Again bombed on 25th and sank
17	STATESMAN ...	S.	7,939	56°44'N. 13°45'W.	A.C.	B.	
17	ELEONORA MAERSK*	M. Tank	10,694	Suda Bay, Crete	A.C.	B.	
18	PIAKO	S.	8,286	07°52'N. 14°57'W.	S.M.	T.	

Date	Name	Type	Gross tons	Position	Cause of loss	How lost	Remarks
MAY, 1941—(Contd.)							
18	BEGERIN	M.	483	295° 17m. from South Bishops	A.C.	B.	
19	EMPIRE RIDGE ...	S.	2,922	90m. W. of Bloody Foreland	S.M.	T.	
19	WINKFIELD ...	S.	5,279	1m. S.W. of B.4 Buoy, Thames Estuary	Mine	—	
19	CITY OF ROCHESTER	Paddle steamer	194	Acorn Yard, Rochester	A.C.	Parachute Mine	
20	DARLINGTON COURT	M.	4,974	57°28′N. 41°07′W.	S.M.	T.	
20	JAVANESE PRINCE...	M.	8,593	59°46′N. 10°45′W.	S.M.	T.	
20	STARCROSS	S.	4,662	51°45′N. 20°45′W.	S.M.	T.	Sunk by Escort.
20	HARPAGUS	S.	5,173	56°47′N. 40°55′W.	S.M.	T.	
20	NORMAN MONARCH	S.	4,718	56°41′N. 40°52′W.	S.M.	T.	
20	BRITISH SECURITY	M. Tank	8,470	57°28′N. 41°07′W.	S.M.	T.	
20	ROTHERMERE ...	S.	5,356	57°48′N. 41°36′W.	S.M.	T.	
20	COCKAPONSET ...	S.	5,996	57°28′N. 41°07′W.	S.M.	T.	
21	TEWKESBURY ...	S.	4,601	05°49′N. 24°09′W.	S.M.	T.	
21	MARCONI	S.	7,402	58°N. 41°W. (Approx.)	S.M.	T.	
22	BARNBY	S.	4,813	60°30′N. 34°12′W.	S.M.	T.	
22	BRITISH GRENADIER*	S. Tank	6,857	06°15′N. 12°59′W.	S.M.	T.	
23	VULCAIN	S.	4,362	09°20′N. 15°35′W.	S.M.	T.	
24	TRAFALGAR... ...	S.	4,530	25°S. 01°E. (Approx.)	Raider	—	
25	HELKA	S. Tank	3,471	E. Mediterranean	A.C.	B.	
26	COLONIAL	S.	5,108	09°13′N. 15°09′W.	S.M.	T.	
29	TABARISTAN ...	S.	6,251	06°32′N. 15°23′W.	S.M.	T.	
29	EMPIRE STORM ...	S.	7,290	55°00′N. 39°50′W.	S.M.	T.	
30	SILVERYEW ...	M.	6,373	16°42′N. 25°29′W.	S.M.	T.	
30	EMPIRE PROTECTOR	S.	6,181	06°00′N. 14°25′W.	S.M.	T.	
30	WESTAVON	S.	2,842	51°36′N. 01°11′E.	Mine	—	
31	CLAN MACDOUGALL	M.	6,843	16°50′N. 25°10′W.	S.M.	T.	
31	GRAVELINES ...	S.	2,491	56°00′N. 11°13′W.	S.M.	T.	
31	SIRE...	S.	5,664	08°50′N. 15°30′W.	S.M.	T.	
	Total ... 92		386,953				
JUNE 1941							
1	SCOTTISH MONARCH	S.	4,719	12°58′N. 27°20′W.	S.M.	T.	
1	ALFRED JONES ...	M.	5,013	08°N. 15°W. (Approx.)	S.M.	T.	
2	MICHAEL E. ...	S.	7,628	48°50′N. 29°00′W.	S.M.	T.	
2	INVERSUIR	M. Tank	9,456	48°28′N. 28°20′W.	S.M.	T. & G.	
2	BEAUMANOIR ...	S.	2,477	180° 8 cables from 19 Buoy, Robin Hood's Bay	A.C.	B.	
2	PRINCE RUPERT CITY	S.	4,749	58°46′N. 04°41′W.	A.C.	B.	
3	ROYAL FUSILIER ...	S.	2,187	55°22′N. 01°21′W.	A.C.	B.	Sank 200° 4m. from May Is.
4	WELLFIELD* ...	M. Tank	6,054	48°34′N. 31°34′W.	S.M.	T.	
4	ROBERT HUGHES ...	Dredger	2,879	Entrance to Lagos, W. Africa	Mine	—	
4	TRECARREL... ...	S.	5,271	47°10′N. 31°00′W.	S.M.	T.	
6	TREGARTHEN ...	S.	5,201	46°17′N. 36°20′W.	S.M.	T.	
6	BARON LOVAT ...	S.	3,395	35°30′N. 11°30′W.	S.M.	T.	
6	SACRAMENTO VALLEY	S.	4,573	17°10′N. 30°10′W.	S.M.	T.	
6	GLEN HEAD ...	S.	2,011	35°40′N. 10°30′W.	A.C.	B.	
6	QUEENSBURY ...	S.	3,911	56°50′N. 02°07′W.	A.C.	B.	
7	KINGSTON HILL ...	S.	7,628	09°35′N. 29°40′W.	S.M.	T.	
7	BARON NAIRN ...	S.	3,164	47°36′N. 39°02′W.	S.M.	T.	
8	ELMDENE	S.	4,853	08°16′N. 16°50′W.	S.M.	T.	

Date	Name	Type	Gross tons	Position	Cause of loss	How lost	Remarks
JUNE, 1941—(*Contd.*)							
8	TREVARRACK ...	S.	5,270	48°46′N. 29°14′W.	S.M.	T.	
8	PHIDIAS	S.	5,623	48°25′N. 26°12′W.	S.M.	G.	
8	ADDA	M.	7,816	08°30′N. 14°39′W.	S.M.	T.	
9	DIANA ... , ...	S.	942	62°04′N. 13°40′W. (Approx.)	A.C.	B.	
9	SILVERPALM ...	M.	6,373	51°N. 26°W. (Approx.)	S.M.*	—	
9	DAGMAR	S.	844	50°35′N. 01°48′W.	A.C.	B.	
10	AINDERBY ...	S.	4,860	55°30′N. 12°10′W.	S.M.	T.	
10	ROYAL SCOT ...	S.	1,444	070° 5 cables from 62 Buoy, Humber entrance	Mine	—	
11	BARON CARNEGIE ...	S.	3,178	51°55′N. 05°34′W.	A.C.	T.	
11	MOORWOOD... ...	S.	2,056	At 20 C Buoy off Hartlepool	A.C.	T.	
12	EMPIRE DEW ...	M.	7,005	51°09′N. 30°16′W.	S.M.	T.	
12	CHINESE PRINCE ...	M.	8,593	56°12′N. 14°18′W.	S.M.	T.	
12	TRESILLIAN ...	S.	4,743	44°40′N. 45°30′W.	S.M.	T.	
13	DJURDJURA ...	S.	3,460	38°53′N. 23°11′W.	S.M.	T.	
13	KINGSTOWN ...	S.	628	9m. N.W. of S. Bishops Lt., Bristol Channel	A.C.	B.	
13	ST. LINDSAY ...	S.	5,370	51°N. 30°W. (Approx.)	S.M.*	—	
13	ST. PATRICK ...	S.	1,922	52°04′N. 05°25′W. (Approx.)	A.C.	B.	
13	SUSAN MAERSK ...	S.	2,355	North Atlantic	C.U	—	
17	TOTTENHAM ...	S.	4,762	07°38′S. 19°12′W.	Raider	—	
17	CATHRINE	M.	2,727	49°30′N. 16°00′W. (Approx.)	S.M.	T.	
18	NORFOLK	S.	10,948	57°17′N. 11°14′W.	S.M.	T.	
19	EMPIRE WARRIOR	S.	1,306	2¾m. off Guadiana Bar, Gulf of Cadiz	A.C.	B.	
21	GASFIRE	S.	3,001	About 10m. due E. of Southwold	Mine	—	
21	KENNETH HAWKSFIELD	S.	1,546	52°18′N. 01°59′E.	Mine	—	
22	BALZAC	S.	5,372	12°S. 29°W. (Approx.)	Raider	—	
23	HULL TRADER ...	S.	717	270° 1m. from No. 57 C. Buoy, Cromer (Approx.)	Mine	—	
23	TRELISSICK ...	S.	5,265	114° 3½m. from Sheringham Buoy, Cromer	A.C.	B.	
23	ARAKAKA* ... (Meteorological Vessel)	S.	2,379	47°N. 40°W. (Approx.)	S.M.*	—	
24	KINROSS	M.	4,956	55°23′N. 38°49′W.	S.M.	T.	
24	BROCKLEY HILL ...	S.	5,297	58°30′N. 38°20′W.	S.M.	T.	
25	DASHWOOD ...	S.	2,154	52°59′N. 01°52′E.	A.C.	B.	
26	MAREEBA	S.	3,472	10°N. 88°E. (Approx.)	Raider	—	
26	RIVER LUGAR ...	S.	5,423	24°N. 21°W. (Approx.)	S.M.	T.	
26	MALAYA II... ...	M.	8,651	59°56′N. 30°35′W.	S.M.	T.	
27	EMPIRE ABILITY ...	S.	7,603	23°50′N. 21°10′W.	S.M.	T.	
27	P.L.M.22 ...	S.	5,646	25°43′N. 22°47′W.	S.M.	T.	
28	AURIS*	M. Tank	8,030	34°27′N. 11°57′W.	S.M.	T.	
28	BARRHILL	S.	4,972	52°50′N. 01°46′E.	A.C.	B.	
29	RIO AZUL	S.	4,088	29°N. 25°W. (Approx.)	S.M.	T.	
29	GRAYBURN	S.	6,342	59°30′N. 18°07′W.	S.M.	T.	
29	CUSHENDALL ...	S.	626	56°57′N. 02°03′W.	A.C.	B.	
30	ST. ANSELM ...	S.	5,614	31°N. 26°W. (Approx.)	S.M.	T.	
	Total ... 60		268,548				

Date	Name	Type	Gross tons	Position	Cause of loss	How lost	Remarks
JULY, 1941							
1	HOMEFIRE ...	S.	1,262	53°05′N. 01°28′E.	A.C.	B.	
2	TORONTO CITY* ... (Meteorological Vessel)	S.	2,486	47°03′N. 30°00′W. (Approx.)	S.M.*	—	
3	ROSME	Sprit-sail Barge	82	51°34′N. 01°03′E.	Mine	—	
4	AUDITOR	S.	5,444	25°53′N. 28°23′W.	S.M.	T.	
4	LUNAN	S.	363	51°27′N. 03°10′W.	Mine	—	
4	BALFRON	S.	362	038° 3½m. from Ravenscar	A.C.	B.	
4	ROBERT L. HOLT ...	S.	2,918	24°15′N. 20°00′W. (Approx.)	C.U.	—	
5	ANSELM	S.	5,954	44°25′N. 28°35′W.	S.M.	T.	
5	BENCRUACHAN ...	S.	5,920	297° 9.8 cables from Mex High Lt. (off Alexandria)	Mine	—	
5	FOWEY ROSE ...	S.	470	51°51′N. 05°28′W.	A.C.	B.	
9	DESIGNER	S.	5,945	42°59′N. 31°40′W.	S.M.	T.	
9	INVERNESS ...	S.	4,897	42°46′N. 32°45′W.	S.M.	T.	
9	BLUE MERMAID ...	S.B.	97	185° 8m. from Clacton (Approx.)	Mine	—	
13	COLLINGDOC ...	S.	1,780	200° 4 cables from Southend Pier	Mine	—	
14	RUPERT DE LARRINAGA	S.	5,358	36°18′N. 21°11′W.	S.M.	T.	
15	FARFIELD	S.	468	250° 5m. from S. Stack	A.C.	B.	
17	GUELMA	S.	4,402	30°44′N. 17°33′W.	S.M.	T.	
19	HOLMSIDE	S.	3,433	19°00′N. 21°30′W.	S.M.	T.	
23	OMFLEET	Steam Barge	130	Hull	Mine	—	
24	MACON	S.	5,135	32°48′N. 26°12′W.	S.M.	T.	
26	HORN SHELL* ...	M. Tank	8,272	33°23′N. 22°18′W.	S.M.	T.	
26	BOTWEY	S.	5,106	55°42′N. 09°53′W. (Approx.)	S.M.	T.	
26	KELLWYN	S.	1,459	43°N. 17°W. (Approx.)	S.M.	T.	
27	HAWKINGE ...	S.	2,475	44°55′N. 17°44′W.	S.M.	T.	
28	ERATO	S.	1,335	43°10′N. 17°30′W.	S.M.	T.	
28	WROTHAM	S.	1,884	43°N. 17°W. (Approx.)	S.M.	T.	
28	LAPLAND	S.	1,330	40°36′N. 15°30′W.	S.M.	T.	
29	SHAHRISTAN ...	S.	6,935	35°19′N. 23°53′W. (Approx.)	S.M.	T.	
29	CHAUCER	S.	5,792	16°46′N. 38°01′W.	Raider	—	
30	ADAM'S BECK ...	S.	2,816	235° 1m. from 20 C. Buoy, Tyne	A.C.	B.	
	Total ... 30		94,310				
AUGUST, 1941							
2	TRIDENT	S.	4,317	Off 20 C Buoy, Tyne	A.C.	B.	
4	TUNISIA	S.	4,337	53°53′N. 18°10′W.	A.C.	B.	
5	KUMASIAN	S.	4,922	53°11′N. 15°38′W.	S.M.	T.	
5	SWIFTPOOL ...	S.	5,205	53°03′N. 16°00′W.	S.M.	T.	
5	HARLINGEN ...	S.	5,415	53°26′N. 15°40′W.	S.M.	T.	
5	BELGRAVIAN ...	S.	3,136	53°03′N. 15°54′W.	S.M.	T.	
5	CAPE RODNEY ...	S.	4,512	53°26′N. 15°40′W.	S.M.	T.	Sank on 9th in position 52°44′N. 11°41′W.
9	CORDENE	S.	2,345	53°01′N. 01°48′E.	A.C.	B.	
11	SIR RUSSELL ...	S.	1,548	349° 6 cables from No. 10 Buoy. Off Dungeness	E-Boat	T.	
11	EMPIRE HURST ...	S.	2,852	36°48′N. 09°50′W.	A.C.	B.	
14	AUSTRALIND ...	M.	5,020	04°13′S. 91°03′W.	Raider	—	
19	CISCAR	S.	1,809	49°10′N. 17°40′W.	S.M.	T.	
19	ALVA	S.	1,584	49°N. 17°W. (Approx.)	S.M.	T.	
19	AGUILA	S.	3,255	49°23′N. 17°56′W.	S.M.	T.	

Date	Name	Type	Gross tons	Position	Cause of loss	How lost	Remarks

AUGUST, 1941—*(Contd.)*

Date	Name	Type	Gross tons	Position	Cause of loss	How lost	Remarks
19	GOLDEN GRAIN ...	Motor Barge	101	51°35′N. 01°03′E.	Mine	—	
19	DEVON	S.	9,036	05°S. 91°W. (Approx.)	Raider	—	
20	TURBO*	S. Tank	4,782	32°08′N. 31°57′E.	A.C.	T.	Seriously damaged Foundered in tow 5th April, 1942.
22	EMPIRE OAK ...	Tug	482	40°43′N. 11°39′W. (Approx.)	S.M.	T.	
22	CLONLARA	S.	1,203	40°43′N. 11°39′W. (Approx.)	S.M.	T.	
23	STORK	M.	787	40°43′N. 11°39′W. (Approx.)	S.M.	T.	
23	ALDERGROVE ...	S.	1,974	40°43′N. 11°39′W. (Approx.)	S.M.	T.	
24	SKAGERAK ...	S.	1,283	River Orwell, Harwich	Mine	—	
27	TREMODA	S.	4,736	53°36′N. 16°40′W. (Approx.)	S.M.	T.	Last seen on 28th in position 54°08′N. 15°28′W.
27	SAUGOR	S.	6,303	53°36′N. 16°40′W. (Approx.)	S.M.	T.	
27	EMBASSAGE ...	S.	4,954	54°N. 13°W. (Approx.)	S.M.	T.	
28	OTAIO	M.	10,298	52°16′N. 17°50′W.	S.M.	T.	
	Total ... 26		96,196				

SEPTEMBER, 1941

Date	Name	Type	Gross tons	Position	Cause of loss	How lost	Remarks
3	FORT RICHEPANSE	M.	3,485	52°15′N. 21°10′W.	S.M.	T.	
5	ABBAS COMBE ...	S.	489	5m. N.N.W. of Bardsey Island	A.C.	B.	
7	DUNCARRON ...	S.	478	3m. East of Sheringham Buoy, Norfolk Coast	E-Boat	T.	
7	MARCREST	S.	4,224	090° 2m. from Yarmouth	A.C.	B.	
7	EMPIRE GUNNER ...	S.	4,492	52°08′N. 05°18′W.	A.C.	B.	
7	TRSAT	S.	1,369	N.E. × E. 7m. from Kinnaird Head	A.C.	B.	
10	EMPIRE SPRINGBUCK	S.	5,591	61°38′N. 40°40′W. (Approx.)	S.M.	T.	
10	BARON PENTLAND...	S.	3,410	61°15′N. 41°05′W.	S.M.	T.	
10	SALLY MAERSK ...	M.	3,252	61°40′N. 40°30′W.	S.M.	T.	
10	MUREFTE (Ferry) ...	S.	691	33°12′N. 34°55′E.	S.M.	G.	
10	THISTLEGLEN ...	S.	4,748	61°59′N. 39°46′W.	S.M.	T.	
10	EMPIRE HUDSON ...	S.	7,465	61°28′N. 40°51′W.	S.M.	T.	
10	MUNERIC	S.	5,229	61°38′N. 40°40′W.	S.M.	T.	
10	GYPSUM QUEEN ...	S.	3,915	63°05′N. 37°50′W.	S.M.	T.	
10	BULYSSES	M. Tank	7,519	62°22′N. 38°22′W.	S.M.	T.	
11	BERURY	S.	4,924	62°40′N. 38°50′W.	S.M.	T.	
11	EMPIRE CROSSBILL	S.	5,463	63°14′N. 37°12′W.	S.M.	T.	
11	STONEPOOL ...	S.	4,815	63°05′N. 37°50′W.	S.M.	T.	
12	TAI KOO*	Tug	688	16°45′N. 40°05′E. (Approx.)	Mine	—	
13	BLOOMFIELD* ...	S.	1,417	61°50′N. 06°00′W.	A.C.	B.	
15	NEWBURY	S.	5,102	54°39′N. 28°04′W.	S.M.	T.	
15	DARU	M.	3,854	51°56′N. 05°58′W.	A.C.	B.	
15	FLYING KITE ...	Tug	260	Off Dalmuir Basin, Clyde	Mine	—	
15	EMPIRE ELAND ...	S.	5,613	54°N. 28°W. (Approx.)	S.M.*	—	
15	BIRTLEY	S.	2,873	53°06′N. 01°17′E.	Mine	—	Sank on 16th in position 53°03′N. 01°18′E.
16	JEDMOOR	M.	4,392	59°N. 10°W. (Approx.)	S.M.	T.	
17	TEDDINGTON	S.	4,762	53°04′N. 01°34′E.	E-Boat	T.	
19	T. J. WILLIAMS ...	S. Tank	8,211	61°34′N. 35°11′W.	S.M.	T.	

Date	Name	Type	Gross tons	Position	Cause of loss	How lost	Remarks

SEPTEMBER, 1941—(Contd.)

Date	Name	Type	Gross tons	Position	Cause of loss	How lost	Remarks
19	Empire Burton ...	S.	6,966	61°30′N. 35°11′W.	S.M.	T.	
19	Bradglen	S.	4,741	230° 2m. from B.3 Buoy, Barrow Deep	Mine	—	
20	Portsdown (Ferry)	S.	342	50°46′N. 01°06′W.	Mine	—	
20	Cingalese Prince	M.	8,474	02°00′S. 25°30′W.	S.M.	T.	
20	Fiona Shell ...	Storage Hulk	2,444	Gibraltar	Italian Assault Craft	—	
20	Baltallinn ...	S.	1,303	49°07′N. 22°07′W.	S.M.	T.	
20	Empire Moat. ...	S.	2,922	48°07′N. 22°05′W. (Approx.)	S.M.	T.	
21	Lissa	S.	1,511	47°N. 22°W. (Approx.)	S.M.*	T.	
21	Runa	S.	1,575	46°20′N. 22°23′W.	S.M.	T.	
21	Rhineland ...	S.	1,381	47°N. 22°W. (Approx.)	S.M.*	T.	
21	Vancouver ...	S. Tank	5,729	51°51′N. 01°31′E.	Mine	—	
21	Walmer Castle* ...	M.	906	47°16′N. 22°25′W.	A.C.	B.	
22	Niceto de Larrinaga	S.	5,591	27°32′N. 24°26′W.	S.M.	T.	
22	Edward Blyden ...	M.	5,003	27°36′N. 24°29′W.	S.M.	T.	
22	Silverbelle ...	M.	5,302	25°45′N. 24°00′W.	S.M.	T.	Abandoned on 29th in position 26°30′N 23°14′W.
23	St. Clair II	S.	3,753	30°25′N. 23°35′W.	S.M.	T.	
24	John Holt ...	S.	4,975	31°12′N. 23°32′W.	S.M.	T.	
24	Lafian	S.	4,876	31°12′N. 23°32′W.	S.M.	T.	
24	Dixcove	M.	3,790	31°12′N. 23°41′W.	S.M.	T.	
25	Avoceta	S.	3,442	47°57′N. 24°05′W.	S.M.	T.	
25	Empire Stream ...	S.	2,922	46°03′N. 24°40′W. (Approx.)	S.M.	T.	
25	Erna III	S.	1,590	51°45′N. 35°15′W. (Est.)	C.U.	—	
26	Petrel	S.	1,354	47°40′N. 23°28′W.	S.M.	T.	
26	Lapwing	S.	1,348	47°40′N. 23°30′W. (Approx.)	S.M.	T.	
26	Cortes	S.	1,374	47°48′N. 23°45′W. (Approx.)	S.M.	T.	
26	British Prince ...	M.	4,979	53°52′N. 00°25′E.	A.C.	B.	
27	Margareta ...	S.	3,103	50°15′N. 17°27′W.	S.M.	T.	
27	Cervantes ...	S.	1,810	48°37′N. 20°01′W. (Approx.)	S.M.	T.	
27	Imperial Star ...	M.	12,427	37°31′N. 10°46′E.	A.C.	T.	
	Total ... 57		214,664				

OCTOBER, 1941.

Date	Name	Type	Gross tons	Position	Cause of loss	How lost	Remarks
2	Empire Wave ...	S.	7,463	59°08′N. 32°26′W.	S.M.	T.	
2	San Florentino*	S. Tank	12,842	52°42′N. 34°51′W.	S.M.	T.	Also torpedoed on 1st in position 52°50′N. 34°40′W.
2	Hatasu	S.	3,198	600m. E. of Cape Race	S.M.	T.	
5	Tynefield* ...	M. Tank	5,856	Suez Canal	Mine	—	
6	Thistlegorm ...	S.	4,898	Anchorage F, Straits of Jubal, Suez	A.C.	B.	
8	Rosalie Moller ...	S.	3,963	Anchorage H, Suez	A.C.	B.	
10	Nailsea Manor ...	S.	4,926	18°45′N. 21°18′W.	S.M.	T.	
12	Chevington ...	S.	1,537	52°59′N. 01°52′E.	E-Boat	T.	
12	Glynn	S.	1,134	52°35′N. 01°56′E.	A.C.	B.	Sunk by gunfire from H.M.S.
15	Empire Heron ...	S.	6,023	54°55′N. 27°15′W.	S.M.	T.	
15	Silvercedar ...	M.	4,354	53°36′N. 30°00′W.	S.M.	T.	
15	Vancouver Island	M.	9,472	53°37′N. 25°37′W.	S.M.	T.	
16	W. C. Teagle ...	S. Tank	9,551	57°N. 25°W. (Approx.)	S.M.	T.	
17	Pass of Balmaha*	S. Tank	758	31°14′N. 28°50′E.	S.M.	T.	

Date	Name	Type	Gross tons	Position	Cause of loss	How lost	Remarks
OCTOBER, 1941—(Contd.)							
18	MAHSEER	S.	7,911	51°41′N. 01°19′E.	Mine	—	
18	EMPIRE GHYLL ...	S.	2,011	221° 4 to 5 cables from B.7 Buoy, Barrow Deep	Mine	—	
19	BARON KELVIN ...	S.	3,081	100° 14m. from Tarifa	S.M.	T.	
19	INVERLEE* ...	M. Tank	9,158	240° 30m. from Cape Spartel	S.M.	T.	
20	BRITISH MARINER...	S. Tank	6,996	07°43′N. 14°20′W.	S.M.	T.	
21	TREVERBYN ...	S.	5,281	51°N. 19°W. (Approx.)	S.M.	T.	
21	SERBINO ... ...,	S.	4,099	51°10′N. 19°20′W.	S.M.	T.	
24	CARSBRECK ...	S.	3,670	36°20′N. 10°50′W.	S.M.	T.	
24	ARIOSTO	S.	2,176	36°20′N. 10°50′W.	S.M.	T.	
24	ALHAMA	S.	1,352	35°42′N. 10°58′W. (Approx.)	S.M.	T.	
24	EMPIRE GUILLEMOT	S.	5,720	W. of Galeta Is., Mediterranean	A.C.	T.	
27	ANTIOPE	S.	4,545	53°13′N. 01°08′E.	A.C.	B.	
28	ULEA	S.	1,574	41°17′N. 21°40′W.	S.M.	T.	
28	HAZELSIDE ...	S.	5,297	23°10′S. 01°36′E.	S.M.	T.	
28	ROSLEA ...	S.	642	Off Belgian Coast	Captured and sunk	—	
29	SARASTONE ...	S.	2,473	37°05′N. 06°48′W.	A.C.	B.	
31	BRITISH FORTUNE	S. Tank	4,696	265° 1m. from Aldeburgh Lt. Buoy	A.C.	B.	
31	KING MALCOLM ...	M.	5,120	Last seen in position 47°40′N. 51°15′W.	S.M.*	—	
	Total ... 32		151,777				
NOVEMBER, 1941.							
1	BRADFORD CITY ...	M.	4,953	22°59′S. 09°49′E.	S.M.	T.	
2	MARIE DAWN ...	S.	2,157	20m. from Spurn Pt.	A.C.	B.	Sank on 3rd, 2m. S.W. of H.2 Buoy, Humber
2	LARPOOL	S.	3,872	250m. E.S.E. of Cape Race	S.M.	T.	
2	BRYNMILL ...	S.	743	210° 4m. from E. Dudgeon Buoy	A.C.	—	Sank 5m. W. of E. Dudgeon Bell Buoy
2	FOREMOST 45 ...	Hopper Barge	824	51°21′N. 03°17′W.	Mine	—	
3	FLYNDERBORG ...	S.	2,022	51°21′N. 51°45′W.	S.M.	T.	
3	GRETAVALE ...	S.	4,586	51°21′N. 51°45′W.	S.M.	T.	
3	EMPIRE GEMSBUCK	S.	5,626	52°18′N. 53°05′W.	S.M.	T.	
3	EVEROJA	S.	4,830	077° 80m. from Belle Isle	S.M.	T.	Sank on 4th
About 3	ROSE SCHIAFFINO ...	S.	3,349	Vicinity Newfoundland, N. Atlantic	S.M.*	—	
4	BRITISHER ...	S.	68	Off Maplin Lt., Thames Estuary	Mine*	—	
7	NOTTINGHAM ...	M.	8,532	53°24′N. 31°51′W.	S.M.	T.	
12	PERU	M.	6,961	01°30′N. 13°20′W.	S.M.	T.	
12	MAURITA	S.	201	Hilbre Swash, Dee Estuary, Liverpool Bay	Mine	—	
14	EMPIRE PELICAN ...	S.	6,463	Between Galeta Is. and Tunisian Coast	A.C.	T.	
15	EMPIRE DEFENDER	S.	5,649	18m. S. of Galeta Is., Mediterranean	A.C.	T.	
15	CORHAMPTON ...	S.	2,495	26m. N.E. of Spurn Head	A.C.	B.	Sank on 16th whilst in tow in position 53°53′N. 00°26′E.
17	BOVEY TRACEY ...	S.	1,212	52°28′N. 02°05′E.	A.C.	B.	
19	ARUBA	S.	1,159	52°51′N. 02°07′E.	E-Boat	T.	
19	WALDINGE	S.	2,462	52°56′N. 02°01′E.	E-Boat	T.	Sank on 20th
24	VIRGILIA	S. Tank	5,723	3m. N.E. of Hearty Knoll Buoy	E-Boat	T.	

Date	Name	Type	Gross tons	Position	Cause of loss	How lost	Remarks
NOVEMBER, 1941—*(Contd.)*							
29	THORNLIEBANK ...	S.	5,569	41°50'N. 29°48'W.	S.M.	T.	
29	ASPERITY	S. Tank	699	53°11'N. 01°07'E.	E-Boat	T.	
29	CORMARSH ...	S.	2,848	53°16'N. 01°04'E.	E-Boat	T.	
30	ASHBY	S.	4,868	36°54'N. 29°51'W.	S.M.	T.	
30	EMPIRE NEWCOMEN	S.	2,840	5m. S. of Dudgeon Lt., off Cromer	E-Boat	T.	
	Total ... 26		90,711				
DECEMBER, 1941							
2	GRELHEAD	S.	4,274	2m. from Punta Negri, Morocco	C.U.	—	
2	BRITISH CAPTAIN ...	S. Tank	6,968	52°13'N. 01°55'E.	Mine	—	
3	MACLAREN	S.	2,330	51°21'N. 03°17'W.	Mine	—	
6	GREENLAND ...	S.	1,281	52°14'N. 01°56'E.	Mine	—	Sank in position 52°14'N. 02°06'E.
6	SCOTTISH TRADER...	S.	4,016	N. Atlantic, S. of Iceland	S.M.	—	
7	WELSH PRINCE ...	S.	5,148	110° 5 cables from No. 59 Buoy, vicinity of Spurn Head	Mine	—	Abandoned in position 53°24'N. 00°59'E.
7	SEVERN TRANSPORT	M.	119	51°27'N. 03°04'W.	Mine	—	
8	FIREGLOW	S.	1,261	3m. S. of Dudgeon Buoy	Mine	—	Sank in position 53°19'N. 01°05'E.
8	EDITH MOLLER* ...	Tender	645	S. of Amoy	Captured	—	
8	MIN-WO	Tug	287	Hankow	Seized	—	
8	WANTUNG	S.	1,061	Shanghai	Seized	—	
8	KINTANG	S.	435	Shanghai	Seized	—	
8	HSIN TSEANGTAH ...	S.	933	Shanghai	Seized	—	
8	SCOT I	Tug	274	Shanghai	Seized	—	
8	MERRY MOLLER ...	Tug	382	Shanghai	Seized	—	
8	DIANA MOLLER ...	Tug	252	Shanghai	Seized	—	
8	CHRISTINE MOLLER	Salvage Tug	800	Shanghai	Seized	—	
8	JESSIE MOLLER ...	Salvage Vessel	530	Shanghai	Seized	—	
8	READY MOLLER ..	Tug	268	Off Amoy	Captured	—	
8	CHEKIANG	S.	2,172	Wangpu River, N. China	Seized	—	
8	MARY MOLLER ...	S.	2,698	Wangpu River, N. China	Seized	—	
8	KIA-WO	S.	1,311	Ichang	Seized	—	
8	ANALOCK	S.	6,638	China Seas	Seized	—	On charter to Japan.
8	KIANG-WO ...	S.	2,209	China Seas	Seized	—	Two crew reported prisoners of war in Japan
8	DESLOCK	S.	5,015	China Seas	Seized	—	On charter to Japan.
8	TUNG ON	S.	1,950	China Seas	C.U.	—	Sunk, seized or captured
8	FEDERLOCK ...	S.	6,607	China Seas	Seized	—	On charter to Japan.
8	MACAU	S.	1,665	China Seas	C.U.	—	Sunk, seized or captured
8	HATTERLOCK ...	S.	5,138	China Seas	Seized	—	⎫
8	MUNLOCK	S.	5,240	China Seas	Seized	—	⎬ On charter to
8	ST. QUENTIN ...	S.	3,528	China Seas	Seized	—	⎬ Japan
8	VITORLOCK ...	S.	5,030	China Seas	Seized	—	⎭
8	WENCHOW	S.	3,113	China Seas	Seized	—	⎫ Masters prisoners of
8	WOOSUNG	S.	3,426	China Seas	Seized	—	⎬ war
8	HSIN CHANG WO ...	S.	582	Ichang	Seized	—	
8	SIANGTAN	S.	1,195	Ichang	Seized	—	⎫ Crew prisoners of
8	SHASI	S.	1,327	In Yangtsze River	Seized	—	⎬ war
8	SUI-TAI	S.	1,816	Shanghai	C.U.	—	Sunk, seized or captured
8	KONG SO	S.	789	Tinghai	Seized	—	Master prisoner of war

B

Date	Name	Type	Gross tons	Position	Cause of loss	How lost	Remarks
DECEMBER, 1941—(Contd.)							
8	CHUEN CHOW ...	S.	1,088	Far Eastern Waters	C.U.	—	
8	CHUNG ON ...	S.	968	Far Eastern Waters	C.U.	—	
8	FOOK ON	M.	738	Far Eastern Waters	C.U.	—	
8	KWONG FOOK CHEUNG	S.	881	Far Eastern Waters	C.U.	—	
8	LING KONG ...	S.	850	Far Eastern Waters	C.U.	—	Sunk, seized or captured
8	ON LEE*	S.	1,026	Far Eastern Waters	C.U.	—	
8	TAI HING	S.	1,068	Far Eastern Waters	C.U.	—	
8	TAI LEE	S.	1,423	Far Eastern Waters	C.U.	—	
8	TAI MING* ...	S.	649	Far Eastern Waters	C.U.	—	
8	TIN YAT	S.	942	Far Eastern Waters	C.U.	—	
8	TAISHAN*	S.	3,174	Far Eastern Waters	C.U.	—	
8	CHANGSHA	S.	2,482	China Seas	Seized	—	
8	KAU TUNG ...	S.	1,665	China Seas	C.U.	—	
8	KWONG SAI ...	S.	1,309	China Seas	C.U.	—	Sunk, seized or captured
8	KWONG TUNG ...	S.	1,218	China Seas	C.U.	—	
8	KUT-WO	S.	2,665	China Seas	Seized	—	
8	LOONGWO	S.	3,923	China Seas	Seized	—	
8	KINSHAN	S.	2,733	China Seas	C.U.	—	Sunk, seized or captured
8	PAOWO	S.	2,517	China Seas	Seized	—	Chief Engineer prisoner of war
8	SAGRES	S.	2,333	China Seas	Seized	—	
8	WUHU	S.	2,938	China Seas	Seized	—	
8	FATSHAN	S.	2,639	Canton	Seized	—	
8	CARMEN MOLLER ...	Tug	366	S. of Amoy	Captured	—	
8	ELSIE MOLLER ...	Tug	1,136	Off Amoy	Captured	—	
8	HSIN PEKING ...	S.	2,104	On voyage Tongku to Hong Kong	Captured	—	
8	KIANGSU	S.	2,676	Off Amoy	Captured	—	
8	MARIE MOLLER ...	Tug	593	Off Ningpo	Captured	—	
8	NANNING	S.	2,486	Hong Kong	Seized	—	
8	ST. DOMINIC* ...	Tug	451	S. of Saddle Is., China Seas	C.U.	—	
8	SOOCHOW	S.	2,604	Hong Kong	Scuttled	—	Salved by Japanese
9	BENNEVIS	S.	5,356	Off Hong Kong	Captured	—	
10	KIRNWOOD ...	S.	3,829	56°57'N. 16°35'W.	S.M.	T.	
10	KURDISTAN ...	S.	5,844	56°51'N. 16°36'W.	S.M.	T.	Sank on 11th
10	HARELDAWINS ...	S.	1,523	Off Luzon Is., Philippines	C.U.	—	
12	DROMORE CASTLE ...	S.	5,242	20m. S.S.E. of Humber	Mine	—	
12	KALGAN	S.	2,655	Bangkok	Seized	—	
12	CAMBAY PRINCE ...	S.	455	Bleak Pier, Hong Kong	Scuttled	—	
12	SHINAI	S.	2,410	Kuching, N. Borneo	Seized	—	
14	ST. VINCENT DE PAUL	S.	1,339	Hong Kong	C.U.	—	
15	EMPIRE BARRACUDA	S.	4,972	35°30'N. 06°17'W.	S.M.	T.	
19	RUCKINGE	S.	2,869	38°20'N. 17°15'W.	S.M.	T.	
20	SUMATRA	S.	984	Hong Kong	Seized	—	Sunk by gunfire by H.M.S. on 20th. Subsequently salved by Japanese
21	BENMACDHUI ...	S.	6,869	53°40'N. 00°30'E.	Mine	—	
23	SHUNTIEN* ...	S.	3,059	32°06'N. 24°46'E.	S.M.	T.	
24	MARGARET ...	M.	248	Kuching, N. Borneo	Seized	—	
24	REJANG	M.	288	Kuching, N. Borneo	Seized	—	
24	GLADYS	S.	358	Kuching, N. Borneo	Seized	—	
24	KIM CHIN SENG ...	Motor Lighter	165	Kuching, N. Borneo	Seized	—	
24	PHENIX*	S. Tank	5,907	Haifa Harbour	Mine	—	
24	STANMOUNT ...	S. Tank	4,468	350° 1m. from No. 6 Buoy, Yarmouth	Mine	—	
24	MERCHANT	S.	4,615	354° 1¼m. from No. 6 Buoy, Yarmouth	Mine	—	
24	FORAFRIC	M.	3,475	In Celebes Sea, S. of Philippine Is.	A.C.	B.	
25	APOEY	S.	2,790	Hong Kong	Scuttled	—	

Date	Name	Type	Gross tons	Position	Cause of loss	How lost	Remarks
DECEMBER, 1941—(Contd.)							
25	Ariadne Moller	S.	1,840	Hong Kong	Scuttled	—	
25	Chengtu	S.	2,219	Hong Kong	Scuttled	—	Salved by Japanese
25	Ethel Moller ...	Salvage Vessel	912	Hong Kong	Scuttled	—	Salved by Japanese
25	Fausang	S.	2,256	Hong Kong	Scuttled	—	
25	Hinsang	M.	4,644	Hong Kong	Scuttled	—	Salved by Japanese
25	Kanchow	S.	2,001	Hong Kong	Scuttled	—	
25	Josephine Moller	Tug	1,274	Hong Kong	Scuttled	—	
25	Kathleen Moller	Salvage Vessel	1,487	Hong Kong	Scuttled	—	
25	Joan Moller ...	S.	2,232	Hong Kong	Scuttled	—	Salved by Japanese
25	Ming Sang ...	S.	3,420	Hong Kong	Scuttled	—	Salved by Japanese
25	Shrivati	M.	389	Hong Kong	Scuttled	—	
25	Shun Chih ...	S.	1,881	Hong Kong	Scuttled	—	
25	Hsin Fuhle ...	Tug	184	Hong Kong	Scuttled	—	
25	Patricia Moller*	Tug	390	Hong Kong	Scuttled	—	
25	Gertrude Moller*	Tug	92	Hong Kong	Scuttled	—	
25	Shinhwa	S.	1,460	Off Hong Kong	Captured	—	
25	Cormead	S.	2,848	350° 3m. from No. 5 Buoy, Lowestoft	Mine	—	Sank on 26th in position 52°25'N. 02°13'E.
25	Yat Shing	S.	2,284	Hong Kong	Scuttled		
26	Tantalus	M.	7,724	Off Manila	A.C.	—	
27	J. B. Paddon ...	S.	570	53°55'N. 00°16'E.	A.C.	B.	
28	Volo	S.	1,587	31°45'N. 26°48'E.	S.M.	T.	
28	Kaiping	S.	2,563	Manila Bay	A.C.	—	
28	Hai Kwang ...	M. Tank	905	Manila Bay	A.C.	—	
28	Seistan	S.	2,455	Manila Bay	A.C.	—	
About 29	Subok	M.	148	Labuan	Seized	—	
About 29	Jitra	M.	122	Labuan	Seized	—	
29	Henry Keswick ...	Tug	671	Corregidor, Philippines	C.U.	—	
31	Cardita	M. Tank	8,237	59°18'N. 12°50'W.	S.M.	T.	Sank 3rd Jan., 1942
	Total ... 120		270,873				
JANUARY, 1942							
1	Penrhos	S.	187	243° 1m. from N. Constable Buoy, Liverpool Bay (Approx.)	Mine	—	
1	Kentwood... ...	S.	2,180	Nr. 56 Buoy, Hearty Knoll Channel	Mine	—	Sank in tow 2 cables N.E. of 56 Buoy, off Yarmouth
2	Waziristan ...	S.	5,135	74°09'N. 19°10'E.	S.M.*	—	
3	Corfen	S.	1,848	1¾m. N.E. of B.8 Buoy, Barrow Deep	Mine	—	Sank in tow in position 51°50'N. 01° 27'E.
3	Robert	S.	1,272	160° 1.5m. from 54 E. Buoy, off Lowestoft	Mine	—	Sank on 4th in position 52°17'N. 02° 00'E.
4	Kwangtung ...	S.	2,626	09°12'S. 111°10'E.	S.M.	G.	
6	Norwich Trader...	S.	217	51°55'N. 01°32'E.	Mine*	—	
10	Baron Erskine ...	S.	3,657	59°15'N. 18°30'W.	S.M.*	—	
11	Cyclops	S.	9,076	41°51'N. 63°48'W.	S.M.	T.	
11	Wulin	M.	2,515	In Muar River, Johore State	A.C.	B.	
11	Baynain	S.	659	Off Tarakan, Dutch East Indies	C.U.	—	Sunk, seized or captured
About 11	Borderdene ...	S.	122	51°18'N. 03°03'W. (Approx.)	Mine	—	
12	Quickstep... ...	S.	2,722	51°46'N. 01°26'E.	Mine	—	
12	Caledonian Monarch	S.	5,851	57°N. 26°W. (Approx.)	S.M.*	—	
13	Lerwick	S.	5,626	54°26'N. 00°24'W.	A.C.	B.	

Date	Name	Type	Gross tons	Position	Cause of loss	How lost	Remarks
JANUARY, 1942—*(Contd.)*							
14	JALARAJAN ...	S.	5,102	00°12′S. 97°00′E.	S.M.	T.	
14	EMPIRE SURF ...	S.	6,641	58°42′N. 19°16′W.	S.M.	T.	
14	DAYROSE ...	S.	4,113	46°32′N. 53°00′W.	S.M.	T.	
14	MERCIA	Tug	94	51°31′N. 02°47′W.	Mine	—	
15	COIMBRA	S. Tank	6,768	40°25′N. 72°21′W.	S.M.	T.	
15	DIALA	M. Tank	8,106	44°50′N. 46°50′W.	S.M.	T.	Derelict, last seen in position 47°N. 37°W. on 19th March
15	EMPIRE BAY ...	S.	2,824	Tees Bay	A.C.	B.	
17	CULEBRA	S.	3,044	40°N. 50°W. (Est.)	S.M.	T. & G.	
19	LADY HAWKINS ...	S.	7,989	35°00′N. 72°30′W. (Approx.)	S.M.	T.	
19	H.K.D.	S.B.	65	130° ½m. from Van Meerlant Wreck Buoy, Thames Estuary	Mine	—	
22	ATHELCROWN ...	M. Tank	11,999	45°06′N. 40°56′W.	S.M.	T.	
22	CHAK-SANG... ...	S.	2,358	15°42′N. 95°02′E.	S.M.	G.	
23	THIRLBY	S.	4,887	43°20′N. 66°15′W. (Approx.)	S.M.	T.	
24	EMPIRE WILDEBEESTE	S.	5,631	39°30′N. 59°54′W.	S.M.	T.	
24	EMPIRE GEM ...	M. Tank	8,139	35°06′N. 74°58′W.	S.M.	T.	Sank in position 35°02′N. 75°33′W. (Approx.)
25	SWYNFLEET ...	S.	1,168	51°55′N. 01°19′E.	Mine	—	
26	TRAVELLER... ...	S.	3,963	40°N. 61°45′W. (Est.)	S.M.*	—	
26	REFAST	S. Tank	5,189	42°41′N. 53°02′W.	S.M.	T.	
29	GIANG SENG ...	S.	1,811	Dutch East Indies	C.U.	—	Sunk, seized or captured
30	JALATARANG ...	S.	2,498	12°59′N. 81°00′E.	S.M.	T. & G.	
30	JALAPALAKA ...	S.	4,215	13°00′N. 81°08′E.	S.M.	G.	
31	SAN ARCADIO ...	M. Tank	7,419	38°10′N. 63°50′W.	S.M.	T. & G.	
	Total ... 37		147,716				
FEBRUARY, 1942							
1	TACOMA STAR ...	S.	7,924	37°33′N. 69°21′W.	S.M.	T.	
3	NORAH MOLLER ...	M.	4,433	Banka Strait	A.C.	B.	
3	KATONG	S.	1,461	4m. from Bar L.V., Palembang	A.C.	G.	
3	LOCH RANZA ...	S.	4,958	00°37′N. 104°14′E.	A.C.	B.	
3	PINNA*	S. Tank	6,121	00°52′S. 104°19′E.	A.C.	B.	Again attacked on 4th and sunk
4	MONTROLITE ...	M. Tank	11,309	35°14′N. 60°05′W.	S.M.	T.	
4	SILVERAY	M.	4,535	43°54′N. 64°16′W.	S.M.	T.	
5	CORLAND	S.	3,431	53°43′N. 00°36′E.	A.C.	B.	
5	EMPRESS OF ASIA...	S.	16,909	Approaches to Singapore	A.C.	B.	
6	OPAWA	M.	10,354	38°21′N. 61°13′W.	S.M.*	—	
7	EMPIRE SUN ...	S.	6,952	44°07′N. 64°16′W.	S.M.	T.	
8	OCEAN VENTURE ...	S.	7,174	37°05′N. 74°46′W.	S.M.	T.	
9	EMPIRE FUSILIER ...	S.	5,408	44°45′N. 47°25′W.	S.M.	T.	
10	VICTOLITE	M. Tank	11,410	36°12′N. 67°14′W.	S.M.	T.	
11	WANYUAN* ...	S.	674	Singapore	Seized	—	Previously immobilised
13	DERRYMORE ...	M.	4,799	05°18′S. 106°20′E.	S.M.	T.	
13	SUBADAR	S.	5,424	Banka Strait	A.C.	B.	
13	HOSANG	S.	5,698	Palembang	Seized	—	Damaged by A.C.
14	BIELA	S.	5,298	42°55′N. 45°40′W.	S.M.	T.	
14	KAMUNING... ...	S.	2,076	08°35′N. 81°44′E.	S.M.	T. & G.	
14	CLAN CHATTAN ...	S.	7,262	35°01′N. 20°11′E.	A.C.	B.	
14	ROWALLAN CASTLE	M.	7,798	34°54′N. 19°40′E.	A.C.	B.	Sunk by H.M.S.

Date	Name	Type	Gross tons	Position	Cause of loss	How lost	Remarks
FEBRUARY, 1942—(Contd.)							
15	REDANG	S.	531	Far Eastern Waters	C.U.	—	Sunk, seized or cap-tured
15	JOHANNE JUSTESEN	S.	4,681	09°04′N. 75°58′E.	S.M.	T.	
15	EMPIRE SPRING ...	M.	6,946	42°N. 55°W. (Approx.)	S.M.*	—	
15	RHU*	M.	254	Singapore	Seized	—	
16	BAGAN (Ferry) ...	S.	244	Palembang	Scuttled	—	
16	SOMME	S.	5,265	40°N. 55°W. (Approx.)	S.M.	T.	
16	ORANJESTAD ...	S. Tank	2,396	At anchor off San Nicholas, Aruba	S.M.	T.	
16	SAN NICOLAS ...	S. Tank	2,391	25m. S.W. of Punta Macolla, Gulf of Venezuela	S.M.	T.	
16	TIA JUANA ...	S. Tank	2,395	25m. S.W. of Punta Macolla, Gulf of Venezuela	S.M.	T.	
16	BRUNEI	M.	101	Singapore	Scuttled	—	
16	TALTHYBIUS ...	S.	10,254	Singapore	Seized	—	Previously damaged by A.C. on 3rd
17	TATUNG	S.	1,560	Tanjong Batoe	Seized	—	Previously immobi-lised
19	EMPIRE SEAL ...	M.	7,965	43°14′N. 64°45′W.	S.M.	T.	
19	EMPIRE COMET ...	M.	6,914	58°15′N. 17°10′W.	S.M.*	—	
19	BRITISH MOTORIST*	M. Tank	6,891	Port Darwin	A.C.	B.	
19	ZEALANDIA ...	S.	6,683	Port Darwin	A.C.	B.	
19	NEPTUNA*	M.	5,952	Port Darwin	A.C.	B.	
20	BHIMA	M.	5,280	07°47′N. 73°31′E.	S.M.	T.	
20	SCOTTISH STAR ...	S.	7,224	13°24′N. 49°36′W.	S.M.	T.	
20	KOOLAMA	M.	4,068.	Off Wyndham, W. Australia	A.C.	B.	
21	CIRCE SHELL* ...	M. Tank	8,207	11°03′N. 62°03′W.	S.M.	T. & G.	
22	GEORGE L. TORIAN	S.	1,754	09°13′N. 59°04′W.	S.M.	T.	
22	KARS	M. Tank	8,888	44°15′N. 63°25′W.	S.M.	T.	
22	ADELLEN* ...	M. Tank	7,984	49°20′N. 38°15′W.	S.M.	T.	
22	HANNE	S.	1,360	31°57′N. 25°26′E.	A.C.	B.	
22	BINTANG ...	M.	2,825	31°50′N. 26°01′E.	A.C.	B.	
23	LENNOX	S.	1,904	09°15′N. 58°30′W.	S.M.	T.	
23	EMPIRE HAIL ...	S.	7,005	44°48′N. 40°21′W.	S.M.	T.	
24	EMPIRE CELT ...	S. Tank	8,032	43°50′N. 43°38′W.	S.M.	T.	Remained afloat. Date and position of sinking uncer-tain
24	ANADARA	M. Tank	8,009	43°45′N. 42°15′W. (Est.)	S.M.	T.	
24	INVERARDER* ...	S. Tank	5,578	44°34′N. 42°37′W.	S.M.	T.	
24	WHITE CREST ...	S.	4,365	43°45′N. 42°15′W. (Approx.)	S.M.*	—	
24	LA CARRIERE* ...	S. Tank	5,685	16°53′N. 67°05′W.	S.M.	T.	Sank on 25th after second attack
27	MACGREGOR ...	S.	2,498	19°50′N. 69°40′W. (Approx.)	S.M.	G.	
27	NAM YONG... ...	S.	1,345	Indian Ocean	C.U.	—	Sunk or captured
27	FERNSIDE	S.	269	Off Banff*	A.C.*	—	
28	CITY OF MANCHESTER	S.	8,917	08°16′S. 108°52′E.	S.M.	T. & G.	
	Total ... 59		314,028				
MARCH, 1942							
1	CARPERBY	S.	4,890	39°57′N. 55°40′W.	S.M.	T.	
1	AUDACITY ...	S. Tank	589	53°33′N. 00°22′E.	Mine	—	
1	POLGARTH	S.	794	2m. S.S.W. of Alde-burgh Lt. Float	Mine	—	

Date	Name	Type	Gross tons	Position	Cause of loss	How lost	Remarks
MARCH, 1942—*(Contd.)*							
2	SHINYU	S.	1,615	Sourabaya	C.U.	—	
2	KULIT	M. Tank	213	Sumatra	C.U.	—	
2	SISUNTHON NAWA...	S.	3,286	Sourabaya	C.U.	—	Sunk or seized
2	RIBOT	M. Tank	237	Sumatra	C.U.	—	
2	TAIYUAN	S.	2,994	Sourabaya	C.U.	—	
3	HELENUS ...	S.	7,366	06°01′N. 12°02′W.	S.M.	T.	
3	RASA	M.	217	D.E.I. Waters	C.U.	—	
3	RIMAU	M.	214	D.E.I. Waters	C.U.	—	
3	PETALING	M.	168	D.E.I. Waters	C.U.	—	
3	PANDAI	M.	166	D.E.I. Waters	C.U.	—	Sunk, seized or captured
3	RIMBA	M.	139	D.E.I. Waters	C.U.	—	
3	INTAN	M.	117	D.E.I. Waters	C.U.	—	
3	RENGAM	M.	185	D.E.I. Waters	C.U.	—	
3	PHASIANELLA ...	M. Tank	855	Batavia	Scuttled	—	
4	FRUMENTON ...	S.	6,675	170° ½m. from 54 E. Buoy, off Orfordness	Mine	—	
5	IPOH	S.	1,279	Batavia	C.U.	—	Sunk or seized
5	KINTA	S.	1,220	Batavia	C.U.	—	
5	AUBY	S.	636	D.E.I. Waters	C.U.	—	Sunk, seized or captured
5	BENMOHR	S.	5,920	06°05′N. 14°15′W.	S.M.	T.	
5	AMPANG	S.	213	D.E.I. Waters	C.U.	—	Sunk, seized or captured
5	RAWANG	S.	198	Malayan Waters	Scuttled	—	Salved by Japanese
5	RANTAU	M.	197	Banka Strait	C.U.	—	
5	RELAU	M.	223	Banka Strait	C.U.	—	Sunk or captured
5	ROMPIN	M.	189	Banka Strait	C.U.	—	
6	MELPOMENE ...	S. Tank	7,011	23°35′N. 62°39′W.	S.M.	T.	
7	CHAUK	S.	419	Rangoon	Scuttled	—	
7	UNIWALECO ...	S. Tank	9,755	13°23′N. 62°04′W.	S.M.	T.	
7	MINBU	S.	139	Rangoon	Scuttled	—	
7	LANYWA	S.	52	Bassein Creek, Burma	C.U.	—	
7	NYOUNGHLA ...	S.	382	Rangoon	Scuttled	—	
7	SADAING	Launch	266	Rangoon	Scuttled	—	
8	HENGIST	S.	984	59°31′N. 10°15′W.	S.M.	T.	
8	BALUCHISTAN ...	S.	6,992	04°13′N. 08°32′W.	S.M.	T. & G.	
10	LAKSHIMI GOVINDA	S.V.	235	13°22′N. 87°27′E.	S.M.	G.	
11	CHILKA	S.	4,360	Indian Ocean, Off Padang, Sumatra	S.M.	G.	
11	HORSEFERRY ...	S.	951	52°52′N. 02°10′E.	E-Boat	T.	
13	DAYTONIAN ...	S.	6,434	26°33′N. 74°43′W.	S.M.	T. & G.	
14	BRITISH RESOURCE	M. Tank	7,209	36°04′N. 65°38′W.	S.M.	T.	
15	MANAQUI	S.	2,802	17°15′N. 61°00′W.	S.M.*	—	
15	SARNIADOC ...	S.	1,940	15°45′N. 65°00′W. (Approx.)	S.M.*	—	
15	ATHELQUEEN ...	M. Tank	8,780	26°50′N. 75°40′W.	S.M.	T. & G.	
15	DAGO	S.	1,757	39°19′N. 09°26′W.	A.C.	B.	
16	BARON NEWLANDS	S.	3,386	04°35′N. 08°32′W.	S.M.	T.	
16	STANGARTH... ...	S.	5,966	22°N. 65°W. (Approx.)	S.M.*	—	
16	CRESSDENE ...	S.	4,270	52°08′N. 01°52′E.	Mine	—	
17	ILE DE BATZ ...	S.	5,755	04°04′N. 08°04′W.	S.M.	T.	
17	SAN DEMETRIO ...	M. Tank	8,073	37°03′N. 73°50′W.	S.M.	T.	
17	SCOTTISH PRINCE ...	M.	4,917	04°10′N. 08°00′W.	S.M.	T.	
17	ALLENDE	S.	5,081	04°00′N. 07°44′W. (Approx.)	S.M.	T.	
22	THURSOBANK ...	S.	5,575	38°05′N. 68°30′W.	S.M.	T.	
23	PEDER BOGEN* ...	S. Tank	9,741	24°41′N. 57°44′W.	S.M.	T.	
23	BRITISH PRUDENCE*	M. Tank	8,620	45°28′N. 56°13′W.	S.M.	T.	

Date	Name	Type	Gross tons	Position	Cause of loss	How lost	Remarks
MARCH, 1942—(Contd.)							
23	Empire Steel ...	M. Tank	8,138	37°45′N. 63°17′W.	S.M.	T. & G.	
23	Clan Campbell ...	S.	7,255	245° 8m. from Filfola Is., Nr. Malta	A.C.	B.	
25	Narragansett ...	M. Tank	10,389	34°46′N. 67°40′W.	S.M.	T.	
25	Tredinnick ...	S.	4,589	27°15′N. 49°15′W. (Approx.)	S.M.*	—	
26	Pampas	M.	5,415	Malta	A.C.	B.	
28	Empire Ranger ...	S.	7,008	72°10′N. 30°00′E.	A.C.	B.	
28	Wellpark	S.	4,649	25°S. 10°W. (Est.)	Raider	—	
29	Hertford	S.	10,923	40°50′N. 63°31′W.	S.M.	T.	
30	Muncaster Castle	M.	5,853	02°02′N. 12°02′W.	S.M.	T.	
30	Induna	S.	5,086	70°55′N. 37°18′E.	S.M.	T.	
31	Eastmoor	S.	5,812	37°33′N. 68°18′W.	S.M.	T.	
ˋ31	San Gerardo* ...	S. Tank	12,915	36°N. 67°W. (Approx.)	S.M.	T.	
	Total ... 67		250,679				
APRIL, 1942							
1	Rio Blanco ...	S.	4,086	35°16′N. 74°18′W.	S.M.	T.	
1	Willesden ...	S.	4,563	16°S. 16°W. (Est.)	Raider	—	
1	Loch Don	S.	5,249	37°05′N. 61°40′W.	S.M.	T.	
1	Robert W. Pomeroy	S.	1,750	53°10′N. 01°10′E.	Mine	—	
2	Clan Ross... ...	S.	5,897	15°58′N. 68°24′E.	S.M.	T.	
2	Glenshiel ...	M.	9,415	01°00′S. 78°11′E.	S.M.	T.	
3	New Westminster City	S.	4,747	Murmansk	A.C.	B.	
3	Empire Starlight	S.	6,850	Murmansk Harbour	A.C.	B.	Bombed again on 15th and repeatedly thereafter until 1st June, when ship became a total loss
5	Harpasa	S.	5,082	19°19′N. 85°46′E.	A.C.	B.	
6	Silksworth ...	S.	4,921	Off Puri, Bay of Bengal	Warship	—	
6	Autolycus ...	S.	7,621	19°40′N. 86°50′E.	Warship	—	
6	Dardanus	S.	7,726	16°00′N. 82°20′E.	Warship	—	
6	Gandara	S.	5,281	16°00′N. 82°20′E.	Warship	—	
6	Ganges	S.	6,246	17°48′N. 84°09′E.	Warship	—	
6	Malda	S.	9,066	19°45′N. 86°27′E.	Warship	—	
6	Indora	S.	6,622	Bay of Bengal	Warship	—	
6	Taksang	S.	3,471	17°52′N. 83°40′E.	Warship	—	
6	Shinkuang ...	S.	2,441	Bay of Bengal	Warship	—	
6	Sinkiang	S.	2,646	Bay of Bengal	A.C.	B.	
7	Fultala	M.	5,051	06°52′N. 76°54′E.	S.M.	T.	
7	British Splendour	M. Tank	7,138	35°07′N. 75°19′W.	S.M.	T.	
7	Bahadur	S.	5,424	19°44′N. 68°28′E.	S.M.	T. & G.	
9	Yu Sang	S.	3,357	Marivales Harbour, Philippine Is.	A.C.	B.	
9	British Sergeant	S. Tank	5,868	08°00′N. 81°38′E.	A.C.	B.	
9	Athelstane* ...	S. Tank	5,571	07°30′N. 81°56′E.	A.C.	B.	
9	Sagaing	S.	7,958	Trincomalee	A.C.*	—	
10	Kirkpool	S.	4,842	33°S. 07°W. (Approx.)	Raider	—	
10	San Delfino ...	M. Tank	8,072	35°35′N. 75°06′W.	S.M.	T.	
10	Empire Prairie ...	S.	7,010	35°N. 60°W. (Approx.)	S.M.*	—	
11	Ulysses	S.	14,647	34°23′N. 75°35′W.	S.M.	T.	
11	Empire Cowper ...	S.	7,164	71°01′N. 36°00′E.	A.C.	B.	
13	Empire Progress	S.	5,249	40°29′N. 52°35′W.	S.M.	T.	
13	Harpalion... ...	S.	5,486	73°33′N. 27°19′E.	A.C.	B.	
14	Empire Amethyst	S. Tank	8,032	16°N. 72°W. (Approx.)	S.M.*	—	

Date	Name	Type	Gross tons	Position	Cause of loss	How lost	Remarks
APRIL, 1942—(Contd.)							
14	EMPIRE THRUSH ...	S.	6,160	35°08'N. 75°18'W.	S.M.	T.	
14	LANCASTER CASTLE	S.	5,172	Anchored in River at Murmansk	A.C.	B.	
16	EMPIRE HOWARD ...	S.	6,985	73°48'N. 21°32'E.	S.M.	T.	
16	CASPIA	S. Tank	6,018	10m. S. of Beirut	S.M.	T.	
18	MEGOHM	Dredger	124	River Irrawaddy	C.U.	—	
19	PATELLA* ...	M. Tank	7,468	23°S. 20°W. (Approx.)	Raider	—	
20	EMPIRE DRYDEN ...	S.	7,164	34°21'N. 69°00'W.	S.M.	T.	
20	HARPAGON	S.	5,719	34°35'N. 65°50'W.	S.M.	T.	
20	VINELAND	S.	5,587	23°05'N. 72°20'W.	S.M.	T.	
20	PLAWSWORTH ...	S.	1,489	½m. S. of Aldeburgh Buoy	Mine	—	
22	DERRYHEEN ...	S.	7,217	31°20'N. 70°55'W.	S.M.	T.	
23	KIRKLAND	S.	1,361	31°51'N. 26°37'E.	S.M.	T.	
23	JERSEY	M.	4,986	Suez	Mine	—	
23	CHATWOOD ...	S.	2,768	53°19'N. 01°00'E.	Mine	—	
24	EMPIRE DRUM ...	M.	7,244	37°00'N. 69°15'W.	S.M.	T.	
25	MODESTA	S.	3,849	33°40'N. 63°10'W. (Approx.)	S.M.	T.	
29	ATHELEMPRESS* ...	M. Tank	8,941	13°21'N. 56°15'W.	S.M.	T. & G.	
29	ALLIANCE*	Tug	81	022° 9.5 cables from Famagusta Lt., off Cyprus	Mine	—	
	Total ... 52		292,882				
MAY, 1942							
About 1	MILDRED PAULINE	Sch.	300	Off Nova Scotia	S.M.	G.	
1	JAMES E. NEWSOM...	Sch.	671	35°50'N. 59°40'W.	S.M.	G.	
2	UNIQUE	S.B.	51	51°38'N. 01°00'E.	Mine	—	
2	CAPE CORSO ...	S.	3,807	73°02'N. 19°46'E.	A.C.	T.	
2	BOTAVON ...	S.	5,848	73°02'N. 19°46'E.	A.C.	T.	
2	JUTLAND	S.	6,153	73°02'N. 19°46'E.	A.C.	T.	
2	CALDERON	S.	1,374	31°05'N. 29°07'E.	A.C.	B.	
3	BRITISH WORKMAN	S. Tank	6,994	44°07'N. 51°53'W.	S.M.	T.	
3	OCEAN VENUS ...	S.	7,174	28°23'N. 80°21'W.	S.M.	T.	
4	FLORENCE M. DOUGLAS	Sch.	119	07°55'N. 58°10'W.	S.M.	G.	
5	KHODAUNG ...	M. Tank	254	River Irrawaddy	C.U.	—	Destroyed by fire
5	STANBANK	S.	5,966	34°55'N. 61°47'W.	S.M.	T.	
5	LADY DRAKE ...	S.	7,985	35°43'N. 64°43'W.	S.M.	T.	
6	ROYAL LADY ...	M.	195	Gozo, Mediterranean	A.C.	B.	
6	EMPIRE BUFFALO ...	S.	6,404	19°14'N. 82°34'W.	S.M.	T.	
8	MONT LOUIS ...	S.	1,905	08°23'N. 58°44'W.	S.M.	T.	
9	CALGAROLITE ...	M. Tank	11,941	19°24'N. 82°30'W.	S.M.	T. & G.	
10	CLAN SKENE ...	S.	5,214	31°43'N. 70°43'W.	S.M.	T.	
10	KITTY'S BROOK ...	S.	4,031	42°56'N. 63°59'W.	S.M.	T.	
10	NANKIN	S.	7,131	26°43'S. 89°56'E.	Raider	—	Taken in prize
10	RAMB IV (Hospital Ship)	M.	3,676	31°17'N. 29°23'E.	A.C.	B.	
11	EMPIRE DELL ...	S.	7,065	53°00'N. 29°57'W.	S.M.	T.	
11	CAPE OF GOOD HOPE	M.	4,963	22°48'N. 58°43'W.	S.M.	T. & G.	
12	CRISTALES	S.	5,389	52°55'N. 29°50'W.	S.M.	T.	
12	LLANOVER	S.	4,959	52°50'N. 29°04'W.	S.M.	T.	
12	NICOYA	S.	5,364	49°19'N. 64°51'W.	S.M.	T.	
12	DENPARK	S.	3,491	22°28'N. 28°10'W.	S.M.	T.	
13	BATNA	S.	4,399	52°09'N. 33°56'W.	S.M.	T.	
13	BRITISH COLONY* ...	S. Tank	6,917	13°12'N. 58°10'W.	S.M.	T.	
13	CITY OF MELBOURNE	S.	6,630	15°00'N. 54°40'W.	S.M.	T.	

Date	Name	Type	Gross tons	Position	Cause of loss	How lost	Remarks
MAY, 1942—*(Contd.)*							
15	SOUDAN	S.	6,677	36°10′S. 20°22′E.	Mine	—	
16	ARDUITY ...	M.	304	53°22′N. 00°30′E.	Mine	—	
17	SAN VICTORIO ...	M. Tank	8,136	11°40′N. 62°33′W.	S.M.	T.	
17	PEISANDER. ...	M.	6,225	37°24′N. 65°38′W.	S.M.	T.	
17	FORT QU'APPELLE...	S.	7,121	39°50′N. 63°30′W.	S.M.	T.	
17	BARRDALE	S.	5,072	15°15′N. 52°27′W.	S.M.	T.	
20	TORONDOC	S.	1,927	14°45′N. 62°15′W. (Est.)	S.M.*	—	
20	EOCENE	S. Tank	4,216	31°56′N. 25°14′E.	S.M.	T.	
20	DARINA	M. Tank	8,113	29°17′N. 54°25′W.	S.M.	T.	
21	NEW BRUNSWICK ...	S.	6,529	36°53′N. 22°55′W.	S.M.	T.	
21	TROISDOC	S.	1,925	18°15′N. 79°20′W.	S.M.	T.	
22	FRANK B. BAIRD...	S.	1,748	28°03′N. 58°50′W.	S.M.	G.	
23	MARGOT	S.	4,545	39°N. 68°W. (Approx.)	S.M.	T.	
24	ZURICHMOOR ...	S.	4,455	39°30′N. 66°00′W.	S.M.*	—	
27	ATHELKNIGHT ...	M. Tank	8,940	27°50′N. 46°00′W.	S.M.	T. & G.	
27	EMPIRE PURCELL ...	S.	7,049	74°00′N. 26°08′E.	A.C.	B.	
27	EMPIRE LAWRENCE	S.	7,457	74°00′N. 25°10′E. (Approx.)	A.C.	B.	
27	LOWTHER CASTLE...	S.	5,171	60m. E.S.E. of Bear Is. (Approx.)	A.C.	T.	
28	WESTERN-HEAD ...	S.	2,599	19°57′N. 74°18′W.	S.M.	T.	
28	MENTOR	S.	7,383	24°11′N. 87°02′W.	S.M.	T.	
28	NORMAN PRINCE ...	S.	1,913	14°40′N. 62°15′W.	S.M.	T.	
28	YORKMOOR ...	S.	4,457	29°30′N. 72°29′W.	S.M.	G.	
29	CHARLBURY ...	S.	4,836	06°22′S. 29°44′W.	S.M.	T. & G.	
29	ALLISTER ...	S.	1,597	18°23′N. 81°13′W.	S.M.	T.	
30	LIVERPOOL PACKET	S.	1,188	43°20′N. 66°20′W. (Approx.)	S.M.	T.	
31	FRED W. GREEN ... (Derrick Ship)	S.	2,292	30°20′N. 62°00′W.	S.M.	T.	
	Total ... 56		258,245				
JUNE, 1942							
1	WESTMORELAND ...	S.	8,967	35°55′N. 63°35′W.	S.M.	T.	
2	MATTAWIN	M.	6,919	40°14′N. 66°01′W.	S.M.	T.	
2	CITY OF BREMEN ...	S.	903	49°57′N. 11°35′W.	A.C.	B.	
3	LILLIAN	Sch.	80	12°25′N. 59°30′W.	S.M.	G.	
3	IRON CHIEFTAIN ...	S.	4,812	33°55′S. 151°50′E.	S.M.	T.	
4	IRON CROWN ...	S.	3,353	38°17′S. 149°44′E.	S.M.	T.	
4	GEMSTONE	S.	4,986	01°52′N. 26°38′W.	Raider	—	
5	ELYSIA	S.	6,757	27°33′S. 37°05′E.	Raider	T.	Sank on 9th
7	CHILE	M.	6,956	04°17′N. 13°48′W.	S.M.	T.	
8	ROSENBORG ...	S.	1,512	18°47′N. 85°05′W.	S.M.	G.	
8	KING LUD	M.	5,224	20°S. 40°E. (Approx.)	S.M.*	—	
10	EMPIRE CLOUGH ...	S.	6,147	51°50′N. 35°00′W. (Approx.)	S.M.	T.	
10	RAMSAY	S.	4,855	51°53′N. 34°59′W.	S.M.	T.	
10	ARDENVOHR ...	M.	5,025	12°45′N. 80°20′W.	S.M.	T.	
10	SURREY	S.	8,581	12°45′N. 80°20′W.	S.M.	T.	
10	HAVRE	S.	2,073	Between Alexandria and Matruh	S.M.	T.	
10	PORT MONTREAL ...	M.	5,882	12°17′N. 80°20′W.	S.M.	T.	
11	GEO. H. JONES ...	S. Tank	6,914	45°40′N. 22°40′W.	S.M.	T.	
11	PONTYPRIDD ...	S.	4,458	49°50′N. 41°37′W.	S.M.	T.	
11	FORT GOOD HOPE...	S.	7,130	10°19′N. 80°16′W.	S.M.	T.	
11	MAHRONDA ...	S.	7,926	14°37′S. 40°58′E.	S.M.	T.	
11	LYLEPARK	S.	5,186	14°S. 10°W. (Approx.)	Raider	—	
12	DARTFORD	S.	4,093	49°19′N. 41°33′W.	S.M.	T.	
12	CLIFTON HALL ...	M.	5,063	16°25′S. 40°10′E.	S.M.	T.	
12	HARDWICKE GRANGE	S.	9,005	25°45′N. 65°45′W.	S.M.	T.	

Date	Name	Type	Gross tons	Position	Cause of loss	How lost	Remarks
JUNE, 1942—(Contd.)							
13	CLAN MACQUARRIE	S.	6,471	05°30′N. 23°30′W.	S.M.	T. & G.	
14	DUTCH PRINCESS ...	Sch.	125	13°46′N. 60°06′W.	S.M.	G.	
14	BHUTAN	S.	6,104	34°00′N. 23°40′E. (Approx.)	A.C.	B.	
14	ETRIB	S.	1,943	43°18′N. 17°38′W.	S.M.	T.	
14	PELAYO	M.	1,346	43°18′N. 17°38′W.	S.M.	T.	
15	CITY OF OXFORD ...	S.	2,759	43°32′N. 18°12′W.	S.M.	T.	
15	THURSO	S.	2,436	43°41′N. 18°02′W.	S.M.	T.	
15	KENTUCKY* ...	S. Tank	9,308	36°37′N. 12°10′E.	A.C.	B.	
15	BURDWAN ...	S.	6,069	35m. S. of Pantellaria Island	A.C.	B.	
16	PORT NICHOLSON ...	S.	8,402	42°11′N. 69°25′W.	S.M.	T.	
17	MACDHUI	M.	4,561	Port Moresby	A.C.	—	Again attacked on 18th and capsized. Later became total loss
18	MOTOREX	M. Tank	1,958	10°10′N. 81°30′W.	S.M.	T. & G.	
19	DALRIADA* ...	S.	973	Edinburgh Channel, Thames Estuary	Mine	—	
20	AFON DULAIS ...	S.	988	50°04′N. 00°23′W.	Mine	—	
24	WILLIMANTIC ...	S.	4,558	25°55′N. 51°58′W.	S.M.	G.	
25	ANGLO CANADIAN ...	M.	5,268	25°12′N. 55°31′W.	S.M.	T.	
26	PUTNEY HILL ...	M.	5,216	24°20′N. 63°16′W.	S.M.	T. & G.	
28	MONA MARIE ...	Sch.	126	12°22′N. 60°10′W.	S.M.	—	
28	QUEEN VICTORIA ...	M.	4,937	21°15′S. 40°30′E. (Approx.)	S.M.*	—	
28	ZEALAND ...	S.	1,433	32°27′N. 34°43′E.	S.M.	T.	
29	EMPIRE MICA ...	S. Tank	8,032	29°25′N. 85°17′W.	S.M.	T.	
29	WAIWERA	M.	12,435	45°49′N. 34°29′W.	S.M.	T.	
30	AIRCREST	S.	5,237	31°49′N. 34°34′E.	A.C.	T.	
	Total ... 48		233,492				
JULY, 1942							
1	MARILYSE MOLLER	S.	786	31°22′N. 33°44′E.	S.M.	T.	
4	NAVARINO	S.	4,841	75°57′N. 27°14′E.	A.C.	T.	
5	BOLTON CASTLE ...	S.	5,203	76°40′N. 36°30′E.	A.C.	B.	
5	RIVER AFTON ...	S.	5,479	75°57′N. 43°00′E.	S.M.	T.	
5	AVILA STAR ...	S.	14,443	38°04′N. 22°46′W.	S.M.	T.	
5	EARLSTON	S.	7,195	74°54′N. 37°40′E.	S.M.	T.	
5	ZAAFARAN* ... (Rescue Ship)	S.	1,559	75°05′N. 43°40′E.	A.C.	B.	
5	EMPIRE BYRON ...	S.	6,645	76°18′N. 33°30′E.	S.M.	T.	
6	MUNDRA	S.	7,341	28°45′S. 32°20′E.	S.M.	T. & G.	
6	DINARIC	S.	2,555	49°30′N. 66°30′W.	S.M.	T.	Sank on 9th in position 49°28′N. 65°38′W.
7	UMTATA	S.	8,141	25°35′N. 80°02′W.	S.M.*	—	
7	HARTLEBURY ...	S.	5,082	72°30′N. 52°00′E. (Approx.)	S.M.	T.	
8	HARTISMERE ...	S.	5,498	18°00′S. 41°22′E.	S.M.	T. & G.	
9	EMPIRE EXPLORER	S.	5,345	11°40′N. 60°55′W.	S.M.	T. & G.	
9	POMELLA	M. Tank	6,766	50°19′N. 03°00′W.	E-Boat	T.	
9	GRIPFAST* ...	S.	1,109	50°26′N. 02°59′W.	A.C.	B.	
9	CAPE VERDE ...	M.	6,914	11°32′N. 60°17′W.	S.M.	T.	
11	PORT HUNTER ...	S.	8,826	31°N. 24°W. (Approx.)	S.M.	T.	
11	CORTONA	S.	7,093	32°45′N. 24°45′W.	S.M.	T.	
12	SHAFTESBURY ...	S.	4,284	31°42′N. 25°30′W.	S.M.	T.	
12	SIRIS	S.	5,242	31°20′N. 24°48′W.	S.M.	T. & G.	
12	HAURAKI	M.	7,113	17°32′S. 80°25′E.	Raider	—	
13	SITHONIA	S.	6,723	29°N. 25°W. (Approx.)	S.M.	T.	
14	BRITISH YEOMAN*	S. Tank	6,990	26°42′N. 24°20′W.	S.M.	T.	
15	EMPIRE ATTENDANT	S.	7,524	23°48′N. 21°51′W.	S.M.	T.	

Date	Name	Type	Gross tons	Position	Cause of loss	How lost	Remarks
JULY, 1942—(Contd.)							
16	GLOUCESTER CASTLE	S.	8,006	08°S. 01°E. (Est.)	Raider	—	
18	GLACIER	Sch.	130	10°50′N. 58°58′W.	S.M.	G.	
18	COMRADE	Sch.	110	11°20′N. 58°50′W.	S.M.	G.	
19	EMPIRE HAWKSBILL	S.	5,724	42°29′N. 25°26′W.	S.M.	T.	
19	LAVINGTON COURT	S.	5,372	42°38′N. 25°28′W.	S.M.	T.	Foundered in tow 1st August in position 49°40′N. 18° 04′W.
20	FREDERIKA LENSEN	S.	4,367	49°22′N. 65°12′W.	S.M.	T.	
20	INDUS	M.	5,187	26°44′S. 82°50′E.	Raider	—	
21	DONOVANIA ...	M. Tank	8,149	10°56′N. 61°10′W.	S.M.	T.	
23	GARMULA	S.	5,254	05°32′N. 14°45′W.	S.M.	T.	
25	BROOMPARK ...	S.	5,136	49°02′N. 40°26′W.	S.M.	T.	Sank in tow on 1st August in position 47°42′N. 51°55′W.
26	EMPIRE RAINBOW...	M.	6,942	47°08′N. 42°57′W.	S.M.	T.	
27	ELMWOOD	S.	7,167	04°48′N. 22°00′W.	S.M.	T.	
27	WEIRBANK ...	M.	5,150	11°29′N. 58°51′W.	S.M.	T.	
29	PACIFIC PIONEER ...	M.	6,734	43°30′N. 60°35′W.	S.M.	T.	
29	PRESCODOC ...	S.	1,938	08°50′N. 59°05′W.	S.M.	T.	
30	DANMARK	M.	8,391	07°00′N. 24°19′W.	S.M.	T. & G.	
	Total ... 41		232,454				
AUGUST, 1942							
1	CLAN MACNAUGHTON	S.	6,088	11°54′N. 54°25′W.	S.M.	T.	
2	FLORA II	S.	1,218	62°45′N. 19°07′W.	S.M.	T.	
2	TREMINNARD ...	S.	4,694	10°40′N. 57°07′W.	S.M.	T.	
3	TRICULA	M. Tank	6,221	11°35′N. 56°51′W.	S.M.	T.	
3	LOCHKATRINE ...	M.	9,419	45°52′N. 46°44′W.	S.M.	T.	
4	RICHMOND CASTLE	M.	7,798	50°25′N. 35°05′W.	S.M.	T.	
4	EMPIRE ARNOLD ...	S.	7,045	10°45′N. 52°30′W.	S.M.	T.	
5	ARLETTA	S. Tank	4,870	44°44′N. 55°22′W.	S.M.	T.	
6	MAMUTU	M.	300	09°11′S. 144°12′E.	S.M.	G.	
8	RADCHURCH ...	S.	3,701	56°15′N. 32°00′W. (Approx.)	S.M.*	—	
8	TREHATA	S.	4,817	56°30′N. 32°14′W.	S.M.	T.	
8	KELSO	S.	3,956	56°30′N. 32°14′W.	S.M.	T.	
8	ANNEBERG	S.	2,537	56°30′N. 32°14′W.	S.M.	T.	Sunk by escort
9	SAN-EMILIANO ...	M. Tank	8,071	07°22′N. 54°08′W.	S.M.	T.	
9	DALHOUSIE ...	M.	7,072	20°22′S. 24°40′W.	Raider	—	
10	MEDON	M.	5,445	09°26′N. 38°28′W.	S.M.	T. & G.	
10	EMPIRE REINDEER	S.	6,259	57°00′N. 22°30′W.	S.M.	T.	
10	OREGON	S.	6,008	57°05′N. 22°41′W.	S.M.	T.	
10	CAPE RACE ...	S.	3,807	56°45′N. 22°50′W.	S.M.	T.	
10	VIVIAN P. SMITH ...	S.V.	130	21°50′N. 68°40′W.	S.M.	G.	
11	VIMEIRA	S. Tank	5,728	10°03′N. 28°55′W.	S.M.	T. & G.	
12	OHIO*	S. Tank	9,514	Between Cap Bon and Malta	A.C.	B.	First attacked by S.M. on 12th 75m. N. of Cap Bon, then continuously attacked by A.C. until arrival at Malta on 15th, when vessel became a total loss
12	CLAN FERGUSON ...	S.	7,347	20m. N. of Zembra Is., Mediterranean	A.C.	T.	
12	DEUCALION... ...	M.	7,516	37°56′N. 08°40′E.	A.C.	B.	Subsequently torpedoed by A.C. on same date in position 270° 5m. from Cani Rocks and sank
12	EMPIRE HOPE ...	M.	12,688	Off Galeta Is., Mediterranean	A.C.	B.	Sunk by Escort

Date	Name	Type	Gross tons	Position	Cause of loss	How lost	Remarks
AUGUST, 1942—(Contd.)							
13	GLENORCHY ...	M.	8,982	5m. N.W. of Kelibia Lt., Tunisia	E-Boat	T.	
13	WAIRANGI	M.	12,436	36°34′N. 11°15′E.	E-Boat	T.	
13	DORSET	M.	10,624	36°12′N. 12°49′E.	A.C.	B.	
13	WAIMARAMA ...	M.	12,843	36°25′N. 12°00′E.	A.C.	B.	
14	SYLVIA DE LARRINAGA	S.	5,218	10°49′N. 33°35′W.	S.M.	T.	
14	EMPIRE CORPORAL	S. Tank	6,972	21°45′N. 76°10′W.	S.M.	T.	
14	MICHAEL JEBSEN ...	S.	2,323	21°45′N. 76°10′W.	S.M.	T.	
17	PRINCESS MARGUERITE	S.	5,875	32°03′N. 32°47′E.	S.M.	T.	
17	FORT LA REINE ...	S.	7,133	18°30′N. 75°20′W.	S.M.	T.	
18	HATARANA ...	S.	7,522	41°07′N. 20°32′W.	S.M.	T.	
18	EMPIRE BEDE ...	M.	6,959	19°41′N. 76°50′W.	S.M.	T.	
18	HAMLA	S.	4,416	04°S. 24°W. (Est.)	Raider	--	
About 18	ARABISTAN ...	S.	5,874	11°30′S. 26°00′W. (Approx.)	Raider		
19	SEA GULL D. ...	Lugger	75	11°38′N. 67°42′W.	S.M.	G.	
19	CITY OF MANILA ...	S.	7,452	43°21′N. 18°20′W.	S.M.	T.	
19	BRITISH CONSUL*...	S. Tank	6,940	11°58′N. 62°38′W.	S.M.	T.	
19	CRESSINGTON COURT	M.	4,971	07°58′N. 46°00′W.	S.M.	T.	
19	EMPIRE CLOUD · ...	S.	5,969	11°58′N. 62°38′W.	S.M.	T.	Sank in tow on 21st in position 10°54′N. 62°10′W.
21	CITY OF WELLINGTON	S.	5,733	07°29′N. 14°40′W.	S.M.	T.	
24	KATVALDIS ...	S.	3,163	48°55′N. 35°10′W.	S.M.	T.	
24	SHEAF MOUNT ...	S.	5,017	48°55′N. 35°10′W.	S.M.	T.	
25	EMPIRE BREEZE ...	S.	7,457	49°22′N. 35°52′W.	S.M.	T.	
25	HARMONIDES ...	S.	5,237	01°47′N. 77°27′E.	S.M.	T.	
25	AMAKURA	S.	1,987	17°46′N. 75°52′W.	S.M.	T.	
25	VIKING STAR ...	S.	6,445	06°00′N. 14°00′W. (Approx.)	S.M.	T.	
26	CLAN MACWHIRTER	S.	5,941	35°45′N. 18°45′W.	S.M.	T.	
26	BEECHWOOD ...	S.	4,897	05°30′N. 14°04′W.	S.M.	T.	
26	EMPIRE KUMARI ...	S.	6,288	31°58′N. 34°21′E.	S.M.	T.	Towed to Haifa; became a total loss
28	SAN FABIAN ...	S. Tank	13,031	18°09′N. 74°38′W.	S.M.	T.	
28	CITY OF CARDIFF...	S.	5,661	40°20′N. 16°02′W.	S.M.	T.	Sank on 29th
31	WINAMAC	S. Tank	8,621	10°36′N. 54°34′W.	S.M.	T.	
	Total ... 56		344,311				
SEPTEMBER, 1942							
1	ILORIN	S.	815	05°N. 01°W. (Approx.)	S.M.	T.	
1	GAZCON	S.	4,224	13°01′N. 50°30′E.	S.M.	T.	
2	OCEAN MIGHT ...	S.	7,173	00°57′N. 04°11′W.	S.M.	T.	
3	PENROSE	S.	4,393	38°N. 09°W. (Approx.)	S.M.	T.	
3	HOLLINSIDE ...	S.	4,172	38°N. 09°W. (Approx.)	S.M.	T.	
3	DONALD STEWART	S.	1,781	50°32′N. 58°46′W.	S.M.	T.	
5	SAGANAGA	S.	5,454	47°35′N. 52°59′W.	S.M.	T.	
5	LORD STRATHCONA	S.	7,335	47°35′N. 52°59′W.	S.M.	T.	
5	MYRMIDON	M.	6,278	00°45′N. 06°27′W.	S.M.	T.	
6	HELEN FORSEY ...	Aux. Sch.	167	28°35′N. 57°35′W.	S.M.	G.	
6	TUSCAN STAR ...	M.	11,449	01°34′N. 11°39′W.	S.M.	T.	
6	ANSHUN	M.	3,188	Milne Bay, New Guinea	Warship	—	
6	JOHN A. HOLLOWAY	S.	1,745	14°10′N. 71°30′W.	S.M.	T.	
7	OAKTON	S.	1,727	48°50′N. 63°46′W.	S.M.	T.	
9	HARESFIELD ...	S.	5,299	13°05′N. 54°35′E.	S.M.	T.	
10	EMPIRE OIL ...	S. Tank	8,029	51°23′N. 28°13′W.	S.M.	T.	

Date	Name	Type	Gross tons	Position	Cause of loss	How lost	Remarks
SEPTEMBER, 1942—(Contd.)							
11	EMPIRE MOONBEAM	S.	6,849	48°55′N. 33°38′W.	S.M.	T.	
11	HEKTORIA	S. Tank	13,797	48°55′N. 33°38′W.	S.M.	T.	
11	EMPIRE DAWN ...	M.	7,241	34°S. 02°E. (Approx.)	Raider	—	
12	TREVILLEY ...	M.	5,296	04°30′S. 07°50′W.	S.M.	T. & G.	
12	LACONIA	S.	19,695	05°05′S. 11°38′W.	S.M.	T.	
13	OCEAN VANGUARD	S.	7,174	10°43′N. 60°11′W.	S.M.	T.	
13	EMPIRE LUGARD ...	M.	7,241	12°07′N. 63°32′W.	S.M.	T.	
13	EMPIRE STEVENSON	S.	6,209	76°10′N. 10°05′E.	A.C.	T.	
13	EMPIRE BEAUMONT	S.	7,044	76°10′N. 10°05′E.	A.C.	T.	
14	ATHELTEMPLAR* ...	M. Tank	8,992	76°10′N. 18°00′E.	S.M.	T.	
14	HARBOROUGH ...	S.	5,415	10°03′N. 60°20′W.	S.M.	T. & G.	
15	KIOTO ...	S.	3,297	11°05′N. 60°46′W.	S.M.	T.	
16	OCEAN HONOUR ...	S.	7,173	12°48′N. 50°50′E.	S.M.	T. & G.	
17	PETERTON	S.	5,221	18°45′N. 29°15′W.	S.M.	T.	
18	FERNWOOD ...	S.	1,892	Dartmouth	A.C.	B.	
18	NORFOLK	S.	1,901	08°36′N. 59°20′W.	S.M.	T.	
19	QUEBEC CITY ...	S.	4,745	02°12′S. 17°36′W.	S.M.	T. & G.	
20	REEDPOOL	S.	4,838	08°58′N. 57°34′W.	S.M.	T.	
20	EMPIRE HARTEBEESTE	S.	5,676	56°20′N. 38°10′W.	S.M.	T.	
22	TENNESSEE... ...	S.	2,342	58°40′N. 33°41′W.	S.M.	T.	
22	ATHELSULTAN ...	M. Tank	8,882	58°24′N. 33°38′W.	S.M.	T.	
22	OCEAN VOICE ...	S.	7,174	71°23′N. 11°03′W.	S.M.*	—	Sunk by H.M.S
23	BRUYERE	S.	5,335	04°55′N. 17°16′W.	S.M.	T.	
25	EMPIRE BELL ...	S.	1,744	62°19′N. 15°27′W.	S.M.	T.	
25	BOSTON	S.	4,989	54°23′N. 27°54′W.	S.M.	T.	
25	NEW YORK ...	S.	4,989	54°34′N. 25°44′W. (Approx.)	S.M.	T.	
26	YORKTOWN ...	S.	1,547	55°10′N. 18°50′W.	S.M.	T.	
28	REGISTAN	S.	6,008	12°37′N. 57°10′W.	S.M.	T.	
28	LIFLAND	S.	2,254	56°40′N. 30°30′W. (Est.)	S.M.*	- -	
29	EMPIRE AVOCET ...	S.	6,015	04°05′N. 13°23′W.	S.M.	T.	
29	BARON OGILVY ...	S.	3,391	02°30′N. 14°30′W.	S.M.	T.	
30	ALIPORE	S.	5,273	07°09′N. 54°23′W.	S.M.	T. & G.	
30	KUMSANG	S.	5,447	04°07′N. 13°40′W.	S.M.	T.	
30	SIAM II	M.	6,637	03°25′N. 15°46′W.	S.M.	T.	
	Total ... 50		274,952				
OCTOBER, 1942							
1	EMPIRE TENNYSON	S.	2,880	09°27′N. 60°05′W.	S.M.	T.	
6	ANDALUCIA STAR ...	S.	14,943	06°38′N. 15°46′W.	S.M.	T.	
7	MANON	S.	5,597	15°00′N. 80°30′E.	S.M.	T.	
7	SHEAF WATER ...	S.	2,730	53°06′N. 01°25′E.	E-Boat	T.	
7	IGHTHAM	S.	1,337	53°32′N. 00°45′E.	Mine	—	Sank in position 55° 33′N. 00°26′E.
7	ILSE	S.	2,874	53°06′N. 01°25′E.	E-Boat	T.	
7	JESSIE MAERSK ...	S.	1,972	53°06′N. 01°25′E.	E-Boat	T.	
7	BORINGIA	M.	5,821	35°09′S. 16°32′E.	S.M.	T.	
8	GLENDENE	S.	4,413	04°29′N. 17°41′W.	S.M.	T.	
8	CITY OF ATHENS ...	S.	6,558	33°40′S. 17°03′E.	S.M.	T.	
8	CLAN MACTAVISH ...	S.	7,631	34°53′S. 16°45′E.	S.M.	T.	
8	SARTHE	S.	5,271	34°50′S. 18°40′E. (Approx.)	S.M.	T.	
9	PENNINGTON COURT	S.	6,098	58°18′N. 27°55′W.	S.M.	T.	
9	CAROLUS	S.	2,375	48°47′N. 68°10′W.	S.M.	T.	
9	ORONSAY	S.	20,043	04°29′N. 2°52′W.	S.M.	T.	
10	DUCHESS OF ATHOLL	S.	20,119	07°03′S. 11°12′W.	S.M.	T.	
10	ORCADES	S.	23,456	35°51′S. 14°40′E.	S.M.	T.	
11	AGAPENOR	S.	7,392	06°53′N. 15°23′W.	S.M.	T.	
11	WATERTON ...	S.	2,140	47°07′N. 59°54′W.	S.M.	T.	
13	EMPIRE NOMAD ...	S.	7,167	37°50′S. 18°16′E.	S.M.	T.	
13	ASHWORTH	S.	5,227	53°05′N. 44°06′W.	S.M.	T.	

Date	Name	Type	Gross tons	Position	Cause of loss	How lost	Remarks
OCTOBER, 1942 (Contd.)							
13	Stornest	S.	4,265	54°25′N. 27°42′W.	S.M.	T.	
13	Southern Empress*	S.	12,398	53°40′N. 40°40′W.	S.M.	T.	
		O.R.					
14	Empire Mersey ...	S.	5,791	54°00′N. 40°15′W.	S.M.	T.	
14	Caribou	S.	2,222	47°19′N. 59°29′W.	S.M.	T.	
16	Newton Pine ...	S.	4,212	55°N. 30°W. (Est.)	S.M.*	—	
16	Castle Harbour*	S.	730	11°00′N. 61°10′W.	S.M.	T.	
17	Empire Chaucer ...	S.	5,970	40°20′S. 18°30′E.	S.M.	T.	
19	Rothley	M.	4,996	13°34′N. 54°34′W.	S.M.	T.	
19	Scalaria	S. Tank	5,683	Ras Gharib, Red Sea	A.C.	T. & B.	
22	Donax	M. Tank	8,036	49°51′N. 27°58′W.	S.M.	T.	Abandoned and sank on 29th
22	Ocean Vintage ...	S.	7,174	21°37′N. 60°06′E.	S.M.	T.	
22	Winnipeg II ...	S.	9,807	49°51′N. 27°58′W.	S.M.	T.	
22	Empire Turnstone	S.	6,113	54°40′N. 28°00′W.	S.M.	T.	
23	City of Johannesburg	S.	5,669	33°20′S. 29°30′E.	S.M.	T.	
23	Empire Star ...	M.	12,656	48°14′N. 26°22′W.	S.M.	T.	
24	Holmpark ...	S.	5,780	13°11′N. 47°00′W.	S.M.	T.	
26	Anglo Maersk ...	M. Tank	7,705	27°50′N. 22°15′W.	S.M.	T.	Again attacked on 27th in position 27° 15′N. 18°50′W. and sank
27	Pacific Star ...	S.	7,951	29°16′N. 20°57′W.	S.M.	T.	Abandoned on 28th in position 29°21′N 19°28′W. Last seen on 30th sinking.
27	Sourabaya* ...	S. Tank	10,107	54°32′N. 31°02′W.	S.M.	T.	
27	Stentor	M.	6,148	29°13′N. 20°53′W.	S.M.	T.	
28	Hopecastle ...	M.	5,178	31°39′N. 19°35′W.	S.M.	T.	
28	Nagpore	S.	5,283	31°30′N. 19°36′W.	S.M.	T. & G.	
29	Primrose Hill ...	S.	7,628	18°58′N. 28°40′W.	S.M.	T.	
29	Bullmouth* ...	M. Tank	7,519	33°20′N. 18°25′W.	S.M.	T.	
29	Bic Island ...	S.	4,000	55°05′N. 23°27′W.	S.M.	T.	
29	Barrwhin	S.	4,998	55°02′N. 22°45′W.	S.M.	T.	
29	Ross	M.	4,978	38°51′S. 21°40′E.	S.M.	T.	
29	Laplace	S.	7,327	40°33′S. 21°35′E.	S.M.	T.	
29	Abosso	M.	11,330	48°30′N. 28°50′W.	S.M.	T.	
29	Brittany	M.	4,772	33°29′N. 18°32′W.	S.M.	T.	
29	Corinaldo ...	S.	7,131	33°20′N. 18°12′W.	S.M.	T.	
30	Tasmania	M.	6,405	36°06′N. 16°59′W.	S.M.	T.	
30	Baron Vernon ...	S.	3,642	36°06′N. 16°59′W.	S.M.	T.	
30	President Doumer	M.	11,898	35°08′N. 16°44′W.	S.M.	T.	
30	Marylyn	S.	4,555	00°46′S. 32°42′W.	S.M.	T.	
30	Silverwillow ...	M.	6,373	35°08′N. 16°44′W.	S.M.	T.	Abandoned 5th November. Foundered 11th November in position 37°24′N. 10°45′W.
31	Aldington Court	M.	4,891	30°20′S. 02°10′W.	S.M.	T.	
31	Empire Guidon ...	S.	7,041	30°10′S. 33°50′E.	S.M.	T.	
	Total ... 59		404,406				
NOVEMBER, 1942							
1	Elmdale	S.	4,872	00°17′N. 34°55′W.	S.M.	T.	
1	Mendoza	S.	8,233	29°20′S. 32°13′E.	S.M.	T.	
2	Llandilo	S.	4,966	27°03′S. 02°59′W.	S.M.	T.	
2	Reynolds	S.	5,113	29°S. 41°E. (Approx.)	Raider	—	
2	Empire Zeal ...	S.	7,009	00°30′S. 30°45′W.	S.M.	T. & G.	
2	Rose Castle ...	S.	7,803	47°36′N. 52°58′W.	S.M.	T.	
2	P.L.M.27	S.	5,633	47°36′N. 52°58′W.	S.M.	T.	
2	Empire Sunrise ...	S.	7,459	51°50′N. 46°25′W.	S.M.	T.	
2	Empire Leopard ...	S.	5,676	52°26′N. 45°22′W.	S.M.	T.	
2	Hartington ...	S.	5,496	52°30′N. 45°30′W. (Approx.)	S.M.	T.	

Date	Name	Type	Gross tons	Position	Cause of loss	How lost	Remarks
NOVEMBER, 1942—*(Contd.)*							
2	MARITIMA	S.	5,801	52°20'N. 45°40'W.	S.M.	T.	
2	DALCROY	S.	4,558	52°30'N. 45°30'W. (Approx.)	S.M.	T.	
2	EMPIRE ANTELOPE	S.	4,945	52°26'N. 45°22'W.	S.M.	T.	
2	EMPIRE GILBERT ...	S.	6,640	Off E. Coast of Iceland	S.M.*	—	
3	GYPSUM EMPRESS...	S.	4,034	12°27'N. 64°04'W.	S.M.	T.	
3	CHR. J. KAMPMANN	S.	2,260	12°06'N. 62°42'W.	S.M.	T.	
3	DAGOMBA	M.	3,845	02°30'N. 19°00'W.	S.M.	T.	
3	JEYPORE	S.	5,318	55°30'N. 40°16'W.	S.M.	T.	
3	EMPIRE LYNX ...	S.	6,379	55°20'N. 40°01'W.	S.M.	T.	
3	HATIMURA	S.	6,690	55°38'N. 39°52'W.	S.M.	T.	
4	TREKIEVE	S.	5,244	25°46'S. 33°48'E.	S.M.	T.	
4	DALEBY	S.	4,640	57°N. 36°W. (Approx.)	S.M.	T.	
4	OUED GROU ...	S.	792	04°33'N. 04°49'E.	S.M.	T.	
5	LA CORDILLERA ...	M.	5,185	12°02'N. 58°04'W.	S.M.	T.	
5	NEW TORONTO ...	S.	6,568	05°57'N. 02°30'E.	S.M.	T.	
6	ARICA	S.	5,431	10°58'N. 60°52'W.	S.M.	T.	
6	OCEAN JUSTICE ...	S.	7,173	10°06'N. 60°00'W.	S.M.	T.	
6	CITY OF CAIRO ...	S.	8,034	23°30'S. 05°30'W.	S.M.	T.	
7	ROXBY	S.	4,252	49°35'N. 30°32'W.	S.M.	T.	
7	D'ENTRECASTEAUX	S.	7,291	15°30'N. 57°00'W.	S.M.	T.	
7	LINDENHALL ...	S.	5,248	11°34'N. 63°26'W.	S.M.	T.	
7	GLENLEA	S.	4,252	50°N. 30°W. (Approx.)	S.M.	T.	
9	CERINTHUS ...	S. Tank	3,878	12°27'N. 27°45'W.	S.M.	T. & G.	
9	ARDEOLA	S.	2,609	Off Bizerta	Captured	—	
9	TADORNA	S.	1,947	1½m. N. of Bizerta	Captured	—	
10	GARLINGE*	S.	2,012	21m. N. of Cape Ivi, Algeria	S.M.	T.	
10	START POINT ...	S.	5,293	13°12'N. 27°27'W.	S.M.	T.	
11	NURMAHAL ...	S.	5,419	14°45'N. 55°45'W. (Est.)	S.M.*	—	
11	CITY OF RIPON ...	S.	6,368	08°40'N. 59°20'W.	S.M.	T.	
11	VICEROY OF INDIA	T.-E.	19,627	36°26'N. 00°24'W.	S.M.	T.	
11	AWATEA	S.	13,482	1m. N. of Bougie Breakwater, Algeria	A.C.	T. & B.	
11	CATHAY	S.	15,225	Bougie, Algeria	A.C.	B.	Sank on 12th
12	BROWNING	S.	5,332	35°53'N. 00°33'W.	S.M.	T.	
13	LOUISE MOLLER ...	S.	3,764	30°50'S. 35°54'E.	S.M.	T.	
13	MARON	M.	6,487	36°27'N. 00°58'W.	S.M.	T.	
14	WARWICK CASTLE...	M.	20,107	39°16'N. 13°25'W.	S.M.	T.	
14	NARKUNDA ...	S.	16,632	36°52'N. 05°01'E.	A.C.	B.	
14	EMPIRE SKY ...	S.	7,455	Off N. Russian Coast	C.U.	—	
15	KING ARTHUR ...	M.	5,224	10°30'N. 59°50'W.	S.M.	T.	
15	ETTRICK	M.	11,279	36°13'N. 07°54'W.	S.M.	T.	
15	IRISH PINE ...	S.	5,621	Off New York	S.M.*	—	
15	LINWOOD ...	S.	992	¼m. East of Longsand Buoy, Thames Estuary	Mine	—	
16	CLAN MACTAGGART	S.	7,622	36°08'N. 07°23'W.	S.M.	T.	
17	CITY OF CORINTH...	S.	5,318	10°55'N. 61°01'W.	S.M.	T.	
17	WIDESTONE ...	S.	3,192	54°30'N. 37°10'W.	S.M.	T.	
18	PRESIDENT SERGENT	S. Tank	5,344	54°07'N. 38°26'W.	S.M.	T.	
18	TOWER GRANGE ...	M.	5,226	06°20'N. 49°10'W.	S.M.	T.	
19	YEWFOREST ...	S.	815	120° 11m. from Eddystone Lt. (Approx.)	E-Boat	T.	
19	BIRGITTE	S.	1,595	118° 5½m. from Eddystone Lt.	E-Boat	T.	
19	SCOTTISH CHIEF* ...	S. Tank	7,006	30°39'S. 34°41'E.	S.M.	T.	
20	GRANGEPARK ...	S.	5,132	35°55'N. 10°14'W.	S.M.	T.	
21	EMPIRE STARLING...	S.	6,060	13°05'N. 56°20'W.	S.M.	T.	
21	EMPIRE SAILOR ...	M.	6,140	43°53'N. 55°12'W.	S.M.	T.	
23	CRANFIELD ...	S.	5,332	08°26'N. 76°42'E.	S.M.	T.	
23	TILAWA	S.	10,006	07°36'N. 61°08'E.	S.M.	T.	Again attacked in position 07°45 N. 61°10'E.

Date	Name	Type	Gross tons	Position	Cause of loss	How lost	Remarks
NOVEMBER, 1942—*(Contd.)*							
23	GOOLISTAN	S.	5,851	75°30′N. 08°00′E.	S.M.*	T.	
23	BENLOMOND ...	S.	6,630	00°30′N. 38°45′W. (Est.)	S.M.	T.	
24	TRENTBANK ...	S.	5,060	10m. N. of Cap Tenes, Algeria	A.C.	T.	
24	DORINGTON COURT	S.	5,281	27°00′S. 34°45′E.	S.M.	T. & G.	Sunk by gunfire after being abandoned.
26	BARBERRYS ...	S.	5,170	50°36′N. 47°10′W.	S.M.	T.	
26	OCEAN CRUSADER...	S.	7,178	50°30′N. 45°30′W.	S.M.*	—	
26	CLAN MACFADYEN...	S.	6,191	08°57′N. 59°48′W.	S.M.	T.	
28	EMPIRE CROMWELL	S.	5,970	09°00′N. 58°30′W.	S.M.	T.	
28	NOVA SCOTIA ...	S.	6,796	28°30′S. 33°00′E.	S.M.	T.	
30	LLANDAFF CASTLE...	S.	10,799	27°20′S. 33°40′E.	S.M.	T.	
30	TREVALGAN ...	M.	5,299	09°40′N. 59°15′W.	S.M.	T.	
	Total ... 76		474,606				
DECEMBER, 1942							
2	SOLON II	S.	4,561	07°45′N. 56°30′W. (Approx.)	S.M.	T.	
2	CITY OF BATH ...	S.	5,079	09°29′N. 59°30′W.	S.M.	T.	
2	WALLSEND ...	S.	3,157	20°08′N. 25°50′W.	S.M.	T.	
3	EMPIRE DABCHICK	S.	6,089	43°00′N. 58°17′W.	S.M.	T.	
3	GATINAIS	M.	383	190° 5m. from Start Pt.	E-Boat	T.	
5	TEESBANK	M.	5,136	03°33′N. 29°35′W.	S.M.	T.	
6	CERAMIC	S.	18,713	40°30′N. 40°20′W.	S.M.	T.	
7	HENRY STANLEY ...	M.	5,026	40°35′N. 39°40′W.	S.M.	—	
7	PETER MAERSK ...	M.	5,476	39°47′N. 41°00′W.	S.M.	T.	
8	NIGERIAN	S.	5,423	09°17′N. 59°00′W.	S.M.	T.	
8	EMPIRE SPENSER ...	M. Tank	8,194	57°04′N. 36°01′W.	S.M.	T.	
9	CHARLES L.D. ...	M.	5,273	59°02′N. 30°45′W.	S.M.	T.	
12	RIPLEY	M.	4,997	00°35′S. 32°17′W.	S.M.	T.	
12	EMPIRE GULL ...	S.	6,408	26°S. 35°E. (Approx.)	S.M.	T.	
12	EMPIRE HAWK ...	S.	5,033	05°56′N. 39°50′W.	S.M.	T.	
12	AVONWOOD ...	S.	1,056	3m. from ·No. 4 Buoy, off Lowestoft	E-Boat	T.	
12	GLEN TILT ...	S.	871	3m. from No. 4 Buoy, off Lowestoft	E-Boat	T.	
12	LINDISFARNE ...	S.	999	3m. from No. 4 Buoy, off Lowestoft	E-Boat	T.	
12	KNITSLEY	S.	2,272	1½m. N. of No. 4 Buoy, Lowestoft	E-Boat	T.	
13	CITY OF BOMBAY ...	S.	7,140	02°43′S. 29°06′W.	S.M.	T.	
14	EDENCRAG* ...	S.	1,592	33°49′N. 01°25′W.	S.M.*	—	
14	ORFOR ...	S.	6,578	16°N. 50°W. (Approx.)	S.M.	T.	
15	HANNAH MOLLER ...	S.	2,931	Benghazi	A.C.	B.	
16	EAST WALES ...	S.	4,358	00°24′N. 31°27′W.	S.M.	T.	
16	OBSERVER ...	S.	5,881	05°30′S. 31°00′W.	S.M.	T.	
18	BRETWALDA ...	S.	4,906	44°35′N. 16°28′W.	S.M.	T.	
19	BANKSIDE ...	Aux. S.B.	77	Nr. Maplin Spit, Thames Estuary	Mine	—	
20	OTINA	M. Tank	6,217	47°40′N. 33°06′W.	S.M.	T.	
21	QUEEN CITY ...	S.	4,814	00°49′S. 41°34′W.	S.M.	T. & G.	
21	STRATHALLAN ...	S.	23,722	36°52′N. 00°34′W.	S.M.	T.	
21	MONTREAL CITY ...	S.	3,066	50°28′N. 38°00′W.	S.M.	T.	
26	EMPIRE UNION ...	S.	5,952	47°30′N. 24°30′W.	S.M.	T.	
27	EMPIRE MARCH ...	S.	7,040	40°S. 05°W. (Approx.)	Raider*	—	
27	KING EDWARD ...	S.	5,224	47°25′N. 25°20′W.	S.M.	T.	
27	MELROSE ABBEY ...	S.	2,473	47°30′N. 24°30′W.	S.M.	T.	
27	OAKBANK	M.	5,154	00°46′S. 37°58′W.	S.M.	T.	
27	GERTRUDE MAY ...	S.B.	72	51°45′N. 01°19′E. (Approx.)	Mine	—	
28	LYNTON GRANGE ...	S.	5,029	43°23′N. 27°14′W.	S.M.	T.	

Date	Name	Type	Gross tons	Position	Cause of loss	How lost	Remarks
DECEMBER, 1942—(Contd.)							
28	ZARIAN	S.	4,871	43°23'N. 27°14'W.	S.M.	T.	
28	BARON COCHRANE...	S.	3,385	43°23'N. 27°14'W.	S.M.	T.	
28	EMPIRE SHACKLETON	S.	7,068	43°20'N. 27°18'W.	S.M.	T.	
28	MELMORE HEAD ...	S.	5,273	43°27'N. 27°15'W.	S.M.	T.	
28	VILLE DE ROUEN ...	S.	5,598	43°25'N. 27°15'W.	S.M.	T.	
28	TREWORLAS ...	S.	4,692	10°52'N. 60°45'W.	S.M.	T.	
28	EMPIRE WAGTAIL...	S.	4,893	43°17'N. 27°22'W. (Approx.)	S.M.	T.	
	Total ... 45		232,152				
JANUARY, 1943							
2	EMPIRE METAL ...	M. Tank	8,201	Bone Harbour	A.C.	B.	
2	ST. MERRIEL ...	S.	4,980	Bone Harbour	A.C.	B.	
3	BARON DECHMONT	S.	3,675	03°11'S. 38°41'W.	S.M.	T.	
3	BRITISH VIGILANCE	M. Tank	8,093	20°58'N. 44°40'W.	S.M.	T.	
7	BENALBANACH ...	S.	7,153	37°07'N. 04°38'E.	A.C.	T.	
8	YORKWOOD... ...	S.	5,401	04°10'S. 35°30'W.	S.M.	T.	
8	OLTENIA II* ...	S. Tank	6,394	27°59'N. 28°50'W.	S.M.	T.	
9	EMPIRE LYTTON ...	S. Tank	9,807	28°08'N. 28°20'W.	S.M.	T.	
9	WILLIAM WILBERFORCE	M.	5,004	29°20'N. 26°53'W.	S.M.	T.	
10	OCEAN VAGABOND...	S.	7,174	57°17'N. 20°11'W.	S.M.	T.	
10	BRITISH DOMINION	M. Tank	6,983	30°30'N. 19°55'W.	S.M.	T.	
11	C. S. FLIGHT ...	Sch.	67	12°25'N. 63°00'W.	S.M.*	—	
13	AILSA	S.B.	67	½m. N.E. of Whittaker Beacon, Burnham-on-Crouch	Mine	—	
15	OCEAN COURAGE ...	S.	7,173	10°52'N. 23°28'W.	S.M.	T.	
17	KALINGO	S.	2,051	34°07'S. 153°15'E.	S.M.	T.	
20	HAMPTON LODGE*	S.	3,645	36°44'N. 01°50'E.	A.C.	B	Sank on 21st
23	LACKENBY	S.	5,112	55°N. 47°W. (Approx.)	S.M.*	—	
28	RESOLUTE	S.B.	76	51°47'N. 01°14'E.	Mine*	—	
	Total ... 18		91,056				
FEBRUARY, 1943							
3	RHEXENOR ...	S.	7,957	24°59'N. 43°37'W.	S.M.	T. & G.	
3	INVERILEN	M. Tank	9,456	56°35'N. 23°30'W.	S.M.	T.	
3	CORDELIA*... ...	M. Tank	8,190	56°37'N. 22°58'W.	S.M.	T.	
7	TOWARD*	S.	1,571	55°13'N. 26°22'W.	S.M.	T.	
7	IRON KNIGHT ...	S.	4,812	36°51'S. 150°38'E.	S.M.	T.	
7	EMPIRE WEBSTER...	S.	7,043	36°47'N. 01°37'E.	S.M.	T.	
7	AFRIKA	M.	8,597	55°16'N. 26°31'W.	S.M.	T.	
7	HARMALA	S.	5,730	55°14'N. 26°37'W.	S.M.	T.	
7	BALTONIA*... ...	S.	2,013	35°58'N. 05°59'W.	Mine	—	
7	MARY SLESSOR ...	M.	5,027	35°58'N. 05°59'W.	Mine	—	
7	EMPIRE MORDRED...	S.	7,024	35°58'N. 05°59'W.	Mine	—	
7	EMPIRE BANNER ...	S.	6,699	36°48'N. 01°32'E.	S.M.	T.	
8	NEWTON ASH ...	S.	4,625	56°25'N. 22°26'W.	S.M.	T.	
10	QUEEN ANNE ...	M.	4,937	34°53'S. 19°51'E.	S.M.	T.	
11	HELMSPEY	S.	4,764	34°22'S. 24°54'E.	S.M.	T.	
17	LLANASHE	S.	4,836	34°00'S. 28°30'E.	S.M.	T.	
21	KYLECLARE ...	S.	700	41°45'N. 11°45'W. (Est.)	S.M.*	—	
21	EMPIRE TRADER ...	S.	9,990	48°25'N. 30°10'W.	S.M.	T.	
21	RADHURST	S.	3,454	48°50'N. 47°00'W. (Est.)	S.M.*	T.	
22	ROXBURGH CASTLE	M.	7,801	38°12'N. 26°22'W.	S.M.	T.	

Date	Name	Type	Gross tons	Position	Cause of loss	How lost	Remarks
FEBRUARY, 1943 —(Contd.)							
22	EMPIRE REDSHANK	S.	6,615	47°00'N. 34°30'W.	S.M.	T.	
23	ATHELPRINCESS ...	M. Tank	8,882	32°02'N. 24°38'W.	S.M.	T.	
23	EMPIRE NORSEMAN	S. Tank	9,811	31°18'N. 27°20'W.	S.M.	T.	
23	FINTRA	S.	2,089	36°57'N. 03°41'E.	S.M.	T.	
23	EULIMA	M. Tank	6,207	46°48'N. 36°18'W.	S.M.	T.	
25	MANCHESTER MERCHANT	S.	7,264	45°10'N. 43°23'W.	S.M.	T.	
25	STOCKPORT* ...	S.	1,683	45°N. 44°W. (Est.)	S.M.*	T.	
27	ST. MARGARET ...	S.	4,312	27°38'N. 43°23'W.	S.M.	T.	
27	MODAVIA	M.	4,858	090° 14m. from Berry Head (Lyme Bay)	E-Boat	T.	
	Total ... 29		166,947				
MARCH, 1943							
3	CITY OF PRETORIA	S.	8,049	41°45'N. 42°30'W. (Est.)	S.M.*	T.	
3	NIRPURA	S.	5,961	32°47'S. 29°47'E.	S.M.	T.	
3	EMPIRE MAHSEER...	S.	5,087	32°01'S. 30°48'E.	S.M.	T.	
4	CALIFORNIA STAR ...	M.	8,300	42°32'N. 37°20'W.	S.M.	T.	
4	MARIETTA E. ...	S.	7,628	31°49'S. 31°11'E.	S.M.	T.	
5	FIDRA	S.	1,574	43°50'N. 14°50'W.	S.M.	T.	
5	EMPIRE TOWER ...	S.	4,378	43°50'N. 14°46'W.	S.M.	T.	
5	TREFUSIS ...	S.	5,299	43°50'N. 14°46'W.	S.M.	T.	
5	GER-Y-BRYN ...	S.	5,108	43°50'N. 14°45'W.	S.M.	T.	
6	EGYPTIAN	S.	2,868	56°25'N. 37°38'W.	S.M.	T.	
6	FORT BATTLE RIVER	S.	7,133	36°33'N. 10°22'W.	S.M.	T.	
7	BARON KINNAIRD...	S.	3,355	50°N. 40°W. (Est.)	S.M.*	—	
7	EMPIRE LIGHT ...	M. Tank	6,537	53°57'N. 46°14'W.	S.M.	T.	
7	SABOR	S.	5,212	34°30'S. 23°10'E.	S.M.	T.	
8	FORT LAMY ...	S.	5,242	58°30'N. 31°00'W. (Approx.)	S.M.	T.	
8	GUIDO	S.	3,921	58°08'N. 32°20'W.	S.M.	T.	
9	ROSEWOOD ...	M. Tank	5,989	58°37'N. 22°32'W.	S.M.	T.	
9	KELVINBANK ...	M.	3,872	07°24'N. 52°11'W.	S.M.	T.	
9	CLARISSA RADCLIFFE	S.	5,754	42°N. 62°W. (Est.)	S.M.*	—	
10	NAILSEA COURT ...	S.	4,946	58°45'N. 21°57'W.	S.M.	T.	
10	TUCURINCA ...	S.	5,412	51°00'N. 30°10'W.	S.M.	T.	
11	EMPIRE LAKELAND	S.	7,015	58°N. 15°W. (Est.)	S.M.*	—	
11	EMPIRE IMPALA ...	S.	6,116	58°N. 15°W. (Est.)	S.M.*	—	
11	AELYBRYN	S.	4,986	28°30'S. 34°00'E.	S.M.	T.	
11	LEADGATE	S.	2,125	58°N. 15°W. (Est.)	S.M.*	—	
13	EMPRESS OF CANADA	S.	21,517	01°13'S. 09°57'W.	S.M.	T.	
13	MARCELLA	S.	4,592	42°45'N. 13°31'W.	S.M.	T.	
13	OPORTO	S.	2,352	42°45'N. 13°31'W.	S.M.	T.	
13	CLAN ALPINE ...	S.	5,442	42°45'N. 13°31'W.	S.M.	T.	Sunk by Escort
13	OCEAN FREEDOM ...	S.	7,173	Murmansk	A.C.	B.	
15	OCEAN SEAMAN ...	S.	7,178	36°55'N. 01°59'E.	S.M.	T.	
16	HADLEIGH ...	S.	5,222	36°10'N. 00°30'W.	S.M.	T.	
17	CORACERO	S.	7,252	51°04'N. 33°20'W.	S.M.	T.	
17	SOUTHERN PRINCESS	S. Tank	12,156	50°36'N. 34°30'W.	S.M.	T.	
17	KINGSBURY ...	S.	4,898	51°55'N. 32°41'W.	S.M.	T.	
17	FORT CEDAR LAKE	S.	7,134	52°14'N. 32°15'W.	S.M.	T.	
17	KING GRUFFYDD ...	S.	5,072	51°55'N. 32°41'W.	S.M.	T.	
17	ZOUAVE	S.	4,256	52°25'N. 30°15'W.	S.M.	T.	
17	PORT AUCKLAND ...	S.	8,789	52°25'N. 30°15'W.	S.M.	T.	
17	NARIVA	S.	8,714	50°40'N. 34°10'W.	S.M.	T.	
18	CANADIAN STAR ...	M.	8,293	53°24'N. 28°34'W.	S.M.	T.	
18	DAFILA	S.	1,940	32°59'N. 22°21'E.	S.M.	T.	
18	KAYING	S.	2,626	32°59'N. 22°21'E.	S.M.	T.	
19	LULWORTH HILL ...	S.	7,628	10°10S. 01°00'E. (Approx.)	S.M.	T.	
19	GLENDALOUGH ...	S.	868	53°16'N. 01°03'W.	Mine	—	

Date	Name	Type	Gross tons	Position	Cause of loss	How lost	Remarks
MARCH, 1943—*(Contd.)*							
19	Ocean Voyager ...	S.	7,174	Tripoli Harbour	A.C.	B.	Sank on 20th
20	Fort Mumford ...	S.	7,132	10°N. 71°E. (Approx.)	S.M.	T.	
21	City of Christchurch	S.	6,009	39°35′N. 12°46′W.	A.C.	B.	Sank on 22nd in position 38°42′N. 10°14′W.
23	Windsor Castle ...	S.	19,141	37°28′N. 01°10′E.	A.C.	T.	
26	Empire Standard	S.	7,047	Algiers Harbour	A.C.	B.	
26	City of Perth ...	S.	6,415	35°50′N. 01°41′W.	S.M.	T.	
27	Empire Rowan ...	M.	9,545	37°16′N. 06°54′E.	A.C.	T.	
27	City of Guildford	S.	5,157	33°00′N. 22°50′E.	S.M.	T.	
28	Silverbeech ...	M.	5,319	25°20′N. 15°55′W.	S.M.	T.	
28	Lagosian	S.	5,449	25°35′N. 15°43′W.	S.M.	T.	
29	Celtic Star ...	S.	5,575	04°16′N. 17°44′W.	S.M.	T.	
29	Umaria	S.	6,852	46°44′N. 16°38′W.	S.M.	T.	Sank on 30th
29	Empire Whale ...	S.	6,159	46°44′N. 16°38′W.	S.M.	T.	
29	Nagara	S.	8,791	46°50′N. 16°40′W.	S.M.	T.	
30	Empire Bowman ...	S.	7,031	47°26′N. 15°53′W.	S.M.	T.	
30	Fort a la Corne...	S.	7,133	36°52′N. 01°47′E.	S.M.	T.	
	Total ... 61		384,898				
APRIL, 1943							
2	Gogra	S.	5,190	41°02′N. 15°39′W.	S.M.	T.	
2	Katha	S.	4,357	41°02′N. 15°39′W.	S.M.	T.	
2	City of Baroda ...	S.	7,129	26°56′S. 15°21′E.	S.M.	T.	
2	Melbourne Star...	M.	12,806	28°05′N. 57°30′W. (Est.)	S.M.	T.	
5	British Ardour*	S. Tank	7,124	58°08′N. 33°04′W.	S.M.	T.	
5	Aloe	S.	5,047	32°37′S. 37°50′E.	S.M.	T.	
5	Shillong	M.	5,529	57°10′N. 35°30′W.	S.M.	T.	
5	Waroonga ...	S.	9,365	57°10′N. 35°30′W.	S.M.	T.	Sank on 6th
6	Josefina Thorden	M. Tank	6,620	Near Sunk Head Buoy, Thames Estuary	Mine	—	Beached ; later became total loss
10	Runo	S.	1,858	32°15′N. 23°55′E.	S.M.*	T.	
11	Empire Whimbrel	S.	5,983	02°31′N. 15°55′W.	S.M.	T. & G.	
11	Lancastrian Prince	S.	1,914	50°18′N. 42°48′W.	S.M.	T.	
12	Fresno City	M.	7,261	54°15′N. 30°00′W.	S.M.	T.	
12	Pacific Grove ...	M.	7,117	54°10′N. 30°00′W.	S.M.	T.	
14	Stanlake*	S.	1,742	060° 12m. from Lizard Head	E-Boat	T.	
17	Fort Rampart ...	S.	7,134	47°22′N. 21°58′W.	S.M.	T.	
17	Dynamo	S.	809	Near B.8 Buoy, Barrow Deep	Mine	—	
18	Manaar	S.	8,007	30°59′S. 33°00′E.	S.M.	T. & G.	
18	Empire Bruce ...	S.	7,459	06°40′N. 13°17′W.	S.M.	T.	
18	Corbis	M. Tank	8,132	34°56′S. 34°03′E.	S.M.	T.	
21	Wanstead ...	S.	5,486	55°46′N. 45°14′W.	S.M.	T.	
21	Ashantian ...	S.	4,917	55°50′N. 44°00′W.	S.M.	T.	
22	Amerika	M.	10,218	57°30′N. 42°50′W.	S.M.	T	
24	Kowarra	S.	2,125	24°26′S. 153°44′E.	S.M.	T.	
24	Rosenborg ...	S.	1,997	61°N. 15°W. (Approx.)	S.M.	T.	
25	Doryssa	M. Tank	8,078	37°03′S. 24°03′E.	S.M.	T. & G	
25	Limerick	M.	8,724	28°54′S. 153°54′E.	S.M.	T.	
29	Wollongbar ...	S.	2,239	31°17′S. 153°07′E.	S.M.	T.	
30	Nagina	S.	6,551	07°19′N. 13°50′W.	S.M.	T.	
30	Corabella ...	S.	5,682	07°15′N. 13°49′W.	S.M.	T.	
30	Bandar Shahpour	S.	5,236	07°15′N. 13°49′W.	S.M.	T.	
30	Port Victor ...	M.	12,411	47°49′N. 22°02′W.	S.M.	T.	
	Total ... 32		194,247				

Date	Name	Type	Gross tons	Position	Cause of loss	How lost	Remarks
MAY, 1943							
1	CLAN MACPHERSON	S.	6,940	07°58′N. 14°14′W.	S.M.	T.	
1	CITY OF SINGAPORE	S.	6,555	07°55′N. 14°16′W.	S.M.	T.	
1	BRITISH TRUST* ...	M. Tank	8,466	32°40′N. 19°53′E.	A.C.	T.	
1	ERINPURA	S.	5,143	32°40′N. 19°53′E.	A.C.	B.	
5	HARBURY	S.	5,081	55°01′N. 42°59′W.	S.M.	T.	
5	SELVISTAN	S.	5,136	53°10′N. 44°40′W.	S.M.	T.	
5	NORTH BRITAIN ...	S.	4,635	55°08′N. 42°43′W.	S.M.	T.	
5	HARPERLEY ...	S.	4,586	55°00′N. 42°58′W.	S.M.	T.	
5	BRISTOL CITY ...	S.	2,864	54°00′N. 43°55′W.	S.M.	T.	
5	WENTWORTH ...	S.	5,213	53°59′N. 43°55′W.	S.M.	T.	
5	DOLIUS	M.	5,507	54°00′N. 43°35′W.	S.M.	T.	
5	GHARINDA	S.	5,306	53°10′N. 44°40′W.	S.M.	T.	
5	LORIENT	S.	4,737	54°N. 44°W. (Approx.)	S.M.*	T.	
5	HOLMBURY ...	S.	4,566	04°30′N. 10°20′W.	S.M.	T. & G.	
8	CAMERATA	S.	4,875	Gibraltar	Italian Assault Craft	—	
8	KANBE	S.	6,244	Off Liberian Coast	S.M.	T.	
11	NAILSEA MEADOW...	S.	4,962	32°04′S. 29°13′E.	S.M.	T.	
11	ANTIGONE	S.	4,545	40°30′N. 32°30′W.	S.M.	T.	
11	TINHOW	S.	5,232	25°15′S. 33°30′E.	S.M.	T.	
12	DORSET COAST ...	M.	646	Algiers	A.C.	B.	
12	FORT CONCORD ...	S.	7,138	46°05′N. 25°20′W.	S.M.	T.	
13	CENTAUR* (Hospital Ship)	M.	3,222	27°17′S. 154°05′E.	S.M.	T.	
15	IRISH OAK	S.	5,589	47°51′N. 25°53′W.	S.M.	T.	
17	NORTHMOOR ...	M.	4,392	28°27′S. 32°43′E.	S.M.	T.	
17	AYMERIC	S.	5,196	59°42′N. 41°39′W.	S.M.	T.	
18	EMPIRE EVE* ...	S.	5,979	36°37′N. 00°46′E.	S.M.	T.	
19	ANGELUS	S.V.	255	38°40′N. 64°00′W.	S.M.	G.	
22	ALPERA	S.	1,777	300° 15m. from Cape St. Vincent	A.C.	B.	
29	HOPETARN	M.	5,231	30°50′S. 39°32′E.	S.M.	T.	
30	LLANCARVAN ...	S.	4,910	2m. S. of Cape St. Vincent	A.C.	B.	
31	CATFORD	S.	1,568	53°37′N. 00°42′E.	Mine	—	
	Total ... 31		146,496				
JUNE, 1943							
5	DUMRA	M.	2,304	28°15′S. 33°20′E.	S.M.	T.	
6	HARRIER	S.	193	29°S. 34°E. (Approx.)	S.M.*	—	
14	EMPIRE MAIDEN ...	S. Tank	813	Pantellaria Island	A.C.	B.	
15	ATHELMONARCH* ...	M. Tank	8,995	32°20′N. 34°39′E.	S.M.	T.	
15	SAN ERNESTO ...	M. Tank	8,078	09°18′S. 80°20′E.	S.M.	T. & G.	
17	YOMA	S.	8,131	33°03′N. 22°04′E.	S.M.	T.	
21	BRINKBURN ...	S.	1,598	36°53′N. 02°22′E.	S.M.*	T.	
23	VOLTURNO	S.	3,424	2m. W.N.W. of Cape St. Vincent	A.C.	B.	
23	SHETLAND	S.	1,846	2½m. W.N.W. of Cape St. Vincent	A.C.	B.	
24	BRITISH VENTURE...	S. Tank	4,696	25°13′N. 58°02′E.	S.M.	T.	
28	VERNON CITY ...	S.	4,748	04°30′S. 27°20′W.	S.M.	T.	
	Total ... 11		44,826				
JULY, 1943							
2	HOIHOW	S.	2,798	19°30′S. 55°30′E. (Approx.)	S.M.	T.	
2	EMPIRE KOHINOOR	S.	5,225	06°20′N. 16°30′W.	S.M.	T.	Torpedoed again on 3rd and sunk

Date	Name	Type	Gross tons	Position	Cause of loss	How lost	Remarks
JULY, 1943 —(Contd.)							
4	St. Essylt ...	M.	5,634	36°44'N. 01°31'E.	S.M.	T.	
4	City of Venice ...	S.	8,762	36°44'N. 01°31'E.	S.M.	T.	
5	Devis	M.	6,054	37°01'N. 04°10'E.	S.M.*	T.	
6	Jasper Park ...	S.	7,129	32°52'S. 42°15'E.	S.M.	T.	
6	Shahjehan ...	S.	5,454	33°01'N. 21°32'E.	S.M.	T.	Sank on 7th in position 32°51'N. 21°10'E.
7	Leana	S.	4,743	25°06'S. 35°33'E.	S.M.	T. & G.	
9	Manchester Citizen	S.	5,343	05°50'N. 02°22'E.	S.M.	T.	
10	Talamba ... ... (Hospital Ship)	S.	8,018	36°55'N. 15°13'E.	A.C.	B.	
11	California ...	S.	16,792	41°15'N. 15°24'W.	A.C.	B.	
11	Duchess of York	S.	20,021	41°18'N. 15°24'W.	A.C.	B.	
12	Rahmani ...	S.	5,463	14°52'N. 52°06'E.	S.M.	T.	
12	Ocean Peace ...	S.	7,173	36°55'N. 15°13'E.	A.C.	B.	
14	Harvard	Aux. Sch.	114	10°05'N. 60°20'W.	S.M.	G.	
15	Harmonic	S.	4,558	23°S. 33°W. (Approx.)	S.M.	T.	
15	Gilbert B. Walters	Sch.	176	09°40'N. 59°50'W.	S.M.	G.	
15	Empire Lake* ...	S.	2,852	21°27'S. 51°47'E.	S.M.	T.	
15	J. B. W.	S.B.	72	N. of N.E. Maplin Buoy, Burnham-on-Crouch	Mine*	—.	
16	Fort Franklin ...	S.	7,135	22°36'S. 51°22'E.	S.M.	T.	
16	City of Canton ...	S.	6,692	13°52'S. 41°10'E.	S.M.	T.	Sank on 17th
18	Incomati	M.	7,369	03°09'N. 04°15'E.	S.M.	T. & G.	
20	Fort Pelly ...	S.	7,131	Augusta, Sicily	A.C.	B.	
21	Empire Florizel...	S.	7,056	Off Augusta, Sicily	A.C.	B.	
24	Henzada	S.	4,161	25°15'S. 44°08'W.	S.M.	T.	
24	Fort Chilcotin ...	S.	7,133	15°03'S. 32°35'W.	S.M.	T.	
26	Fishpool	M.	4,950	Syracuse, Sicily	A.C.	B.	
26	El Argentino ...	M.	9,501	39°50'N. 13°38'W.	A.C.	B.	
27	Halizones ...	S.	5,298	38°04'N. 12°59'W.	A.C.	B.	Sank on 30th in position 37°22'N. 13°03'W.
29	Cornish City ...	M.	4,952	27°20'S. 52°10'E.	S.M.	T.	
	Total ... 30		187,759				
AUGUST, 1943							
1	Uskside	S.	2,708	Palermo	A.C.	B.	
2	City of Oran ...	S.	7,323	13°45'S. 41°16'E.	S.M.	T.	Sunk by Escort on 3rd
4	Dalfram	S.	4,558	20°53'S. 56°43'E.	S.M.	T.	
6	Fort Halkett ...	S.	7,133	09°30'S. 26°50'W.	S.M.	T.	
6	Macumba	S.	2,526	11°30'S. 134°40'E.	A.C.	B.	
7	Contractor ...	S.	6,004	37°15'N. 07°21'E.	S.M.*	T.	
7	Umvuma	S.	4,419	20°18'S. 57°14'E.	S.M.	T.	
11	Clan MacArthur	S.	10,528	23°00'S. 53°11'E.	S.M.	T.	
15	Warfield	S.	6,070	39°59'N. 12°58'W.	A.C.	B.	
16	Empire Kestrel ...	S.	2,689	37°10'N. 04°35'E.	A.C.	T.	
17	Empire Stanley ...	M.	6,921	27°08'S. 48°15'E.	S.M.	T.	
19	Sai On	S.	1,950	Macau (Portuguese China)	Seized	---	
20	Namaz	Sch.	50	33°42'N. 34°43'E.	S.M.	---	
20	Panikos	Sch.	21	33°42'N. 34°43'E.	S.M.	---	
	Total ... 14		62,900				
SEPTEMBER, 1943							
6	Sellinge*	S.	2,327	Off Hurd Bank, Malta	Mine	—	
9	Larchbank ...	M.	5,151	07°38'N. 74°00'E.	S.M.	T.	
13	Newfoundland (Hospital Ship)	S.	6,791	40°13'N. 14°21'E.	A.C.	B.	Sunk on 14th by gunfire
13	Fort Babine ...	S.	7,135	41°31'N. 14°39'W.	A.C.	B.	

Date	Name	Type	Gross tons	Position	Cause of loss	How lost	Remarks
SEPTEMBER, 1943—(Contd.)							
19	Fort Longueuil ...	S.	7,128	10°S. 68°E. (Est.)	S.M.*	T.	
20	St. Usk	S.	5,472	16°30′S. 29°28′W.	S.M.	T.	
20	Almenara	S.	1,851	20 to 25m. S.S.E. of Taranto	Mine	—	
23	Fort Jemseg ...	S.	7,134	53°18′N. 40°24′W.	S.M.	T.	
29	Banffshire ...	S.	6,479	09°26′N. 71°20′E.	S.M.	T.	
30	Empire Commerce	M. Tank	3,722	37°19′N. 06°40′E.	S.M.	T.	
30	Fort Howe ...	S.	7,133	37°19′N. 06°40′E.	S.M.	T.	
	Total ... 11		60,323				
OCTOBER, 1943							
1	Tahsinia	M.	7,267	06°51′N. 73°48′E.	S.M.	T. & G.	
1	Stanmore	S.	4,970	36°41′N. 01°10′E.	S.M.	T.	
2	Haiching	S.	2,183	18°46′N. 71°55′E.	S.M.	T.	
4	Fort Fitzgerald...	S.	7,133	36°42′N. 01°17′E.	A.C.	T.	
11	Ocean Viking ...	S.	7,174	40°20′N. 17°00′E.	Mine	—	
11	Jalabala	S.	3,610	11°40′N. 75°19′E.	S.M.	T.	
16	Essex Lance ...	S.	6,625	57°53′N. 28°00′W.	S.M.	T.	
19	Penolver	S.	3,721	47°19′N. 52°27′W.	Mine	—	
21	Saltwick	S.	3,775	36°55′N. 01°36′E.	A.C.	T.	
24	Congella	M.	4,533	01°02′N. 71°14′E.	S.M.	G.	
31	New Columbia ...	S.	6,574	04°25′N. 05°03′E.	S.M.	T.	
	Total ... 11		57,565				
NOVEMBER, 1943							
2	Baron Semple ...	S.	4,573	05°S. 21°W. (Est.)	S.M.*	—	
2	Dona Isabel ...	S.	1,179	16m. W.S.W. of Dungeness	E-Boat	T.	
2	Master Standfast	M.	150	North Sea area	Captured	—	
2	Storaa	S.	1,967	Off Hastings	E-Boat	T.	
2	Foam Queen ...	S.	811	Between Dungeness and Beachy Head	E-Boat	T.	
4	British Progress	S. Tank	4,581	52°55′N. 02°00′E. (Approx.)	E-Boat	T.	Towed to port but subsequently broken up
10	Sambo	S.	7,176	12°28′N. 43°31′E.	S.M.	T.	
11	Birchbank ...	M.	5,151	36°10′N. 00°06′W.	A.C.	T.	
11	Indian Prince ...	M.	8,587	36°13′N. 00°05′W.	A.C.	T.	
13	Cormount	S.	2,841	Off Harwich	Mine	—	
18	Sambridge ...	S.	7,176	11°25′N. 47°25′E.	S.M.	T.	
18	Empire Dunstan...	S.	2,887	39°24′N. 17°40′E.	S.M.	T.	
21	Marsa	S.	4,405	46°40′N. 18°18′W.	A.C.	B.	
26	Morar	S.	1,507	51°50′N. 01°34′E.	Mine	—	
26	Rohna	S.	8,602	36°56′N. 05°20′E.	A.C.	B.	
	Total ... 15		61,593				
DECEMBER, 1943							
2	Testbank	S.	5,083	Bari	A.C.	—	⎱ Blew up or caught fire following explosion of ammunition ship
2	Devon Coast ...	M.	646	Bari	A.C.	—	
2	Lars Kruse ...	S.	1,807	Bari	A.C.	—	
2	Fort Athabaska ...	S.	7,132	Bari	A.C.	—	
9	Cap Padaran ...	S.	8,009	39°15′N. 17°30′E.	S.M.	T.	
13	Daisy Moller ...	S.	4,087	16°21′N. 82°13′E.	S.M.	T.	
17	Kingswood ...	S.	5,080	05°57′N. 01°43′E.	S.M.	T.	
19	Phemius	S.	7,406	05°01′N. 00°17′W.	S.M.	T.	
23	Peshawur	S.	7,934	11°11′N. 80°11′E.	S.M.	T.	
24	Dumana	M.	8,427	04°27′N. 06°58′W.	S.M.	T.	
	Total ... 10		55,611				

Date	Name	Type	Gross tons	Position	Cause of loss	How lost	Remarks
JANUARY, 1944							
3	Empire Housman...	M.	7,359	60°50'N. 22°07'W.	S.M.	T.	Previously torpedoed on 31st December. Torpedoed again 3rd January in position shown. Sank on 5th
6	Polperro	M.	403	49°57'N. 05°28'W. (Approx.)	E-Boat	T.	
6	Underwood ...	M.	1,990	49°57'N. 05°28'W. (Approx.)	E-Boat	T.	
10	Ocean Hunter ...	S.	7,178	36°07'N. 00°11'W.	A.C.	T.	
16	Perseus	S.	10,286	12°00'N. 80°14'E.	S.M.	T.	
20	Fort Buckingham	S.	7,122	08°50'N. 66°25'E. (Est.)	S.M.	T.	
24	St. David (Hospital Carrier)	S.	2,702	41°10'N. 12°21'E.	A.C.	B.	
25	Fort La Maune ...	S.	7,130	13°04'N. 56°30'E.	S.M.	T.	
25	Fort Bellingham	S.	7,153	73°25'N. 25°10'E.	S.M.	T.	
26	Samouri	S.	7,219	13°04'N. 55°45'E.	S.M.	T.	
26	Surada	S.	5,427	13°00'N. 55°15'E.	S.M.	T.	
31	Emerald	S.	806	S.E. of Beachy Head	E-Boat	T.	
31	Caleb Sprague ...	S.	1,813	10m. S.E. of Beachy Head	E-Boat	T.	
	Total ... 13		66,588				
FEBRUARY, 1944							
7	Margit*	S.	1,735	61°30'N. 10°30'W. (Est.)	S.M.*	—	
10	El Grillo* ...	S. Tank	7,264	Seidis Fjord, Iceland	A.C.	B.	
12	Khedive Ismail ...	S.	7,513	00°57'N. 72°16'E.	S.M.	T.	
15	Fort St. Nicholas	S.	7,154	40°34'N. 14°37'E.	S.M.	T.	
22	British Chivalry	S. Tank	7,118	00°50'S. 68°00'E.	S.M.	T.	
23	San Alvaro ...	M. Tank	7,385	13°46'N. 48°55'E.	S.M.	T.	
24	Philipp M. ...	S.	2,085	Nr. Hearty Knoll Buoy, off Gt. Yarmouth	E-Boat	T.	
26	Silvermaple ...	M.	5,313	04°44'N. 03°20'W.	S.M.	T.	
26	Sutlej	M.	5,189	08°S. 70°E. (Approx.)	S.M.	T.	
29	Palma	M.	5,419	05°51'N. 79°58'E.	S.M.	T.	
29	Ascot	S.	7,005	05°S. 63°E. (Approx.)	S.M.	T. & G.	
	Total ... 11		63,180				
MARCH, 1944							
3	Fort McLeod ...	S.	7,127	02°01'N. 77°06'E.	S.M.	T. & G.	
4	Empire Tourist ...	S.	7,062	73°25'N. 22°11'E.	S.M.	T.	
5	John Holt ...	S.	4,964	03°56'N. 07°36'E.	S.M.	T.	
9	Behar	M.	7,840	20°32'S. 87°10'E.	Raider	—	
16	El Madina ...	S.	3,962	20°54'N. 89°36'E.	S.M.	T.	
18	Nancy Moller ...	S.	3,916	02°14'N. 78°25'E.	S.M.	T.	
20	Matadian ...	S. Tank	4,275	05°07'N. 04°47'E.	S.M.	T.	
22	Watuka	S.	1,621	44°30'N. 62°51'W.	S.M.	T.	
27	Tulagi*	M.	2,281	11°00'S. 78°40'E.	S.M.	T.	
30	City of Adelaide	S.	6,589	12°01'S. 80°27'E.	S.M.	T. & G.	
	Total ... 10		49,637				
APRIL, 1944							
1	Dahomian	S.	5,277	34°25'S. 18°19'E.	S.M.	T.	
8	Nebraska	S.	8,262	11°55'S. 19°52'W.	S.M.	T.	
20	Royal Star ...	S.	7,900	37°02'N. 03°41'E.	A.C.	T.	
	Total ... 3		21,439				

Date	Name	Type	Gross tons	Position	Cause of loss	How lost	Remarks
MAY, 1944							
1	JANETA	S.	5,312	18°10′S. 20°00′W.	S.M.	T.	
6	ANADYR	S.	5,321	10°55′S. 27°30′W.	S.M.	T.	
11	EMPIRE HEATH ...	S.	6,644	19°S. 31°W.	S.M.	T.	
19	FORT MISSANABIE...	S.	7,147	38°20′N. 16°28′E.	S.M.	T.	
30	NORDEFLINGE* ...	S.	2,873	37°02′N. 03°47′E.	A.C.	B.	
	Total ... 5		27,297				
JUNE, 1944							
5	HELEN MOLLER ...	S.	5,259	04°28′S. 74°45′E.	S.M.	T.	
6	SAMBUT	S.	7,219	51°08′N. 01°33′E.	C.U.	---	
10	DUNGRANGE ...	S.	621	S. of St. Catherine's Pt., I.O.W.	E-Boat	T.	
10	BRACKENFIELD ...	S.	657	50m. S. of Nab. L.V.	E-Boat	T.	
10	ASHANTI	M.	534	Off St. Catherine's Pt., I.O.W.	E-Boat	T.	
16	COLUMBINE... ...	S.	3,268	32°44′S. 17°22′E.	S.M.	T.	
16	ALERT (Trinity House Vessel)	S.	793	49°25′N. 00°40′W.	Mine	-/-	
18	ALBERT C. FIELD...	S.	1,764	50°28′N. 01°46′W.	A.C.	T.	
20	WESTDALE	S.	424	49°24′N. 00°38′W.	Mine	---	
22	DUNVEGAN HEAD...	S.	638	Off Assault Beaches, Normandy	C.U.	---	
24	FORT NORFOLK ...	S.	7,131	Off Assault Beaches, Normandy	Mine	---	
24	EMPIRE LOUGH ...	S.	2,824	51°06′N. 01°16′E.	C.U.	---	
24	DERRYCUNIHY ...	M.	7,093	Off Assault Beaches, Normandy	Mine	---	
28	MAID OF ORLEANS	S.	2,386	50°10′N. 00°40′W.	S.M.	T.	
29	NELLORE	S.	6,942	07°51′S. 75°20′E.	S.M.	T.	
29	EMPIRE PORTIA ...	S.	7,058	50°33′N. 00°35′W.	S.M.	T.	
	Total ... 16		54,611				
JULY, 1944							
2	EMPIRE BROADSWORD	S.	7,177	49°25′N. 00°54′W.	Mine	---	
5	GLENDINNING ...	S.	1,927	50°32′N. 00°22′W.	S.M.	T.	
9	SHAHZADA	S.	5,454	15°30′N. 65°30′E.	S.M.	T.	
12	NAJA	Tug	72	Upper Pool, Wapping, London	Flying Bomb	---	
14	DIRECTOR	S.	5,107	24°30′S. 35°44′E.	S.M.	T.	
15	TANDA	S.	7,174	13°22′N. 74°09′E.	S.M.	T.	
19	KING FREDERICK ...	S.	5,265	09°29′N. 71°45′E.	S.M.	T.	
20	No. 36	Hopper Barge	772	Cherbourg	Mine	---	
30	SAMWAKE	S.	7,219	50°40′N. 00°31′E. (Approx.)	E-Boat	T.	
	Total ... 9		40,167				
AUGUST, 1944							
4	T.C.C. HOPPER NO. 1	Hopper Barge	604	Cherbourg	Mine	---	
5	EMPIRE CITY ...	M.	7,295	11°33′S. 41°25′E.	S.M.	T.	
7	EMPIRE DAY ...	M.	7,242	07°06′S. 42°00′E.	S.M.	T.	
7	AMSTERDAM (Hospital Carrier)	S.	4,220	49°25′N. 00°35′W.	Mine*	---	
13	RADBURY	S.	3,614	24°20′S. 41°45′E.	S.M.	T.	
16	EMPIRE LANCER ...	S.	7,037	15°S. 45°E. (Approx.)	S.M.	T.	
17	IDDESLEIGH ...	S.	5,205	¾m. S. of 90 Buoy. Off Langrune, Assault area, Normandy	One man torpedo	---	Previously damaged by torpedo on 10th
18	NAIRUNG	S.	5,414	15°S. 42°E. (Est.)	S.M.*	T.	
19	WAYFARER ...	S.	5,068	14°30′S. 42°20′E. (Est.)	S.M.	T.	

Date	Name	Type	Gross tons	Position	Cause of loss	How lost	Remarks
AUGUST, 1944—(Contd.)							
19	St. Enogat ...	S.	2,360	50°16′N. 00°50′W. (Approx.)	S.M.*	T.	
20	Berwickshire ...	S.	7,464	30°58′S. 38°50′E.	S.M.	T.	
20	Coral	S.	638	50°13′N. 00°48′W.	S.M.	T.	
23	Fort Yale ...	S.	7,134	50°23′N. 00°55′W.	S.M.	T.	Previously damaged by mine on 8th
24	Empire Rosebery	S. Tank	2,370	49°22′N. 00°36′W.	Mine	—	
25	Orminster ...	S.	5,712	50°09′N. 00°44′W.	S.M.	T.	
26	Ashmun J. Clough	S.	1,791	50°10′N. 01°41′W.	S.M.	T.	
31	Troilus	S.	7,422	14°10′N. 61°04′E.	S.M.	T.	
	Total ... 17		80,590				
SEPTEMBER, 1944							
3	Livingston ...	S.	2,140	46°15′N. 58°05′W.	S.M.	T.	
8	Empire Heritage	S. Tank	15,702	55°27′N. 08°01′W.	S.M.	T.	
8	Pinto	M.	1,346	55°27′N. 08°01′W.	S.M.	T.	
29	Samsuva	S.	7,219	72°58′N. 23°59′E.	S.M.	T.	
	Total ... 4		26,407				
OCTOBER, 1944							
26	Rouseville ...	M. Tank	1,155	49°26′N. 00°36′E. In River Seine, off Vieux Port	Mine	—	
NOVEMBER, 1944							
2	Rio Bravo ...	M. Tank	1,141	Ostend Roads	E-Boat	T.	
5	Marion Moller ...	S.	3,827	10°40′N. 81°10′E.	S.M.	T.	
10	Shirvan	S. Tank	6,017	64°08′N. 22°50′W. (Approx.)	S.M.	T.	
10	Empire Wold* ...	Tug	269	64°08′N. 22°38′W.	S.M.*	—	
	Total ... 4		11,254				
DECEMBER, 1944							
1	Empire Dace (Ferry)	S.	716	Entrance to Missolonghi, Greece	Mine	—	
3	Cornwallis ...	S.	5,458	43°59′N. 68°20′W. (Approx.)	S.M.	T.	
7	Samsip	S.	7,219	298° 1m. from N.F.11 Buoy, Scheldt Estuary	Mine	—	Sunk by gunfire
15	Fort Maisonneuve	S.	7,128	105° 8.5m. from N.F.14 Buoy, Scheldt Estuary	Mine	—	
18	Silverlaurel ...	S.	6,142	50°07′N. 04°40′W.	S.M.	T.	
23	Dumfries	S.	5,149	50°23′N. 01°43′W.	S.M.*	T.	
23	Slemish	S.	1,536	49°45′N. 01°42′W.	S.M.*	T.	
23	Tid 70	Tug	50	50°12′N. 00°52′W.	Mine	—	
24	Empire Path ...	S.	6,140	51°22′N. 02°52′E.	Mine	—	
28	Empire Javelin ...	S.	7,177	50°04′N. 01°00′W.	S.M.	T.	
	Total ... 10		46,715				
JANUARY, 1945							
10	Blackheath ...	S.	4,637	35°49′N. 06°03′W.	S.M.*	T.	
11	Normandy Coast...	S.	1,428	53°19′N. 04°48′W.	S.M.	T.	
14	Athelviking ...	M. Tank	8,779	44°20′N. 63°24′W.	S.M.	T.	

Date	Name	Type	Gross tons	Position	Cause of loss	How lost	Remarks
JANUARY, 1945—(Contd.)							
14	BRITISH FREEDOM*	M. Tank	6,985	44°28'N. 63°28'W.	S.M.	T.	
15	MAJA	M. Tank	8,181	53°40'N. 05°14'W.	S.M.	T.	
15	D	Hopper Barge	262	109° 1.53m. from Eastham Pumping Chimney, Mersey	Mine	—	
15	DALEMOOR	S.	5,835	53°22'N. 00°50'E. (Approx.)	Mine	—	
18	SAMVERN	S.	7,219	51°22'N. 03°02'E.	Mine	—	
22	HALO	S.	2,365	51°22'N. 02°24'E. (Approx.)	E-Boat	T.	
	Total ... 9		45,691				
FEBRUARY, 1945							
6	EVERLEIGH ...	S.	5,222	50°30'N. 01°48'W.	S.M.	T.	
17	REGENT LION ...	M. Tank	9,551	35°56'N. 05°45'W.	S.M.	T.	
22	ALEXANDER KENNEDY	S.	1,313	50°06'N. 04°50'W.	S.M.*	T.	
22	GOODWOOD ...	S.	2,780	52°53'N. 02°12'E. (Approx.)	E-Boat	T.	
22	BLACKTOFT ...	S.	1,109	52°52'N. 02°36'E.	E-Boat	T.	
23	POINT PLEASANT PARK	S.	7,136	29°42'S. 09°58'E.	S.M.	T. & G.	
24	ORISKANY	S.	1,644	50°05'N. 05°51'W.	S.M.	T.	
24	ALERT*	Cable Ship	941	51°21'N. 01°37'E.	C.U.	—	
25	EGHOLM	S.	1,317	55°50'N. 01°52'W.	S.M.*	T.	
26	AURETTA	S.	4,571	51°24'N. 02°49'E.	Mine	—	
27	SAMPA	S.	7,219	9m. N. of Ostend (Approx.)	Mine	—	
28	NORFOLK COAST ...	M.	646	51°58'N. 05°25'W.	S.M..	T.	
	Total ... 12		43,449				
MARCH, 1945							
2	KING EDGAR ...	M.	4,536	52°05'N. 05°42'W.	S.M.	T.	
8	LORNASTON ...	S	4,934	50°35'N. 00°03'W.	S.M.*	T.	
10	BARON JEDBURGH...	S.	3,656	10°02'S. 25°00'W.	S.M.	T.	
13	TABER PARK ...	S.	2,878	52°22'N. 01°53'E.	Midget S.M.*	—	
16	INGER TOFT ...	S.	2,190	57°25'N. 06°52'W.	S.M.	T.	
19	SAMSELBU	S.	7,253	51°23'N. 03°06'E.	Mine	—	
19	EMPIRE BLESSING...	S.	7,062	51°24'N. 03°17 E.	Mine	—	
19	CRICHTOUN ...	S.	1,097	Off Lowestoft	E-Boat	T.	
19	ROGATE	S.	2,871	070° 3m. from No. 4 Buoy (off Lowestoft)	E-Boat	T.	
22	EMPIRE KINGSLEY...	S.	6,996	50°08'N. 05°51'W.	S.M.	T.	
26	NEWLANDS ...	S.	1,556	51°28'N. 01°25'E. (Approx.)	Midget S.M.	—	
30	JIM	S.	833	52°08'N. 01°40'E.	Midget S.M.*	—	
	Total ... 12		45,862				
APRIL, 1945							
5	GASRAY	S.	1,406	2m. from St. Abb's Head	S.M.	T.	
6	CUBA	S.	11,420	50°36'N. 00°57'W.	S.M.	T.	
9	SAMIDA „ ...	S.	7,219	50°57'N. 01°03'E. (Approx.)	S.M.	T.	
16	MONARCH*. .	Cable Ship	1,150	52°08'N. 01°52'E.	S.M.*	T.	
16	ATHELDUKE .	M Tank	8,966	55°39'N. 01°31'W.	S.M.	T.	

Date	Name	Type	Gross tons	Position	Cause of loss	How lost	Remarks
APRIL, 1945—(Contd.)							
16	Gold Shell ...	M. Tank	8,208	51°22′N. 02°55′E.	Mine	—	
18	Empire Gold ...	S. Tank	8,028	47°47′N. 06°26′W.	S.M.	T.	
18	Filleigh	S.	4,856	51°20′N. 01°42′E.	S.M.	T.	
24	Monmouth Coast...	S.	878	80m. from Sligo	S.M.*	T.	
	Total ... 9		52,131				
MAY, 1945							
7	Avondale Park ...	S.	2,878	1m. S.E. of May Is., Firth of Forth	S.M.	T.	

LIST II

BRITISH FISHING VESSELS LOST BY ENEMY ACTION

Date	Name	Type	Gross tons	Position	Cause of loss	How lost	Remarks
SEPTEMBER, 1939							
13	DAVARA	S.T.	291	21m. N.W. × N. of Tory Is.	S.M.	G.	
16	RUDYARD KIPLING	S.T.	333	53°50′N. 11°10′W.	S.M.	Time Bombs	
18	ARLITA	S.T.	326	57°51′N. 09°28′W.	S.M.	G.	
18	LORD MINTO ...	S.T.	295	57°51′N. 09°28′W.	S.M.	G.	
24	CALDEW	S.T.	287	60°47′N. 06°20′W.	S.M.	G.	
	Total ... 5		1,532				
OCTOBER, 1939							
28	ST. NIDAN	S.T.	565	60°N. 05°W. (Approx.)	S.M.	G. and explosive charge	
28	LYNX II	S.T.	250	60°N. 05°W. (Approx.)	S.M.	G.	
	Total ... 2		815				
NOVEMBER, 1939							
12	CRESSWELL ...	S.T.	275	18m. N.W. × N. of Flannan Is., Outer Hebrides	S.M.	G.	
18	WIGMORE	S.T.	345	25m. N. × W. of Rattray Head	S.M.	T.	
20	SEA SWEEPER ...	S.T.	329	25m. N.W. × W. of Tory Is.	S.M.	G.	
20	DELPHINE	S.T.	250	18m. N. × E. of Tory Is.	S.M.	G.	
20	THOMAS HANKINS...	S.T.	276	14m. N.W. of Tory Is.	S.M.	G.	
21	SULBY	S.T.	287	75m. N.W. of Rathlin Is.	S.M.	G.	
21	WILLIAM HUMPHRIES	S.T.	276	75m. N.W. of Rathlin Is.	S.M.	G.	
	Total ... 7		2,038				
DECEMBER, 1939							
17	PEARL	S.T.	198	65m. E. ½S. of Outer Dowsing L.V.	A.C.	B.	
17	COMPAGANUS ...	S.T.	270	150m. E. × N. of May Is.	A.C.	B.	
17	ISABELLA GREIG ...	S.T.	210	145m. E. × N. of May Is.	A.C.	B.	
17	TRINITY N.B. ...	S.T.	203	57°50′N. 01°30′W.	A.C.	B.	
18	ACTIVE	S.T.	185	48m. N.N.W. of Rattray Head	A.C.	T.	
18	ZELOS	S.T.	227	112m. E. × N. of May Is.	A.C.	B.	
19	DANEDEN	S.T.	210	12m. E.S.E. of Fetlar, Shetlands	A.C.	B.	
19	RIVER EARN ...	S.T.	202	58°30′N. 02°00′E.	A.C.	B.	
28	BARBARA ROBERTSON	S.T.	325	35m. N.W. of Butt of Lewis	S.M.	G.	
28	RESERCHO ...	S.T.	258	6m. S.E. × E. of Flamboro' Head	Mine	—	
	Total ... 10		2,288				

Date	Name	Type	Gross tons	Position	Cause of loss	How lost	Remarks
JANUARY, 1940							
6	ETA	M.T.	81	6m. N. ½W. of Outer Gabbard L.V.	Mine	—	
11	LUCIDA	S.T.	251	55°00'N. 00°53'W.	Mine	—	
11	CROXTON	S.T.	195	53°20'N. 02°40'E.	A.C.	B.	
12	WILLIAM IVEY ...	S.T.	202	15 to 16m. N. ½E. of Longstone L.H.	A.C.	B.	
15	NEWHAVEN... ...	S.T.	162	18m. S.S.E. of Lowestoft (Est.)	Mine	—	
	Total ... 5		891				
FEBRUARY, 1940							
10	THERESA BOYLE ...	S.T.	224	115m. E. × N. of Aberdeen	A.C.	B.	
11	TOGIMO	S.T.	290	50°40'N. 11°02'W.	S.M.	G,	
27	BEN ATTOW ...	S.T.	156	7m. E. ½S. of May Is.	Mine	—	
	Total ... 3		670				
MARCH, 1940							
10	LEUKOS	S.T.	216	N.W. of Tory Is.	C.U.	—	
11	HALIFAX	S.T.	165	3m. S.E. of Aldeburgh L.V.	Mine	—	
	Total ... 2		381				
APRIL, 1940							
3	GORSPEN	S.T.	208	31m. N.E. of Outer Skerries	A.C.	B.	
3	SANSONNET... ...	S.T.	212	18m. E. × S. of Muckle Flugga	A.C.	B.	
	Total ... 2		420				
MAY, 1940							
22	TEASER	Motor Fishing Smack	9	400 yds. W. of Tollesbury Pier, R. Blackwater, Essex	Mine	—	
About 30	CORENNIE	S.T.	203	North Sea	C.U.	—	
	Total ... 2		212				
JUNE, 1940							
1	SLASHER	S.T.	195	70m. N.E. ½E. of Humber	A.C.	B.	
1	RENOWN	F.V.	9	Near Sandetti L.V.	Mine	—	
2	GREYNIGHT ...	S.T.	96	54°40'N. 01°30'E.	A.C.	B. & G.	
3	OCEAN LASSIE ...	Drifter	96	055° 2¾ cables from Outer Ridge Buoy, Harwich	Mine	—	
10	RIVER NESS ...	S.T.	203	8m. N.E. × N. of Skerries	A.C.	B.	
28	CASTLETON ...	S.T.	211	Vicinity of Orkneys	C.U.	—	
	Total ... 6		810				
JULY, 1940							
4	REMEMBRANCE ...	F.V.	7	51°53'N. 01°22'E.	Mine	—	
12	VOLANTE	S.T.	255	10m. E. of Hvalbam, Iceland	A.C.	B.	
29	LEACH'S ROMANCE	F.V.	44	10½m. due S. of Kemp Town	Mine	—	
	Total ... 3		306				

Date	Name	Type	Gross tons	Position	Cause of loss	How lost	Remarks
AUGUST, 1940							
18	VALERIA	S.T.	189	035° 8m. from Smalls	A.C.	B.	
28	FLAVIA	S.T.	202	North Sea	C.U.	—	
	Total ... 2		391				
SEPTEMBER, 1940							
7	SALACON	S.T.	211	114° 5.3m. from Spurn Pt. L.H.	Mine	—	
11	BEATHWOOD ...	S.T.	209	1m. E. of Montrose Coast Guard Look-out	A.C.	B.	
11	RESPONDO ...	S.T.	209	Off Old Head of Kin-sale	C.U.	—	
24	BASS ROCK ...	S.T.	169	Off Old Head of Kin-sale	A.C.	B.	
	Total ... 4		798				
OCTOBER, 1940							
16	PRIDE	Motor F.V.	25	Off Scarborough	Mine	—	
17	ALBATROSS ...	F.V.	15	Off Grimsby	Mine	—	
25	ENCOURAGE ...	Motor F.V.	45	210° 6¼ cables from Breakwater Fort, Plymouth	Mine	—	
25	WINDSOR ...	S.T.	222	174° 2.1m. from Spurn Pt.	Mine	—	
25	CARLTON	Steam Drifter	207	131½° 3.5m. from Spurn Pt.	Mine	—	
	Total ... 5		514				
NOVEMBER, 1940							
12	LORD HALDANE ...	S.T.	91	Neighbourhood of Bristol Channel	C.U.	—	
DECEMBER, 1940							
2	KILGERRAN CASTLE	S.T.	276	51°21'N. 08°35'W.	A.C.	B.	
17	CARRY ON ...	Steam Drifter	93	E. of Nore Sand L.V.	Mine	—	
	Total ... 2		369				
JANUARY, 1941							
12	STRATHRYE... ...	S.T.	212	50°35'N. 03°59'W.	Mine	—	
12	OYAMA	S.T.	340	North Atlantic	C.U.	—	
27	CAERPHILLY CASTLE	S.T.	275	52°35'N. 12°00'W.	A.C.	B.	
	Total ... 3		827				
FEBRUARY, 1941							
11	JOHN DUNKIN ...	S.T.	202	13m. N. × E. of Buckie	A.C.	B.	
11	EAMONT	S.T.	227	58°15'N. 03°26'W.	A.C.	B.	
16	THOMAS DEAS ...	S.T.	276	273° 4m. from Spurn Pt.	Mine	—	
16	NANIWA ...	S.T.	340	52°15'N. 12°30'W.	A.C.	B.	
	Total ... 4		1,045				
MARCH, 1941							
11	ABERDEEN	S.T.	163	Cardigan Bay	A.C.	B. & G.	
14	PEACEFUL STAR ...	Steam Drifter	94	17m. E.S.E. of Rock-abill L.H.	A.C.	B.	
20	JOAN MARGARET* ...	F.V.	25	River Humber	Mine	—	
20	BIANCA	S.T.	174	Irish Sea	A.C.	T.	
23	ELMIRA	S.T.	197	59°55'N. 03°40'W.	A.C.	B.	

Date	Name	Type	Gross tons	Position	Cause of loss	How lost	Remarks
MARCH, 1941—(Contd.)							
25	ALASKAN	F.V.	21	54°49′N. 01°07′W.	Mine	—	
26	MILLIMUMUL ...	S.T.	287	Nr. Newcastle, N.S.W.	Mine	—	
27	KINCLAVEN ...	S.T.	178	Off Faroes	C.U.	—	
28	KESTREL ..: ...	S.T.	75	N.E. of N. Lundy Lt.	A.C.	B.	
29	KIMBERLEY ...	S.T.	190	Near 62D Buoy, 22m. S.E.of Flamborough Head	A.C.	B.	
29	EXETER	S.T.	165	5m. S.W. of Ballycotton	A.C.	B.	
29	HORACE E. NUTTEN	S.T.	209	Moray Firth	C.U.	—	
30	NISUS	S.T.	210	Faroese Waters	C.U.	—	
31	HELPMATE	Steam Drifter	76	Off Newlyn, Cornwall	C.U.	—	
31	ONTARIO	S.T.	208	60°15′N. 11°00′W.	A.C.	B. & G.	
	Total ... 15		2,272				
APRIL, 1941							
4	WHITBY	S.T.	164	3m. S.S.E. of Blackwater L.V.	A.C.	B.	
6	DANELAND	S.T.	289	30m. N. ¼W. of Rathlin O'Birne Is.	A.C.	B.	
7	SYLVIA	S.T.	213	61°27′N. 05°48′W.	A.C.	B.	
26	COMMANDER HORTON	S.T.	227	Off Iceland	C.U.	—	
	Total ... 4		893				
MAY, 1941							
7	WATERLILY ...	F.V.	12	Bessom Creek, West Mersea	A.C.	B.	
8	WELCOME HOME ...	Ketch	38	Hull	A.C.	B.	
9	TANKERTON TOWERS	S.T.	97	Off St. Goven's L.V.	A.C.	B.	
13	FORT RONA ...	S.T.	203	15m. W.S.W. of Bardsey Is.	A.C.	B.	
	Total ... 4		350				
JUNE, 1941							
5	LAVINIA L.* ...	Steam Drifter	73	Sheerness	A.C.	B.	
15	AUDACIOUS ...	F.V.	7	51°28′N. 00°51′E.	Mine	—	
18	DORIS II	F.V.	6	Off Sheerness	Mine*	—	
	Total ... 3		86				
JULY, 1941							
1	STRATHGAIRN ...	S.T.	211	20m. S.W. of Barra Head (Approx.)	Mine	—	
6	WESTFIELD	S.T.	140	Off St. Goven's Head	A.C.*	—	
10	ISABELLA FOWLIE...	S.T.	196	7m. E.N.E. of Longstone	A.C.	B.	
17	BEN GLAMAIR ...	S.T.	198	Vicinity of Dunstanburgh	C.U.	—	
27	BEN STROME ...	S.T.	198	15m. S.E. of Fuglo Is., Faroes	A.C.	B.	
28	STRATHLOCHY ...	S.T.	212	180m. N.W. of Rosa Head, Orkneys	A.C.	B.	
	Total ... 6		1,155				
AUGUST, 1941							
4	ROBERT MAX ...	F.V.	172	36°47′N. 21°15′W.	S.M.	G.	
8	OCEAN VICTOR ...	S.T.	202	Off Iceland	A.C.*	—	

Date	Name	Type	Gross tons	Position	Cause of loss	How lost	Remarks
AUGUST, 1941—(Contd.)							
12	EXPRESS	Motor Fishing Smack	16	1m. S.W. of E. Spaniard Buoy, off Whitstable	Mine	—	
20	JULIET	S.T.	173	30m. S. of Old Head of Kinsale	A.C.	B.	
30	LADYLOVE	S.T.	230	Off Iceland*	C.U.	—	
	Total ... 5		793				
SEPTEMBER, 1941							
7	OPHIR II	S.T.	213	About 15m. from Spurn Pt. in Northern Approach Channel	Mine	—	
8	KING ERIK ...	S.T.	228	Off Iceland	C.U.	—	
19	GLEN ALVA ...	F.V.	6	Off Jenkins Buoy, Southend	Mine	—	
28	MURIELLE	S.T.	96	Approx. 9m. S.W. × S. of Morecambe L.V.	Mine	—	Sank 3m. W. × N. of Blackpool Tower whilst in tow
	Total ... 4		543				
NOVEMBER, 1941							
2	CALIPH	S.T.	226	12m. S. of Old Head of Kinsale	A.C.	B.	
8	CRADOCK	S.T.	204	14m. N.N.E. of St. Abb's Head	A.C.	B.	
16	FERNBANK	S.T.	211	12m. N.W. of Myggenaes, Faroes	A.C.	B.	
	Total ... 3		641				
DECEMBER, 1941							
1	ST. LEONARD No. 1	S.T.	210	60°58′N. 01°10′W. (Approx.)	A.C.	B.	
8	LORD SHREWSBURY	S.T.	167	Entrance to River Humber	Mine*	—	
10	KINCORTH	Steam Drifter	148	082° 7m. from Lynas Pt.	Mine	—	
19	MOUETTE	F.V.	3	Blue Anchor Bay, Minehead	Mine	—	
	Total ... 4		528				
JANUARY, 1942							
29	BRACONBUSH ...	S.T.	204	Off Duncansby Head	Mine*	—	
FEBRUARY, 1942							
22	BELLEVUE	S.T.	156	Off Turnberry L.H. Near Ailsa Craig (Est.)	C.U.	—	
MAY, 1942							
4	LITTLE EXPRESS ...	F.V.	9	½m. S.E. of West Pansand Buoy, Kentish Flats	Mine	—	
14	OUR JANIE... ...	F.V.	19	Brixham	A.C.	—	
	Total ... 2		28				

Date	Name	Type	Gross tons	Position	Cause of loss	How lost	Remarks
JUNE, 1942							
17	MAGGIE	F.V.	6	25m. N.N.E. of N. Foreland	Mine	—	
About 25	BROMELIA	S.T.	242	Off Iceland	C.U.	—	
	Total ... 2		248				
JULY, 1942							
2	WHINNYFOLD ...	S.T.	210	15m. S.E. of Langanaes L.V., Iceland	A.C.	B.	
25	LUCILLE M. ...	Motor F.V.	54	42°02′N. 65°38′W.	S.M.	G.	
	Total ... 2		264				
AUGUST, 1942							
2	DUREENBEE ...	S.T.	223	35°55′S. 150°30′E.	S.M.	G.	
About 6	BOMBAY	S.T.	229	62°N. 18°W. (Est.)	C.U.	—	
	Total ... 2		452				
DECEMBER, 1942							
About 25	BEN SCREEL ...	S.T.	195	Off St. Abb's Head	Mine*	—	
MARCH, 1943							
17	E.V.G. (No. RX. 152)	F.V.	16	5m. S. of Rye	Mine	—	
APRIL, 1943							
10	BOY BILLY ...	F.V.	5	235° 6m. from Dungeness	Mine	—	
JUNE, 1943							
26	CRYSTAL	S.T.	149	12m. off Scarborough	Mine	—	
SEPTEMBER, 1943							
1	STRATHLYON ...	S.T.	218	Off Iceland	Mine*	—	
JANUARY, 1944							
30	ALONSO	S.T.	172	North Sea Fishing Grounds	C.U.	—	
JULY, 1944							
5	NOREEN MARY ...	S.T.	207	58°30′N. 05°23′W.	S.M.	G.	
27	ROCHESTER ...	S.T.	165	53°54′N. 00°42′E. (Est.)	Mine	—	
	Total ... 2		372				

Date	Name	Type	Gross tons	Position	Cause of loss	How lost	Remarks
FEBRUARY, 1945							
25	AQUARIUS	S.T.	187	15m. S.E. × E. of Outer Dowsing L.V. (Approx.)	Mine	—	
APRIL, 1945							
20	ETHEL CRAWFORD...	S.T.	200	55°13′N. 05°14′W.	Mine	—	

LIST III

BRITISH MERCHANT AND FISHING VESSELS DAMAGED BY ENEMY ACTION BUT NOT LOST

(Vessels only superficially damaged have not been included).

Date	Name	Type	Gross tons	Position	Cause of damage	How damaged	Remarks
SEPTEMBER, 1939							
16	CITY OF PARIS ...	S.	10,902	52°14′N. 01°43′E.	Mine	—	
21	TEAKWOOD ...	S. Tank	6,014	49°39′N. 06°39′W.	S.M.	T.	
OCTOBER, 1939							
5	MARWARRI	S.	8,063	190° 3½m. from Scarweather L.V.	Mine	—	
6	LOCHGOIL	M.	9,462	51°24′N. 04°00′W.	Mine	—	
13	STONEPOOL ...	S.	4,803	48°40′N. 15°30′W. (Approx.)	S.M.	G.	
NOVEMBER, 1939							
18	JAMES J. MAGUIRE	M. Tank	10,525	51°46′N. 01°40′E.	Mine	—	
23	DAVISIAN	S.	6,433	Off Nore L.V.	Mine	—	
24	SUSSEX	M.	11,063	S.E. of Southend	Mine	—	
DECEMBER, 1939							
2	ESKDENE	S.	3,829	56°30′N. 01°40′W. (Approx.)	C.U.	—	Mine or S.M. T.
14	ATHELTEMPLAR ...	M. Tank	8,939	55°05′N. 01°07′W.	Mine	—	
17	AGNITA	M. Tank	3,552	50°42′N. 00°44′E.	A.C.	B.	
17	EILEEN WRAY ...	S.T.	227	Off Hartlepool	A.C.	B. & G.	
17	CRAIGIELEA ...	S.T.	211	90m. N.E. × E. ½E. of Aberdeen	A.C.	B. & G.	
18	ASTROS	S.T.	275	115m. E. × N. of May Island	A.C.	B.	
18	NEW CHOICE ...	S.T.	236	115m. E. × N. of May Island	A.C.	B. & G.	
18	ETRURIA	S.T.	373	20m. S.E. ½E. of Duncansby Head	A.C.	B. & G.	
19	STAR OF SCOTLAND	S.T.	203	10m. S.E. of Fetlar Is., Shetlands	A.C.	B. & G.	
21	DOSINIA	M. Tank	8,053	½m. S.W. of Haisboro' L.V.	Mine	—	
22	GRYFEVALE ...	S.	4,434	3m. E. of Tyne Piers	Mine	—	
26	ADELLEN	M. Tank	7,984	51°30′N. 01°43′E.	Mine	—	
28	SAN DELFINO ...	M. Tank	8,072	In Humber	Mine	—	
JANUARY, 1940							
6	CITY OF MARSEILLES	S.	8,317	1½m. S.E. of No. 1 Black Buoy, River Tay	Mine	—	
9	CHRYSOLITE ...	S.T.	251	8m. N.W. × N. of Smith's Knoll L.V.	A.C.	B. & G.	
9	RECULVER (Trinity House Vessel)	M.	683	Off Great Yarmouth	A.C.	B. & G.	
9	NORTHWOOD ...	S.	1,146	Off Whitby	A.C.	B. & G.	

C*

Date	Name	Type	Gross tons	Position	Cause of damage	How damaged	Remarks
JANUARY, 1940—*(Contd.)*							
11	Flavia	S.T.	202	90m. N.E. × E. of Buchanness	A.C.	B. & G.	
11	Pitwines	S.	932	25m. S.E. × S. of Flamboro' Head	A.C.	B. & G.	
12	Persian Empire ...	S.T.	195	7m. E. × N. of Filey	A.C.	B.	
12	Blythmoor ...	S.	6,582	54°16′N. 00°10′W.	A.C.	B.	
15	Gracia	S.	5,642	5m. W.S.W. of Bar L.V., Mersey	Mine	—	
15	Kildale	S.	3,877	2m. E. of S. Ship-head Buoy, off the Naze	Mine	—	
29	Imperial Monarch	S.	5,831	062° 10m. from Scurdyness	A.C.	B. & G.	
29	Gripfast	S.	1,109	10m. S.E. × E. ½S. of Flamboro' Head	A.C.	B. & G.	
30	Royal Crown ...	S.	4,364	15m. S. of Smith's Knoll L.V.	A.C.	B. & G.	
30	Jersey Queen	S.	910	53°06′N. 01°30′E.	A.C.	B. & G.	
FEBRUARY, 1940							
3	Kildale	S.	3,877	53°47′N. 00°34′E.	A.C.	B. & G.	
3	Yewdale	S.	823	4m. N.N.E. of Scarborough	A.C.	B. & G.	
3	Beechwood ...	S.	4,897	3m. E. of Smith's Knoll L.V.	A.C.	B. & G.	
3	Harley	S.	400	8m. S.S.E. of Flamboro' Head	A.C.	B. & G.	
3	Newminster ...	S.	967	54°49′N. 01°03′E.	A.C.	B. & G.	
3	Rose of England	S.T.	223	5 to 6m. E. of Scarborough Castle	A.C.	B. & G.	
3	Nairana	S.T.	225	54°00′N. 02°20′E.	A.C.	B. & G.	
9	Boston Trader ...	M.	371	½m. S.E. × S. of Blakeney Bell Buoy	A.C.	B. & G.	
9	Foremost 102 ...	Hopper Barge	833	4m. W. of Bell Rock	A.C.	B. & G.	
9	Clintonia	S.	3,106	2m. E. of Flamboro' Head	A.C.	B. & G.	
9	Laurieston ...	S.	1,304	7m. E. of Coquet Island	A.C.	B. & G.	
9	Cree	S.	4,791	5m. E. of Rattray Head	A.C.	B. & G.	
9	Lowdock	S.T.	276	2½m. E. of Scarborough	A.C.	B. & G.	
11	Imperial Transport	M. Tank	8,022	59°N. 12°W. (Approx.)	S.M.	T.	
MARCH, 1940							
2	Domala	M.	8,441	30m. E. of St. Catherine's Pt., I.O.W.	A.C.	B.	
4	Charles F. Meyer	M. Tank	10,516	50°28′N. 00°16′E.	Mine	—	
17	Emerald	S.T.	150	80m. E. × N. of Spurn Lt.	A.C.	G.	
20	Thistlebrae ...	S.	4,747	North Sea	A.C.	B.	
20	Northern Coast...	S.	1,211	58°53′N. 02°00′W. (Approx.)	A.C.	B. & G.	Attacked again on 29th
28	Princess Royal ...	S.T.	213	40m. S.S.W. of Bressay Lt., Shetlands	A.C.	B. & G.	
29	Northern Coast...	S.	1,211	10m. N.N.E. of Kinnaird Head	A.C.	B. & G.	Previously attacked on 20th
APRIL, 1940							
20	Western Prince...	M.	10,926	Near Edinburgh Channel L.V., Thames Estuary	A.C.	G.	
25	Seminole	M. Tank	10,389	51°29′N. 04°07′W.	Mine	—	

Date	Name	Type	Gross tons	Position	Cause of damage	How damaged	Remarks
APRIL, 1940—(Contd.)							
26	CREE	S.	4,791	52°53′N. 02°19′E.	Mine	—	
27	SCOTTISH AMERICAN	S. Tank	6,999	58°41′N. 04°40′W.	S.M.	T.	
27	DELIUS	M.	6,065	Romsdalsfjord	A.C.	B.	Attack continued on 28th
MAY, 1940							
20	BALTEAKO	S.	1,328	Narvik	A.C.	B.	
22	DUNSTER GRANGE...	M.	9,494	49°20′N. 08°40′W.	S.M.	T. & G.	
26	YEWDALE	S.	823	French Channel Coast	Shelled by shore battery	—	Shelled again and attacked by A.C. on 28th
27	BIARRITZ	S.	2,388	Dunkirk	Shelled by shore battery	—	
30	FULHAM IV ...	S.	1,584	Off Orfordness	A.C.	B.	
30	PRINCESS MAUD ...	S.	2,883	Off Gravelines	Shelled by shore battery	—	
JUNE, 1940							
1	PRAGUE	S.	4,220	115° 13m. from N. Foreland	A.C.	B.	
2	KATREEN	S.T.	104	54°30′N. 01°40′E.	A.C.	B. & G.	
2	ROYAL DAFFODIL ...	M.	2,060	51°13′N. 02°00′E.	A.C.	B. & G.	
3	WORTHING (Hospital Ship)	S.	2,294	Off Dunkirk	A.C.	B.	
7	EROS	T.-E.	5,888	55°33′N. 08°26′W.	S.M.	T.	
11	ATHELPRINCE ...	M. Tank	8,782	43°24′N. 13°20′W.	S.M.	T.	
19	GOLDEN GRAIN ...	M. Barge	101	Felixstowe	A.C.	—	
24	CLAN ROSS...	S.	5,897	43°54′N. 01°53′W.	A.C.	B.	
30	CLAN OGILVY ...	S.	5,802	46°17′N. 14°35′W.	S.M.	T.	
30	HELDER	S.	979	Off St. Catherine's Pt., I.O.W.	E.-Boat	T. & G.	
JULY, 1940							
1	ZARIAN	S.	4,871	48°03′N. 11°11′W.	S.M.	T.	
2	BARON RUTHVEN ...	S.	3,178	50°25′N. 01°27′W.	A.C.	B.	
4	BRITISH CORPORAL	S. Tank	6,972	50°13′N. 02°35′W. (Approx.)	E-Boat	T.	
4	FAIRWATER ...	S.	4,108	50°16′N. 02°14′W.	A.C.	B. & G.	
4	FLIMSTON	S.	4,674	Off Portland	A.C.	B.	
4	ANTONIO	S.	5,225	20m. S.S.W. of Portland Bill	A.C.	B.	
4	EASTMOOR	S.	5,812	314° 12m. from Portland Bill	A.C.	B.	
4	ARGOS HILL ...	S.	7,178	Off Portland	A.C.	B. & G.	
4	CITY OF MELBOURNE	S.	6,630	In Portland Harbour	A.C.	B.	
4	KING FREDERICK ...	S.	5,106	50°10′N. 02°33′W.	A.C.	B.	
4	IRENE MARIA ...	S.	1,860	50°30′N. 02°00′W. (Approx.)	A.C.	B.	
4	BRIARWOOD ...	S.	4,019	Off Portland	A.C.	B.	
4	LIFLAND	S.	2,254	Off Portland	A.C.	B.	
4	EAST WALES ...	S.	4,358	In Portland Harbour	A.C.	B.	
4	WILLIAM WILBERFORCE	M.	5,004	In Portland Harbour	A.C.	B.	
5	HARTLEPOOL ...	S.	5,500	16m. S.S.W. of Portland Lt.	E-Boat	T.	
6	APRICITY	M.	402	South of Portland Bill	A.C.	B.	Previously attacked by aircraft on 4th
8	EASTWOOD	S.	1,551	1m. N. of 20D Buoy, Hartlepool	A.C.	B.	
8	CORUNDUM ...	S.	929	7m. S.W. of Folkestone	A.C.	B.	
9	SAN FELIPE ...	S.	5,919	Roath Docks, Cardiff	A.C.	B.	

Date	Name	Type	Gross tons	Position	Cause of damage	How damaged	Remarks
JULY, 1940—(*Contd.*)							
9	KENNETH HAWKSFIELD	S.	1,546	Dover Area	A.C.	B.	
9	POLGRANGE ...	S.	804	51°46′N. 01°46′E.	A.C.	B. & G.	
9	EMPIRE DAFFODIL	M.	398	13m. S.S.W. of Portland	A.C.	B.	
10	BRITISH CHANCELLOR	S. Tank	7,085	Off Falmouth	A.C.	B.	
11	KYLEMOUNT ...	S.	704	10m. W. of Dartmouth	A.C.	B.	
11	PERU	M.	6,961	Portland Harbour	A.C.	B.	
11	ELEANOR BROOKE...	S.	1,037	Portland	A.C.	B.	
12	JOSEWYN	S.	1,926	8m. W.N.W. of St. Catherine's Pt., I.O.W.	A.C.	B. & G.	
14	MONS	S.	641	1½m. S. of Dover Pier	A C.	B. & G.	
18	LODDON	S.T.	200	51°05′ N. 08°35′ W.	A.C.	B.	
18	GENERTON	S.	4,797	North Sea	A.C.	B.	
20	WESTOWN	S.	710	Off Dover	A.C.	B.	
22	SWYNFLEET ...	S.	1,168	53°33′N. 00°56′E.	A.C.	B.	
24	ALERT (Trinity House Vessel)	S.	793	Nr. S. Goodwin L.V.	A.C.	B. & G.	
25	TAMWORTH ...	S.	1,332	Off Dover	A.C.	B.	
25	NEWMINSTER ...	S.	967	Off Dover	A.C.	B.	
25	HODDER	S.	1,016	Off Dover	A.C.	B.	
25	SUMMITY	M.	554	Off Dover	A.C.	B.	
25	GRONLAND	S.	1,264	Off Dover	A.C.	B. & G.	Attacked again by aircraft on 29th and sunk
27	WESTAVON	S.	2,842	52°01′N. 01°51′E.	A.C.	B.	
28	MATHURA	S.	8,890	Aden	A.C.	B.	
AUGUST, 1940							
1	CITY OF CANBERRA	S.	7,484	52°06′N. 01°52′E.	Mine	—	
1	KERRY HEAD ...	S.	825	4m. E.S.E. of Old Head of Kinsale (Approx.)	A.C.	B.	
1	GOTHIC	S. Tank	2,444	310° 12m. from Flamboro' Head	A.C.	B.	
1	HIGHLANDER ...	S.	1,216	56°56′N. 02°04′W.	A.C.	B. & G.	
2	ALEXIA	M. Tank	8,016	55°30′N. 15°30′W.	S.M.	T. & G.	
2	LUCERNA	M. Tank	6,556	55°18′N. 16°39W.	S.M.	T.	
4	WHITE CREST ...	S.	4,365	Off Cape Wrath	A.C.	B.	
8	POLLY M.	M.	380	190° 15m. from Newhaven	E-Boat	G.	
8	SCHELDT	M.	497	15m. W. of St. Catherine's Pt., I.O.W.	A.C.	B.	
8	BALMAHA	S.	1,428	15m. W. of St. Catherine's Pt., I.O.W.	A.C.	B.	
8	JOHN M.	M.	500	10m. S. of Needles, I.O.W.	E-Boat	G.	Also bombed by aircraft
10	BLAIRCLOVA ...	S.	5,083	20m. N.N.E. of Holyhead	A.C.	B.	
11	KIRNWOOD ...	S.	3,829	52°27′N. 02°10′E.	A.C.	B.	
11	OILTRADER ...	S. Tank	5,550	071° 3½m. from Shipwash L.V.	A.C.	B.	
12	ERMINE	S.T.	181	Off Smalls	A.C.	B. & G.	
12	KERNEVAL	S.T.	172	Off Smalls	A.C.	B. & G.	
12	RIVER YTHAN ...	S.T.	161	Off Smalls	A.C.	B. & G.	
16	CLAN FORBES ...	S.	7,529	Tilbury Dock	A.C.	B.	
16	LOCH RYAN ...	Aux.	210	40m. N.W. × N. of Longships Lt.	A.C.	B. & G.	
17	ST. PATRICK ...	S.	1,922	St. George's Channel	A.C.	B. & G.	
17	YEWKYLE	S.	824	52°27′N. 05°45′W.	A.C.	B. & G.	
18	LYSTER	Dredger	619	Brunswick Dock, Liverpool	A.C.	B.	
19	WALDINGE	S.	2,462	Milford Haven	A.C.	B.	

Date	Name	Type	Gross ·tons	Position	Cause of damage	How damaged	Remarks
AUGUST, 1940—*(Contd.)*							
20	MACVILLE	S.	666	Blacksod Bay	A.C.	B.	
20	PEEBLES	M.	4,982	20m. E. of Tuskar Rock, Irish Sea	A.C.	B. & G.	
20	OUR MAGGIE ...	M.T.	17	Brixham	A.C.	B.	
21	ALACRITY	M.	554	Falmouth	A.C.	B.	
21	WOLSELEY	S.T.	159	9m. W. of Smalls Lt. (Approx.)	A.C.	G.	
23	BEACON GRANGE ...	M.	10,119	58°17′N. 02°27′W.	A.C.	B.	
23	HAVILDAR	S.	5,407	55°39′N. 07°18′W.	S.M.	T.	
23	OVERTON	S.	426	Off Bardsey Island	A.C.	B.	
25	STAKESBY	S.	3,900	23m. N. of Butt of Lewis	S.M.	T.	
25	HAMPSHIRE COAST	M.	485	6m. S.W. of St. Ann's Lt.	A.C.	B. & G.	
25	OSSIAN	S.	1,514	51°39′N. 05°51′W.	A.C.	B. & G.	
25	SANFRY	S.	946	50°26′N. 00°22′W.	A.C.	B.	Subsequently attacked by E-Boat on 26th
26	CITY OF HANKOW...	S.	7,360	Off Peterhead	A.C.	B.	
27	SIR JOHN HAWKINS	S.	930	Plymouth	A.C.	B.	
28	HARTISMERE ...	S.	5,498	56°04′N. 13°06′W.	S.M.	T.	
29	BALTISTAN	S.	6,803	55°06′N. 15°39′W.	A.C.	G.	
30	S.H.3	Hopper Barge	389	Victoria Dock, Hull	A.C.	B.	
30	ANADARA	M. Tank	8,009	56°15′N. 09°10′W.	S.M.	T.	
31	CORNWALL	S.	11,288	258° 6m. from Elephonisi Island (S. of Crete)	A.C.	B.	
31	BRITISH ENERGY ...	M. Tank	7,209	Birkenhead	A.C.	B.	
31	ATHELVISCOUNT ...	M. Tank	8,882	Cammell Laird Yd., River Mersey	A.C.	B.	
SEPTEMBER, 1940							
2	LAGOSIAN	S.	5,412	13m. E.S.E. of Peterhead	A.C.	B.	
2	ASHBY	S.	4,868	Off Rattray Head	A.C.	B.	
4	EWELL	S.	1,350	North Sea	E-Boat	G.	
5	MELBOURNE STAR...	M.	12,806	53°27′N. 15°12′W.	A.C.	B. & G.	
6	GANNET	S.	1,336	57°25′N. 01°45′W.	A.C.	B.	
6	IWATE	S.T.	314	53°30′N. 14°00′W.	A.C.	G.	
6	ILFRACOMBE ...	S.T.	165	51°20′N. 11°22′W.	A.C.	G.	
7	BARONESA	S.	8,663	Port of London	A.C.	B.	
7	GOTHLAND	S.	1,286	Port of London	A.C.	B.	
7	BENNEVIS	S.	5,264	Port of London	A.C.	B.	
7	UMGENI	S.	8,180	Port of London	A.C.	B.	
7	GLENSTRAE... ...	S.	9,460	Port of London	A.C.	B.	
7	KNITSLEY	S.	2,272	Port of London	A.C.	B.	
7	UMTALI	S.	8,162	Port of London	A.C.	B.	Attacked again by aircraft on 11th
7	INANDA	S.	5,985	Port of London	A.C.	B.	Attacked again by aircraft on 8th and 9th
7	INKOSI	S.	6,618	Port of London	A.C.	B.	
7	FRUMENTON ...	S.	6,675	Port of London	A.C.	B.	
7	HETTON	S.	2,714	Port of London	A.C.	B.	
7	EASTWOOD	S.	1,551	Port of London	A.C.	B.	
7	WILLIAM CASH ...	S.	1,186	Port of London	A.C.	B.	
7	OTAIO	M.	10,298	Port of London	A.C.	B.	
8	TYNEMOUTH ...	S.	3,168	Port of London	A.C.	B.	
8	SHERWOOD	S.	1,530	Port of London	A.C.	B.	
9	RYAL	M.	367	Port of London	A.C.	B.	
11	NORMAN QUEEN ...	S.	957	Port of London	A.C.	B.	
11	ALEXIA	M. Tank	8,016	57°56′N. 02°02′E.	A.C.	B.	
11	HARPENDEN ...	S.	4,678	55°34′N. 15°56′W.	S.M.	T.	
12	GLENROY	M.	9,809	Liverpool	A.C.	B.	
12	TINTERN ABBEY ...	S.	2,471	270° 6m. from Chicken Rock, Isle of Man	A.C.	B. & G.	

Date	Name	Type	Gross tons	Position	Cause of damage	How damaged	Remarks
SEPTEMBER, 1940—(Contd.)							
13	INISHTRAHULL ...	S.	869	Belfast Lough	A.C.	B.	
15	CORONDA ...	S. Tank	7,503	58°07'N. 09°24'W.	A.C.	B.	
15	REGENT LION ...	M. Tank	9,551	N. Channel, off Mull of Kintyre	A.C.	B. & G.	
15	STANWOLD ...	S.	1,020	Southampton	A.C.	B.	
15	WEST HARSHAW ...	S.	5,756	North Channel, Irish Sea	A.C.	B. & G.	
18	RUDMORE ...	S.	969	Gravesend Reach	A.C.	B.	
18	LING	S.B.	164	N. Morpeth Docks, Liverpool	A.C.	B.	
19	WEST KEDRON ...	S.	5,621	North Channel, Irish Sea	A.C.	B. & G.	
20	BHIMA	M.	5,280	13°57'N. 42°53'E.	A.C.	B.	
21	BROOMPARK ...	S.	5,136	55°08'N. 18°30'W.	S.M.	T.	
21	ENCHANTRESS ...	S.B.	56	London Docks	A.C.	B.	
22	COLLEGIAN ...	S.	7,886	320m. W. of Malin Head	S.M.	G.	
23	CORINIA	S.	870	Gravesend Reach	A.C.	B.	
23	PACIFIC GROVE ...	M.	7,117	5m. N.W. of Tory Island	A.C.	B. & G.	
26	ASHANTIAN ...	S.	4,917	55°10'N. 11°00'W. (Approx.)	S.M.	T.	
26	WELSH PRINCE ...	S.	5,148	57°37'N. 01°34'W.	A.C.	B.	
26	DIPLOMAT ...	S.	8,240	Brunswick Dock, Liverpool	A.C.	B.	
26	PETERTON	S.	5,221	Brunswick Dock, Liverpool	A.C.	B.	
26	WELLINGTON ...	Tug	285	Liverpool	A.C.	B.	
26	WEST KEDRON ...	S.	5,621	Liverpool	A.C.	B.	
26	SUVA ...	S.	4,873	57°30'N. 01°32'W.	A.C.	B.	
28	QUEEN CITY ...	S.	4,814	58°10'N. 02°19'W.	A.C.	B.	
30	SUSSEX	M.	11,063	54°20'N. 15°32'W.	A.C.	B. & G.	
30	MOUNTPARK ...	S.	4,648	57°24'N. 01°35'W.	A.C.	B.	
30	EMPIRE SUCCESS ...	S.	6,009	5m. E. of Peterhead	A.C.	B.	
30	BARON VERNON ...	S.	3,642	52°40'N. 17°56'W.	A.C.	B. & G.	
30	KERMA	S.	4,333	57°24'N. 01°35'W.	A.C.	B.	
30	HENRY DUNDAS ...	M. Tank	10,448	Mersey River Anchorage	A.C.	B.	
OCTOBER, 1940							
2	TREHATA	S.	4,817	Off Peterhead	A.C.	B.	
3	FRAMLINGHAM ...	S.T.	169	20m. S. of Fastnet	A.C.	B.	
3	IWATE	S.T.	314	5m. N.W. of Mizzen Hd.	A.C.	B. & G.	
5	ORTOLAN	S.	489	Free Trade Wharf, Stepney	A.C.	B.	
6	HULL TRADER ...	S.	717	London Docks	A.C.	B.	
6	FIRECREST	S.	538	2½m. S.W. of Sunk L.V., Thames Estuary	A.C.	B. & G.	
8	ORONSAY	S.	20,043	56°N. 10°W. (Approx.)	A.C.	B. & G.	
10	TILL	M.	367	51°36'N. 01°12'E.	Mine	—	
11	THYRA II	S.	1,088	Off East Barrow L.V., Thames Estuary	Mine	—	
11	CLAN MacTAGGART	S.	7,622	Liverpool	A.C.	B.	
11	CLAN CUMMING ...	S.	7,264	Liverpool	A.C.	B.	
11	HIGHLAND CHIEFTAIN	M.	14,135	Liverpool	A.C.	B.	
11	VIRGILIA	S. Tank	5,723	Liverpool	A.C.	B.	
11	INVER	S.	1,543	Straits of Dover	Shelled by Shore Battery	—	
11	BANNTHORN ...	S.	429	Rathlin O'Birne Sound, Eire	A.C.	G.	
12	STARLING	S.	1,320	4m. S.W. of San Sebastian Lt.	A.C.	B. & G.	

Date	Name	Type	Gross tons	Position	Cause of damage	How damaged	Remarks
OCTOBER, 1940—(Contd.)							
12	LONGSCAR	S.T.	215	Off Hartlepool	A.C.	B.	
13	CARGO FLEET No. 2	Hopper Barge	1,130	1 cable W. of Datum Buoy, off Tees	Mine	—	
15	BRITISH GLORY ...	M. Tank	6,993	57°10′N. 08°36′W.	S.M.	T.	
16	ACTIVITY	M.	358	51°31′N. 00°55′E.	Mine	—	
17	ETHYLENE	S.	936	½m. N.N.E. of East Oaze Lt. Buoy	Mine	—	
17	GEORGE BALFOUR...	S.	1,570	230° 12,900 yds. from Aldeburgh L.V.	Mine	—	
17	P.L.M. 14	S.	3,754	52°52′N. 02°06′E.	E-Boat	T.	
17	GASFIRE	S.	2,972	52°52′N. 02°06′E.	E-Boat	T.	
17	CARSBRECK ...	S.	3,670	58°46′N. 14°11′W.	S.M.	T.	
18	KING ATHELSTAN ...	S.T.	159	About 15m. off Mizzen Head	A.C.	B. & G.	
18	BLAIRSPEY	S.	4,155	57°55′N. 11°10′W.	S.M.	T.	Torpedoed again on 19th
20	CONAKRIAN... ...	S.	4,876	130° 9m. from Girdleness	A.C.	T.	
20	ATHELMONARCH ...	M. Tank	8,995	56°45′N. 15°58′W.	S.M.	T.	
20	CITY OF ROUBAIX...	S.	7,108	Alexandria Dock, Liverpool	A.C.	B.	
23	EMPIRE ABILITY ...	S.	7,603	Gareloch	A.C.	B.	
25	JANET	Motor F.V.	25	Montrose Quay	A.C.	B.	
27	ALFRED JONES ...	M.	5,013	56°00′N. 12°08′W.	A.C.	B.	
27	CONISTER	S.	411	Queen's Dock, Liverpool	A.C.	B.	
27	NEWLANDS ...	S.	1,556	45°10′N. 10°00′W.	A.C.	B.	
31	STARSTONE ...	S.	5,702	54°12′N. 15°32′W.	A.C.	B.	
NOVEMBER, 1940							
3	EROS	T.E.	5,888	57°48′N. 01°54′W.	A.C.	T.	
3	WINDSOR CASTLE ...	S.	19,141	54°12′N. 13°18′W.	A.C.	B.	
3	CAIRNGORM... ...	M.	394	Bristol Channel	Mine	—	
5	SAN DEMETRIO ...	M. Tank	8,073	52°48′N. 32°15′W.	Raider	—	
5	ANDALUSIAN ...	S.	3,082	North Atlantic	Raider	—	
6	HARBOROUGH ...	S.	5,415	076° 9m. from Noss Head	A.C.	B.	
7	DAGO II	S.	1,993	51°32′N. 01°06′E.	A.C.	B.	
7	MEDEE	S.	2,163	51°10′N. 01°12′E.	A.C.	B.	
8	EMPIRE DORADO ...	S.	5,595	55°07′N. 16°50′W.	A.C.	B.	
8	FIREGLOW	S.	1,261	S.W. of Swin Buoy, Thames Estuary	A.C.	B. & G.	
8	EWELL	S.	1,350	51°43′N. 01°23′E.	A.C.	B. & G.	
8	CATFORD	S.	1,568	S.W. of Swin Buoy, Thames Estuary	A.C.	G.	
9	EMPRESS OF JAPAN	S.	26,032	53°54′N. 14°28′W.	A.C.	B.	
9	BEAL	M.	504	Off Tees	Mine	—	
9	SHELBRIT II ...	M. Tank	695	Alongside Cleveland Wharf, Shoreham	A.C.	B.	
11	CORSEA	S.	2,764	Barrow Deep	A.C.	B.	
11	COLONEL CROMPTON	S.	1,495	Barrow Deep	A.C.	B.	
11	PITWINES	S.	932	N.E. of Yarmouth	A.C.	B.	
11	CORDUFF	S.	2,345	Barrow Deep Channel	A.C.	B.	
11	HARLAW	S.	1,141	Off Aberdeen	A.C.	B.	
11	GRIT	M.	501	200 yds. S.W. × S. of Margate Buoy	Mine	—	
11	IWATE	S.T.	314	35m. S. × W. of Old Head of Kinsale	A.C.	B. & G.	
13	BRITISH PRESTIGE...	M. Tank	7,106	Off Humber Boom	Mine	—	
14	FAIRY	M.	207	Nr. Chequer Buoy, off Mouth of Humber	Mine	—	
14	FISHPOOL.	M.	4,950	55°00′N. 17°04′W. (Approx.)	A.C.	B.	

Date	Name	Type	Gross tons	Position	Cause of damage	How damaged	Remarks
NOVEMBER, 1940—(Contd.)							
16	SHERBROOKE ...	S.	2,052	8m. S.E. of Orford-ness	A.C.	B. & G.	
16	DAGENHAM ...	S.	2,178	2½ cables E.N.E. of Mouse L.V.	Mine*	—	
18	S.N.A.8	S.	2,569	Off Swin L.V.	A.C.	B.	
18	LANGLEETARN ...	S.	4,908	Thames Estuary	A.C.	B.	
18	BIELA	S.	5,298	52°26′N. 16°31′W.	A.C.	B.	
18	EL NAWRAS ...	S. Tank	323	Alexandria	A.C.	B.	
19	FOLDA	S.	1,165	51°47′N. 01°30′E.	A.C.	B.	
20	CHESAPEAKE ...	M. Tank	8,955	Off Lizard	A.C.	B. & G.	
22	ZAHRA	S. Tank	821	Alexandria	A.C.	B.	
23	LLANDOVERY CASTLE	S.	10,640	Southampton	A.C.	B.	
23	DUCHESS OF CORNWALL	S.	302	Alongside Royal Pier, Southampton	A.C.	B.	
24	CAMROUX IV ...	M.	590	045° 1m. from East Oaze L.V.	Mine	—	Previously slightly damaged by air-craft on 20th
24	LENT LILY ...	M.T.	44	6m. E.S.E. of Wolf Rock	E-Boat*	G.	
27	GALACUM ...	S.	585	51°34′N. 01°09′E.	Mine	—	
27	CHARMOUTH ...	S.T.	195	Off Milford Haven	A.C.	B. & G.	
27	RATTRAY	S.T.	182	Off Milford Haven	A.C.	G.	
27	CHARLES F. MEYER	M. Tank	10,516	56°00′N. 13°52′W.	S.M.	T.	
28	SKIPJACK ...	S.	1,167	Dover	Shelled by Shore Battery	—	
29	FERMAIN	S.	759	Dover	Shelled by Shore Battery	—	
DECEMBER, 1940							
1	LOCH RANZA ...	S.	4,958	54°37′N. 18°54′W.	S.M.	T.	
2	DUNSLEY	S.	3,862	54°41′N. 18°41′W.	S.M.	G.	
3	ROBRIX	M.	292	110° 2m. from Spurn Pt. L.H.	Mine	—	
3	WILLIAM DOWNES...	S.T.	275	5m. W.N.W. of Skel-ligs	A.C.	B. & G.	
3	SLEBECH	S.T.	222	5m. W.N.W. of Skel-ligs	A.C.	G.	
3	QUEBEC CITY ...	S.	4,745	North Atlantic, off Irish Coast	A.C.	G.	
5	WATERLAND ...	S.	1,107	Dover	Shelled by Shore Battery	—	
7	YEWARCH	S.	827	Off Dudgeon Buoy, Humber	A.C.	B. & G.	
7	HERTFORD	S.	10,923	35°30′S. 135°25′E.	Mine	—	
8	TREVERBYN ...	S.	5,281	59°00′N. 14°24′W.	A.C.	B. & G.	
11	SAXON QUEEN ...	M.	482	Near Sunk Head Buoy, Thames Es-tuary	A.C.	B.	
13	ORARI	M.	10,350	49°50′N. 20°55′W.	S.M.	T.	
14	EMPIRE RAZORBILL	S.	5,118	59°31′N. 13°15′W.	S.M.	G.	
16	BIC ISLAND ...	S.	3,921	54°12′N. 17°45′W.	A.C.	B.	
18	TWEED	S.	2,697	53°40′N. 04°40′W.	A.C.	B. & G.	
20	OVERDALE	Hopper Barge	315	Liverpool	A.C.	B.	
20/21	EUROPA	M.	10,224	Liverpool	A.C.	B.	
20/21	LAPLACE	S.	7,327	Liverpool	A.C.	B.	
20/21	EASTERN PRINCE ...	M.	10,926	Liverpool	A.C.	—	
20/21	JOHN A. BROWN ...	M. Tank	10,455	Liverpool	A.C.	B.	Also struck a mine on same date
20/21	ROXBURGH CASTLE	M.	7,801	Liverpool	A.C.	B.	
21	ALPERA	S.	1,777	Liverpool	A.C.	B.	
21	CITY OF CORINTH...	S.	5,318	Liverpool	A.C.	B.	
21	DEMETERTON ...	S.	5,251	Liverpool	A.C.	B.	

Date	Name	Type	Gross tons	Position	Cause of damage	How damaged	Remarks
DECEMBER, 1940—(Contd.)							
21/22	Llangibby Castle	M.	11,951	Liverpool	A.C.	B.	
21/22	Mahronda ...	S.	7,926	Liverpool	A.C.	B.	
21/22	Deucalion... ...	M.	7,516	Liverpool	A.C.	B.	
22	Elax	M. Tank	7,403	Off No. 10 Buoy, Liverpool	Mine	—	
22	Pardo	M.	5,400	Liverpool	A.C.	B.	
22	Llandilo	S.	4,966	Between Nos. 2 and 3 Yantlet Buoys, Thames Estuary	Mine	—	
22	Almeda Star ...	S.	14,935	Liverpool	A.C.	B.	
22	No. 9	Hopper Barge	671	Liverpool	A.C.	B.	
23	Pacific Pioneer ...	M.	6,734	Manchester	A.C.	B.	
23	Iwate	S.T.	314	52°55′N. 12°20′W.	A.C.	B. & G.	
23	Flynderborg ...	S.	2,022	Oban	A.C.	B. & G.	
23	Lupina	Drifter	88	Oban	A.C.	B.	
24	Peterton	S.	5,221	54°51′N. 13°13′W.	A.C.	B. & G.	
25	Empire Trooper ...	S.	13,994	43°58′N. 24°15′W.	Raider	—	
27	Lady Connaught...	S.	2,284	53°37′N. 03°43′W.	Mine	—	
27	Victoria	S.	1,641	290° 8m. from Bar L.V., Mersey	Mine	—	
28	Lochee	M.	964	4m. N.E. × N. of Bar L.V., Mersey	Mine	—	
28	Canute	Tug	271	Southampton	A.C.	B.	
29	Trevarrack ...	S.	5,270	55°34′N. 09°30′W.	A.C.	B. & G.	
29	Catrine	M.	5,218	Liverpool Bay	Mine	—	Struck a second mine on 30th near Q.1 Buoy Queen's Channel, Liverpool
30	Dorcasia	M. Tank	8,053	250° 3m. from Bar L.V., Mersey	Mine	—	
31	British Zeal ...	M. Tank	8,532	15°40′N. 20°43′W.	S.M.	T.	
JANUARY, 1941							
1	Attendant ...	S.	1,016	1 cable E. of 9 Buoy, Sheerness	Mine	—	
2	Loch Dee	S.	5,252	Cardiff	A.C.	B.	
5	Temple Moat ...	S.	4,427	55°29′N. 18°55′W.	A.C.	B. & G.	
9	Dorset Coast ...	M.	646	51°24′N. 03°08′W.	Mine	—	
11	British Fidelity...	M. Tank	8,465	51°22′N. 03°05′W.	Mine	—	
11	Greyfriars ...	S.	1,142	1m. W. of 59A Buoy, off Grimsby	A.C.	B.	
13	Wooler	M.	507	Victoria Wharf, Plymouth	A.C.	B.	
15	Maywood	S.	1,823	51°21′N. 03°16′W.	Mine	—	
15	Karri	M.	354	2m. N. of Bar L.V., Mersey	Mine	—	
15	Stalker	S.T.	197	Hawke Roads, Grimsby	A.C.	B.	
16	Gladonia	M.	360	Off Sunk L.V., Thames Estuary	A.C.	B.	
16	Romsey	S.	509	51°41′N. 05°09′W.	Mine	—	
16	Skjold	S.	1,345	N. of Lundy Island	A.C.	B.	
16	Llanwern	S.	4,966	Avonmouth	A.C.	B.	
16/17	Essex	M.	11,063	Malta	A.C.	B.	
17	Athelduke ...	M. Tank	8,966	51°21′N. 03°20′W.	Mine	—	
19	Clan Cumming ...	S.	7,264	Off Piræus	S.M.	T.	
19	Zelo	S.	2,294	Off Sunk L.V., Thames Estuary	A.C.	B.	
20	Vasco	S.	2,878	Athens	A.C.	B.	
20	Tregarthen ...	S.	5,201	55°54′N. 07°00′W.	A.C.	B.	
22	Jamaica Planter...	M.	4,098	196° 2,500 yds. from Nell's Pt., Barry Island	Mine	—	
24	Tasmania	M.	6,405	090° 11½m. from Rattray Head	Mine*	—	

Date	Name	Type	Gross tons	Position	Cause of damage	How damaged	Remarks
JANUARY, 1941—(Contd.)							
26	Gwynwood	S.	1,177	Abreast No. B.3 Buoy, Barrow Deep	A.C.	B.	
26	Catford	S.	1,568	Off Ooze Bank	Mine	—	
26	Grangetoft	S.	975	Off B.4 Buoy, Barrow Deep	A.C.	B. & G.	
26	Sandhill	M.	586	53°43′N. 03°15′W.	Mine	—	
28	Tafelberg	S. O.R.	13,640	51°21′N. 03°16′W.	Mine	—	Reconstructed as tanker and renamed EMPIRE HERITAGE
28	Baron Renfrew	S.	3,635	55°50′N. 10°18′W.	A.C.	B.	
29	Westmoreland	S.	8,967	270° 3m. from Bar L.V., Mersey	Mine	—	
31	Dorsetshire (Hospital Ship)	M.	9,717	Gulf of Sollum	A.C.	B.	Attacked again on 1st February
31	Desmoulea	M. Tank	8,120	35°31′N. 02°34′E.	Destroyer or E-Boat	T.	
FEBRUARY, 1941							
2	Waziristan	S.	5,135	61°21′N. 11°12′W.	A.C.	B.	
3	Derwenthall	M.	4,934	Suez Canal	Mine	—	
3	Calyx	M.	212	8m. N.E. of Bar L.V., Mersey	Mine	—	
7	Scottish Co-operator	M.	513	2m. S.W. of Workington Pier, Solway Firth	Mine	—	
9	Crista	M.	2,590	Tobruk Harbour	Mine	—	
10	Benmacdhui	S.	6,869	52°42′N. 02°00′E.	A.C.	B.	
11	Cantick Head	S.	488	30m. N.W. of Kinnaird Head	A.C.	G.	
12	Lornaston	S.	4,934	37°12′N. 21°20′W.	Raider	—	
13	Westcliffe Hall	S.	1,900	010° 2½m. from Whitby High Lt.	A.C.	B.	
13	Cape Rodney	S.	4,512	Off Girdleness	A.C.	B.	
14	Moorlands	S.	420	2m. N. of Sands End Bay, off Banff	A.C.	B. & G.	Bombed again on 20th in Buckie Harbour
15	Stock Force	S.	983	Nr. Outer Dowsing Float, Humber	A.C.	B.	
19	Fulham II	S.	1,596	Off Tyne Piers	Mine	—	
19	Athelsultan	M. Tank	8,882	120° 2½m. from May Island	A.C.	B.	
19/20	Queenforth	Tug	204	Swansea	A.C.	B.	
20	D. L. Harper	M. Tank	12,223	58°50′N. 12°12′W.	A.C.	B.	
20	Scarborough	S.T.	162	52°15′N. 11°45′W.	A.C.	B. & G.	
20	British Splendour	M. Tank	7,138	1½m. S. of Black Head, Nr. Lizard	A.C.	B.	
20	St. Rosario	S.	4,312	58°50′N. 11°40′W.	A.C.	B. & G.	Bombed again on 22nd in position 59°40′N. 12°40′W.
20	Rosenborg	S.	1,997	58°49′N. 11°40′W.	A.C.	B. & G.	
22	Luxor	M. Tank	6,554	Swansea	A.C.	B.	
22	Kingston Hill	S.	7,628	59°44′N. 12°33′W.	A.C.	B.	
22	Keila	S.	3,621	59°44′N. 12°33′W.	A.C.	B.	
25	Tynefield	M. Tank	5,856	Tobruk	A.C.	B.	
26	Empire Steelhead	S.	7,744	080° 10m. from Cromarty	A.C.	B. & G.	
26	Diala	M. Tank	8,106	55°50′N. 14°00′W.	S.M.	T.	
26	Melmore Head	S.	5,273	55°07′N. 16°00′W.	A.C.	B.	
26	Leeds City	S.	4,758	54°00′N. 17°45′W.	A.C.	B.	
26	Hopton	S.T.	202	6m. E.S.E. of Girdleness	A.C.	B. & G.	
27	Blacktoft	S.	1,109	51°57′N. 01°40′E.	A.C.	B.	
27	Cape Clear	M.	5,085	53°27′N. 04°01′W.	Mine	—	
27	Newlands	S.	1,556	Barrow Deep	A.C.	B.	

Date	Name	Type	Gross tons	Position	Cause of damage	How damaged	Remarks
MARCH, 1941							
1	FORTHBANK	S.	5,057	57°53′N. 01°57′W.	A.C.	B.	
1	EMPIRE SIMBA	S.	5,691	52°21′N. 05°23′W.	A.C.	B.	
1	ATHELTEMPLAR	M. Tank	8,949	57°04′N. 01°50′W.	A.C.	B.	
4	RUTH II	M.	321	2 cables N.N.E. of Bar L.V., Mersey	Mine	—	
4	EAST COAST	S.T.	192	Off Fastnet	A.C.	B. & G.	
4	ANGLIAN COAST	M.	594	075° 2 cables from Bar L.V., Mersey	Mine	—	
4	LYNDIS KITWOOD	Pilot Cutter	20	Off Skegness	Mine	—	
6	EILIAN HILL	S.	781	Off Nell's Point, Barry Island	Mine	—	
7	DELILIAN	S.	6,423	60°28′N. 13°38′W.	S.M.	T.	
9	ESMOND	S.	4,976	57°21′N. 01°38′W.	A.C.	B.	
9	SYLVIA BEALE	S.	1,040	5m. E.N.E. of Dungeness	A.C.	B.	
11	ROYAL STAR	S.	7,900	Stonehaven	A.C.	B. & G.	
11/12	CONTRACTOR	S.	6,004	Manchester	A.C.	B.	
11/12	NOVELIST	S.	6,133	Manchester	A.C.	B.	
11/12	MARKHOR	S.	7,917	Manchester	A.C.	B.	
12	CAMROUX I	M.	324	Off Blyth	Mine	—	
12	ESSEX LANCE	S.	6,625	51°03′N. 01°38′E.	A.C.	B. & G.	
12/13	CATRINE	M.	5,218	Liverpool	A.C.	B.	
12/13	IMPERIAL STAR	M.	12,427	Liverpool	A.C.	B.	
12/13	ELAX	M. Tank	7,403	Liverpool	A.C.	B.	
12/13	EL MIRLO	M. Tank	8,092	Liverpool	A.C.	B.	
13	NGATIRA	M.	525	51°21′N. 03°17′W.	Mine	—	
13	WEARWOOD	S.	4,597	Liverpool	A.C.	B.	
13	MYRMIDON	M.	6,278	Liverpool	Mine	—	
13	MOUNTSTEWART	S.	1,099	Liverpool	A.C.	B.	
13/14	CLERMISTON	S.	1,448	Glasgow	A.C.	B.	
13/14	TREVARRACK	S.	5,270	Clyde	A.C.	B.	
14	MINEGARTH	Tug	179	Liverpool	A.C.	B.	
14	SCOTTISH CHIEF	S. Tank	7,006	Liverpool	A.C.	B.	
14	EMPIRE SIMBA	S.	5,691	Liverpool	Mine	—	
15	WARRIOR	Tug	249	Clyde	Mine	—	
15	ERODONA	M. Tank	6,207	61°20′N. 17°00′W.	S.M.	T.	
16	FRANCHE COMTE	M. Tank	9,314	61°15′N. 12°30′W.	S.M.	T.	
17	CORMEAD	S.	2,848	52°20′N. 02°00′E.	A.C.	B. & G.	
17	PIONEER (Trinity House Vessel)	Pilot Cutter	281	B.3 Buoy, Thames Estuary	A.C.	B. & G.	
19	NAILSEA MEADOW	S.	4,962	Victoria Dock, London	A.C.	B.	
19	TOTTENHAM	S.	4,762	Southend Anchorage	Mine	—	
19/20	TELESFORA DE LARRINAGA	S.	5,780	Victoria Dock, London	A.C.	B.	
19/20	LINDENHALL	S.	5,248	Victoria Dock, London	Mine	—	
20	CHARLIGHT	Tug	40	Off Le Bas Wharf, Millwall	A.C.	B.	
20	MARI II	S.	1,395	Plymouth	A.C.	B.	
21	HALO	S.	2,365	Off Beckton Pier	Mine	—	
22	DASHWOOD	S.	2,154	Barrow Deep	A.C.	B.	
23	CITY OF LINCOLN	S.	8,039	Grand Harbour, Malta	A.C.	B.	
23	PERTHSHIRE	S.	10,496	Grand Harbour, Malta	A.C.	B.	
23	SAMURAI	S.T.	221	30m. N.N.W. of St. Kilda	A.C.	B. & G.	
24	MARIE MAERSK	M. Tank	8,271	Eastern Mediterranean	A.C.	B.	
26	KINGSWAY	S.T.	211	10m. E. of Bell Rock	A.C.	B.	
26	BALUCHISTAN	S.	6,992	Eastern Mediterranean	A.C.	B.	
26	THE LADY BELLE	S.	331	10m. S. of Grassholm Island	A.C.	B. & G.	

Date	Name	Type	Gross tons	Position	Cause of damage	How damaged	Remarks
MARCH, 1941—(Contd.)							
27	PALMSTONE ...	Salvage Vessel	430	2m. S.E. of St. Goven's L.V.	A.C.	B.	
27	FORT DEE	S.T.	212	61°31'N. 05°04'W.	A.C.	B. & G.	
28	STAFFORDSHIRE ...	M.	10,683	59°30'N. 10°18'W.	A.C.	B.	
29	GRENAA	S.	1,262	Off Rotherhithe	Mine	—	
31	RATTRAY	S.T.	182	2m. S.E. × E. of Hook Pt.	A.C.	B. & G.	
APRIL, 1941							
1	ADELLEN	M. Tank	7,984	7 cables from Sea Buoy, Milford Haven	A.C.	B.	
1	CHESAPEAKE ...	M. Tank	8,955	10m. S.W. of St. Goven's Head	A.C.	B. & G.	Also attacked earlier same day 15m. N. of Smalls
2	MELROSE ABBEY ...	S.	1,908	River Ythan (N. of Aberdeen)	Mine	—	
2	WILD ROSE ...	S.	873	12m. S.E. of Tuskar L.H.	A.C.	B.	
3	GEDDINGTON COURT	S.	6,903	56°25'N. 02°13'W.	A.C.	B.	
3	ASSUAN	S.	499	56°42'N. 02°26'W.	A.C.	B. & G.	
4	CAPE VERDE ...	M.	6,914	52°12'N. 05°42'W.	A.C.	B. & G.	
6	GLENFINLAS ...	S.	7,572	52°01'N. 01°47'E. (Approx.)	A.C.	B. & G.	
6	CINGALESE PRINCE	M.	8,474	Piraeus	A.C.	B.	
6	DEVIS	M.	6,054	Piraeus	A.C.	B.	
7	KIRNWOOD ...	S.	3,829	51°47'N. 01°30'E.	A.C.	B. & G.	
8	CORMARSH	S.	2,848	Off Sheringham Buoy	A.C.	B.	
8	CHAUCER	S.	5,792	Nr. Humber L.V.	A.C.	B.	Attacked again on 9th
9	KYLEGORM ...	S.	622	245° 4m. from St. Ann's Head	A.C.	B.	
9	BRITISH WORKMAN	S. Tank	6,994	58°31'N. 02°40'W.	A.C.	B. & G.	
9	ABERHILL	S.	1,516	54°37'N. 00°48'W.	A.C.	B. & G.	
9	PERSIA	Tug	165	Shellhaven, London	Mine	—	
9	BRITISH STATESMAN	S. Tank	6,991	Off Harwich	A.C.	B.	
9	PANDORIAN ...	S.	4,159	140° 15m. from Duncansby Head	A.C.	B.	
10	THIRLBY	S.	4,887	140m. N.N.W. of Butt of Lewis	A.C.	B. & G.	
10	BUSIRIS	S.	943	Off Runnelstone, Mounts Bay	A.C.	B.	
12	DARTFORD	S.	4,093	1½m. S. of Mumbles Lt.	A.C.	B.	
13	BARON BELHAVEN	S.	6,591	51°33'N. 05°32'W.	A.C.	B.	
16	KING ATHELSTAN ...	S.T.	159	3m. off Ballinskelligs	A.C.	B.	
17	ETHEL RADCLIFFE	S.	5,673	Near Cross Sands L.V., off Great Yarmouth	E-Boat	T.	Subsequently sunk by A.C. on May 16th
18	SCOTTISH MUSICIAN	M. Tank	6,998	205° 3m. from St. Ann's Head	A.C.	B.	
20	R. S. JACKSON ...	Spritsail Barge	60	London	A.C.	B.	
21	BRITISH LORD ...	S. Tank	6,098	34°35'N. 23°32'E.	A.C.	B.	
21	BRITISH RENOWN ...	M. Tank	6,997	3m. S.E. of Dartmouth	A.C.	B.	
21	REGENCY	Tug	76	Off Ford's, Dagenham	Mine	—	
21	ALPHA	F.V.	11	Whittaker Channel, Essex	Mine	—	
21	MAIDSTONE	S.	688	Plymouth	A.C.	B.	
22	ANTONIO	S.	5,225	Off T.2 Buoy, Tyne	A.C.	B.	
22	CROHAM	S.	391	Peterhead	A.C.	B.	
23	MISS ELAINE ...	Salvage Vessel	364	Plymouth	A.C.	B.	
24	DOLIUS	M.	5,507	56°35'N. 02°11'W.	A.C.	B. & G.	
26	SCOTTISH PRINCE ...	M.	4,917	36°07'N. 24°30'E.	A.C.	B.	

Date	Name	Type	Gross tons	Position	Cause of damage	How damaged	Remarks
APRIL, 1941—(Contd.)							
28	Marie Dawn ...	S.	2,157	Off Sheringham Buoy	A.C.	B. & G.	
28	Empire Strait ...	S.	2,824	Off Yarmouth	A.C.	B.	
29	Corglen	S.	2,822	½m. N.N.E. of T.2 Buoy, Tyne	A.C.	B.	
29	Prowess	M.	207	Off Projector Buoy, Humber	Mine	—	
MAY, 1941							
1	Sea Fisher ...	S.	2,950	55°34'N. 01°28'W.	Mine*	—	
3	Tacoma Star ...	S.	7,924	Liverpool	A.C.	B.	
3	Cantal	S.	3,178	Liverpool	A.C.	—	
3/4	Baronesa	S.	8,663	Liverpool	A.C.	B.	
3/4	Lobos	M.	6,479	Liverpool	A.C.	B.	
3/4	Wapiti	Tug	208	Liverpool	A.C.	B.	
3/4	Mahout	S.	7,921	Liverpool	A.C.	—	
3/4	San Fabian ...	S. Tank	13,031	Stanlow, Liverpool	A.C.	B.	
3/4	Busiris	S.	943	Liverpool	A.C.	B.	
3/4	Limpet	S.B.	164	Liverpool	A.C.	B.	
3/4	Oyster	S.B.	133	Liverpool	A.C.	—	
3/4	Clam	S.B.	159	Liverpool	A.C.	B.	
3/4	Glitto	S.B.	166	Liverpool	A.C.	B.	
4	Bison	Tug	274	Liverpool	A.C.	B.	
4	Talthybius ...	S.	10,254	Liverpool	A.C.	B.	Bombed again on the 8th
4	Hornby	Tug	201	Liverpool	A.C.	—	
4	Enid Blanch ...	Tug	99	Liverpool	A.C.	—	
4	No. 33	Hopper Barge	718	Liverpool	A.C.	B.	
4	Roxburgh Castle	M.	7,801	Liverpool	A.C.	B.	
4/5	Bongo	S.B.	46	LIVERPOOL	A.C.	B.	
5	Shepperton Ferry	S.	2,839	Belfast	A.C.	B.	
5	Silversandal ...	M.	6,770	Liverpool	A.C.	B.	Previously slightly damaged on 3rd
5	Clan Macinnes ...	S.	4,672	Liverpool	A.C.	B.	
5	Cape Breton ...	S.	6,044	Belfast	A.C.	B.	
6	Industria ...	S.	4,861	Liverpool	A.C.	B.	
8	Royal Daffodil II (Ferry)	M.	591	Liverpool	A.C.	B.	
8	Baron Inchcape ...	S.	7,005	Liverpool	A.C.	B.	Previously slightly damaged between 3rd and 6th
8	No. 20	Camel Barge	703	Liverpool	A.C.	B.	
9	Ostrevent... ...	S.	1,737	E. of Helwick L.V.	A.C.	B.	
9	Empire Cloud ...	S.	5,969	61°00'N. 32°30'W.	S.M.	T.	
9	Alexandra ...	S.B.	84	Hull	A.C.	B.	
9	Dan-y-Bryn ...	S.	5,117	Hull	A.C.	B.	
9	Castilian	S.	3,067	Hull	A.C.	B.	
9	Fishpool	M.	4,950	Barrow	A.C.	B.	
9/10	San Roberto ...	S. Tank	5,890	22m. E. × N. of Spurn Pt.	A.C.	B.	
9/10	British Statesman	S. Tank	6,991	22m. E. × N. of Spurn Pt.	A.C.	B.	
10	Aelybryn	S.	4,986	59°23'N. 35°25'W.	S.M.	T.	
10	Tower Field ...	S.	4,241	Off Outer Dowsing Buoy	A.C.	B.	
10	Henry Ward ...	Sludge Vessel	1,438	In Dry Dock, Green & Silley Weir, London	A.C.	B.	
11	Caithness	M.	4,970	52°03'N. 05°24'W.	A.C.	B.	
11	Dencade	Tug	58	Brixham	A.C.	B.	
11	Silver Lining ...	F.V.	40	Brixham	A.C.	B.	
13	Lottinge	S.	2,468	Off Tyne	A.C.	B. & G.	
14	Cape Horn ...	M.	5,643	Port Said	A.C.	B. & G.	
16	Joffre Rose ...	S.	715	Off St. David's Head	A.C.	B. & G.	Bombed again on 18th in Dale Bay
16	Obsidian	S.	811	52°06'N. 05°25'W.	A.C.	B. & G.	

Date	Name	Type	Gross tons	Position	Cause of damage	How damaged	Remarks
MAY, 1941—(*Contd.*)							
17	ARTHUR WRIGHT ...	S.	1,091	5m. S. of Shoreham	A.C.	B. & G.	
17	ABA (Hospital Ship)	M.	7,938	50m. S. of Crete	A.C.	B.	
18	ESKBURN	S.	472	Off Blyth	A.C.	B.	
19	DIXCOVE	M.	3,790	51°36′N. 01°11′E.	Mine	—	
20	SAN FELIX ...	S. Tank	13,037	57°32′N. 40°21′W.	S.M.	T.	
22	EMPIRE PROGRESS...	S.	5,249	3m. S.W. of Needles	A.C.	B. & G.	
24	OCTANE	M. Tank	2,034	50°08′N. 05°02′W.	Mine	—	
24	SARNIA	S.	711	Milford Haven	A.C.	B. & G.	
24	CRESSDENE ...	S.	4,270	Mumbles Roads	A.C.	B. & G.	
26	GROS PIERRE ...	S.	297	Off Sunderland	A.C.	B.	
26	H. E. STROUD ...	S.T.	214	135° 10m. from Lamb Head, Stromsay	A.C.	B. & G.	
30	KYLECLARE ...	S.	700	Off Limerick	A.C.	B.	
30	SANGARA	M.	5,445	Accra Harbour	S.M.	T.	
JUNE, 1941							
2	BEN SCREEL ...	S.T.	195	55°30′N. 01°30′W.	A.C.	B.	
3	DENNIS ROSE ...	S.	1,600	About 5m. W. × S. of Start Pt.	A.C.	B.	
6	EMULATOR	S.T.	168	7 to 8m. E. of Scarborough	A.C.	B.	
8	ENSIS	M. Tank	6,207	48°46′N. 29°14′W.	S.M.	T.	
8/9	REMAGIO	S.T.	174	Nr. Bamburgh	A.C.	B.	
10	CLEARPOOL ...	S.	5,404	Off 18B Buoy, Scarborough	A.C.	B. & G.	
10	DURENDA	M.	7,241	Approaching Port Said	A.C.	B.	
11	WESTBURN ...	S.	2,842	3m. N. of Skinningrove, off Hartlepool	A.C.	B.	
13	EMPIRE CREEK ...	S.	332	57°16′N. 01°43′W.	A.C.	B.	
13	DALEMOOR ...	S.	5,796	57°04′N. 01°51′W.	A.C.	B.	
16	ATLANTIC	S.T.	167	3m. S.E. of Eddystone	A.C.	B.	
17	JIM	S.	833	Off T.2 Buoy, Tyne	A.C.	B.	
20	INVERARDER ...	S. Tank	5,578	Off Isle of Wight	A.C.	B.	
20	ILSE	S.	2,844	W. side of Hartlepool Approach Channel	Mine	—	
20	CORMOUNT	S.	2,841	Off Outer Dowsing L.V.	A.C.	T.	
23	CAMROUX 11 ...	M.	324	1m. N.E. of No. 17 Buoy, Flamboro' Head	Mine	—	
23	TOLWORTH ...	S.	1,351	53°05′N. 01°25′E.	A.C.	D.	
24	LEVENWOOD ...	S.	803	Tees Bay	A.C.	B.	
25	ISLE OF WIGHT ...	S.T.	176	Off Scarborough	A.C.	B.	
29	SILVERLAUREL ...	S.	6,142	King George Dock, Hull	A.C.	B.	
29	EMPIRE METEOR ...	S.	7,457	53°05′N. 01°30′E.	A.C.	B.	
30	EMPIRE LARCH ...	Tug	487	Off Gt. Yarmouth	A.C.	B.	
JULY, 1941							
1	HIGHWOOD ...	S.	1,177	Barry	A.C.	B.	
1	JAMAICA PLANTER...	M.	4,098	Barry	A.C.	B.	
4	GOLDFINCH ...	M.	454	270° 10m. from St. Bee's Head, Solway Firth	Mine	—	
5	NORTH DEVON ...	S.	3,658	Off Sheringham	A.C.	B.	
11	RIVER TRENT ...	M.	246	53°00′N. 01°15′E.	Mine	—	
13	SCORTON	S.	4,813	2m. off 57C Buoy, Smith's Knoll	A.C.	B.	
14	GEORGIC	M.	27,759	Suez Bay	A.C.	B.	
16	ELIZABETE	S.	2,039	Between 20C Buoy and T.2 Buoy, Tyne	A.C.	B.	

Date	Name	Type	Gross tons	Position	Cause of damage	How damaged	Remarks
JULY, 1941—(*Contd.*)							
17	EMERALD QUEEN ...	M.	481	54°39'N. 00°48'W.	A.C.	B.	
18	PILAR DE LARRINAGA	S.	7,046	54°23'N. 16°53'W.	A.C.	B. & G.	
20	CANADIAN STAR ...	M.	8,293	49°15'N. 21°00'W.	S.M.	G.	
20	UMVUMA	S.	4,419	Nr. 57 Buoy, off Humber	A.C.	B.	
23	ADAMANT	Barge	80	Hull	Mine	--	
23	SOAVITA	Barge	80	Hull	Mine	—	
24	SYDNEY STAR ...	M.	12,696	Mediterranean	E-Boat	T.	
26	ATLANTIC CITY ...	M.	5,133	55°42'N. 09°58'W.	S.M.	T.	
31	ONWARD	S.T.	209	20m. E. of Nolso, Faroes	A.C.	B. & G.	
AUGUST, 1941							
2	KOOLGA	S.	1,110	Nr. 54D Buoy, Smith's Knoll	A.C.	B.	
3	DESMOULEA ...	M. Tank	8,120	Off W. Beacon, Suez	A.C.	T.	
8	GOLD SHELL ...	M. Tank	8,208	53°05'N. 01°32'E.	A.C.	B.	
9	GLENDALOUGH ...	S.	868	52°59'N. 01°53'E.	A.C.	B.	
12	EAGLESCLIFFE HALL	S.	1,900	2m. E. of Sunderland (Approx.)	A.C.	B.	
17	KINDERSLEY ...	S.	1,999	3m. S.E. × E. of B.1 Buoy, off Blyth	A.C.	B.	
20	DALEWOOD ...	S.	2,774	53°11'N. 01°05'E.	E-Boat	T.	
22	DURHAM	M.	10,893	W. of Pantellaria	Mine	—	
28	DONOVANIA ...	M. Tank	8,149	3m. S.S.W. of St. Ann's Head	A.C.	B.	
SEPTEMBER, 1941							
3/4	HARPALYCUS ...	S.	5,629	Off Ashrafi Reef, Gulf of Suez	A.C.	B.	
6	STANMOUNT ...	S. Tank	4,468	Off Gt. Yarmouth	A.C.	B.	
7	NAIRANA	S.T.	225	7 to 8m. off Myggenaes, Faroes	A.C.	B.	
10	TAHCHEE	S. Tank	6,508	61°15'N. 41°05'W.	S.M.	T.	
11	CORMEAD	S.	2,848	52°33'N. 02°05'E.	A.C.	B.	Attacked again on 12th
11	WAR GREY ...	S.T.	246	Off Sunderland	A.C.	B.	
15	PONTFIELD ...	M. Tank	8,290	53°03'N. 01°20'E.	Mine	—	
15	ATLANTIC COCK ...	Tug	182	Off Dalmuir Basin, Clyde	Mine	—	
17	TETELA	S.	5,389	53°04'N. 01°34'E.	E-Boat	T.	
19	PRESTATYN ROSE ...	S.	1,151	3m. N.E. of Sunk Buoy, off Harwich	A.C.	B.	
20	DURHAM	M.	10,893	Gibraltar	Italian Assault Craft	—	
24	DALTONHALL ...	M.	7,253	51°45'N. 05°16'W.	Mine	—	
26	ORIOLE	M.	489	Off S. Bishops, Cardigan Bay	Mine	—	
30	CEDARWOOD ...	S.	899	Off Dover	A.C.	B.	
OCTOBER, 1941							
1	SERENITY	M.	557	10m. S.E. × E. of St. Goven's L.V.	A.C.	B. & G.	
2	SOUTHPORT ...	S.	572	South Shields	A.C.	B.	
6	SALAMAUA	M.	6,676	Anchorage, Straits of Jubal, Suez	A.C.	B.	
7	SVEND FOYN ...	S. O.R.	14,795	60°37'N. 21°44'W.	S.M.	T.	
11	ICEMAID	S.	1,964	Nr. Shipwash L.V., off Harwich	Mine	—	

Date	Name	Type	Gross tons	Position	Cause of damage	How damaged	Remarks
OCTOBER, 1941—(Contd.)							
16	EDENVALE	M.	444	Off Old Head of Kinsale	A.C.	B.	
20	CORDELIA	M. Tank	8,190	In convoy Anchorage, Milford	Mine	—	
NOVEMBER, 1941							
1	KINGSLAND ...	S.	3,669	North Sea	A.C.	B.	
2	THYRA III ...	S.	828	Great Yarmouth Roads	A.C.	B.	
2	AGILITY	S. Tank	522	Great Yarmouth Roads	A.C.	B.	
5	GLENCREE ...	S.	481	15m. S.W. of Bishops Lt.	A.C.	B. & G.	
8	GASLIGHT	S.	1,696	2 cables S.E. of S.1 Buoy, off Sunderland	A.C.	B.	
12	BEN SCREEL ...	S.T.	195	14m. N.E. × N. of St. Abb's Head	A.C.	B.	
24	BLAIRNEVIS ...	S.	4,155	52°20′N. 01°59′E.	E-Boat	T.	
24	ARDENZA	S.	933	10m. S.E. of Orfordness	A.C.	B.	
DECEMBER, 1941							
10	ANSHUN	M.	3,188	Manila Harbour	A.C.	B.	
10	ANHUI	S.	3,494	Outer Harbour, Manila	A.C.	B.	
13	MYRIEL	S. Tank	3,560	31°03′N. 29°00′E.	S.M.	T.	
19	LUCELLUM	M. Tank	9,425	270° 5m. from Bardsey Island	A.C.	B.	
22	NAM YONG... ...	S.	1,345	Port Swettenham, Malaya	A.C.	B.	
24	EASTWOOD	S.	1,551	270° 2½m. from Aldeburgh Lt.	Mine	—	
25	CHARLES PARSONS...	S.	1,554	8m. N. of Hartlepool (Approx.)	A.C.	B.	
25	SHEAF MOUNT ...	S.	5,017	North Atlantic	A.C.	B.	
JANUARY, 1942							
5	SCOTTISH MUSICIAN	M. Tank	6,998	52°16′N. 01°59′E.	Mine	—	
5	LARGO	S.	2,209	1m. S.E. × E. of 54E Buoy, off Southwold	Mine	—	
6	LODDON ,,, ,,,	S.T.	200	N.W. of 18D Buoy, off Whitby	A.C.	B.	
8	CRAIG-AN-ERAN ...	S.T.	202	Off Old Head of Kinsale	A.C.	B. & G.	
13	EMPIRE MASEFIELD	S.	7,023	54°22′N. 00°19′W.	A.C.	B.	
16	TOORAK	S. Tank	8,627	47°54′N. 52°11′W.	S.M.	T.	
16	LLANGIBBY CASTLE	M.	11,951	46°04′N. 19°06′W.	S.M.	T.	
17	HARMATRIS... ...	S.	5,395	69°16′N. 36°08′E.	S.M.	T.	
28	IDAR	S.	391	10°12′N. 80°13′E.	S.M.	G.	Also set on fire by boarding party
29	FAIRNILEE	Tug	226	Falmouth	A.C.	B.	
29	NORTHGATE SCOT ...	Tug	174	Falmouth	A.C.	B.	
31	EMPIRE REDSHANK	S.	6,615	63°24′N. 02°24′W.	A.C.	B. & G.	
31	LONGWOOD ...	M. Tank	9,463	290° 20m. from Outer Buoy, Colombo	S.M.	T.	
FEBRUARY, 1942							
1	SEDULITY	M.	490	Off Cromer	A.C.	B. & G.	
3	SPONDILUS	M. Tank	7,402	06°16′N. 79°38′E.	S.M.	T. & G.	

Date	Name	Type	Gross tons	Position	Cause of damage	How damaged	Remarks
FEBRUARY, 1942—(*Contd.*)							
3	MADURA	S.	9,032	Dutch East Indies	A.C.	B.	
4	AQUARIUS	S.T.	187	5m. E. × N. of Aberdeen	A.C.	B. & G.	
5	HELDER	S.	979	3½m. E. of Humber Light Float	A.C.	B. & G.	
6	BLUSH ROSE ...	S.	645	3m. S. of St. Ann's Head	A.C.	B.	
10	LIEUTENANT ROBERT MORY	S.	3,176	5m. W. of Trevose Head	A.C.	B.	
12 About	JALAVIHAR	S.	5,330	Off Singapore	A.C.	B. & G.	
12	ANGLO INDIAN ...	S.	5,609	Dutch East Indies	A.C.	B.	
12	EMPIRE STAR ...	M.	12,656	Durian Straits, Dutch East Indies	A.C.	B.	
13	CLAN CAMPBELL ...	S.	7,255	32°22'N. 24°22'E.	A.C.	B.	
15	EMPIRE HEAD ...	M.	489	34°42'N. 00°54'W.	A.C.	B.	
16	PEDERNALES ...	S. Tank	4,317	Off San Nicholas, Aruba	S.M.	T.	
18	BRITISH CONSUL ...	S. Tank	6,940	10°37'N. 61°34'W.	S.M.	T.	
19	BAROSSA	S.	4,239	Port Darwin	A.C.	B.	
19	MANUNDA (Hospital Ship)	M.	9,115	Port Darwin	A.C.	B. & G.	
20	JALAKRISHNA ...	S.	4,991	Dutch East Indies	A.C.	B.	
22	ENSEIGNE MARIE ST. GERMAIN	S.	3,139	Off Yarmouth	Mine	—	
24	DILOMA	M. Tank	8,146	43°51'N. 43°41'W.	S.M.	T.	
28	BRITISH JUDGE ...	S. Tank	6,735	10m. S. of Princes Island, Dutch East Indies	S.M.	T.	
MARCH, 1942							
5	ALACRITY	M.	554	7m. N.W. of Bishop Rock	A.C.	B.	
7	CERION	M.	2,588	Tobruk	A.C.	B.	
9	LADY NELSON ...	S.	7,970	Castries Harbour, St. Lucia, W. Indies	S.M.	T.	
9	UMTATA	S.	8,141	Castries Harbour, St. Lucia, W. Indies	S.M.	T.	
17	CRISTA	M.	2,590	32°21'N. 25°00'E.	S.M.	T.	
21	ATHELVISCOUNT ...	M. Tank	8,882	38°46'N. 55°44'W.	S.M.	T.	
21	SAN CIRILO ...	M. Tank	8,012	00°40'N. 79°40'E.	S.M.	T.	
24	LANCASTER CASTLE ...	S.	5,172	Murmansk	A.C.	B.	
25	IMPERIAL TRANSPORT	M. Tank	8,022	46°26'N. 41°30'W.	S.M.	T.	
27	DESTRO	S.	3,553	Tobruk	A.C.	B.	
29	OLTENIA II ...	S. Tank	6,394	18°36'N. 85°33'E.	A.C.	B.	
APRIL, 1942							
5	BENLEDI	S.	5,943	Colombo	A.C.	B.	
6	ANGLO CANADIAN ...	M.	5,268	Vizagapatam Roads, Bay of Bengal	A.C.	B.	
6	ELMDALE	S.	4,872	06°52'N. 78°50'E.	S.M.	G.	
7	SOMERSETSHIRE (Hospital Ship)	M.	9,716	32°13'N. 26°34'E.	S.M.	T.	
9	EMPIRE MOONRISE ...	S.	6,854	Colombo	A.C.	B.	
15	GOLLY	S.	627	Malta	A.C.	B.	Again damaged by aircraft on 4th May
MAY, 1942							
1	THISTLEFORD ...	S.	4,781	Port Said	A.C.	B.	
1	LA PAZ	M.	6,548	28°15'N. 80°20'W.	S.M.	T.	

Date	Name	Type	Gross tons	Position	Cause of damage	How damaged	Remarks
MAY, 1942—(Contd.)							
2	DALFRAM	S.	4,558	34°10′S. 17°49′E.	Mine	—	
3	GEO. W. McKNIGHT	M. Tank	12,502	11°18′N. 61°19′W.	S.M.	T. & G.	
4	ECLIPSE	S. Tank	9,767	26°30′N. 80°00′W.	S.M.	T.	
11	BEN IVER	S.T.	197	59°39′N. 09°25′W.	Mine	—	
12	FANO	S.	1,889	Southampton	A.C.	B.	
14	OUR MAGGIE ...	M.T.	17	Brixham Harbour	A.C.	B.	
14	DENCADE	Tug	58	Brixham Harbour	A.C.	B.	
14	BREADWINNER ...	M.T.	59	Brixham Harbour	A.C.	B.	
18	SAN ELISEO ...	M. Tank	8,042	15°30′N. 54°16′W.	S.M.	T.	Further attacks on 19th in positions 14°42′N. 55°02′W. and 14°20′N. 56°22′ W.
20	E. P. THERIAULT ...	Sch.	326	24°30′N. 83°55′W.	S.M.	G. and time bombs	
30	BRITISH LOYALTY...	M. Tank	6,993	037° 5 cables from Antsivana L.H., Diego Suarez,Madagascar	S.M.	T.	
JUNE, 1942							
12	CITY OF CALCUTTA...	S.	8,063	Off Mersa Matruh, Mediterranean	A.C.	B.	
14	POTARO	M.	5,410	450m. E. of Malta	A.C.	B.	
16	ORARI	M.	10,350	Entrance to Malta	Mine	—	
20	FORT CAMOSUN ...	S.	7,100	47°22′N. 125°30′W.	S.M.	T.	
22	RECTOR	Tug	106	Southampton	A.C.	B.	
27	BRITISH FREEDOM...	M. Tank	6,985	34°45′N. 75°22′W.	S.M.	T.	
JULY, 1942							
7	MANX KING ...	S.T.	235	10m. N.E. of Fuglo Head, Faroes	A.C.	B. & G.	
14	SHUNA	S.	1,575	Gibraltar	Mine	—	Limpet*
14	EMPIRE SNIPE ...	S.	2,497	120° 1½m. from North Mole Lt., Gibraltar	Mine	—	Limpet*
14	BARON DOUGLAS ...	S.	3,899	343° 14 cables from North Mole Lt., Gibraltar	Mine	—	Limpet
18	SAN GASPAR ...	S. Tank	12,910	10°30′N. 60°27′W.	S.M.	T.	
22	ALLARA	S.	3,279	33°03′S. 152°22′E.	S.M.	T.	
25	BRITISH MERIT ...	M. Tank	8,093	49°03′N. 40°36′W.	S.M.	T.	
AUGUST, 1942							
3	G. S. WALDEN ...	M. Tank	10,627	45°45′N. 47°17′W.	S.M.	T.	
3	EL CIERVO ...	S. Tank	5,841	229° 7m. from Start Pt.	A.C.	T.	
4	KATOOMBA	S.	9,424	300m. E.S.E. of Albany, S.W. Pacific	S.M.	G.	
9	ALEXIA	M. Tank	8,016	16°50′N. 60°40′W.	S.M.	T.	Attacked again in position 16°47′N. 60°27′W.
12	BRISBANE STAR ...	M.	12,791	Off Skuki Channel, Mediterranean	A.C.	T.	
13	ROCHESTER CASTLE	M.	7,795	36°28′N. 11°47′E.	E-Boat	T.	Also bombed by A.C.
14	STANDELLA ...	M. Tank	6,197	21°41′N. 76°09′W.	S.M.	T.	
17	LAGUNA	M.	6,466	18°45′N. 75°04′W.	S.M.	T.	
25	KYLOE	S.	2,820	52°27′N. 02°01′E.	Mine	—	
29	MALAITA	M.	3,310	09°50′S. 142°55′E.	S.M.	T.	

Date	Name	Type	Gross tons	Position	Cause of damage	How damaged	Remarks
SEPTEMBER, 1942							
8	Nephrite	S.	927	4½m. E. of Ramsgate	A.C.	B.	
10	F. J. Wolfe ...	M. Tank	12,190	51°30'N. 28°25'W.	S.M.	T.	
11	Cornwallis ...	S.	5,458	13°05'N. 59°36'W.	S.M.	T.	
15	Ravens Point ...	S.	1,787	330° 7 cables from North Mole Lt., Gibraltar	Mine	—	Limpet
16	Essex Lance ...	S.	6,625	49°03'N. 67°08'W.	S.M.	T.	
29	Ocean Vagabond...	S.	7,174	47°31'N. 52°27'W.	S.M.	T.	
OCTOBER, 1942							
13	Martaban	S.	4,161	06°31'N. 82°03'E.	S.M.	T.	
14	George Balfour...	S.	1,570	Vicinity of 58 Buoy, S.E. of Dudgeon Shoal	E-Boat	T.	
NOVEMBER, 1942							
8	Benalder	S.	5,161	04°19'N. 02°44'W.	S.M.	T.	
8	Capo Olmo ...	S.	4,712	10°56'N. 61°14'W.	S.M.	T.	
9	Wandle	S.	1,482	2m. N. of 3C Buoy, Lowestoft	E-Boat	T.	
13	Glenfinlas ...	S.	7,479	Bougie Harbour	A.C.	B.	
14	Lalande	S.	7,453	36°08'N. 03°46'W.	S.M.	T.	
15	Adviser	S.	6,348	32°03'S. 33°52'E.	S.M.	T.	
21	Forest	M.	4,998	Bougie	A.C.	B.	Again bombed at Gibraltar on 11th Dec.
21	British Promise ...	M. Tank	8,443	43°53'N. 55°02'W.	S.M.	T.	
21	British Renown...	M. Tank	6,997	43°53'N. 55°02'W.	S.M.	T.	
23	Scythia	S.	19,761	Off Algiers	A.C.	T.	
28	Empire Glade ...	M.	7,006	17°16'N. 48°44'W.	S.M.	G.	
DECEMBER, 1942							
1	Hindustan ...	M.	5,245	Bone	A.C.	B.	
6	Ousel	S.	1,533	Philippeville	A.C.	B. & G.	Attacked again on 11th
12	Empire Centaur...	S.	7,041	Algiers Bay	Italian Assault Craft	--	
12	Harmattan ...	S.	4,558	36°48'N. 03°04'E.	S.M.	T.	
12	Ocean Vanquisher	S.	7,174	36°48'N. 03°04'E.	S.M.	T.	
13	Hororata	S.	13,945	42°03'N. 34°33'W.	S.M.	T.	
15	Period	S.	2,791	Timor Sea	A.C.	B.	
16	Regent Lion ...	M. Tank	9,551	50°49'N. 24°07'W.	S.M.	T.	
22	Cameronia... ...	S.	16,297	37°03'N. 05°24'E.	A.C.	T.	
27	Scottish Heather	S. Tank	7,087	46°15'N. 26°20'W.	S.M.	T.	
JANUARY, 1943							
1	Novelist	S.	6,133	Bone Harbour	A.C.	B.	
1	Harpalyce ...	M.	7,269	Bone Harbour	A.C.	B.	
2	Dalhanna	S.	5,571	Bone Harbour	A.C.	B.	
7	Ville de Strasbourg	S.	7,159	37°04'N. 04°06'E.	S.M.*	T.	Subsequently bombed in Algiers Harbour
10	San Cipriano ...	M. Tank	7,966	Off Veleki Point, Kola Inlet	A.C.	B.	
17	Recorder	S.	5,982	Bone	A.C.	B.	
21	Ocean Rider ...	S.	7,178	4½m. W. of Cape Caxine, Algiers	A.C.	T.	

D*

Date	Name	Type	Gross tons	Position	Cause of damage	How damaged	Remarks
FEBRUARY, 1943							
6	FORT BABINE ...	S.	7,135	36°15′N. 00°15′E.	A.C.	T.	
23	BRITISH FORTITUDE	M. Tank	8,482	31°10′N. 27°30′W.	S.M.	T.	
26	EMPIRE PORTIA ...	S.	7,058	69°17′N. 33°20′E.	A.C.	B.	
27	SEMINOLE	M. Tank	10,389	35°53′N. 02°33′W.	S.M.	T.	
MARCH, 1943							
4	SHEAF CROWN ...	S.	4,868	31°49′S. 31°11′E.	S.M.	T.	
4	CHATEAUROUX ...	S.	4,765	41°10′N. 15°10′W.	A.C.	B.	
6	FORT PASKOYAC ...	S.	7,134	36°27′N. 10°17′W.	S.M.	T.	
6	EMPIRE KINSMAN...	S.	6,744	Murmansk	A.C.	B.	
9	FORT NORMAN ...	S.	7,133	36°51′N. 01°09′E.	S.M.	T.	
9	EMPIRE STANDARD	S.	7,047	36°51′N. 01°09′E.	S.M.	T.	
9	COULMORE	S.	3,670	58°48′N. 22°00′W.	S.M.	T.	
14	DUCHESS OF YORK	S.	20,021	305m. S.W. × W. of Cape Finisterre	A.C.	B.	
16	MERCHANT PRINCE	M.	5,229	36°10′N. 00°30′W.	S.M.	T.	
26	BECKENHAM ...	S.	4,636	32°56′N. 13°19′E.	Mine	—	
29	OCEAN VICEROY ...	S.	7,174	46°44′N. 16°38′W.	S.M.	T.	
APRIL, 1943							
4	DOVER HILL ...	S.	5,815	Mishukov Anchorage, Kola Inlet	A.C.	B.	
4	BRITISH GOVERNOR	S. Tank	6,840	Mishukov Anchorage, Kola Inlet	A.C.	B.	
11	NOORA	S.	1,072	Port Harvey, Australia	A.C.	B.	
11	HANYANG ...	S.	2,876	15m. E. of Oro Bay, New Guinea	A.C.	B.	
14	GORGON	M.	3,533	Milne Bay, New Guinea	A.C.	B.	
23	SILVERMAPLE ...	M.	5,313	59°05′N. 35°40′W.	S.M.	T.	
26	EMPIRE MORN ...	S.	7,092	33°52′N. 07°50′W.	Mine*	—	
MAY, 1943							
8	MAHSUD	S.	7,540	Gibraltar	Italian Assault Craft	—	
9	ISLANDER	S.	1,598	Near Cape Arnhem, Northern Territory, Australia	A.C.	B.	
12	ORMISTON	S.	5,832	30°16′S. 153°23′E.	S.M.	T.	
15	CORMULL	S.	2,865	¼ cable W of No 7 Buoy, 14m. N.E. of Yarmouth	Mine	—	
18	FORT ANNE ...	S.	7,134	36°35′N. 01°01′E.	S.M.	T.	
24	DENEWOOD... ...	S.	7,280	River Wear, Sunderland	A.C.	B.	
24	EMPIRE DEED ...	S.	6,766	Sunderland	A.C.	B.	
JUNE, 1943							
2	STANDELLA ...	M. Tank	6,197	07°25′N. 13°26′W.	S.M.	T.	
18	LALANDE	S.	7,453	220° 16m. from Cape Espichel, Portugal	A.C.	B.	
JULY, 1943							
9	STANHOPE ...	S.	2,337	37°10′N. 09°00′W.	A.C.	B.	
12	PORT FAIRY ...	M.	8,337	37°18′N. 14°37′W.	A.C.	B.	
12	DORSETSHIRE ... (Hospital ship)	M.	9,717	286° 13m. from Cape Passaro Lt., Sicily	A.C.	B.	

Date	Name	Type	Gross tons	Position	Cause of damage	How damaged	Remarks
JULY, 1943—(Contd.)							
15	TWICKENHAM ...	S.	4,762	28°36′N. 13°18′W.	S.M.	T.	
16	KAIPARA	M.	5,882	13°30′N. 17°43′W.	S.M.	T.	
19	KAITUNA	M.	4,914	35°15′N. 35°35′E.	Mine	—	Limpet
21	OCEAN VIRTUE ...	S.	7,174	Augusta, Sicily	A.C.	B.	
22	EMPIRE MOON ...	S.	7,472	36°43′N. 15°20′E.	S.M.	T.	
24	LLANDAFF ...	S.	4,825	20m. N.E. of Kildin Island, entrance to Kola Inlet	A.C.	B.	
26	EMPIRE BRUTUS ...	S.	7,233	39°50′N. 13°38′W.	A.C.	B.	
27	EMPIRE HIGHWAY...	M.	7,166	38°04′N. 12°59′W.	A.C.	B.	
29	EMPIRE DARWIN ...	S.	6,765	44°52′N. 16°00′W.	A.C.	B.	
AUGUST, 1943							
4	STANRIDGE ...	S.	5,975	Gibraltar	Italian Assault Craft	—	
13	EMPIRE HAVEN ...	S.	6,852	36°15′N. 02°23′W.	A.C.	T.	
15	BARON FAIRLIE ...	S.	6,706	39°59′N. 12°58′W.	A.C.	B.	
15	OCEAN FAITH ...	S.	7,173	39°05′N. 12°54′W.	A.C.	B.	
23	SPEEDFAST	S.	1,898	Palermo	A.C.	B.	
SEPTEMBER, 1943							
6	FORT DREW ...	S.	7,134	35°52′N. 14°47′E.	Mine	—	
12	LYMINGE	S.	2,499	Off Salerno	A.C.	B.	
25	NAIRANA	S.T.	225	53°54′N. 00°30′E.	A.C.	B.	
OCTOBER, 1943							
4	SAMITE	S.	7,219	36°42′N. 01°17′E.	A.C.	B.	
7	LAURELWOOD ...	M. Tank	7,347	Off Taranto	Mine	—	
20	BRITISH PURPOSE...	M. Tank	5,845	11°49′N. 74°54′E.	S.M.	T.	
23	KERLOGUE	M.	335	100m. S. of Ireland	A.C.	B.	
NOVEMBER, 1943							
4	FIRELIGHT	S.	2,841	52°55′N. 02°00′E. (Approx.)	E.Bt.	T.	
21	DELIUS	M.	6,065	46°46′N. 18°30′W.	A.C.	B.	
DECEMBER, 1943							
2	CRISTA	M.	2,590	Bari	A.C.	⊤	⎫ Damaged by bombs
2	FORT LAJOIE ...	S.	7,134	Bari	A.C.	—	⎪ or by debris fol-
2	BRITTANY COAST ...	S.	1,389	Bari	A.C.	—	⎬ lowing explosion of ammunition ⎭ ship
3	FORT CAMOSUN ...	S.	7,126	11°23′N. 46°03′E.	S.M.	T.	
5	CLAN MATHESON ...	S.	5,613	Calcutta	A.C.	B.	
31	TORNUS	M. Tank	8,054	19°45′N. 59°10′E.	S.M.	T. & G.	
31	EMPIRE HOUSMAN...	M.	7,359	60°30′N. 24°35′W.	S.M.	T.	Torpedoed again on 3rd Jan., 1944, and sunk
JANUARY, 1944							
2	LARGS BAY ...	S.	14,182	Approaches to Naples	Mine	—	
11	TRIONA	S.	7,283	00°03′N. 80°43′E.	S.M.	T.	
24	LEINSTER ... ... (Hospital Carrier)	M.	4,303	41°19′N. 12°36′E.	A.C.	B.	
24	ST. ANDREW ... (Hospital Carrier)	S.	2,702	41°10′N. 12°26′E.	A.C.	B.	
29	FORT LOUISBOURG	S.	7,130	Surrey Commercial Dock, London	A.C.	B.	

Date	Name	Type	Gross tons	Position	Cause of damage	How damaged	Remarks
FEBRUARY, 1944							
9	KELMSCOTT ...	S.	7,039	47°31′N. 52°23′W.	S.M.	T.	
11	ASPHALION ...	S.	6,274	17°28′N. 83°32′E.	S.M.	T.	
12	CORFIRTH ...	S.	1,803	170° 1m. from Ajaccio	Mine	—	
20	NOLISEMENT ...	S.	5,084	270° 3¼m. from Monopoli L.H.	Mine	—	
29	ENSIS	M. Tank	6,207	35°36′N. 35°33′E.	S.M.	T.	
MARCH, 1944							
6	CORUNDUM ...	S.	929	Off Dover	Shelled by Shore Batteries	—	
9	BRITISH LOYALTY...	M. Tank	6,993	Addu Atoll Harbour	S.M.	T.	
15	ABA ... ... (Hospital Ship)	M.	7,938	Naples	A.C.	B.	
APRIL, 1944							
20	SAMITE	S.	7,219	37°02′N. 03°41′E.	A.C.	T.	
MAY, 1944							
14	G. S. WALDEN ...	M. Tank	10,627	36°45′N. 00°55′E.	S.M.	T.	
14	FORT FIDLER ...	S.	7,127	36°45′N. 00°55′E.	S.M.	T.	
JUNE, 1944							
7	ST. JULIEN... ... (Hospital Carrier)	S.	1,952	49°35′N. 00°32′W.	Mine	—	
7	DINARD ... ... (Hospital Carrier)	S.	2,313	49°35′N. 00°35′W.	Mine	—	
11	FORT McPHERSON...	S.	7,132	50°02′N. 00°36′W.	A.C.	B.	
12	BRITISH ENGINEER	S. Tank	6,993	50°10′N. 00°59′W.	Mine	—	
13	THE VICEROY ...	S.	824	Off Assault Beaches, Normandy	Mine	—	
23	EMPIRE TRISTRAM...	S.	7,167	Surrey Commercial Dock, London	Flying bomb	—	Again hit by Flying bomb on 12th July
24	GURDEN GATES ...	S.	1,791	Off Folkestone	Shelled by shore battery	—	
27	SHELL SPIRIT I ...	M. Tank	440	Beckton	Flying bomb	—	
28	DALEGARTH FORCE	S	825	1m. S.W. of Dover	Shelled by shore battery	—	
28	VIKING	S.	1,957	Rotherhithe	Flying bomb	—	
28	JACOB	Tug	65	Rotherhithe	Flying bomb	—	
28	TORO	Tug	87	Rotherhithe	Flying bomb	—	
JULY, 1944							
6	EMPIRE HALBERD...	S.	7,177	006° 3.8 miles from Longships Lt.	Mine	—	
8	EMPIRE BRUTUS ...	S.	7,233	075° 2¼ cables from Juno L.V., Normandy	Mine	—	
17	ORANMORE... ...	S.	495	49°37′N. 00°28′W.	Mine	—	
19	ABBOTSBURY ...	Tug	92	Albert Dock Hoists, R. Thames	Flying bomb	—	
24	SAMNEVA	S.	7,219	50°14′N. 00°47′W.	S.M.	T.	
26	FORT McPHERSON...	S.	7,132	Victoria Dock, London	Flying bomb		

Date	Name	Type	Gross tons	Position	Cause of damage	How damaged	Remarks
JULY, 1944—(Contd.)							
27	Fort Perrot ...	S.	7,171	50°50′N. 00°44′E.	E-Boat	T.	
27	Empire Beatrice...	S.	7,046	50°55′N. 01°02′E.	E-Boat	T.	
30	Ascanius	S.	10,048	50°15′N. 00°48′W.	S.M.	T.	
30	Ocean Courier ...	S.	7,178	50°42′N. 00°36′W.	E-Boat	T.	
30	Fort Dearborn ...	S.	7,160	50°40′N. 00°31′E. (Approx.)	E-Boat	T.	
30	Fort Kaskaskia ...	S.	7,187	50°38′N. 00°27′E.	E-Boat	T.	
30	Ocean Volga ...	S.	7,174	50°41′N. 00°32′E.	E-Boat	T.	
AUGUST, 1944							
3	Samlong	S.	7,219	49°24′N. 00°28′W.	One man torpedo	---	
3	Fort Lac la Ronge	S.	7,131	49°22′N. 00°21′W.	One man torpedo	—	
4	Samsylarna ...	S.	7,100	33°05′N. 20°16′E.	A.C.	T.	
8 10	Fort Yale ...	S.	7,134	49°26′N. 00°33′W. (Approx.)	Mine	---	Torpedoed on 23rd August and sunk
	Iddesleigh ...	S.	5,205	½m. from 90 Buoy, Sword Beach, Normandy	S.M.*	T.	Torpedoed again on 17th August and became a total loss
18	Fort Gloucester...	S.	7,127	082° 10½m. from Dungeness	E-Boat	T.	
18	Samdel	S.	7,219	West India Dock, London	Flying bomb	—	
19	Harpagus	M.	7,271	1½m. N. of W. Breakwater, Arromanches Harbour	Mine*	—	
20	Daronia	M. Tank	8,139	31°10′S. 38°00′E.	S.M.	T.	
SEPTEMBER, 1944							
21	Morialta	M.	1,379	42°55′N. 05°30′E.	Mine	—	
23	Wolseley	S.T.	159	22m. E.N.E. of Gt. Yarmouth	Mine	—	
OCTOBER, 1944							
4	Cotton Valley ...	M. Tank	1,179	190° 6m. from Port du Bouc	Mine	—	
21	Guernsey Queen	M.	567	Entrance to Boulogne	Mine	—	
NOVEMBER, 1944							
2	Fort Thompson ...	S.	7,134	48°55′N. 67°41′W.	S.M.	T.	
10	Fort La Baye ...	S.	7,162	31°25′N. 32°23′E.	Mine	---	
12	Fairplay I ...	Salvage Tug	162	Ostend Harbour	Mine	---	
21	Empire Cutlass ...	S.	7,177	294° 700 yds. from Digue Nord Lt., Le Havre	S.M.	T.	
DECEMBER, 1944							
20	Empire Osborne...	S.	2,906	190° 3½m. from Cap de la Heve, R. Seine (Approx.)	Mine	—	
21	Samtucky	S.	7,219	44°22′N. 63°23′W.	S.M.	T.	
JANUARY, 1945							
4	Nipiwan Park ...	M. Tank	2,373	44°30′N. 63°00′W.	S.M.	T.	

Date	Name	Type	Gross tons	Position	Cause of damage	How damaged	Remarks
FEBRUARY, 1945							
19	CITY OF LINCOLN ...	S.	8,039	300° 8 cables from 14 Buoy, off Humber	Mine	—	
22	SKJOLD	S.	1,345	52°53′N. 02°08′E.	E-Boat	G.	
28	CYDONIA	S.	3,517	53°17′N. 00°57′E.	Mine	—	
MARCH, 1945							
6	EMPIRE GERAINT...	S.	6,991	090° 1m. from St. Goven's Lt., off Milford Haven	S.M.	T.	
8	KYLE CASTLE ...	S.	845	Granville	Damaged in sea-borne raid	—	
8	PARKWOOD ...	S.	1,049	Granville		—	
8	NEPHRITE	S.	927	Granville		—	
8	ESKWOOD	S.	791	Granville		—	
APRIL, 1945							
11	PORT WYNDHAM ...	M.	8,580	Off Outer Lade Buoy, Dungeness	Midget S.M.*	—	
15	CONAKRIAN... ...	S.	4,876	51°20′N. 02°36′E.	Mine	—	
23	RIVERTON	S.	7,345	50°25′N. 05°25′W.	S.M.	T.	
30	SAMCLYDE	S.	7,219	40°22′N. 22°51′E.	Mine	—	
MAY, 1945							
4	EMPIRE UNITY ...	M. Tank	6,386	64°23′N. 22°37′W.	S.M.*	T.	

LIST IV

BRITISH MERCHANT AND FISHING VESSELS LOST BY MISCELLANEOUS WAR CAUSES OTHER THAN ENEMY ACTION

(*Note :* The majority of these vessels were lost by striking British or Allied mines. Though their loss was due to war causes it could not be attributed to enemy action.

BRITISH

Date	Name	Type	Gross tons	Position
13 November, 1939	Sirdhana	S.	7,745	Off Singapore
6 January, 1940	British Liberty	M. Tank	8,485	4m. N.E. of Dyck L.V.
6 June, 1940	Lapwing	S.T.	217	54°00′N. 01°10′E.
9 September, 1940	John Baptish	S.T.	290	S. of Coningbeg L.V.
23 September, 1940	Tacoma	M.	5,905	Dakar
24 November, 1940	Alma Dawson	S.	3,985	55°32′N. 06°44′W.
25 November, 1940	Patria	S.	11,885	Haifa Anchorage
11 December, 1940	Robinia	S.T.	208	65°20′N. 12°40′W.
6 January, 1941	Gadra	S.T.	219	1½m. off Myling Head, Faroes
11 January, 1941	Oriole	F.V.	172	2½m. N. of Stakken North Pt., Faroes
31 January, 1941	Botusk	S.	3,091	Off North Rona Island
16 February, 1941	Empire Otter	S. Tank	4,670	25m. S.W. of Hartland Pt.
27 February, 1941	Christabelle	S.T.	203	61°27′N. 06°05′W.
8 June, 1941	Hopton	S.T.	202	Off Iceland
13 July, 1941	Pegasus	S. Tank	3,597	Beirut, Syria
8 December, 1941	Gertie	S.	341	Off Tuskar Lt.
24 January, 1942	Tai Sang	S.	3,555	00°55′N. 103°35′E.
27 January, 1942	Harpa	M. Tank	3,007	Main Strait, Singapore
5 April, 1942	Empire Beacon	M.	872	250° 6m. from St. Ann's Head
12 July, 1942	Heron	S.T.	223	Nr. Faroes Bank
4 October, 1942	Athelbrae	S. Tank	681	10°02′N. 61°51′W.
1 January, 1943	Empire Panther	S.	5,600	8m. off Strumble Head
24 July, 1944	Portsea	S.	1,583	43°28′N. 13°44′E.
24 July, 1944	Auk	S.	1,338	43°48′N. 13°44′E.
7 December, 1944	Glenmaroon	S.	745	54°05′N. 03°53′W.
12 April, 1945	Falmouth	S.T.	165	6m. E.N.E. of No. 62 F. Buoy, off Humber
28 April, 1945	Dinorah	S.T.	192	Off Bridlington
1 May, 1945	Neuralia	S.	9,182	40°11′N. 17°44′E.
24 July, 1945	Gozo	S.T.	172	Off Old Head of Kinsale

APPENDIX A

CASUALTIES TO PERSONNEL OF BRITISH MERCHANT SHIPS

(1)   Deaths (at sea or ashore) and supposed deaths (at sea) which have been notified to the Registrar General of Shipping and Seamen and recorded as due to enemy action or other causes arising out of the war, comprising :

(1) seamen of all nationalities who served in British ships, and

(2) British seamen who served in foreign ships chartered or requisitioned by His Majesty's Government, from the outbreak of war to 31st August, 1945, were as follows :—

In Merchant Vessels	*In Fishing Vessels*	*Total*
29,180	814	29,994

APPENDIX B

Table showing Number and Gross Tonnage of British, Allied and Neutral Merchant and Fishing Vessels lost through Enemy Action during each month of the war, 3rd September, 1939, to 2nd September, 1945, inclusive, showing cause of loss.

(Thousands of Tons)

Month	U-BOAT		MINE		SURFACE CRAFT		AIRCRAFT		CAUSE UNCERTAIN		TOTAL	
	No.	Gross tonnage	No.	Gross tonnage	No.	Gross tonnage	No.	Gross tonnage	No.	Gross tonnage	No.	Gross tonnage
1939												
Sept. ...	40	153	9	31	1	5	—	—	—	—	50	189
Oct. ...	27	135	10	29	8	32	—	—	—	—	45	196
Nov. ...	18	61	27	108	2	2	—	—	3	3	50	174
Dec. ...	18	72	37	89	4	22	10	3	1	1	70	187
Total ...	103	421	83	257	15	61	10	3	4	4	215	746
1940												
Jan. ...	31	91	23	81	—	—	12	25	4	16	70	213
Feb. ...	35	153	14	51	1	2	2	1	4	8	56	215
March ...	15	47	16	37	—	—	5	7	3	7	39	98
April ...	6	31	11	20	2	6	4	6	20	74	43	137
May ...	10	48	18	48	2	7	36	154	14	17	80	274
June ...	58	284	22	86	9	61	25	106	20	35	134	572
July ...	38	196	14	35	17	81	33	70	—	—	102	382
August ...	56	268	5	12	13	63	15	53	2	1	91	397
Sept. ...	59	295	7	8	17	88	14	56	—	—	97	447
Oct. ...	63	352	23	33	5	32	6	9	6	17	103	443
Nov. ...	32	147	24	47	19	115	18	66	2	1	95	376
Dec. ...	37	213	24	54	11	64	7	15	3	12	82	358
Total ...	440	2,125	201	512	96	519	177	568	78	188	992	3,912
1941												
Jan. ...	21	127	10	17	12	94	20	78	—	—	63	316
Feb. ...	38	195	9	17	21	89	27	89	6	12	101	402
March ...	41	243	19	23	32	156	40	113	7	2	139	537
April ...	43	249	6	25	9	48	84	296	13	36	155	654
May ...	58	326	8	23	3	15	55	136	—	—	124	500
June ...	61	310	9	14	4	18	25	62	9	27	108	431
July ...	22	94	7	9	1	6	11	9	3	3	44	121
August ...	23	80	3	2	5	25	9	24	—	—	40	131
Sept. ...	53	203	9	14	5	16	12	41	4	12	83	286
Oct. ...	32	157	4	20	2	3	10	35	3	4	51	219
Nov. ...	12	62	5	2	7	17	10	23	—	—	34	104
Dec. ...	25	116	19	64	1	6	20	64	122	236	187	486
Total ...	429	2,162	108	230	102	493	323	970	167	332	1,129	4,187

Month	U-BOAT		MINE		SURFACE CRAFT		AIRCRAFT		CAUSE UNCERTAIN		TOTAL	
	No.	Gross tonnage	No.	Gross tonnage	No.	Gross tonnage	No.	Gross tonnage	No.	Gross tonnage	No.	Gross tonnage
1942												
JAN.	62	328	11	10	1	3	15	57	9	20	98	418
FEB.	82	470	2	7	—	—	29	139	17	36	130	652
MARCH	94	532	5	17	10	23	12	48	103	169	224	789
APRIL	75	438	8	15	25	131	16	83	4	6	128	673
MAY	125	607	6	18	3	20	14	59	—	—	148	704
JUNE	144	700	7	20	7	49	11	54	—	—	169	823
JULY	96	476	2	9	11	54	18	74	—	—	127	613
AUGUST	108	544	—	—	8	59	6	61	2	1	124	665
SEPT.	98	486	—	—	4	24	12	58	—	—	114	568
OCT.	93	614	3	5	3	8	1	6	—	—	100	633
NOV.	117	718	1	1	5	10	7	62	4	16	134	807
DEC.	61	337	3	1	8	19	2	4	—	—	74	361
TOTAL	1,155	6,250	48	103	85	400	143	705	139	248	1,570	7,706
1943												
JAN.	37	203	5	19	—	—	6	26	2	6	50	254
FEB.	63	359	7	34	1	5	—	—	1	5	72	403
MARCH	108	627	2	1	—	—	10	65	—	—	120	693
APRIL	56	328	5	12	1	2	2	3	—	—	64	345
MAY	50	265	1	2	—	—	5	21	2	12	58	300
JUNE	20	96	5	4	2	18	3	6	—	—	30	124
JULY	45	245	—	—	1	7	13	106	—	—	59	358
AUGUST	16	86	—	—	1	8	5	14	3	19	25	127
SEPT.	20	119	3	4	—	—	4	23	2	1	29	147
OCT.	20	97	5	20	—	—	4	23	—	—	29	140
NOV.	14	67	3	7	4	8	7	62	—	—	28	144
DEC.	13	87	1	6	—	—	17	75	—	—	31	168
TOTAL	462	2,579	37	109	10	48	76	424	10	43	595	3,203
1944												
JAN.	13	92	1	7	5	7	4	24	1	1	24	130
FEB.	18	93	—	—	1	2	3	22	—	—	22	117
MARCH	23	143	1	7	2	8	—	—	—	—	26	158
APRIL	9	62	—	—	—	—	3	20	—	—	12	82
MAY	4	24	—	—	—	—	1	3	—	—	5	27
JUNE	11	58	6	25	3	2	2	9	3	10	25	104
JULY	12	63	3	8	1	7	—	—	—	—	16	79
AUGUST	18	99	3	7	—	—	—	—	3	13	24	119
SEPT.	7	43	1	2	—	—	—	—	—	—	8	45
OCT.	1	7	2	4	—	—	—	—	—	—	3	11
NOV.	7	30	—	—	1	1	1	7	—	—	9	38
DEC.	9	59	8	35	—	—	5	36	1	4	23	134
TOTAL	132	773	25	95	13	27	19	121	8	28	197	1,044
1945												
JAN.	11	57	4	17	1	2	1	7	—	—	17	83
FEB.	15	65	5	18	2	4	1	7	1	1	24	95
MARCH	12	58	6	36	2	4	—	—	4	6	24	104
APRIL	13	73	4	8	—	—	3	23	—	—	20	104
MAY	3	10	—	—	—	—	—	—	—	—	3	10
JUNE to SEPT.	Nil	Nil	Nil	Nil	Nil	Nil	Nil	Nil	Nil	Nil	Nil	Nil
TOTAL	54	263	19	79	5	10	5	37	5	7	88	396
GRAND TOTAL 3rd SEPT., 1939 to 2nd SEPT., 1945	2,775	14,573	521	1,385	326	1,558	753	2,828	411	850	4,786	21,194

PART IX

INDEX OF VESSELS LOST OR DAMAGED

98